MACMILLAN

LANGUAGE ARTS TODAY

Great literature is an inspiration. *The Secrets of a Tomb* by Carolyn Meyer
and Charles Gallenkamp inspired artist Don Daily to create the illustration
on the cover of your book. The selection begins on page 480. We hope that
you enjoy the selection and the illustration!

SENIOR AUTHORS

ANN McCALLUM   WILLIAM STRONG   TINA THOBURN   PEGGY WILLIAMS

Literature Consultant for Macmillan Language Arts and Macmillan Reading   Joan Glazer

Macmillan Publishing Company   New York
Collier Macmillan Publishers   London

ACKNOWLEDGMENTS

The publisher gratefully acknowledges permission to reprint the following copyrighted material:

"Charles" from *The Lottery and Other Stories* by Shirley Jackson. Copyright 1948, 1949 by Shirley Jackson. Copyright © renewed 1976, 1977 by Laurence Hyman, Barry Hyman, Mrs. Sarah Webster, and Mrs. Joanne Schnurer. Reprinted and recorded by permission of Farrar, Straus & Giroux, Inc. Reprinted also by permission of Brandt & Brandt Literary Agents, Inc.

"Homesick" is an excerpt from *Homesick* by Jean Fritz. Copyright © 1982 by Jean Fritz. Reprinted by permission of G. P. Putnam's Sons and Gina Maccoby Literary Agency. Recorded by permission of Gina Maccoby Literary Agency.

"The Incredible Journey" is an excerpt from *The Incredible Journey* by Sheila Burnford. Copyright © 1960, 1961 by Sheila Burnford. By permission of Little, Brown and Company and Hodder & Stoughton Limited. Recorded by permission of Caedmon and David Higham Associates Ltd.

"The Marriage of Sea and Space" from *Under the High Seas* by Margaret Poynter and Donald Collins. Copyright © 1983 Margaret Poynter and Donald Collins. Reprinted with the permission of Atheneum Publishers, an imprint of Macmillan Publishing Company. Recorded by permission of the publisher.

"The Secrets of a Tomb" is an excerpt from *The Mystery of the Ancient Maya* by Carolyn Meyer and Charles Gallenkamp. Copyright © 1985 Carolyn Meyer and Charles Gallenkamp. Reprinted with the permission of Margaret K. McElderry Books, an imprint of Macmillan Publishing Company. Reprinted also and recorded by permission of Writers House Inc.

"The Story of Stevie Wonder" is abridged from *The Story of Stevie Wonder* by James Haskins. Copyright © 1976 by James Haskins. Used by permission of the author.

"This Farm for Sale" by Jesse Stuart. Copyright © 1982 The Jesse Stuart Foundation. All rights reserved. Reprinted and recorded by permission of Marian Reiner for the Jesse Stuart Foundation, P. O. Box 391, Ashland, KY 41114.

Poems, Brief Quotations, and Excerpts

"Where the Stars Come From" is excerpted from *African Folktales* (where it was titled "The Universe and Its Beginnings") edited by Paul Radin. Copyright 1952 by Bollingen Foundation Inc., New York, N.Y. All rights reserved. Published by Princeton University Press and reprinted with their permission.

"Who Am I?" from *At the Top of My Voice and Other Poems* by Felice Holman. Published by Charles Scribner's Sons. Copyright © Felice Holman. Reprinted by permission of the author.

"Good or Bad" by Calvin O'John, excerpt from "Once Again" by Liz Schappy, and excerpt from "Endless Search" by Alonzo Lopez are from *The Whispering Wind*, edited by Terry Allen. Copyright © 1972 by The Institute of American Indian Arts. Reprinted by permission of Doubleday, a division of Bantam, Doubleday, Dell Publishing Group, Inc.

Quotation by Carolyn Meyer is used by permission of Writers House.

Excerpt from "Primer Lesson" in *Slabs of the Sunburnt West* by Carl Sandburg. Copyright 1922 by Harcourt Brace Jovanovich, Inc., renewed 1950 by Carl Sandburg. Reprinted by permission of the publisher.

(Acknowledgments continued on page 603.)

Cover Design: Barnett-Brandt Design
Cover Illustration: Don Daily

Macmillan Publishing Company
866 Third Avenue
New York, N.Y. 10022
Collier Macmillan Canada, Inc.

Printed in the United States of America

ISBN: 0-02-243509-3

9 8 7 6 5 4 3

MACMILLAN

LANGUAGE ARTS TODAY

C O N T E N T S
THEME: *JOURNEYS*

Writer to Writer.................................... xii

LANGUAGE STUDY Unit 1: SENTENCES   xii

1 Kinds of Sentences.................................. 2
2 Complete Subjects and Complete Predicates.......... 4
3 Simple Subjects and Simple Predicates 6
4 Compound Subjects and Compound Predicates 8
5 Compound Sentences 10
6 Correcting Fragments and Run-on Sentences 12
7 Mechanics: Punctuating Sentences................... 14
8 Vocabulary Building: Using Context Clues 16
Grammar and Writing Connection:
    Combining Sentences 18
Unit Checkup....................................... 20
Enrichment... 22
Extra Practice with Practice Plus 24

WRITING Unit 2: WRITING PERSONAL
                 NARRATIVES   34

Literature: Reading Like a Writer 36
    "Homesick" by Jean Fritz
Responding to Literature.............................. 43
Pictures: Seeing Like a Writer............................. 44
1 Group Writing: A Personal Narrative................. 46
2 Thinking and Writing: General and Specific 50
3 Independent Writing: A Personal Narrative........... 52
Prewrite □ Write □ Revise □ Proofread □ Publish
The Grammar Connection: Correcting Fragments and
    Run-on Sentences 58
The Mechanics Connection: Punctuating Sentences ... 58
4 Speaking and Listening: Telling an Anecdote......... 60
Curriculum Connection Writing About Social Studies 62
Unit Checkup....................................... 64
Theme Project Futuristic Fair 65

AWARD WINNING
SELECTION

THEME: *EXPRESSIONS*

Unit 3: NOUNS

LANGUAGE STUDY

1 Kinds of Nouns 68
2 Singular and Plural Nouns 70
3 Possessive Nouns 72
4 Collective and Compound Nouns 74
5 Appositives 76
6 Mechanics: Forming Possessive Nouns and
    Contractions 78
7 Mechanics: Capitalizing Proper Nouns 80
8 Vocabulary Building: How Language Changes 82
  Grammar and Writing Connection:
    Combining Sentences 84
  Unit Checkup 86
  Enrichment 88
  Extra Practice with Practice Plus 90
  Maintenance: Units 1, 3 100

Unit 4: WRITING SHORT STORIES   102

WRITING

Literature: Reading Like a Writer 104
    "Charles" from The Lottery and Other Stories
    by Shirley Jackson
Responding to Literature 111
Pictures: Seeing Like a Writer 112
1 Group Writing: A Short Story 114
2 Thinking and Writing: Understanding Point of View .. 118
3 Independent Writing: A Short Story 120
  Prewrite □ Write □ Revise □ Proofread □ Publish
  The Grammar Connection: Possessive Nouns 126
  The Mechanics Connection: Quotation Marks 126
4 Speaking and Listening: Having a Class Discussion ... 128
  Curriculum Connection Writing About Literature 130
  Unit Checkup 132
  Theme Project Photo Gallery 133

THEME: *CROSSCURRENTS*

LANGUAGE STUDY | Unit 5: VERBS   134

1 Action Verbs 136
2 Verbs with Direct Objects............................ 138
3 Verbs with Indirect Objects 140
4 Linking Verbs 142
5 Present, Past, and Future Tenses 144
6 Verb Phrases 146
7 Present and Past Progressive Forms................. 148
8 Perfect Tenses 150
9 Irregular Verbs I 152
10 Irregular Verbs II................................. 154
11 Subject-Verb Agreement 156
12 Mechanics: Using Commas to Separate Parts of a
      Sentence.. 158
13 Vocabulary Building: Word Choice 160
    Grammar and Writing Connection:
      Using Active and Passive Voices................. 162
    Unit Checkup..................................... 164
    Enrichment....................................... 166
    Extra Practice with Practice Plus 168

WRITING | Unit 6: WRITING EXPLANATIONS   182

Literature: Reading Like a Writer 184
    "The Marriage of Sea and Space"
      from Under the High Seas
      by Margaret Poynter and Donald Collins
Responding to Literature.............................. 191
Pictures: Seeing Like a Writer............................ 192
1 Group Writing: An Explanatory Paragraph........... 194
2 Thinking and Writing: Comparing and Contrasting.... 198
3 Independent Writing: An Explanation................ 200
    Prewrite □ Write □ Revise □ Proofread □ Publish
    The Grammar Connection: Using Tenses Correctly 206
    The Mechanics Connection: Using Commas Correctly 206
4 Speaking and Listening: Giving Instructions 208
    Curriculum Connection   Writing About Science 210
    Unit Checkup..................................... 212
    Theme Project   Sea Stories 213

AWARD WINNING
SELECTION

THEME: *CHALLENGES*

Unit 7: PRONOUNS   214

LANGUAGE STUDY

1 Personal Pronouns 216
2 Pronouns and Antecedents......................... 218
3 Using Pronouns Correctly.......................... 220
4 Possessive Pronouns 222
5 Indefinite Pronouns 224
6 Subject-Verb Agreement with Indefinite Pronouns 226
7 Reflexive and Intensive Pronouns 228
8 Interrogative and Demonstrative Pronouns 230
9 Mechanics: Using Abbreviations.................... 232
10 Vocabulary Building: Homophones and Homographs 234
   Grammar and Writing Connection:
     Combining Sentences 236
   Unit Checkup....................................... 238
   Enrichment... 240
   Extra Practice with Practice Plus 242
   Maintenance: Units 1, 3, 5, 7..................... 253

Unit 8: WRITING BIOGRAPHICAL
SKETCHES   256

WRITING

Literature: Reading Like a Writer 258
   from The Story of Stevie Wonder
   by James Haskins
Responding to Literature............................. 265
Pictures: Seeing Like a Writer....................... 266
1 Group Writing: A Biographical Sketch 268
2 Thinking and Writing: Understanding Sequence 272
3 Independent Writing: A Biographical Sketch 274
   Prewrite □ Write □ Revise □ Proofread □ Publish
   The Grammar Connection: Using Subject and Object
    Pronouns 280
   The Mechanics Connection: Using Abbreviations 280
4 Speaking and Listening: Conducting an Interview..... 282
   Curriculum Connection   Writing About Health 284
   Unit Checkup....................................... 286
   Theme Project   Characters...................... 287

AWARD WINNING
SELECTION

THEME: *VISIONS*

LANGUAGE STUDY

Unit 9: ADJECTIVES AND ADVERBS   288

1 Adjectives.. 290
2 Articles and Proper Adjectives 292
3 Comparative and Superlative Adjectives I 294
4 Comparative and Superlative Adjectives II 296
5 Demonstrative Adjectives........................... 298
6 Adverbs.. 300
7 Comparative and Superlative Adverbs 302
8 Avoiding Double Negatives 304
9 Using Adjectives and Adverbs 306
10 Mechanics: Commas with Dates, Addresses, and
 Names.. 308
11 Vocabulary Building: Synonyms and Antonyms 310
 Grammar and Writing Connection:
 Combining Sentences 312
 Unit Checkup.. 314
 Enrichment....................................... 316
 Extra Practice with Practice Plus 318

WRITING

Unit 10: WRITING DESCRIPTIONS   330

Literature: Reading Like a Writer 332
 from The Incredible Journey by Sheila Burnford
Responding to Literature.............................. 339
Pictures: Seeing Like a Writer.............................. 340
1 Group Writing: A Description 342
2 Thinking and Writing: Classifying 346
3 Independent Writing: A Description 348
 Prewrite □ Write □ Revise □ Proofread □ Publish
 The Grammar Connection: Using Adjectives and
 Adverbs 354
 The Mechanics Connection: Capitalizing Proper
 Adjectives 354
4 Speaking and Listening: Listening for Details 356
 Curriculum Connection   Writing About Art 358
 Unit Checkup...................................... 360
 Theme Project   Landscapes 361

AWARD WINNING
SELECTION

THEME: *OUTLOOKS*

Unit 11: PREPOSITIONS, CONJUNCTIONS, AND INTERJECTIONS 362

LANGUAGE STUDY

1 Prepositions and Prepositional Phrases............... 364
2 Using Pronouns in Prepositional Phrases............. 366
3 Prepositional Phrases as Adjectives or Adverbs 368
4 Using Verbs After Prepositional Phrases............. 370
5 Conjunctions 372
6 Making Verbs Agree with Compound Subjects........ 374
7 Interjections 376
8 Mechanics: Using Semicolons and Colons............ 378
9 Vocabulary Building: Prefixes 380
  Grammar and Writing Connection:
    Combining Sentences 382
  Unit Checkup....................................... 384
  Enrichment... 386
  Extra Practice with Practice Plus 388

Unit 12: WRITING EDITORIALS 398

WRITING

Literature: Reading Like a Writer 400
    "This Farm for Sale" by Jesse Stuart
Responding to Literature.............................. 411
Pictures: Seeing Like a Writer.......................... 412
1 Group Writing: An Editorial 414
2 Thinking and Writing: Faulty Methods
    of Persuasion..................................... 418
3 Independent Writing: An Editorial................. 420
  Prewrite □ Write □ Revise □ Proofread □ Publish
  The Grammar Connection: Using Verbs After
    Prepositional Phrases 426
  The Mechanics Connection: Using Semicolons and
    Colons.. 426
4 Speaking and Listening: Having a Debate............ 428
  Curriculum Connection Writing About Media 430
  Unit Checkup....................................... 432
  Theme Project Class Campaign 433

THEME: *TRADITIONS*

LANGUAGE STUDY

Unit 13: COMPLEX SENTENCES AND VERBALS   434

1 Sentences and Clauses............................. 436
2 Complex Sentences 438
3 Adjective Clauses 440
4 Adverb Clauses 442
5 Participles and Participial Phrases.................. 444
6 Gerunds.. 446
7 Infinitives 448
8 Mechanics: Using Commas with Clauses 450
9 Vocabulary Building: Suffixes 452
  Grammar and Writing Connection:
    Parallel Structure 454
  Unit Checkup..................................... 456
  Enrichment....................................... 458
  Extra Practice with Practice Plus 460
  Maintenance: Units 1, 3, 5, 7, 9, 11, 13.............. 470

WRITING

Unit 14: WRITING RESEARCH REPORTS   478

Literature: Reading Like a Writer 480
  "The Secrets of a Tomb"
    from The Mystery of the Ancient Maya
    by Carolyn Meyer and Charles Gallenkamp
Responding to Literature............................ 485
Pictures: Seeing Like a Writer................................ 486
1 Group Writing: A Research Report................... 488
2 Thinking and Writing: Cause and Effect............. 494
3 Independent Writing: A Research Report............. 496
  Prewrite □ Write □ Revise □ Proofread □ Publish
  The Grammar Connection: Placing Participial
    Phrases 504
  The Mechanics Connection: Using Commas with
    Clauses 504
4 Speaking and Listening: Giving an Effective Oral
    Report 506
  Curriculum Connection   Writing About Mathematics   508
  Unit Checkup..................................... 510
  Theme Project   Crafts 511

AWARD WINNING
SELECTION

WRITER'S REFERENCE

Language Study Handbook 513

Grammar

    Sentences.. 513

    Nouns... 515

    Verbs... 515

    Pronouns 516

    Adjectives 517

    Adverbs 518

    Prepositions 518

    Conjunctions... 519

    Interjections 519

    Verbals... 519

Punctuation 520

    Periods... 520

    Colons 520

    Commas.. 520

    Apostrophes 520

    Semicolons 521

    Dashes, Hyphens, and Titles 521

    Writing Quotations and Abbreviations...................... 522

Capitalization 523

Usage.. 525

Thesaurus for Writing 527

Letter Models 545

Spelling Strategies.. 547

Overview of the Writing Process 551

Writer's Resources

    Study Strategies... 552

    Using Parts of a Textbook 556

    Using a Dictionary... 557

    Using the Library.. 560

    Skimming and Scanning 564

    Note Taking 566

    Outlining... 568

    Atlases and Almanacs 570

Sentence Structure: Diagraming Guide....................... 574

Glossary 583

INDEX 591

WRITER TO WRITER

I'm here to answer some questions about writing, writer to writer, you might say. Ready? Let's begin!

How can I get ideas for writing?

This book can really help you there. There's great literature between these covers. I noticed that after reading a good story, biography, or poem, I wanted to respond. Sometimes I wanted to write about the same topic or in a similar style. Sometimes I wanted to write a journal entry.

Writers are readers, and readers are writers!

What will I write about today?

I know that sometimes, no matter how hard I try, the ideas won't come. Reading a story doesn't work. Talking with my friends doesn't help. Then, I take a look at the **PICTURES** *SEEING LIKE A WRITER* section in this book, and presto! Ideas start to flow. The pictures turn up the volume on my imagination.

IMAGINE

Writers observe, and observers can find lots of ideas for writing.

How will I remember all my ideas?

 JOURNAL

Personally, I don't know how I'd keep all my ideas straight without my journal. I write in it every day— facts, thoughts, feelings. I write down new and interesting words, too. A journal is a great place to keep track of what you've learned.

A journal is a writer's best friend.

How does working with a group help?

Writing doesn't have to be something that you do alone. I get lots of ideas when I work with my classmates. During group writing, we write and conference together. When it's time to write on my own, I'm all warmed up and ready to go.

Writing together builds confidence; conferences get the ideas flowing.

How do thinking and writing go together?

I really give my brain a workout when I write. I can't help it. To write, you have to think about many things: sequence; main idea; cause and effect; and likenesses and differences.

Writing is thinking on paper.

Writing isn't something that just happens 1-2-3. It takes time to write. The writing process allows me the time I need.

What is the writing process, and how will it help me?

Prewrite

At this stage I can get ideas and plan my writing. I need to think about my purpose and audience. Graphic organizers can really help here.

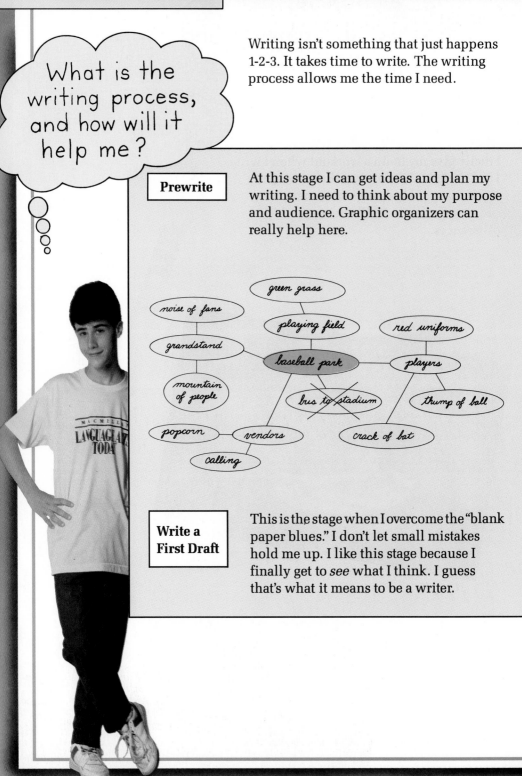

Write a First Draft

This is the stage when I overcome the "blank paper blues." I don't let small mistakes hold me up. I like this stage because I finally get to *see* what I think. I guess that's what it means to be a writer.

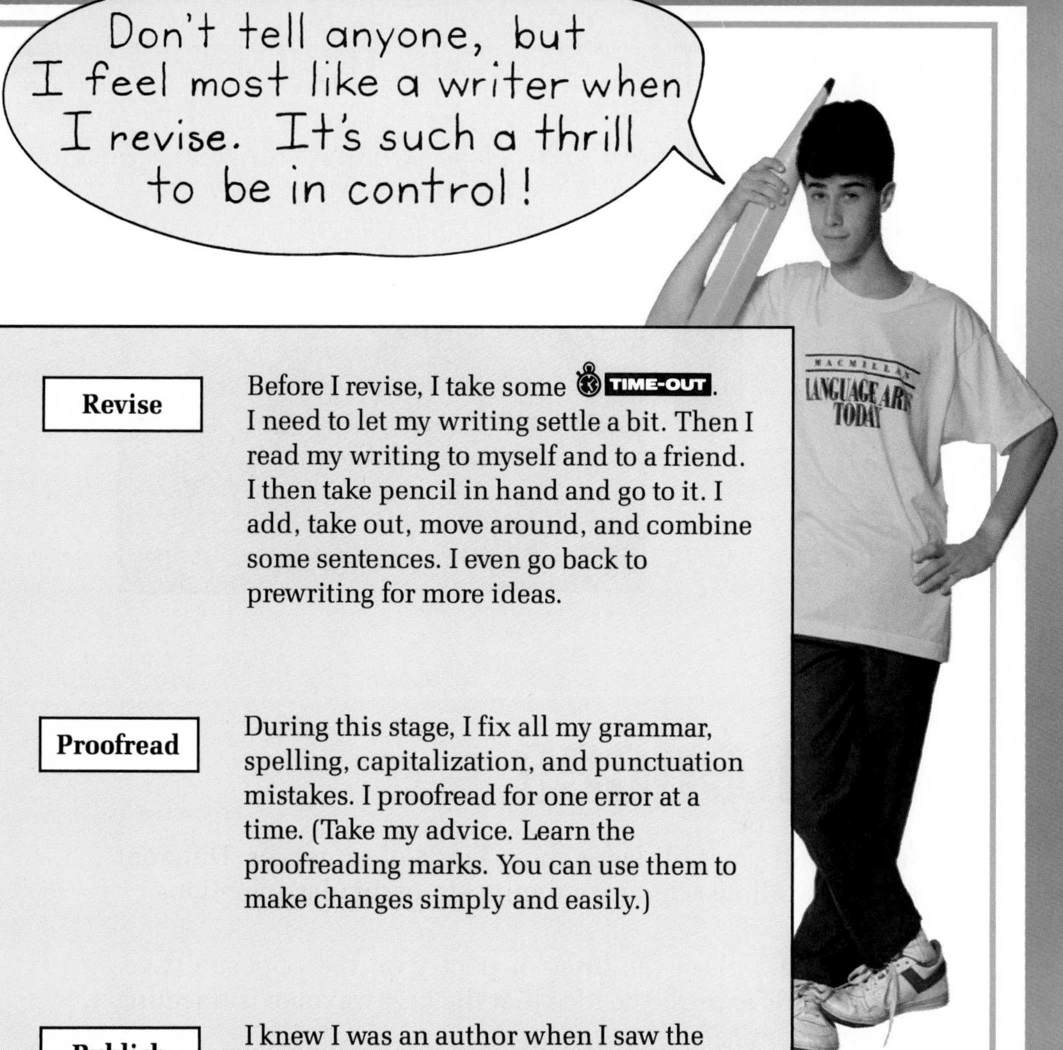

Don't tell anyone, but I feel most like a writer when I revise. It's such a thrill to be in control!

Revise

Before I revise, I take some 🕐 **TIME-OUT**. I need to let my writing settle a bit. Then I read my writing to myself and to a friend. I then take pencil in hand and go to it. I add, take out, move around, and combine some sentences. I even go back to prewriting for more ideas.

Proofread

During this stage, I fix all my grammar, spelling, capitalization, and punctuation mistakes. I proofread for one error at a time. (Take my advice. Learn the proofreading marks. You can use them to make changes simply and easily.)

Publish

I knew I was an author when I saw the word "publish." Publishing can mean reading your writing to friends or taking it home to show your family— anything that involves sharing your writing with your audience.

Sentences

In this unit you will learn about kinds of sentences. Different sentences allow you to communicate particular intentions.

Discuss Read the lines of poetry on the opposite page. What words express the idea that the highwayman is traveling a great distance?

Creative Expression The unit theme is *Journeys*. A journey often involves a search or a quest. In your journal write about a journey you would like to undertake.

THEME: *JOURNEYS*

The road was a ribbon of moonlight over the purple moor,
And the highwayman came riding—
Riding—riding—

—Alfred Noyes, from "The Highwayman"

1 KINDS OF SENTENCES

A sentence is a group of words that expresses a complete thought.

You have learned from everyday conversation the importance of expressing yourself in complete sentences. A **sentence** is a group of words that expresses a complete thought.

The four kinds of sentences are listed below. Notice that every sentence begins with a capital letter and ends with a punctuation mark.

Declarative Sentence	Exclamatory Sentence
Purpose: makes a statement	Purpose: expresses strong feeling
Example: Our class traveled to Chicago.	Example: How huge the museum seemed!
End Mark: period	End Mark: exclamation mark
Interrogative Sentence	**Imperative Sentence**
Purpose: asks a question	Purpose: commands or requests
Example: Did you enjoy our museum trip?	Examples: Sit down near me. Please stay here.
End Mark: question mark	End Mark: period

Guided Practice

Tell whether each sentence is declarative, interrogative, exclamatory, or imperative.

Example: I like class trips. *declarative*

1. Please tell me more about your museum trip.
2. At 9:30 three school buses arrived.
3. Did teachers from other classes go along, too?
4. We spent the entire day at the Field Museum.
5. What interesting discoveries our class made there!

?! THINK

- How can using different kinds of sentences make my writing more interesting?

REMEMBER

- A **declarative sentence** makes a statement and ends with a period.
- An **interrogative sentence** asks a question and ends with a question mark.
- An **exclamatory sentence** expresses strong feeling and ends with an exclamation mark.
- An **imperative sentence** gives a command or makes a request and ends with a period.

More Practice

A. Write whether each sentence is declarative, interrogative, exclamatory, or imperative.

Example: Where is the museum?   *interrogative*

  6. We could see the museum from Lake Shore Drive.
  7. Walk with us along Lake Michigan.
  8. Which exhibits were part of the tour?
  9. A wonderful tour guide led us.
  10. How ancient some of the items were!
  11. We gathered at a tall pair of totem poles.
  12. Have you studied Native American culture?

B. Write each sentence, using the correct capitalization and punctuation marks. Then write whether it is declarative, interrogative, exclamatory, or imperative.

Example: show us your photographs
        Show us your photographs. imperative

  13. last year Jason traveled through the Southwest
  14. what exciting discoveries he made
  15. describe the landscape for us
  16. did Native Americans always live there
  17. in New Mexico Jason visited a pueblo village
  18. how beautiful the sunsets were
  19. a native woman told stories about her people
  20. her costume was authentic, wasn't it

Extra Practice, page 24

WRITING APPLICATION A Letter

Imagine you visited another part of the country. Write a brief letter describing your visit. Then meet with a classmate and find examples of the four kinds of sentences.

2 COMPLETE SUBJECTS AND COMPLETE PREDICATES

Every sentence you write needs two sentence parts to express a complete thought. The **complete subject** includes all the words that tell whom or what the sentence is about. The **complete predicate** includes all the words that tell what the subject does or is.

COMPLETE SUBJECT	COMPLETE PREDICATE
My classmate	comes from Peru.
Anita Montoya's parents	are proud of their birthplace.

In interrogative sentences the complete subject usually comes after part of the complete predicate.

Does | Anita's family | enjoy their new home?

Did | their possessions | arrive safely?

In imperative sentences the complete subject is not stated directly. *You* is the understood complete subject of an imperative sentence.

(You) | Ask Anita about her homeland.

(You) | Please tell me about your heritage.

Guided Practice

Identify the complete subject and the complete predicate in each sentence.

Example: Foreign countries interest me.
Foreign countries   complete subject
interest me   complete predicate

1. Anita's family visited Peru again last summer.

2. Did your friend learn more about her birthplace?

3. The souvenirs from her trip are fascinating.

4. Anita learned more about her homeland.

5. Listen to her stories about Peru's past.

 THINK

■ How do I decide if a sentence is complete?

REMEMBER

- The **complete subject** includes all the words that tell whom or what the sentence is about.
- The **complete predicate** includes all the words that tell what the subject does or is.

More Practice

A. Write each sentence. Underline the complete subject once and the complete predicate twice. Write (*You*) to identify the complete subject of an imperative sentence.

Example: <u>That girl</u> <u><u>travels often</u></u>.

  6. Did Anita travel to the city of Lima?
  7. Her parents took her to the Andes Mountains.
  8. These mountains are truly majestic.
  9. Machu Picchu is an Inca city.
 10. The discovery of Machu Picchu made headlines.
 11. Look at Anita's pictures of this huge fortress.
 12. Did the Montoya family explore this place?

B. Write each sentence. Draw a line between the complete subject and the complete predicate. If necessary, reorder the words in the sentence.

Example: Some students | are from South America.

 13. Anita traveled also to Bolivia.
 14. She explored its beautiful terrain.
 15. This country has the highest freshwater lake in the world.
 16. The family took a ferry between Peru and Bolivia.
 17. Imagine the Montoya family on the ferry.
 18. Did Anita tell you other stories about her trip?
 19. My friend learned an important lesson.
 20. Never forget the value of your family's heritage.

Extra Practice, page 25

 WRITING APPLICATION A Story

Do you or a friend of yours have relatives who are from foreign countries? Do you have neighbors or classmates who were not born in this country? Write a brief story that tells about how they left their home. Then exchange stories with a classmate and identify the complete subjects and complete predicates in each other's sentences.

3 SIMPLE SUBJECTS AND SIMPLE PREDICATES

You have learned that a sentence contains a complete subject and a complete predicate. The main word or words in the complete subject is called the **simple subject.** The main word or words in the complete predicate are called the **simple predicate.**

SIMPLE SUBJECT SIMPLE PREDICATE

Our **teacher** **spent** his vacation in Japan.

David **has visited** the Far East.

The simple predicate of an interrogative sentence is usually divided by the subject.

Did David's **teacher** **learn** Japanese?

The simple predicate of an imperative sentence is usually the first word. The simple subject is not stated but is understood to be *you.*

(You) **Speak** a few words for us.

In the sentence below, the simple subject is *guidebook.* The simple predicate is *is.*

Here **is** a Japanese **guidebook.**

Guided Practice

Identify the simple subject and the simple predicate.

Example: One student described his journal.
   student *simple subject*
   described *simple predicate*

1. Red and white banners hung from the ceiling.
2. Did Ms. Anderson arrange the posters on the wall?
3. Here is David's drawing of Mt. Fuji.
4. Read his story about a ride on a Japanese train.

 THINK

■ How can I decide which words are the simple subject and the simple predicate of a sentence?

REMEMBER

- The **simple subject** is the main word or words in the complete subject.
- The **simple predicate** is the main word or words in the complete predicate.

More Practice

A. Write each sentence. Then underline the simple subject once and the simple predicate twice.

Example: One <u>student</u> <u>comes</u> from Japan.

5. Every student in my class attended this program.
6. Does the program include any Japanese songs?
7. A girl sang a song about cherry blossoms.
8. David welcomed some visitors in Japanese.
9. A report on the country's history followed.
10. Have you read any novels about ancient Japan?
11. The whole class discussed its colorful history.
12. Traces of old Japan exist even now.

B. Write each sentence. Then underline the simple subject once and the simple predicate twice. Write *You* for the simple subject of an imperative sentence.

Example: <u>Tell</u> us about Japan. (You)

13. There was much interest in Oriental culture.
14. Describe a Kabuki play.
15. There were questions about this form of drama.
16. Study Japanese legends.
17. There is some truth to these stories.
18. Try these Japanese snacks.
19. Here is a photograph of him in Tokyo.
20. Is there a shot of David at a tea ceremony?

Extra Practice, page 26

WRITING APPLICATION An Advertisement

COOPERATIVE LEARNING

Imagine that you own a travel agency. With a partner write an advertisement for a special cruise that your agency is offering. What exotic location will the cruise visit, and what special services will be provided? Identify the simple subject and simple predicate in your sentences.

4 COMPOUND SUBJECTS AND COMPOUND PREDICATES

Sometimes you may write a sentence that has a **compound subject,** or more than one simple subject. Other times you may write a sentence that has a **compound predicate,** or more than one simple predicate. The parts of a compound subject or compound predicate are joined by a **coordinating conjunction,** or connecting word, such as *and, or,* or *but.*

| Tisha and Alex | bicycled around the city.

The two friends | stopped and ate | lunch.

Guided Practice

Tell whether each sentence contains a compound subject or a compound predicate.

Example: The streets and squares were busy.
    compound subject

1. Tisha carried a camera and took many photographs.
2. Alex's bicycle ran over a nail and got a flat tire.
3. The park and the riverside are good places for bicycle trips.
4. The tour stimulated Tisha but exhausted Alex.
5. Bicyclists and skateboarders filled the park's sidewalks.

 THINK

■ How can I tell if a sentence has a compound subject or a compound predicate?

REMEMBER

- A **compound subject** is two or more simple subjects with the same predicate.
- A **compound predicate** is two or more simple predicates with the same subject.
- A **coordinating conjunction** such as *and, or,* or *but* connects the parts of a compound subject or predicate.

More Practice

A. Write whether each sentence contains a compound subject or a compound predicate. Then write the simple subjects or simple predicates in each compound.

Example: The girl and boy have new bicycles.
> *compound subject   girl   boy*

6. Tisha and Alex bicycled slowly around the park.
7. Alex admired the foliage but strained his neck.
8. They checked their tires and asked a policeman for directions.
9. The gorillas and the chimpanzees at the zoo were popular.
10. The zookeepers fed the animals or cleaned the cages.

B. Rewrite each sentence so that it contains either a compound subject or a compound predicate.

Example: Alex rode each day.   (compound subject)
> *Alex and his friend rode each day.*

11. Tisha rode across the field and around the lake.
    (compound subject)
12. Canadian geese glided over the smooth lake.
    (compound subject)
13. Tisha photographed the birds. (compound predicate)
14. The bicyclists enjoyed their outing in the park.
    (compound predicate)
15. Children of all ages pedaled past the playground.
    (compound subject and compound predicate)

Extra Practice, page 27

WRITING APPLICATION A Paragraph

Write a paragraph that describes an important discovery you have made with the help of a friend or relative. Then exchange papers with a classmate. Identify compound subjects and predicates in each other's work.

5 COMPOUND SENTENCES

You often write sentences that contain only one subject and one predicate. This kind of sentence is called a **simple sentence.** A simple sentence may contain a compound subject or a compound predicate, or both.

| Mom | was planning a trip |

| Mom and I | found a location and planned a trip. |

Sometimes you may combine two simple sentences to form a **compound sentence.** A compound sentence has two or more complete subjects and two or more complete predicates.

| Mom | was planning a trip | , and | I | helped her. |

You usually use a coordinating conjunction such as *and, but,* or *or* to connect ideas in a compound sentence. Use a comma before the conjunction in a compound sentence.

If the two parts of a compound sentence are not joined by a conjunction, use a semicolon to separate the parts.

I bought a map; we both studied it.

Guided Practice

Tell whether each sentence is a simple sentence or a compound sentence.

Example: Dad and Mom discussed our travel plans.
            simple sentence

1. Mom chose Chicago, and I measured the distance.
2. It was 600 miles away; we needed a closer spot.
3. Larry and Dad considered some interesting places in South Carolina and Mississippi.
4. Mom read about these states in my tour book, but we couldn't make a decision.
5. We studied the map again after dinner, but no one could make a decision.

 THINK

■ How can I decide if a sentence is simple or compound?

REMEMBER

- A **simple sentence** has one complete subject and one complete predicate.
- A **compound sentence** contains two or more simple sentences joined by *and*, *but*, or *or*.

More Practice

A. Write whether each sentence is **simple** or **compound**.

Example: The entire family needed a relaxing vacation.
　　　　simple sentence

6. Dad preferred a location with a warm climate.
7. Mom's sister lives in Florida, and she will give us a tour.
8. I had always dreamed about a tropical beach with palm trees.
9. Dad interrupted my daydream; a decision had finally been reached.
10. Our trip to Florida would take us to Cape Canaveral.

B. Complete each sentence so that it is a compound sentence. Use the coordinating conjunction in parentheses. Add commas where necessary.

Example: Mom likes seaside locations ____. (but)
　　　　Mom likes seaside locations, but Larry prefers the mountains.

11. Larry mentioned California ____. (and)
12. His suggestion sounded good ____. (but)
13. Mom and Dad had promised us a trip to Orlando ____. (and)
14. We could have a great time at Disney World ____. (or)
15. I have a pen pal in Tampa ____. (and)
16. Mom was planning our budget ____. (and)
17. We must keep our travel expenses low ____. (or)
18. Would we see the Everglades ____? (or)
19. We could see the alligators ____. (but)
20. There is so much to see in Disney World ____. (and)

Extra Practice, page 28

WRITING APPLICATION Instructions

Plan an ideal vacation. How would you get there? Write a paragraph that tells about your plans. Then exchange paragraphs with a classmate and identify the simple and compound sentences in each other's work.

6 CORRECTING FRAGMENTS AND RUN-ON SENTENCES

A group of words that does not express a complete thought is called a **sentence fragment.** A sentence fragment lacks either a subject part or a predicate part.

SENTENCE FRAGMENTS: Two of my best friends.
Spent a whole month in Africa.

COMPLETE SENTENCE: Two of my best friends spent a whole month in Africa.

Do not run sentences together without the correct punctuation. This kind of error is called a **run-on sentence.**

How to Correct a Run-on Sentence

■ Rewrite each sentence as a complete thought.
■ Be sure to begin each sentence with a capital letter.
■ Use the correct end mark for each sentence.

RUN-ON: Aretha took many photographs on her trip and she also wrote detailed letters to her parents but the letters never arrived.

CORRECT: Aretha took many photographs on her trip. She also wrote detailed letters to her parents, but the letters never arrived.

Guided Practice

Tell whether each item is a sentence fragment or a run-on.

Example: Took many photographs. *fragment*

1. Aretha's father worked for an international company, he was sent to Sudan in Africa for a project.
2. The exotic capital city of Khartoum.
3. Is situated near the Nile River.
4. Mr. James enjoys warm places and Khartoum is one of the world's hottest capitals and the average January temperature can reach 90°.
5. After spending several months in Khartoum.

 THINK

■ How can I correct a run-on sentence?

REMEMBER

- A **sentence fragment** is a group of words that is only part of a sentence. It does not express a complete thought.
- A **run-on sentence** joins two or more sentences that should be written separately.

More Practice

A. Write whether each item is a sentence fragment or a run-on sentence. Then correct it.

Example: Collected many possessions over the years.
sentence fragment   My grandparents collected many possessions over the years.

6. Grandpa brought a box down from the attic, it was filled with letters from Mom.
7. Many old stamps with unusual designs.
8. The first letter was postmarked in Egypt my parents had stayed there for a month.
9. Whenever my parents talk about Egypt.
10. A trip they took to the Pyramids.
11. Grandpa opened the letter from Egypt he read it to me.
12. Their first camel ride.
13. Across the desert to the pyramids.
14. The Pyramids stand majestically on the Nile and my parents were thrilled at the sight but they also felt humbled.
15. I imagined my parents at the Sphinx, next Grandpa read Mom's letter about King Tutankhamen's tomb.
16. Many kings of Egypt built tombs for themselves and their followers and thieves looted the tombs repeatedly so priceless objects were lost forever.
17. Saw furniture and beautiful dishes in Tutankhamen's tomb.
18. His mummy.
19. Mummies have always interested me and I've seen one in a museum my parents took the whole family.
20. When my little sister saw the mummy.

Extra Practice, Practice Plus, pages 29–31

 WRITING APPLICATION A Post Card

Imagine what it might be like to live in Africa. Write a post card to describe your impressions. Then check your writing for sentence fragments and run-on sentences.

COOPERATIVE
LEARNING

7 MECHANICS: Punctuating Sentences

Punctuation marks serve different purposes in different kinds of sentences.

Use end marks to signal the end of a sentence.

Type of Sentence	End Mark	Example
Declarative	period	Our ancestry is important.
Imperative	period	Ask your parents.
Interrogative	question mark	Where are they?
Exclamatory	exclamation mark	How curious I am!

Use a comma or a semicolon to separate parts of a compound sentence.

Punctuation	When to Use	Example
Comma (,)	with conjunction (*and*, *or*, *but*)	Sue traced her family's heritage, and her grandparents helped her.
Semicolon (;)	without conjunction	Their stories fascinated her; she listened intently.

Guided Practice

Tell what punctuation marks are needed in the following.

Example: Look at these historical documents   *period*

1. How do you create a family tree
2. Sue began a diagram of her family tree on it she wrote the names of her parents and grandparents
3. What an enormous family she had
4. Sue gathered all of her notes but they were not sufficient
5. Imagine Sue's determination in her search

?! THINK

■ What purposes do punctuation marks serve?

REMEMBER

- End declarative and imperative sentences with a period. End interrogative sentences with a question mark. End exclamatory sentences with an exclamation mark.
- Join ideas in a compound sentence by using either (1) a conjunction preceded by a comma or (2) a semicolon.

More Practice

A. Write each sentence. Add the correct punctuation.

Example: Sue has many relatives but I have few
    Sue has many relatives, but I have few.

6. She hoped for more information from her Canadian relatives she wrote letters to several of them
7. Would any of them reply to her request
8. A letter came from one cousin and Sue opened it excitedly
9. It might be helpful or it could frustrate her efforts
10. What a complex jigsaw puzzle her family story was

B. Write each sentence and add the correct punctuation marks. Explain your answer.

Example: Did Sue find many facts
    Did Sue find many facts? interrogative sentence

11. Sue sat on the edge of her bed then she read about a previously unknown relative
12. Did her parents know about her Italian great-aunt or had they never heard of Teresa Mastrangello
13. How surprised they were by this unexpected news
14. The photograph showed a family resemblance
15. Other letters from Canada arrived soon afterward and Sue learned much more about her ancestry
16. Sue did not stop tracing her family tree she did research at the library and she consulted the town records

Extra Practice, page 32

WRITING APPLICATION An Explanation

What do you know about your family history? Write a factual or imaginative paragraph that explains your ancestry. Then exchange papers with a classmate and check to make sure that punctuation marks have been used correctly.

8 VOCABULARY BUILDING: Using Context Clues

When you find an unfamiliar word in your reading, you may use a dictionary to find the word's meaning. You can also guess at a word's meaning by looking at the **context** of the word, that is, the other words in the sentence or in nearby sentences.

> Uncle Miguel, the family **raconteur**, tells wonderful stories about his travels. Some people shrink from the thought of adventures. Our **dauntless** uncle, however, welcomes new challenges. "People fear only the things they don't understand," he says.

Suppose you did not know the meaning of the word *raconteur* in the first sentence above. The second part of the sentence tells you that Uncle Miguel tells stories. This gives you a clue to the meaning of *raconteur*, which means a "skillful storyteller."

Can you guess the meaning of the word *dauntless*, used above? If you study the context of this word by examining the other words and sentences near it, you can tell that the word *dauntless* means "unafraid."

Guided Practice

Tell the meaning of each underlined word by using context clues. Use a dictionary to check your work.

Example: Rob is so <u>gullible</u>; he believes everyone's stories.   *believing*

1. Uncle Miguel has <u>chronicled</u> his travels by describing them in a diary.
2. He might travel as far away as the Amazon River or the Sahara Desert, but his diary accompanies him on every <u>excursion</u>.
3. Both lengthy stories about his experiences and brief <u>anecdotes</u> fill the pages of the diary.
4. How many delightful hours we have dreamed away listening to his <u>beguiling</u> stories!

 THINK

- How can I figure out the meaning of an unfamiliar word without using a dictionary?

REMEMBER

- You can sometimes figure out the meaning of an unfamiliar word by looking at its **context.**

More Practice

A. Write the meaning of each underlined word. Use context clues to help you. Then use a dictionary to check your work.

Example: My uncle's <u>odysseys</u> have taken him around the world.   *voyages*

5. In his flights to the Orient, Uncle Miguel has <u>traversed</u> the Pacific Ocean many times.
6. He has also taken many <u>transatlantic</u> cruises to Europe.
7. He talks enthusiastically of those lands but speaks most <u>fervently</u> of Indonesia, his favorite country.
8. He enjoys telling of his adventures there, particularly one <u>exploit</u> on the island of Sumatra.
9. Uncle Miguel always <u>prefaces</u> the story by first telling us that the tale is absolutely true.

B. Write the meaning of each underlined word. Use context clues to help you. Then check your answers in a dictionary.

I was walking down a **(10)** <u>teeming</u> street when a woman in the busy crowd stopped me. People talked openly all around us, but she whispered **(11)** <u>furtively</u>, "What will you give me in exchange for this valuable jewel?" Although the clear stone she held gleamed with the **(12)** <u>semblance</u> of fire, it felt as **(13)** <u>frigid</u> as ice. We **(14)** <u>negotiated</u> quickly, and I placed a small amount of money in her hand. As she disappeared into the pressing **(15)** <u>throng</u> with this **(16)** <u>pittance</u>, I stood there amazed at the speed of our **(17)** <u>transaction</u>. However, when I went to put the stone away, I was **(18)** <u>disheartened</u> to find that while I had been so **(19)** <u>mesmerized</u>, someone had **(20)** <u>filched</u> my wallet. Later I learned that the "jewel" was only glass!

Extra Practice, page 33

WRITING APPLICATION Definitions

Cut out a newspaper article and circle three words that are unfamiliar to you. Using context clues, write what you think each word means. Check the meanings in a dictionary. Then write two sentences using each word.

Combining Sentences

When you write narratives, you need to tell when events happened in time. Sometimes you can combine sentences to show a relationship of events in time.

> **SEPARATE:** We played tennis. We had a picnic.
>
> **COMBINED:** We played tennis after we had a picnic.
>
> **COMBINED:** After we had a picnic, we played tennis.

Use connecting words such as *after*, *before*, *since*, *until*, *when*, and *while* to combine sentences to show a relationship of events in time. When the connecting word begins the sentence, use a comma at the end of the clause.

You can often shorten a clause that shows time.

> We played tennis **after our picnic.**

You may also combine sentences to show a relationship of reason or condition by using connecting words such as *because*, *if*, *so that*, or *since*.

> **SEPARATE:** It was a beautiful day. We decided to have a picnic.
>
> **COMBINED:** Because it was a beautiful day, we decided to have a picnic.

Working Together

COOPERATIVE
LEARNING

Tell how you would combine each of the following pairs of sentences. Use one of the connecting words listed in the lesson.

Example: It may rain. We will postpone the picnic.
If it rains, we will postpone the picnic.

1. We had sandwiches and milk. Then everyone took a hike.
2. The picnic ground is near the zoo. We went to see the monkeys.
3. We may walk briskly. We may have time to see the aviary.

Revising Sentences

In his journal Delbert wrote down sentences for a story he was planning to write. Help him revise his work by combining each pair of sentences to show a relationship of ideas. Use the connecting words listed in the lesson.

4. The zookeeper would not let us in.
   A small monkey had escaped.
5. She made the announcement.
   We were filled with disappointment.
6. We discussed the situation.
   Several offered their help.
7. The zoo needed assistance.
   The zookeeper accepted our offer.
8. She instructed us.
   We started on our search.
9. We were looking in a small cave.
   Bert saw the monkey in a tree.
10. He moved very carefully.
    The monkey would not be frightened.
11. Bert cornered the monkey.
    Clair picked it up.
12. We got back to the picnic.
    Our food had all been eaten!

Think about the different kinds of journeys you read and wrote about in Unit 1. Which kinds of journeys are most important to you? Write a paragraph telling why those journeys have meaning for you.

When you revise your writing, look for pairs of sentences to combine to show the relationships between ideas. Be sure to use a comma when one is needed.

UNIT CHECKUP

Kinds of Sentences (page 2)   Write each sentence, using the correct punctuation and capitalization. Then write whether it is **declarative, interrogative, exclamatory,** or **imperative.**

1. imagine a trip across America in the last century
2. canals connected rivers and lakes for boat traffic
3. did people dig these canals by hand
4. what an enormous amount of work that was
5. we studied the canals in social studies class

LESSONS

Complete Subjects and Complete Predicates; Simple Subjects and Simple Predicates (pages 4, 6)   Write each sentence. Underline the complete subject once and the complete predicate twice. Then write each simple subject and simple predicate.

6. Do canals interest you?
7. My grandfather remembers the days of canals.
8. Fewer canals exist today.
9. When did the period of railway travel begin?
10. Imagine the cost of building highways.

LESSON

4

Compound Subjects and Compound Predicates (page 8) Write each sentence. Underline a compound subject once and a compound predicate twice.

11. Elena and Mark have traveled on a canal.
12. Carlos and Amy visited the Erie Canal.
13. They returned and described it to the class.
14. Albany and Buffalo were also interesting to them.
15. Their stories amused the class and impressed the teacher.

LESSON

5

Compound Sentences (page 10)   Write each sentence and label it **simple** or **compound.** Underline each complete subject once and each complete predicate twice.

16. Cameras are useful; they assist our memory.
17. Some people record their travels with a camera.
18. Dorothea Lange traveled throughout the country.
19. Lange began her career in California; her work later took her around the United States.
20. I enjoy Lange's work, but Marilyn has not seen it.

LESSON 6

Correcting Fragments and Run-on Sentences (page 12)   Read each item and write whether it is a **sentence fragment** or a **run-on sentence**. Then correct it.

21. The topic of my research report last year.
22. Found a fascinating article about photographers.
23. In 1935 Dorothea Lange went to Oklahoma, there she photographed life in the "Dust Bowl."
24. Pictures of everyday life during World War II.
25. Lange photographed news stories but she also had an interest in human-interest pictures and she remained active in her work until her death.

LESSON 7

Mechanics: Punctuating Sentences (page 14)   Write each sentence, using the correct punctuation.

26. How vast the world is
27. Ana has a book collection I collect maps
28. Can you name the world's smallest countries
29. Come along with me on an imaginary tour
30. How incredibly small the nation of Tuvalu is
31. Tuvalu is tiny but Vatican City is smaller

LESSON 8

Vocabulary Building: Using Context Clues (page 16)   Write the definition of each underlined word. Use context clues to help you.

32. We were <u>apprehensive</u> about the flight, but we were not nervous about the upcoming boat trip.
33. The <u>itinerary</u> for our trip through Italy included two days in Rome.
34. Known as the residence of the Pope, Vatican City includes the <u>Papal</u> Gardens.
35. The <u>autonomy</u> of Vatican City was recognized in 1929; before then, it was a part of Italy.
36. The soldiers of Vatican City do not come from Italy; they are <u>recruited</u> from Switzerland.

Writing Application: Sentences (pages 2–15)   The following paragraph contains 7 sentence errors. Rewrite the paragraph correctly.

37.–43.   when would Justin ever arrive The bus was hot and traffic clogged the highway. Dozing and reading for hours and hours. His parents and brothers and sisters far away. How wonderful he would feel at the end of this endless trip Relieved to be home at last.

Sentence Squares

Fold a sheet of paper in half and then in half again. Label each square as one of the four kinds of sentences. Then under each heading write a sentence about a special place you would like to visit. You may wish to add art, cut out the squares, and share with classmates.

In Other Words

The English language has many colorful expressions called **idioms.** The meaning of an idiom is different from the meanings of the individual words. Examples are *raining cats and dogs* (raining very hard) and *throw your hat into the ring* (announce you are running for office). Working with a partner, think of four idioms and write them down. Then write a humorous dialogue using the idioms.

Scrambled Sentences

Write a paragraph about what makes up a nutritious breakfast, or any other meal. Then scramble the words in each sentence and write them out. Exchange papers with a partner and unscramble each other's sentences. Then for each sentence circle the simple subject and underline the simple predicate.

News of the Day

Imagine you are a news reporter. With a small group of classmates, prepare a broadcast that highlights the major news events of the day. Be sure you use complete sentences. Share your broadcast with the rest of the class.

MAKE YOUR MARK

Write four sentences, one of each kind, leaving out the punctuation marks. Exchange your papers with a partner. Add the correct punctuation marks to each other's sentences and read them aloud.

SPORTS SHOTS

Cut out four pictures of people playing your favorite sport. Attach the pictures to blank sheets of paper. Below the pictures, write descriptions of the athletes using the four different kinds of sentences. Exchange papers with a partner and read your descriptions aloud. Identify each sentence by type.

EXTRA PRACTICE

Three levels of practice

Kinds of Sentences (page 2)

LEVEL

A. Write whether each sentence is **declarative, interrogative, exclamatory,** or **imperative.**

1. Did your grandfather come from Scandinavia?
2. The Vikings lived there ten centuries ago.
3. What powerful warriors they were!
4. Consider the Vikings' other accomplishments, too.
5. They were excellent shipbuilders and sailors.
6. Did they travel far from their Scandinavian home?
7. How boldly they sailed across the Atlantic!
8. I wish I could have joined them.

LEVEL

B. Write each sentence, using the correct capitalization and punctuation marks. Then write whether it is **declarative, interrogative, exclamatory,** or **imperative.**

9. we have studied the Vikings this year
10. have you read about the Vikings' voyages
11. some Vikings left home in search of better land
12. imagine yourself as a Viking at sea
13. each ship sailed under a large square sail
14. do not forget about the crew of rowers
15. where did the Vikings keep their shields
16. how fierce their dragon-shaped figureheads looked

LEVEL

C. Rewrite each sentence so that it is the kind of sentence indicated in parentheses. Use the correct end punctuation.

17. You have traveled in many kinds of boats. (interrogative)
18. The Vikings' royal barges were grand. (exclamatory)
19. Did the Vikings study navigation? (declarative)
20. Can you plot your course by the stars? (imperative)
21. The 4,000-mile voyage to North America was difficult. (exclamatory)
22. The Vikings realized the value of ships. (interrogative)
23. Would Hector like to have been a Viking? (declarative)
24. The Vikings lived long ago. (exclamatory)
25. Did they have magnificent ships? (declarative)

EXTRA PRACTICE

Three levels of practice

Complete Subjects and Complete Predicates (page 4)

LEVEL

A. Write each sentence. Underline each complete subject once and each complete predicate twice. If the complete subject is understood, write (**You**).

1. Would you enjoy a visit to the Himalayas?
2. Look for these mountains on a map of Asia.
3. Annie Taylor visited this part of the world.
4. She explored during the early part of this century.
5. Was Isabella Bishop another such explorer?
6. Her courage is beyond doubt.
7. Remember other Himalayan explorers, too.
8. Several explorers have become world famous.

LEVEL

B. Write each sentence. Draw a line to separate the complete subject from the complete predicate. If necessary, rewrite the sentence so that the complete subject comes first.

9. Tibet is a country in the Himalayas.
10. Alexandra David-Neel went to Tibet in 1924.
11. Did she cross the Gobi Desert completely on foot?
12. Try a long, hot journey like that sometime.
13. The explorer approached a "forbidden" city in the desert.
14. Could a European woman gain entrance?
15. This clever adventurer disguised herself as a peasant.
16. Was David-Neel's book about this trip popular?

LEVEL

C. Write whether each group of words could be the complete subject or the complete predicate of a sentence. Then write a complete sentence using the words.

17. a trip to the distant land of Tibet
18. could learn many things there
19. have traveled outside of the United States
20. three of the books in our school library
21. will travel to the Himalayas someday
22. my younger but very intelligent brother
23. were collecting stories about mountain-climbing
24. the students in my class
25. studied maps and articles about these mountains

EXTRA PRACTICE

Three levels of practice

Simple Subjects and Simple Predicates (page 6)

LEVEL

A. Write each sentence. Underline the simple subject once and the simple predicate twice.

1. My family saw a documentary film last night.
2. The title of the program was *Oh Canada.*
3. The first few scenes showed Vancouver.
4. This city lies almost on the American border.
5. The filmmaker took a spectacular airplane trip.
6. Sunlight gleamed from glaciers and snowy peaks.
7. My sister is writing a story about Canada.
8. This country has a very interesting history.

LEVEL

B. Write each sentence. Underline the simple subject once and the simple predicate twice. If the simple subject is understood, write (**You**).

9. Have you visited this unique land?
10. The young writer described the city of Montreal.
11. Did the farmlands of Alberta come next?
12. There are many similarities to the American landscape.
13. Is the city of Calgary in the province of Alberta?
14. Remember the 1988 Winter Olympics.
15. Huge crowds traveled to Calgary for the events.
16. Would many people enjoy life in the town of Medicine Hat?

LEVEL

C. Rewrite each sentence by adding words to the subject and predicate parts. Then underline the simple subject once and the simple predicate twice.

17. The documentary continued.
18. A ranger spoke.
19. Trees towered.
20. Vacationers wandered.
21. Moose appeared.
22. Vera gathered travelogues.
23. We are making plans.
24. Students researched.
25. Books helped.

EXTRA PRACTICE

Three levels of practice

Compound Subjects and Compound Predicates (page 8)

LEVEL
A. Write each sentence. Underline each compound subject once. Underline each compound predicate twice.

1. Maria and Gloria wanted to take a long train ride.
2. First they talked and chose an interesting location.
3. Their parents and friends advised them.
4. Maria's brother and sister also like train rides.
5. They telephoned and asked Maria a question.
6. Their questions and concerns were numerous.

LEVEL
B. Rewrite each sentence so that it contains either a compound subject or a compound predicate.

7. A lifeguard surveyed the ocean. (compound predicate)
8. Suddenly he blew his whistle. (compound predicate)
9. Boys dove from a raft. (compound subject)
10. Wind surfers paddled out to sea. (compound predicate)
11. They rode the waves. (compound predicate)
12. Small crabs lay on the sand. (compound subject)
13. Beachcombers looked for unusual shells. (compound predicate)
14. A little girl walked slowly to the water's edge. (compound subject)

LEVEL
C. Write each pair of sentences as a single sentence that has either a compound subject or a compound predicate.

15. John wants to go to Maine.
    I want to go to Maine.
16. Friends might enjoy the trip together.
    Relatives might also enjoy the trip.
17. The two girls spoke with other travelers.
    The girls visited the dining car for lunch.
18. Maria had never been to Ocean Beach before.
    Gloria had never been there either.
19. Colorful umbrellas lined the shore.
    Beach blankets were everywhere.
20. Beachcombers were scurrying over rocks.
    They were also wading into tide pools.

EXTRA PRACTICE

Three levels of practice

Compound Sentences (page 10)

LEVEL
A. Write whether each sentence is **simple** or **compound.**

1. People use many modes of transportation, but we often don't appreciate their convenience.
2. Can you imagine the life of an inventor?
3. My name is Elisha Otis; I built a factory in New York.
4. Our business needed a lifting machine, and I created a design.
5. My invention pleased me, but would it transport people?
6. I finally produced a machine from the plan.

LEVEL
B. Write each sentence. Underline each complete subject once and each complete predicate twice. Then write whether it is **simple** or **compound.**

7. I named my machine the "safety hoister"; you know it as the elevator today.
8. There was a demonstration of the elevator.
9. Several assistants hoisted me high on a platform, and then they cut the rope at my command.
10. Would the safety device hold, or would I fall?
11. The audience screamed, but their panic waned.
12. The success of this demonstration resulted in the first passenger elevator in a hotel.

LEVEL
C. Rewrite each simple sentence so that it becomes a compound sentence.

13. My older sister rang for the elevator.
14. We waited for quite some time.
15. Every button on the panel was lit.
16. Reiko understood the problem immediately.
17. The elevator had stopped on every floor.
18. Would a staircase have been faster?
19. Reiko looked impatiently at her watch.
20. The elevator door finally opened.
21. Everyone crowded into the car.
22. I pushed the fifth-floor button.
23. The car shot up with a jerk.
24. It creaked to a stop on five.

EXTRA PRACTICE

Three levels of practice

Correcting Fragments and Run-on Sentences (page 12)

LEVEL

A. Write whether each group of words is a **sentence fragment**, a **run-on sentence**, or a **correct** sentence.

1. You write well.
2. The journey of mail from one place to another.
3. Quick delivery once seemed an impossibility, cross-country mail could take weeks.
4. That kind of wait for a letter from a friend!
5. Our freight company wanted a faster method we considered various plans.
6. Riders were hired, and the Pony Express was born.
7. Did not last very long.
8. The greatest advantage of this new system.

LEVEL

B. Write whether each group of words is a **sentence fragment** or a **run-on sentence.** Then correct each item.

9. Wondered about the origins of the Pony Express.
10. Several students in my class.
11. Read this story, it is about the Pony Express.
12. Stretched from Missouri to California.
13. Each rider changed ponies every ten miles, the riders themselves were changed every 75 miles.
14. Leather boxes on a special saddle blanket.
15. The plan worked well, the average delivery now took just a week.
16. The Pony Express was a valuable service but it lasted less than two years and it was replaced by the telegraph.
17. This fact surprised me, I thought the Express lasted longer.

LEVEL

C. Correct sentence fragments and run-on sentences.

(18.) The requirements of light weight and riding skill. **(19.)** Most of the riders were small in size, many of them were only teenagers. **(20.)** Named him "Buffalo Bill" Cody. **(21.)** Riders met harsh conditions and they rode through unknown wilderness lands and sometimes they were attacked along the way. **(22.)** Riders with few family ties. **(23.)** Even placed in one advertisement the note, "Orphans preferred." **(24.)** These young adventurers. **(25.)** Must have grown up quickly on the Express!

PRACTICE + PLUS

Three levels of additional practice for a difficult skill

Correcting Fragments and Run-On Sentences (page 12)

LEVEL
A. Write whether each group of words is a **sentence fragment**, a **run-on sentence,** or a **correct** sentence.

1. In 1842 my parents and I left Maine, we joined a wagon train in Missouri.
2. Our journey to California took five months.
3. Kept a journal of the events of each day.
4. We crossed the Rocky Mountains on the Oregon Trail and then ran into a blizzard and it delayed us for two days and we lost three oxen, a mule, and a horse.
5. The Plains Indians traded with us and let us pass through their hunting grounds.
6. Sunrise in the Rockies and sunset on the prairie.
7. New opportunities in California.
8. Suffered many hardships and setbacks.
9. Snowstorms swirled for days on end, the bitter cold was relentless.
10. Sometimes Plains Indians guided us and helped us at dangerous river crossings they traded vegetables and buffalo meat for tobacco.
11. We started our journey with eighty other families, few turned back.
12. The heroic men and women in the history of America.

LEVEL
B. Write whether each group of words is a **sentence fragment**, a **run-on sentence**, or a **correct** sentence. Correct each fragment and run-on.

13. Transportation has changed remarkably since ancient times.
14. Ancient Chinese civilization developed a network of roads and these roads connected major cities and merchants used these direct routes for travel throughout the countryside.
15. Most early roads between cities were only dirt tracks.
16. The first extensive system of paved roads.
17. Roman roads were paved with stone blocks.
18. Consisted of several layers of crushed stones and gravel.

19. The Romans transported troops and military supplies on their roads and messengers in horse-drawn carts carried government communications between provinces and the paved roads connected Rome with almost every part of its empire.

20. Most Roman roads fell into ruin in later centuries.

21. Not many roads.

22. A few dirt roads had been worn through the forests, these wide clearings allowed wagons access to other lands.

23. The first hard-surfaced road in America.

24. It connected Philadelphia and Lancaster, Pennsylvania.

LEVEL

C. Rewrite the paragraphs, correcting sentence fragments and run-on sentences.

For most of the trip, we lived in a canvas-covered wagon. **(25.)** We called the wagons "prairie schooners," the white tops resembled the sails of a ship. **(26.)** Traveled with our livestock. **(27.)** Our scout had guided other wagon trains on the long journey to California and he knew the route and he also was familiar with the best places for campsites. **(28.)** Hugged one another at the sight of our destination. **(29.)** Will never forget the beauty of the mountains, rivers, and prairies. **(30.)** A majestic country!

(31.) Life on the Oregon Trail in the 1800s. **(32.)** We realized that we were on a great highway of pioneer travel to the West, the trail ran about 2,000 miles between the Missouri and Columbia rivers. **(33.)** The longest of the frontier highways in the period of westward emigration. **(34.)** Struggled in the dangerous mountain sections west of the continental divide. **(35.)** The skeletons of oxen and horses could be seen along this part of the highway they were the sad signs of how difficult the journey west was at times.

(36.) One main rule. **(37.)** We left home in the spring and made few stops along the way so that we could get through the western mountains before snowstorms blocked the passes, and we would be snowbound. **(38.)** We stopped for two days at Fort Laramie so we could fix our equipment and buy supplies, but after that we only stopped at noon and at night. **(39.)** Travel 15 or 20 miles a day. **(40.)** Happiest day of my life.

EXTRA PRACTICE

Three levels of practice

Mechanics: Punctuating Sentences (page 14)

LEVEL

A. Write each sentence using the correct punctuation marks.

1. Louise's aunt knows much about bird life
2. Migration is a seasonal journey from one part of the world to another
3. Are birds the best known of all migratory animals
4. Imagine the flight of the Arctic tern
5. What tremendous fliers these birds must be
6. Do they really fly from one pole to the other
7. I read an encyclopedia article about terns
8. Do you have any interest in bird life

LEVEL

B. Write each sentence. Add any missing punctuation marks.

9. Where did you learn so much about migration patterns
10. I know some facts but my mother is an expert
11. My mother was part of a bird-banding project and I learned a lot about migration from her
12. Look at the numbers on this aluminum band
13. Do scientists band young birds as well as adults
14. Mom works with both kinds of birds and she handles every bird carefully
15. Could she trace the route of every bird or did some birds disappear during the journey
16. How fascinated I have become with birds

LEVEL

C. Rewrite each simple sentence so that it is the kind of sentence shown in parentheses. Use the correct punctuation.

17. My grandfather told you a story about birds. (interrogative)
18. One stork flies from Europe to Africa each fall. (compound)
19. Does its return mean the beginning of spring? (declarative)
20. Swallows travel great distances without stopping. (exclamatory)
21. Some European gulls migrate along a southeasterly route. (compound)
22. Does grandfather keep a journal of bird stories? (declarative)
23. My favorite story is about a young crane that got lost. (imperative)
24. The crane ended up with a flock of geese. (interrogative)
25. Was the ending of the story happy? (declarative)

EXTRA PRACTICE

Three levels of practice

Vocabulary Building: Using Context Clues (page 16)

LEVEL

A. Write the meaning of each underlined word. Use context clues to help you. Check your definitions in a dictionary.

1. Would you leave Earth and explore the cosmos?
2. Galactic trips interest me, but exploring the galaxy has never captured Rob's imagination.
3. Were the hazards of ancient sea voyages as great as the dangers of space travel?
4. I have no trepidations about space travel, but Margo is nervous even in an airplane.
5. Are you enthusiastic or apathetic about science fiction?

LEVEL

B. Write the meaning of each underlined word. Then write a sentence to explain how you used context clues to determine the meaning. Check your definitions in a dictionary.

6. If you could choose two other planets to study, which would you want to scrutinize?
7. The russet tones of the Martian landscape fascinate me; therefore, the "Red Planet" is my first choice.
8. Frequent dust storms would present a perpetual problem.
9. Because of the thin atmosphere, special breathing equipment would be a prerequisite.
10. Many people have speculated about the "canals" of Mars, but I would like to know the facts.

LEVEL

C. Write the meaning of each underlined word or group of words. Use context clues. Then check your definitions in a dictionary.

Although Mars could **(11.)** captivate my interest for a while, eventually I would want to leave for Jupiter. This **(12.)** colossus of a planet, one of the "gas giants," deserves special study. The **(13.)** Jovian atmosphere contains methane and ammonia; therefore, humans would find it not merely **(14.)** noxious but downright deadly. The mysterious "Red Spot," along with the thin rings that **(15.)** wreathe Jupiter, might contain some real surprises. Some people may fear such a place, but I would remain **(16.)** intrepid.

UNIT

Writing Personal Narratives

Read the quotation and look at the picture on the opposite page. Talk about ways you can relive a special moment in your life.

When you compose a personal narrative, you will want to recapture in writing a meaningful experience that you can share with your audience.

Focus A personal narrative provides a true account of an experience in your life.

What experience would you like to share? On the following pages you will find a story about one person's experience. You will see some photographs, too. You can use both to find ideas for writing.

THEME: *JOURNEYS*

When I was young, reading books was always a chance for me to go somewhere else. (It still is.)

—Jean Fritz

AWARD WINNING SELECTION

Have you ever spent time away from home, in a place where people spoke and behaved in ways that were different from yours?

Jean Fritz spent her childhood in China. In 1927 she sailed home to the United States, along with her parents, her friend Andrea, and Andrea's family. Despite her eagerness to reach America, however, she took pleasure in the long sea voyage and the unusual experience of being "in between" two very different places.

As you read the following selection from her book *Homesick: My Own Story*, look for the events that reveal what the journey meant to her.

from

HOMESICK

by Jean Fritz

It took twenty-eight days to go from Shanghai to San Francisco, and on that first morning I thought I'd be content to lie on my deck chair and stare at the ocean and drink beef tea the whole time.[1] Not Andrea. She thought the ocean was one big waste. We should be watching the people, she said, and sizing them up as they went by. So we did. We found that mostly they

1. The beginning sentence states the main event of the story.

fit into definite types. There were the Counters, for instance: fast-walking men, red-cheeked women, keeping score of how many times they walked around the deck, reveling in how fit they were. Then there were the Stylish Strollers, the Huffers and Puffers, the Lovebirds, leaning on each other, the Queasy Stomachs who clutched the railing and hoped for the best.

"You notice there's no one our age," Andrea said.

That was true. We had seen young people who were probably in their twenties, children who were Edward's age, and of course the majority who were our parents' age or older. But no one who might be in seventh or eighth grade or even high school.

Andrea jumped from her chair. "I'm going to explore."

Normally I would have gone with her but I hadn't had a chance yet to get my fill of the ocean. It was the same ocean as I'd had in Peitaiho[1] and I looked and looked. I walked up to the top deck where I could see the whole circle of water around me. I was smack in the middle of no place, I thought. Not in China, not in America, not in the past, not in the future. In between everything. It was nice.

By the time I went back to my chair, Andrea had returned from her explorations.

"There really is no one our age on board," she reported.

"Well, we can play shuffleboard and deck tennis. There are lots of things we can do."

Andrea sighed. "I was hoping for some boys."

I knew that Andrea had begun to like boys. She said that everyone at the Shanghai American School had a crush on someone else and when your love was requited[2]—well, that was the cat's.[3] What I couldn't understand was how someone could be in love with John Gilbert[4] and a kid in knickers[5] at the same time.

I suppose Andrea could see that I was trying to figure out the boy business. She gave me a curious look. "Just how do you picture your school in Washington, P.A.?" she asked.

---

1. Peitaiho [Bǎ dī hu]: summer seaside resort in northeast China.
2. requited [ri kwī′ tid]: returned
3. the cat's: short for "The cat's meow": anything that is remarkable or excellent.
4. John Gilbert: (1897–1936) American silent film star.
5. kid in knickers: In the 1920s children wore short trousers called knickers.

Well, I knew exactly what it would be like, so I told her: I'd be an American in a class with nothing but Americans in it. When we fought the American Revolution, we'd all fight on the same side. When we sang "My country, 'tis of thee," we'd yell our heads off. We'd all be the same. I would *belong*.

"There'll be boys in your class," Andrea pointed out.

"Naturally. I've seen boys before. So what?"

"Well, I think you're going to be surprised."

I didn't want to be surprised. For years I'd planned my first day at school in America.

"So how do you picture your school in Los Angeles, California?" I asked.

Andrea looked out at the ocean as if she expected to see her school sitting out there on the water. Then suddenly she shut her eyes and dropped her head in her hands. "Oh, Jean," she whispered, "I can't picture anything anymore. All I keep thinking about is my father. Alone in Shanghai."

This was as close as I'd ever seen Andrea come to crying. I put my hand on her shoulder. "I'm sorry," I said. Sorry! Such a puny word. You'd think the English language could give you something better. "I'm so sorry," I repeated.

Andrea dropped her hands and took a deep breath. "Well, let's play shuffleboard," she said.

From then on we played a lot of shuffleboard. Sometimes David joined us, but mostly he stayed in the ship's library, reading books about boys with real families. Edward kept busy in programs planned for children his age and the grown-ups made friends and talked their usual boring grown-up talk.[2]

On the whole, Andrea and I had a good time on the *President Taft*. In the evenings we often watched movies. In the afternoons we made pigs of ourselves at tea where we had our pick of all kinds of dainty sandwiches, scones, macaroons, chocolate bonbons, and gooey tarts. Actually, I even liked going to bed on shipboard. I'd lie in my bunk and feel the ship's engines throbbing and know that even when I fell asleep I wouldn't be wasting time. I'd still be on the go, moving closer to America every minute.

Still, my "in-between" feeling stayed with me. One evening after supper I took Andrea to the top deck and told her about

2. Events are told in chronological order.

the feeling. Of course the "in-between-ness" was stronger than ever in the dark with the circle of water rippling below and the night sky above spilling over with stars. I had never seen so many stars. When I looked for a spot where I might stick an extra star if I had one, I couldn't find any place at all. No matter how small, an extra star would be out of place, I decided. The universe was one-hundred-percent perfect just as it was.[3]

And then Andrea began to dance. She had slipped off her shoes and stockings and she was dancing what was obviously an "in-between" dance, leaping up toward the stars, sinking down toward the water, bending back toward China, reaching forward toward America, bending back again and again as if she could not tear herself away, yet each time dancing farther forward, swaying to and fro. Finally, her arms raised, she began twirling around, faster and faster, as if she were trying to out-spin time itself. Scarcely breathing, I sat beside a smokestack and watched. She was making a poem and I was inside the

3. The writer describes her central feelings about the voyage.

poem with her. Under the stars, in the middle of the Pacific Ocean. I would never forget this night, I thought. Not if I lived to be one hundred.

Only when we came to the international date line did my "in-between" feeling disappear. This is the place, a kind of imaginary line in the ocean, where all ships going east add an extra day to that week and all ships going west drop a day. This is so you can keep up with the world turning and make time come out right. We had two Tuesdays in a row when we crossed the line and after that when it was "today" for me, I knew that Lin Nai-Nai was already in "tomorrow." I didn't like to think of Lin Nai-Nai so far ahead of me. It was as if we'd suddenly been tossed on different planets.

On the other hand, this was the first time in my life that I was sharing the same day with my grandmother.

Oh, Grandma, I thought, *ready or not, here I come!*

It was only a short time later that Edward saw a couple of rocks poking out of the water and yelled for us to come. The rocks could hardly be called land, but we knew they were the beginning of the Hawaiian Islands and we knew that the Hawaiian Islands were a territory belonging to the United States. Of course it wasn't the same as one of the forty-eight states; still, when we stepped off the *President Taft* in Honolulu (where we were to stay a couple of days before going on to San Francisco), we wondered if we could truthfully say we were stepping on American soil.[6] I said no. Since the Hawaiian Islands didn't have a star in the flag, they couldn't be one-hundred-percent American, and I wasn't going to consider myself on American soil until I had put my feet flat down on the state of California.

We had a week to wait. The morning we were due to arrive in San Francisco, all the passengers came on deck early, but I was the first. I skipped breakfast and went to the very front of the ship where the railing comes to a point. That morning I would be the "eyes" of the *President Taft*, searching the horizon for the first speck of land. My private ceremony of greeting, however, would not come until we were closer, until we were sailing through the Golden Gate. For years I had heard about

---

6. Hawaiian . . . soil: Hawaii became the 50th state on August 21, 1959.

the Golden Gate, a narrow stretch of water connecting the Pacific Ocean to San Francisco Bay. And for years I had planned my entrance.

Dressed in my navy skirt, white blouse, and silk stockings, I felt every bit as neat as Columbus or Balboa and every bit as heroic when I finally spotted America in the distance. The decks had filled with passengers by now, and as I watched the land come closer, I had to tell myself over and over that I was HERE. At last.

Then the ship entered the narrow stretch of the Golden Gate and I could see American hills on my left and American houses on my right, and I took a deep breath of American air.

" 'Breathes there the man, with soul so dead,' " I cried,
" 'Who never to himself hath said,
This is my own, my native land!' "[7]

I forgot that there were people behind and around me until I heard a few snickers and a scattering of claps, but I didn't care. I wasn't reciting for anyone's benefit but my own.

Next for my first steps on American soil, but when the time came, I forgot all about them. As soon as we were on the dock, we were jostled from line to line. Believe it or not, after crossing thousands of miles of ocean to get here, we had to prove that it was O.K. for us to come into the U.S.A. We had to show that we were honest-to-goodness citizens and not spies. We had to open our baggage and let inspectors see that we weren't smuggling opium or anything else illegal. We even had to prove that we were germ-free, that we didn't have smallpox or any dire disease that would infect the country. After we had finally passed the tests, I expected to feel one-hundred-percent American. Instead, stepping from the dock into the city of San Francisco, I felt dizzy and unreal, as if I were a made-up character in a book I had read too many times to believe it wasn't still a book.

---

7. "Breathes . . . land!": quote from the poem "The Lay of the Last Minstrel" (1805) by the Scottish author Sir Walter Scott (1771–1832).

Thinking Like a Reader

1. What are Jean's feelings during the journey?
2. Why does she feel the way she does?
3. How would you feel on this kind of trip?

Write your responses in your journal.

Thinking Like a Writer

4. What sequence of events does the writer describe?
5. How do these events reveal the way she feels?
6. Which events do you think are described best?
7. If you were writing about a trip or journey you have taken, even a short one, what events would you include?

Write down your ideas in your journal.

Brainstorm *Vocabulary*

In "Homesick" Jean Fritz tells about a long journey by sea. A *sea voyage* is only one of many kinds of journeys. There are *airplane rides*, *treks*, and *climbs*, for example, as well as *expeditions* and just plain *walks*.

Flights into outer space. Voyages to the bottom of the ocean. Adventures of self-discovery. Journeys can take many forms. How many different ways to make a journey can you think of? In your journal list all the words or phrases that come to mind that refer to any kind of journey. As you come across more such terms, add them to your list. You can then use this personal vocabulary list as a source of ideas when you write.

Talk It Over
Be a Broadcaster

When Jean Fritz came home to America in the 1920s, the golden age of radio broadcasting had just begun. If there had been a radio announcer on board, the ship's arrival in San Francisco would have made a lively broadcast. Present a radio broadcast of this event to your class; or think about something exciting that has happened to you and turn it into an on-the-scene radio broadcast. Make the events come alive for your listeners.

Quick Write *Write a Letter*

Jean and Andrea kept busy aboard ship in their own way, while young Edward was involved in different activities "planned for children his age." Stories, too, must be planned differently for an audience of young children. Characters and plots that appeal to teenagers might not necessarily be of interest to a six-year-old.

Write a letter to a child in which you tell about an amusing incident that has happened to you. Write about the events so that a child would enjoy it. If possible, write about an incident that involves a child. Include details that will entertain your reader. If possible, send your letter to a child that you know.

Idea Corner
Think of Journeys

You have read about one person's journey across the Pacific Ocean. Jean Fritz's journey carried her to a different continent as well as into a new phase of her life. What journey might you write about? To help you think about a topic of your own, make a list in your journal of favorite places you have visited. Your journeys may have been close to home or far away. They may have been voyages that merely covered ground or journeys of discovery in which you learned something new about yourself or the world.

PICTURES  SEEING LIKE A WRITER

Finding Ideas for Writing

Look at the pictures on these pages. Think about what you see. What ideas for writing a personal narrative do the pictures give you? Write your ideas in your journal.

Launching of space shuttle *Discovery* from Cape Canaveral, Florida

1 GROUP WRITING: A PERSONAL NARRATIVE

COOPERATIVE
LEARNING

A **narrative** is a story. If the events are true and based on your own experience, it is a **personal narrative.**

When you plan a personal narrative or any other kind of writing, ask yourself why you are writing and who your readers will be. The **purpose** of a narrative is to entertain the reader. Your **audience** can be your classmates, your friends, your family, or yourself. Remembering your purpose and audience will help you to decide both what to say and how to say it. To write an effective personal narrative, you will need to keep the following points in mind.

- Beginning Sentence
- Supporting Details
- Order of Details

Beginning Sentence and Supporting Details

Here is a narrative paragraph that tells about one student's experience. Notice the underlined sentence.

> I discovered the power of the printed word the day I stepped onto the school bus and was greeted by a chorus of "Hi, string bean!" Since I am tall and skinny and wear a green coat, I figured that this was my friends' poor attempt at humor. I just plunked myself into a seat and opened the school newspaper to look at the article I had written. Before I had a chance, my friend Adam presented me with a carrot, declaring, "Say hello to Julia!" The bus exploded with laughter. Then others called out: "You're a broccoli!" "Just call me cauliflower!" "Turnip!" I began to suspect that it might have something to do with my article on how students were becoming more health-conscious, turning away from junk food and eating more vegetables. I still didn't see anything funny about it—until I opened the paper. There was my headline: "STUDENTS TURN TO VEGETABLES"!

A good beginning sentence for a narrative captures the reader's interest. Often the first sentence also states the main idea of the story. When it does this, the sentence is called a **topic sentence**. Reread the personal narrative above.

■ What does the beginning sentence tell you about the story?

A good opening sentence promises the reader a good story. To keep that promise, the writer must complete the paragraph with details that support the beginning sentence. In a narrative, the supporting details are usually events. Every incident is composed of many smaller events and observations. One of the most important challenges in writing a narrative paragraph is to select just those events that capture the experience you want to relate to your audience. Now look back at the narrative above.

■ What are the main details in the paragraph?
■ How do they support the beginning sentence?

Guided Practice: Composing a Beginning Sentence

As a class, use the list below to help you think of a topic about which you could write a brief narrative. Your purpose will be to entertain an audience of students your age. Together, explore your ideas about the topic. Then write a good beginning sentence.

| a holiday | field trip | guest speaker | performance |
| fire drill | lost item | class crisis | sports event |

Ordering Details

When you describe an experience, the clearest way to present the events is in the order in which they occurred. By arranging events in **chronological order**, or time order, you help the reader to follow your story.

Merely ordering the events chronologically may not be enough, however. To clarify when events occurred and help move the action along, you can use **transition words** and phrases like those below.

| soon | before | now | next | every day | the last time |
| later | after | then | finally | at night | a minute later |

■ Look again at the narrative on page 46. What words help to tell you when events occurred?

The last event in a narrative may or may not make an appropriate last sentence for the paragraph. In the sample narrative, the final event does provide a strong conclusion. It ties up the preceding events and leaves the reader with something to think about.

If the final event in your narrative does not make a strong ending, you need to add a sentence that does.

> My visit to my old neighborhood was like a journey back in time. As soon as I got off the subway, I spotted Mr. Diaz at his newsstand, and I felt seven years old again. Later, walking past my elementary school, I thought I recognized every crack in the sidewalk. At last I stood in front of the gray brick building I once called home. *I would not have been surprised to hear my mother calling me for supper.*

Guided Practice: Chronological Order

As a class, make a list of events that are part of the incident that you chose to describe. Then arrange the events in chronological order.

Putting a Personal Narrative Together

With the help of your classmates you have written a beginning sentence for a narrative and arranged events in time order. Recall what the purpose and audience for your story will be. Then look at your list of events. Considering your topic, what details would you include?

One student's notes are shown below.

> **Beginning Sentence:** When our class played "extras" in a movie, we learned that movie acting should be called movie waiting.
>
> ✔ Chartered bus drove us all to studio at 6:00 A.M.
> Josie had strep throat and couldn't participate
> ✔ Spent almost three hours being made up
> About half liked the way they looked; others didn't
> ✔ Stood around for hours while lighting adjusted
> ✔ Two-minute scene shot eight times

Guided Practice: Writing a Personal Narrative

Look over the list of events you wrote for a class narrative. Decide which details best support the beginning sentence. Then use them to write a narrative. Begin with an opening sentence that states your main point and arouses the interest of your audience. Then make sure you have arranged the events of your narrative in chronological order. Make sure your story has an effective ending. Share your narrative with a friend. Which part does your friend think was written most effectively?

Checklist A Personal Narrative

To help you remember the important elements of a narrative, use a checklist when you write. Copy and complete the checklist below. Keep it in your writing folder. You can use your checklist when you write personal narratives.

> **CHECKLIST**
>
> - Think about purpose.
> - Choose an audience.
> - Write a good beginning sentence.
> - Include supporting details.
> - Use chronological order.
> - _____

2 THINKING AND WRITING: General and Specific

When you talk about *sports*, you are using a term that refers to many different activities, including baseball, swimming, and hockey. When you talk about the *weather*, you are using a term that covers a variety of features, such as temperature and wind speed.

Sports is a **general** term. *Baseball, swimming,* and *hockey* are **specific** sports. *Weather* is also a general term. *Temperature, barometric pressure,* and *wind speed* are specific features of the weather.

GENERAL	SPECIFIC	MORE SPECIFIC
clothing	pants	jeans
food	cereal	oatmeal
verb	move	sprint

Ideas in sentences can also be general or specific. Read these sentences from a writer's journal, telling about the events of an unusual day.

Even the trees and flowers looked strange.
The airplane ride took five hours.
Today I began another life.
I opened the door to my new home and stepped inside.

Thinking Like a Writer

■ Which sentence expresses a general idea?
■ Which sentences express specific ideas?

The beginning sentence of a narrative often states the general idea of the story. In the notes from the writer's journal, the sentence that could be used as a beginning sentence of a narrative is "Today I began another life." It states a general idea.

Other sentences in a paragraph express specific ideas. They support the beginning sentence by providing additional details.

When you write a paragraph, be sure that all of the specific details you include relate to the general idea you express in the beginning sentence. Eliminate details that do not develop the general idea of the paragraph.

THINKING APPLICATION General and Specific

Each of the writers below is planning to write a personal narrative. Help each student to decide on the main idea and specific details. You may wish to discuss your thinking with other students.

1. In his journal Julio has jotted down some general ideas, but he has forgotten the specific details. What details might he include under each general idea? Write them on a separate sheet of paper.

   train trip to the capital   walking dogs can be dangerous
   a puzzling phone call   trying out for the class play

2. Help Joy state a general idea to cover each set of details listed below.

   a. waited all week—biked to pond with friends—cast line—sat under tree to wait—fell asleep—awoke hours later—others had piles of fish—I had empty line—forgot to put bait on line

   b. last drive to zoo had been series of disasters—this one started out on time—little traffic—lunch in nice place—waited for catastrophe like flat tire but never happened—got there early—no long lines to wait in to buy tickets—zoo closed

   c. made potato salad with Dad—helped Mom make chicken—packed plates, silverware, and food in the picnic basket—found our big blanket—gathered together my little brothers and sisters—opened the door—walked outside—it began raining

3. Robert wrote down some ideas for a paragraph about whales. He needed to list his ideas from the most general to the most specific. Make a list showing how you would do this.

   Most of the largest whales eat only plankton.
   Whales are the largest living animals.
   The size of whales varies from 13 to 100 feet.
   Among the largest whales, only the sperm whale eats fish.
   Only whales that eat fish have teeth.

3 INDEPENDENT WRITING: A Personal Narrative

Prewrite: Step 1

Now you can begin to write your own personal narrative. You will be following a process of writing that begins with jotting down your first thoughts and ends with sharing your finished work.

Prewriting is the first stage in the writing process. It refers to everything you do to prepare yourself to write, particularly choosing a topic and exploring your ideas.

Choosing a Topic

To start her ideas flowing, a student named Leona first **brainstormed** a list of interesting experiences that she might write about. Then she wrote down some general ideas.

> losing wallet in store   getting off train in wrong town
> taking trip to Cape Cod   waiting for actor at stage door

Cape Cod was so exciting that Leona decided that it was the topic she wanted to write about. But in a single paragraph she could relate only one incident. There was one that stood out—whale watching.

Exploring Ideas: Clustering Strategy

Leona made this **cluster** to explore her topic idea.

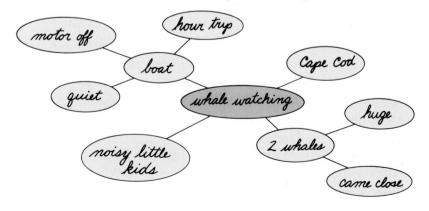

Leona decided that since few of her classmates had ever seen any whales, they would be entertained by the incident. She had her audience and her purpose for writing.

To help make the narrative lively and entertaining, Leona wanted to add more specific information. She thought about her experience for a while and recalled as much as she could. Then she added details to her cluster.

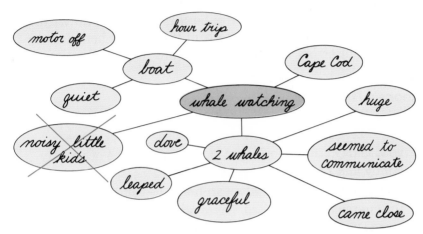

Thinking Like a Writer
- What did Leona add?
- What did she decide to omit?
- Why do you think she made these changes?

YOUR TURN

Choose a topic for a narrative paragraph.

JOURNAL

- Make a list of journeys you have taken or interesting places you have visited. Look through your journal. Perhaps **Pictures** or the reading selection provided in this unit have given you some ideas.
- Choose one topic that you want to write about and that you think will entertain your audience.
- Focus on a single incident.
- Think about your purpose.

Now make a cluster to explore your idea. Then try to recall further details about the incident. Add information to your cluster, or cross out details that do not support your topic. You may change your cluster at any time.

Write a First Draft: Step 2

Leona used what she learned about narrative paragraphs to prepare a planning checklist. In her checklist she included points about purpose, audience, a good beginning sentence, supporting details, and chronological order. She could use her planning checklist as she wrote her first draft.

After she thought about the important parts of a personal narrative, Leona began to write her first draft. While writing her first draft, she did not interrupt the flow of her ideas to worry about errors. She knew she could make corrections and changes later.

Leona's First Draft

Last summer I saw some whales. We took a boat with thirty other people and sailed out into the ocean. My family and I had driven to Cape cod in Massachussetts. My father was born there. After an hour the captin turned off the engine and we waited. There was nothing. Except the ocean. Were there really Whales out there. Someone shouted "Look!" Two enormous shapes were swimming closer and closer everyone kept quiet. The whales dove, flipped, and jumped. These huge creatures were amazingly graceful. They turned back one more time. They leaped out of the water. The whales seemed to be saying good-by.

YOUR TURN

Write the first draft of your personal narrative. As you write, ask yourself these questions about the important parts of a narrative.

- How can I best achieve my purpose? What would my audience want to know?
- What details are most important? What specific events should I describe?
- Are events described in chronological order?

Planning Checklist
- Think about purpose.
- Choose an audience.
- Write a good beginning sentence.
- Include supporting details.
- Use chronological order.

TIME-OUT You might want to take some time out before you revise your narrative. That way you will be able to revise your writing with a fresh eye.

Revise: Step 3

When her first draft was finished, Leona read it over and made some changes that she thought would improve it. Then, since she was writing the paragraph for her classmates, she decided to ask one of them what he thought. Perhaps he could suggest some further improvements.

> I really liked reading about the whales. I wish I could've been there. I didn't get interested at the beginning, though.

> Hmm, I guess my first sentence isn't so great. Maybe I need to try another one. Thanks.

Next, Leona looked back at her planning checklist. She realized that there was one point she had missed—the point about arranging details in chronological order. She put a check mark next to it to remind her to take care of it.

As Leona revised her first draft, she concentrated on important matters like those covered in her planning checklist. Could she improve the beginning? Were the events in chronological order? Did she need to **elaborate**, or add further details to develop her ideas? She would worry about smaller errors like spelling and capitalization later.

Leona also thought more about her **purpose** and **audience**. Since her purpose was to entertain her readers, she asked herself if she had left out any amusing details from her narrative. She tried to recall specific moments of the experience she had chosen for her writing.

Leona made all her changes on the first draft, crossing out some words and adding or moving others. Look at Leona's revised draft on the next page.

Revising Checklist
- Think about purpose.
- Choose an audience.
- Write a good beginning sentence.
- Include supporting details.
- ✔ Use chronological order.

> *two whales sent me a greeting.*
> Last summer I saw some whales. We took a boat
>
> with thirty other people and sailed out into the ocean. My
>
> family and I had driven to Cape cod in Massachussetts. My
>
> father was born there. After an hour the captin turned off
>
> the engine and we waited. There was nothing. Except the
>
> *Then suddenly*
> ocean. Were there really Whales out there. Someone
>
> shouted "Look!" Two enormous shapes were swimming
>
> closer and closer everyone kept quiet. The whales dove,
>
> flipped, and jumped. These huge creatures were amazingly
> *After a while they swam away.*   *and*
> graceful. They turned back one more time. They leaped out
>
> of the water. The whales seemed to be saying good-by.

Thinking Like a Writer

- How did Leona revise the beginning sentence? Do you think it is better?
- What sentence did Leona add? Why?
- Why did she change the position of one sentence?
- Which sentences did she combine? Why do you think she combined them?

YOUR TURN

Read over your first draft. Ask yourself these questions.

1. How can I improve the beginning sentence?
2. What details do I need to add to help the reader understand and enjoy my story?
3. What events need to be rearranged in chronological order?
4. How can I improve the flow of my writing by combining sentences?

If you wish, ask a friend to read the revised draft of your personal narrative and make suggestions for improvements. Then revise your narrative.

Proofread: Step 4

After Leona finished revising her work, she still had to proofread it. Proofreading means correcting errors in spelling, grammar, capitalization, and punctuation. To help her remember what to look for when she proofread, Leona prepared the checklist below. Then she proofread her paragraph, using special marks to indicate corrections.

Leona's Proofread Draft

Last summer ~~I saw some whales.~~ *two whales sent me a greeting.* We took a boat with thirty other people and sailed out into the ocean. My family and I had driven to Cape cod in Massachussetts *Massachusetts*. My ~~father was born there.~~ After an hour the captin *captain* turned off the engine and we waited. There was nothing Except the ocean. Were there really Whales out there Someone *? Then suddenly* shouted "Look!" Two enormous shapes were swimming closer and closer everyone kept quiet. The whales dove, flipped, and jumped. These huge creatures were amazingly graceful. *After a while they swam away.* They turned back one more time. ~~They~~ *and* leaped out of the water. The whales seemed to be saying good-by.

YOUR TURN

Proofreading Practice

Find the errors below. Then write the paragraph correctly.

I was expecting a nigtmare but instead my first baby-sitting job was a dreem. My brother had warned me about this child. I prepared games, rehersed stories, and got some Toys. When I arrived at the Wilbur's house, Linda was asleep. In fact linda stayed asleep all evening I never even got to meet her.

Proofreading Checklist
- Did I indent the paragraph?
- Did I spell each word correctly?
- Did I punctuate sentences correctly?
- Did I use capital letters correctly?
- Did I correct sentence fragments and run-on sentences?

Applying Your Proofreading Skills

Proofread your own narrative. Review your checklist, as well as **The Grammar Connection** and **The Mechanics Connection** below. Use the proofreading symbols.

THE GRAMMAR CONNECTION

Remember these rules about writing sentences correctly.

- Correct a **sentence fragment** by adding the missing subject or predicate part.

  FRAGMENT: Carlos and the man beside him.
  CORRECTED: Carlos and the man beside him waved.
  FRAGMENT: Ran toward us.
  CORRECTED: Then they ran toward us.

- Correct a **run-on sentence** by forming separate sentences or a compound sentence.

  RUN-ON: We waved to Carlos then he ran toward us.
  CORRECTED: We waved to Carlos. Then he ran toward us.
  CORRECTED: We waved to Carlos, and then he ran
                        toward us.

Check your writing. Have you corrected sentence fragments and run-on sentences?

THE MECHANICS CONNECTION

Remember this rule about punctuating sentences correctly.

- Use **periods, question marks, exclamation marks,** and **commas** to punctuate your sentences correctly.

  Declarative Sentence:
  The train roared into the station.

  Interrogative Sentence:
  Would Carlos be waiting for me in the station?

  Imperative Sentence:
  Remember his message about where to meet him.

  Exclamatory Sentence:
  What a long trip that was!

  Compound Sentence:
  We traveled far, but the journey was worth it.

Review your writing. Have you punctuated your sentences correctly?

Proofreading Marks
Indent ⁋
Add ∧
Add a comma ⩘
Add quotation marks ⱽ ⱽ
Add a period ⊙
Take out ⌐
Capitalize ≡
Lower-case letter /
Reverse the order ∿

Publish: Step 5

Leona had written her narrative so that she could share her whale-watching experience with the other students in her class. She copied the paragraph neatly and pasted it on a large sheet of colored paper. Above it she attached a picture of a whale from a brochure that she had received on her whale-watching trip. She hung her poster in the classroom alongside those that her classmates had written. Several students later asked her how they could find out more information about taking a whale-watching excursion.

YOUR TURN

Make a neat final copy of your narrative. Think of a good way to share your story. You may wish to use one of the ideas in the **Sharing Suggestions** box below.

> ### SHARING SUGGESTIONS
>
> | | | |
> |---|---|---|
> | Include your narrative in a letter to a friend. | With your classmates, assemble a book of narratives. Illustrate it and display it in the school library. | Read your narrative aloud, or record it on tape. |

4 SPEAKING AND LISTENING: Telling an Anecdote

Most of us enjoy hearing people tell entertaining stories about events in their lives. Brief stories or narratives such as these are called **anecdotes**. Although it may seem easy, there is an art to telling anecdotes.

To tell a story effectively you need to do a bit of planning. You must consider your purpose. The purpose of most anecdotes is to entertain the listener. Will your audience find your story entertaining? In what ways could you draw out the humor in your story?

You must also consider your audience. Will your story interest them? What details must your audience know to appreciate your anecdote?

After choosing a topic, write down the main points of your story on a note card, as shown below.

First flight -- spent more time on ground
  -- plane to Arizona to visit grandparents
  -- snowed on way to airport
  -- waited for plane to come in -- waited for de-icing
  -- on runway when airport closed -- five hour wait
  -- slept through flight

Here are some guidelines to keep in mind when you are telling a story.

> **SPEAKING GUIDELINES: An Anecdote**
>
> 1. Write your main points on a note card. Practice telling your story.
> 2. Begin with a sentence that tells what the story is about and that also grabs the listener's attention.
> 3. Give details in chronological order. Include a strong ending.
> 4. Adjust your tone of voice, volume, and rate of speaking according to the content of your story.
> 5. Look at your listeners as you speak.
> 6. When appropriate, use physical gestures or facial expressions to bring your story to life.

- Why is it important to capture my listener's attention right at the beginning?
- How does arranging details in chronological order help my listener?

Remember to think about your **purpose** and **audience** when you are telling an anecdote. To achieve your purpose, you need to entertain your listeners with amusing details or a witty perception. The more you practice telling stories, the easier it becomes.

SPEAKING APPLICATION Telling an Anecdote

Think about a story you can share with the class. It might be about a travel experience you have had. Prepare a note card and practice telling your story orally. Use the speaking guidelines to help you. Your classmates will be using the following guidelines as they listen to your story.

> **LISTENING GUIDELINES: An Anecdote**
>
> 1. Listen for the main idea of the story.
> 2. Listen for the sequence of events. Pay close attention to *what* happens *when*.
> 3. Listen for important details. Make pictures in your mind as you listen.

THE CURRICULUM CONNECTION

Writing About Social Studies

Social studies is a broad field of study that includes history, geography, current events, and government. Maps, dates, charts, and documents are all important in social studies, but they are only important because they reflect the lives of real people. How do people govern themselves? How do they handle their resources? How do groups relate to each other? How do geographical features affect the ways societies operate? These are the kinds of questions that social studies tries to answer.

By studying how people interact in groups, social scientists help us understand ourselves as individuals. The true stories of human life they uncover are not only instructive but also can often be more fascinating than any fictional narrative. Facts about societies different from our own can be used to enrich and diversify our own culture.

ACTIVITIES

Create a Travel Brochure
Make a travel brochure that advertises trips to an exotic country. Include facts about the climate, geographical features, language, customs, food, and history of the country. You might also add quotations from fictional tourists who tell about experiences they have had on the tour. Illustrate your brochure and share it with classmates. Use photographs from old newspapers or magazines.

Visit the Past
Imagine that you are living during the period of the Old West. Write a personal narrative about a journey you are taking in a stagecoach. Do research to learn information about life in early 19th-century America. How was life different then? What important events happened? Use some of the information you learn to write your narrative. You may wish to include your narrative in a story or a fictional letter. Share your work with a classmate or family member.

Respond to Literature

Anthropologists study social and cultural developments of the past and present. As part of her research, the anthropologist Margaret Mead in 1925 went to live with the natives of Tau, one of the Samoan Islands in the Pacific Ocean. She made some surprising discoveries. After reading the selection below, write about your reactions to the ideas that are discussed in it. Write your response in the form of an essay, a story, or a poem.

The Samoan Teenager

Through her careful research, Mead had discovered that the Samoan teenage girl was very different from her American counterpart. In the unhurried, relaxed existence of Tau, the adolescent years were the best years of a Samoan girl's life. She experienced no stress, no restlessness, no rebellion. The Samoan teenager suffered none of the tensions and unhappiness of the American, Mead said in *Coming of Age in Samoa*, because the Samoan girl had no sense of competition, did not form deep relationships with others her age, was free to move from family to family, and had no fears of adulthood, since she knew just what life would be when she grew up. The turmoil of adolescence results not from our nature but from our culture.

Margaret Mead had shown that by studying another culture, we can learn much about our own.

UNIT CHECKUP

LESSON 1

Group Writing: A Personal Narrative (page 46)   Rewrite the following paragraph, arranging the events in chronological order. Add transition words where they are needed.

We discovered that half the city was on its way to the beach. When I woke up this morning, the temperature and humidity were already well above the comfort range. My older sister suggested we drive to the beach. Just getting out of bed was an effort. There were thousands of cars on the road, and traffic was at a standstill. We finally turned around and came home again and swam in our neighbors' pool! We turned on the radio and learned that the day would get hotter and hotter. We grabbed our bathing suits and headed out the door.

LESSON 2

Thinking: General and Specific (page 50)   Write a topic sentence for a personal narrative that includes the following details.

Want to be commercial artist—do small jobs for friends—neighbors asked me to letter a sign for their sandwich shop window—turned out well—customers began asking for strange sandwiches—sign read "Turkey $2.95, Ham $2.95, Roast Beef $3.50, Children $2.00"

LESSON 3

Writing a Personal Narrative (page 52)   Respond to the following notice.

Explorations Book Store announces...
A Contest
to celebrate the publication of the exciting new book
Journey into the Unknown by Carrie A. Wey
WRITE ABOUT *YOUR* JOURNEY INTO THE UNKNOWN
WIN A $100 GIFT CERTIFICATE!
Just write a personal narrative of one paragraph, telling the true story of a journey you once made to an unknown place. See if *you* can be our winner!

LESSON 4

Speaking and Listening: Telling an Anecdote (page 60)   In a paragraph summarize the important points for telling an anecdote effectively.

THEME PROJECT  FUTURISTIC FAIR

You have now read and written narratives about different kinds of journeys, some to exotic, faraway places and others to familiar places near home.

Now imagine that you could enter a time machine and take a journey into the future. What will life be like in the next century? What changes will there be in our homes and cities? How will modes of transportation be different? Will we have the same joys and worries? Look at the picture below.

Use the picture as the basis for a discussion with your classmates about life in the future. What might a typical day in your life be like?

Create a project for a "Life in the Future" fair.

- Make a tape recording of a personal narrative told by a seventh grader of the future.
- Present a newscast from the year 2050.
- Write a letter you might compose fifty years from now.
- Tell the "life" story of a robot through its own eyes.

UNIT

3

Nouns

In this unit you will learn about kinds of nouns. You will find out that there are many different ways to name a person, place, thing, or idea.

Discuss Read the lines of poetry on the opposite page. How does the poet make the reader a part of her poem?

Creative Expression The unit theme is *Expressions*. Picture your favorite room in your mind. What makes this room special to you? In your journal write about the ways in which the things in the room are an expression of yourself.

THEME: *EXPRESSIONS*

*When walking in a tiny rain
Across the vacant lot,
A pup's a good companion—
If a pup you've got.*

—Gwendolyn Brooks

1 KINDS OF NOUNS

A noun names a person, place, thing, or idea.

In daily conversation, you must use many words that name persons, places, things, or ideas. These words are called **nouns.** A **common noun** names a general person, place, thing, or idea. A **proper noun** names a specific person, place, thing, or idea.

Common Nouns	Proper Nouns	Common Nouns	Proper Nouns
sister	Andrea	river	Nile River
composer	Beethoven	game	Scrabble
city	Galveston	mountain	Mount Everest
planet	Mercury	period	Stone Age

Concrete nouns name things that you can see or touch. **Abstract nouns** name things that you cannot see or touch, such as emotions or ideas.

CONCRETE NOUNS		ABSTRACT NOUNS	
friend	neighborhood	happiness	imagination
author	notebook	surprise	time

Guided Practice

Name each noun and tell whether it is common or proper.

Example: Dave likes historical novels.
Dave proper, novels common

1. Three friends received an assignment.
2. Mr. Rojas publishes stories by students.
3. Joey thought of an adventure last night.
4. Would the discovery of an ancient tomb in Egypt make a good tale?
5. Martin and Anya discussed some ideas.

?! **THINK**

- How do I know if a word is a common noun or a proper noun?

REMEMBER

- A **noun** names a person, place, thing, or idea.
- A **common noun** names a non-specific, or general, person, place, thing, or idea. A **proper noun** names a specific person, place, thing, or idea.

More Practice

A. Write and identify each common and proper noun.

Example: Did Mark Twain write this book?
Mark Twain   proper   book   common

6. The class discussed characters from literature.
7. Anya told Joey about one subject for a story.
8. The plot would include facts about her family.
9. Her grandparents came to America long ago.
10. Anya would call Grandpa in Miami for details.
11. "My tale is a mystery about two doctors," Martin said.
12. Will the setting be Florida or Maine?

B. Write each noun and label it either **common** or **proper**. Label each common noun either **concrete** or **abstract**.

Example: Justin had unique ideas.
Justin proper, ideas common abstract

13. The students used their imagination.
14. Martin asked Joey for assistance.
15. Their classmate spoke with enthusiasm.
16. A boy and a girl travel to Mexico.
17. The friends have talent as swimmers.
18. The two divers compete in a contest by the sea.
19. The story will contain mystery and excitement.
20. Will Kate earn highest honors for her ability, or will Juan leave Acapulco with the prize?

Extra Practice, page 90

WRITING APPLICATION A Summary

Imagine that you have been asked to write a story for a class magazine. What kind of story would you write? Write a summary of the story. Then exchange papers with a classmate and identify the common and proper nouns in each other's work.

2 SINGULAR AND PLURAL NOUNS

A **singular noun** names one person, place, thing, or idea. A **plural noun** names more than one.

Singular Nouns	To Form Plural	Examples
most singular nouns	add **s**	pencil idea orange pencils ideas oranges
nouns ending with **s, ss, x, zz, ch, sh**	add **es**	kiss box ditch kisses boxes ditches
nouns ending with a **consonant and y**	change **y** to **i** and add **es**	story party lobby stories parties lobbies
nouns ending with a **vowel and y**	add **s**	bay turkey decoy bays turkeys decoys
nouns ending with **f** or **fe**	most add **s**; some change **f** to **v**, add **es**	staff belief wife staffs beliefs wives
nouns ending with a **vowel and o**	add **s**	radio ratio video radios ratios videos
nouns ending with a **consonant and o**	most add **es** some add **s**	tomato veto solo tomatoes vetoes solos
some irregular nouns	change spelling	man goose ox men geese oxen
a few irregular nouns	keep the same spelling	deer salmon corps deer salmon corps

Guided Practice

Tell whether each noun is singular or plural. If it is singular, spell its plural form.

Example: box   *singular   boxes*

1. classes	**3.** hero	**5.** surfs	**7.** reflexes
2. branch	**4.** child	**6.** piano	**8.** alley

?! THINK

- How can I remember how to spell the plural forms of nouns?

REMEMBER

- A **singular noun** is a noun that names one person, place, thing, or idea.
- A **plural noun** is a noun that names more than one person, place, thing, or idea.
- Add **s** or **es** to form most plural nouns.

More Practice

A. Write the plural form of each noun. Check your answers in a dictionary.

Example: potato   *potatoes*

9. half   **12.** crutch   **15.** tray
10. sheep   **13.** veto   **16.** bass
11. woman   **14.** wax   **17.** splash

B. Write each sentence, using the plural form of each noun in parentheses.

Example: We painted the (bench).
               We painted the benches.

18. In "The Sneaker Crisis," one of my favorite (story), the family (member) conduct (search) for a pair of (shoe).
19. It is not in any of the (box), with the (toy), or on the (shelf) in the (bedroom).
20. All morning the (child) watch Mom's (activity).
21. She doesn't appreciate her many (boss); so she asks them to search their (memory) for (clue).
22. Their (suspicion) are that Laurie had them (day) ago.
23. When they ask her to look among the (bushel) of glassware in the (pantry), Mom rolls her (eye) with impatience.
24. Playing their (radio), Sally and Barry then came in, followed by the family dog Jumper, who held the missing sneaker between his (tooth).
25. What family (crisis) will happen next?

Extra Practice, page 91

WRITING APPLICATION An Advertisement

Imagine that you are holding a tag sale of used items at your school. With a small group of classmates, write an advertisement that mentions some of the items. Check to make sure you have spelled plural nouns correctly.

COOPERATIVE
LEARNING

3 POSSESSIVE NOUNS

Sometimes you use nouns that name who or what owns or has something. These are called **possessive nouns.** Possessive nouns can be singular or plural.

Noun	To Form Possessive	Example
most singular nouns	add **apostrophe** and **s ('s)**	This **child** has a book. This **child's** book . . .
plural nouns ending with **s**	add **apostrophe** (')	These **girls** have pets. These **girls'** pets . . . Some **adults** own cars. Some **adults'** cars . . .
plural nouns not ending with **s**	add **apostrophe** and **s ('s)**	Two **children** spend time reading. Two **children's** time . . . Two **women** wrote novels. Two **women's** novels . . .

Remember that apostrophes are used with possessive nouns but not with plural nouns.

> The **characters** talk to each other. (plural noun)
> One **character's** name is Wilbur. (singular possessive)
> We read several **characters'** parts. (plural possessive)

Guided Practice

Name each possessive noun and tell whether it is **singular** or **plural**.

Example: What is the writer's name? *writer's   singular*

1. This author's story is my sister's favorite book.
2. *Charlotte's Web* is many librarians' choice, too.
3. My parents' memories include this children's tale.
4. Wilbur's adventures hold readers' attention.

 THINK

■ Where do I place the apostrophe in a possessive noun?

REMEMBER

- A **possessive noun** is a noun that names who or what has something.
- Use an **apostrophe** and **s ('s)** to form the possessive of most singular nouns and of plural nouns that do not end with *s*.
- Use only an **apostrophe (')** to form the possessive of plural nouns that end with *s*.

More Practice

A. Write the possessive form of each noun.

Example: classmates *classmates'*

5. farmer	**8.** month	**11.** visitors
6. lambs	**9.** geese	**12.** Chris
7. Gloria	**10.** Denver	**13.** sheep

B. Write each sentence, using the correct possessive form of each underlined noun.

Example: What are these <u>characters</u> names?
        What are these characters' names?

14. Despite <u>Avery</u> jokes and her <u>parents</u> misgivings, Fern took care of Wilbur.
15. Uncle <u>Homer</u> barn became the <u>piglet</u> home.
16. <u>Fern</u> visits became less frequent, and the other <u>animals</u> interest in Wilbur lessened.
17. Charlotte A. <u>Cavatica</u> arrival changed <u>Wilbur</u> life.
18. When the <u>Zuckermans</u> plans for Wilbur became clear, the large gray <u>spider</u> mind went to work.
19. Soon <u>men</u> shouts and <u>toddlers</u> voices rang in the yard as visitors read the words SOME PIG in the web.
20. This famous <u>writer</u> masterpiece has been many <u>children</u> and <u>adults</u> favorite book.

Extra Practice, page 92

 WRITING APPLICATION A Script

With a partner write a brief skit for a school production. Think about a series of events; then make a list of characters, props, and costumes. Then write your script. Exchange papers with other classmates and check to make sure that possessive nouns are used correctly.

4 COLLECTIVE NOUNS AND COMPOUND NOUNS

Most of the nouns you use can be easily identified as either singular or plural, but one kind of noun can have a singular or a plural meaning. A **collective noun** names a group of people or things.

family	staff	company	band	army	public
team	flock	chorus	bunch	jury	congress

When the collective noun refers to a group as a whole, use the singular form of a verb after it. When the collective noun refers to the individual members of a group, use the plural form of a verb.

Our **club** *meets* every Thursday afternoon. (singular)
The **jury** quietly *discuss* the evidence among themselves. (plural)

Compound nouns are another special kind of noun. They are formed from two or more words that work together as a single noun. Your full name is a compound noun. To form the plural of a compound noun, you usually change the most important word in the compound.

living room/ living rooms	toothbrush/ toothbrushes	kilowatt-hour/ kilowatt-hours
prime number/ prime numbers	penknife/ penknives	sister-in-law/ sisters-in-law
attorney general/ attorneys general	cupful/ cupfuls	editor-in-chief/ editors-in-chief

Guided Practice

Tell whether each noun is a **collective noun** or a **compound noun**.

Example: teacup *compound noun*

1. herd
2. committee
3. mountain lion
4. audience
5. storyteller
6. great-aunt
7. gingerbread
8. orchestra
9. Doris Troy

?! THINK

- How do I decide if a word is a collective noun or a compound noun?

GRAMMAR

REMEMBER

- A **collective noun** names a group of people or things.
- A **compound noun** is made up of two or more words that act as a single noun.

More Practice

A. Write and label each **collective noun** and **compound noun.** Then write whether the meaning of each collective noun is **singular** or **plural.**

Example: The family discuss issues often.
       family   collective noun   plural

10. The crowd was alert as the vice-president spoke.
11. "This afternoon we will discuss a folk tale."
12. Was the group familiar with this masterpiece?
13. Everyone knew about Washington Irving.

B. Write and label each **collective** and **compound noun.** Write whether each collective noun is **singular** or **plural.** If the compound noun is singular, write its plural form.

Example: The flock flies over the seashore.
       flock   collective noun   singular,
       seashore   compound   seashores

14. Rip lived in the Catskill Mountains.
15. Some villagers called him a good-for-nothing, but most of the townsfolk were his friends.
16. Rip and Wolf hunted until sunset.
17. The pair were each surprised when an aged seafarer in strange clothes passed by.
18. He had a head start, but Rip caught up with the old-timer.
19. There a group were playing a friendly game of ninepins.
20. As Rip viewed the showdown, his eyelids closed, and soon the odd crew was lost in his dreams.

Extra Practice, page 93

 WRITING APPLICATION A Story

COOPERATIVE
LEARNING

Imagine that you awoke after several years of sleep. Write a brief story describing what might have changed. Then exchange papers with a classmate and identify any compound nouns or collective nouns in each other's stories.

5 APPOSITIVES

Sometimes you use a noun to give additional information about another noun in a sentence. This kind of noun is called an **appositive**.

My uncle, **a scholar**, is an expert on Greek myths.

An appositive can include more than one word. Appositives can also appear anywhere in a sentence.

My uncle, **an expert on Greek myths**, has written several books on the subject.

My uncle has written several books on Greek myths, **a fascinating subject for many people**.

Use commas to set off most appositives from the rest of the words in a sentence. However, if the sentence would not make sense without the appositive, do not use commas.

The Greek hero **Ulysses** takes a long voyage.

Guided Practice

Name the appositive in each sentence and the word that the appositive identifies or explains.

Example: Chris, my brother, reads constantly.
     brother   Chris

1. Our teacher, Mr. Sawyer, described some Greek gods.
2. Zeus, the king of the gods, ruled from Mt. Olympus.
3. Apollo and Artemis, twins, were children of Zeus.
4. Did the god Hermes fly on winged sandals?
5. This messenger, the god of traders, traveled the earth and knew its people well.

?! THINK

- How do I decide when to use commas to set off an appositive in a sentence?

REMEMBER

- An **appositive** is a word or group of words that immediately follows a noun and identifies or explains it.
- Use commas to set off most appositives.

More Practice

A. Write the appositive in each sentence and the noun that the appositive identifies.

Example: Jan, my sister, loves myths.

       sister Jan

  6. Some myths contain morals, lessons about life.

  7. Hermes, the messenger god, appears with Zeus in one tale.

  8. This story, a lesson about hospitality, is clever.

  9. The two gods disguised themselves as travelers and walked through Phrygia, a hilly land.

10. The citizens, unfriendly people, refused to help them.

B. Write each sentence and underline the appositive. Then add commas where they are needed.

Example: Mr. Hernandez our teacher read the myth aloud.

      Mr. Hernandez, <u>our teacher</u>, read the myth aloud.

11. The two strangers were welcomed by Baucis and Philemon an elderly couple.

12. Philemon a farmer brought a cabbage for them.

13. Baucis Philemon's wife offered them a bench by the fire.

14. The farmer and his wife generous people offered the strangers a feast.

15. Zeus and Hermes the honored guests were quick to reward their hosts' kindness.

16. How strange it seems that this story a Greek tale appears only in the writings of the roman poet Ovid!

Extra Practice, page 94

WRITING APPLICATION A News Article

Imagine that you are a reporter for a school newspaper. Write a brief news article that tells about a recent event at school. Then exchange papers with a classmate. Discuss how information could be added to some sentences by using appositives.

6 MECHANICS: Forming Possessive Nouns and Contractions

You know that possessive nouns are nouns that show ownership. You need to use an apostrophe to form all possessive nouns.

1. Use an **apostrophe** and an **s ('s)** to form the possessive of a singular noun.

> girl + **'s** = girl's   man + **'s** = man's
> Joan + **'s** = Joan's   jury + **'s** = jury's
> James + **'s** = James's   Bess + **'s** = Bess's

2. Use an **apostrophe** alone to form the possessive of a plural noun that ends in **s**.

> boys + **'** = boys'   ponies + **'** = ponies'
> monkeys + **'** = monkeys'   brides + **'** = brides'

3. Use an **apostrophe** and an **s ('s)** to form the possessive of a plural noun that does not end in **s**.

> women + **'s** = women's   mice + **'s** = mice's
> children + **'s** = children's   oxen + **'s** = oxen's

Do not use an apostrophe with plural nouns that are not possessive.

> The *boys* are watching the *monkeys*.

4. Use an **apostrophe** to replace a letter or letters that have been omitted in a contraction. A **contraction** is a word made by combining two words into one by leaving out one or more letters.

> **Gloria's** a friend of mine.
> (*Gloria is* a friend of mine.)

Guided Practice

Tell how you would form the possessive of each noun.

Example: cousins   cousins'

1. bugs   **2.** city   **3.** goose   **4.** babies

 THINK

- How do I decide where to use apostrophes in possessive nouns and contractions?

REMEMBER

- Use an **apostrophe** and **s** to form the possessive of a singular noun and of a plural noun that does not end in *s*.
- Use an **apostrophe** alone to form the possessive of a plural noun that ends in *s*.
- Use an **apostrophe** to indicate where a letter or letters have been left out in a contraction.

More Practice

A. Write the possessive form of each noun below.

Example: children *children's*

5. student	**12.** ladies
6. students	**13.** child
7. cities	**14.** people
8. city	**15.** committees
9. Jules	**16.** neighbors
10. Jess	**17.** deer
11. Linda	**18.** men

B. Write each sentence, adding apostrophes where needed.

Example: Those girls books are new.
            Those girls' books are new.

19. Have you read Julies story about the interesting life of Abigail Adams?
20. Abigails husband was John Adams.
21. The storys a fictional account of their marriage.
22. The presidents farm was in Massachusetts.
23. Does the story describe Mrs. Adamss personality and her many accomplishments?
24. The future first ladys management was excellent.
25. Her intellectual gifts matched her husbands, and its generally agreed she was a great asset to him.

Extra Practice, Practice Plus, pages 95–97

WRITING APPLICATION A Summary

Think of a historical figure you admire. Summarize the person's accomplishments in a paragraph. You may wish to work with a partner. Check your work to make sure that you have written possessive nouns and contractions correctly.

7 MECHANICS: Capitalizing Proper Nouns

Proper nouns are always capitalized.

Types of Proper Nouns	Examples
names of people and initials of names	Sam Houston Phineas T. Barnum
titles that precede names	Chief Joseph Dr. Jonas E. Salk Mayor Carter Mrs. King
abbreviated titles and terms that follow names	Yuko Katagiri, R.N. Frank Johnson, Jr.
names of cities, states, countries, and continents	Dallas West Virginia Australia South America
names of geographical features	Rio Grande Cape May Gulf of Mexico Gobi Desert
names of streets	State Street Park Avenue
names of buildings, bridges, and monuments	Lincoln Memorial Town Hall Betsy Ross Bridge
names of days, months, holidays, historical events, and eras	Tuesday Labor Day Stone Age August World War II
names of nationalities and languages	Mexican Iroquois American Egyptian Spanish Old English
names of organizations	National Football League Citicorp

Guided Practice

Tell which letters should be capitalized.

Example: Are you spanish?   *Spanish*

1. Last year I visited rome, italy.
2. The mediterranean sea is nearby.
3. The people speak italian and english.
4. Did mr. lyle a. evans, sr. meet you?

 THINK

- How do I decide when to capitalize a noun?

■ A **proper noun** is a noun that names a particular person, place, thing, or idea. Capitalize all proper nouns.

More Practice

A. Write each proper noun using the correct capitalization.

Example: amazon river   *Amazon River*

5. fort worth, texas
6. mary c. hopkins, ph.d.
7. louisiana purchase
8. hancock high school
9. grandparents' day
10. ohio river bridge
11. queen elizabeth II

12. south carolina
13. gen. robert e. lee
14. leaning tower of pisa
15. gulf of mexico
16. norwegian
17. metromedia, inc.
18. st. clair shores, michigan

B. Write each sentence. Capitalize each proper noun.

Example: Is cape cod near new york city?
            Is Cape Cod near New York City?

19. Diana wrote a story set here in lexington, massachusetts, just north of boston.
20. It told of the two children of joshua f. claypool, an agent for the east india company.
21. Andrew and miriam had often crossed vine brook.
22. In westfield woods they had met john swiftarrow, and he had taught them to speak oneida, his native language.
23. As the american revolution approached, claypool offered sam adams his help against the british.
24. At a meeting at munroe tavern, john offered the aid of his people.
25. Did this knowledge encourage mr. adams as he went to philadelphia in september to be part of the first continental congress?

Extra Practice, page 98

WRITING APPLICATION A Letter

Write a letter to a famous person in American history. Inquire about particular events, and people of the period. Then exchange papers with a classmate and check to make sure that all proper nouns have been capitalized correctly.

8 VOCABULARY BUILDING: How Language Changes

The English language is constantly changing. Like a living thing, the language grows when new words are formed. **Compound nouns** are created when words are joined together. Compound nouns can be written as separate words. Long words are sometimes shortened to form **clipped words**. Some new words are **blends**, or words created by joining parts of existing words. Many other new words are **borrowed words**; they come into English from other languages.

Clipped Words
gym (from *gymnasium*)   piano (from *pianoforte*)
bus (from *omnibus*)   phone (from *telephone*)

Blends
splatter (*splash* + *spatter*)   dumfound (*dumb* + *confound*)
motorcade (*motor* + *cavalcade*)

Borrowed Words
noodle (German)   skunk (Algonquian)   banjo (Bantu)
umbrella (Italian)   flamingo (Portuguese)   tycoon (Chinese)
coupon (French)   geyser (Icelandic)   tulip (Turkish)
algebra (Arabic)   lasso (Spanish)   shawl (Persian)

Many dictionary definitions include notes about the sources of words. Other reference books are also available that describe word origins in greater detail.

Guided Practice

Tell whether each word is a clipped word, a blend, or a borrowed word. Use a dictionary to help you.

Example: telethon   *blend*

1. math	**3.** restaurant	**5.** lasagna	**7.** paratrooper
2. poncho	**4.** newscast	**6.** ad	**8.** tundra

?! THINK

■ How do I decide whether a word is a clipped word, a blend, or a borrowed word?

REMEMBER

- A **clipped word** is a shortened form of a longer word.
- A **blend** is a word formed from the parts of other words.
- A **borrowed word** comes from a language other than English.

More Practice

A. Write whether each underlined noun is a **clipped word**, a **blend**, or a **borrowed word**. Use a dictionary to help you.

Example: Do you ride the bus? *clipped word*

9. A story in this magazine describes the exciting saga of an adventurer.

10. He crossed the entire continent of Europe using an auto and a balloon!

11. A photo shows him enjoying a splendid picnic on top of a glacier.

12. When chased by a tiger, he hid beneath a tarp until he could run to a waiting van.

13. With what flair he told that story on a local telecast about people's brushes with danger!

B. Write whether each word below is a **clipped word**, a **blend**, or a **borrowed word.** Use a dictionary to help you. Then write a sentence using each word.

Example: smog *blend*

14. lemon
15. zoo
16. moose
17. opera
18. travelogue
19. brunch
20. cello
21. slogan
22. pagoda
23. flu
24. pants
25. yam

Extra Practice, page 99

WRITING APPLICATION An Interview

Think of several questions that you would want to ask a historian about how language changes. Then write an imaginary interview in which your interviewee answers your questions. Use a dictionary to find specific information to include in your interview.

GRAMMAR —AND WRITING CONNECTION

Combining Sentences

When you write a story, you may write several sentences that describe a single character. To avoid repeating words and to connect ideas in your writing, you can combine related sentences. Sometimes you can combine two related sentences by turning one of them into a word or group of words that describes or explains more about a noun in the other sentence.

SEPARATE: The man in the robes has a sword. The man is King Arthur.

COMBINED: The man in the robes, **King Arthur**, has a sword.

Use commas to set off an added word or group of words that is not essential to the meaning of the sentence. Do not use commas if the word or group of words is essential to the meaning of the sentence.

I like the name **Galahad.**

Working Together

COOPERATIVE
LEARNING

Combine each pair of sentences by making the second sentence into a word or group of words that describes a noun in the first sentence.

Example: Our teacher discussed *The Tales of King Arthur.*
Our teacher is Ms. Chang.
Our teacher, Ms. Chang, discussed The Tales of King Arthur.

1. The king's sword protected Arthur from injury.
   The name of the king's sword was Excalibur.
2. The Lady of the Lake gave Excalibur to Arthur.
   The Lady of the Lake was an enchantress.
3. Galahad was a noble knight.
   Galahad was the son of Lancelot.

Revising Sentences

Combine each pair of sentences by making the second sentence into a word or group of words that describes a noun in the first sentence. Use commas where they are needed.

4. Merlin was Arthur's companion and teacher.
   Merlin was a magician.
5. The Celts developed a rich mythology.
   The Celts are an ancient people.
6. Merlin created a famous piece of furniture for Arthur's knights.
   The piece of furniture was the Round Table.
7. Morgan le Fay was not harmful in the early stories.
   Morgan le Fay was King Arthur's sister.
8. Morgan le Fay is destructive in modern fantasies.
   Morgan le Fay was originally a healer.
9. Lancelot betrayed Arthur.
   Lancelot was a courageous knight.
10. Guinevere fell in love with Lancelot.
    Guinevere was Arthur's wife and queen.
11. Gawain fought the Green Knight.
    The Green Knight was an axe-wielding giant.
12. Camelot may have existed at Cadbury Hill in England.
    Camelot was Arthur's castle.

You have read about many different stories in Unit 3, including the tales of King Arthur. Choose a character from a book you have enjoyed and think of a new story for the character. Then write a brief story using your ideas.

When you are ready to revise your story, exchange papers with a classmate. Look for sentences that could be improved by combining them in the manner taught in this lesson. Use commas correctly.

UNIT CHECKUP

LESSON 1

Kinds of Nouns (page 68)   Write the nouns in each sentence. Then write whether the noun is **common** or **proper.** Next to each common noun write whether it is **concrete** or **abstract.**

Proper nouns are underlined twice.

1. Carolyn is at the library, surrounded by books.   con., con.

2. My cousin has begun doing research about Mali, a country in Africa.   con., abs., con.

3. Information about the city of Bamako will appear in a story that she is writing.   abs., con., con.

4. How the librarian encourages her efforts!   con., abs.

LESSON 2

Singular and Plural Nouns (page 70)   Write the plural form of each singular noun.

5. beach   es

6. glass   es

7. buoy   s

8. mouse   mice

9. loaf   ves

10. policy   ies

11. series   series

12. delivery   ies

13. foot   feet

14. folio   s

15. monkey   s

16. igloo   s

LESSON 3

Possessive Nouns (page 72)   Write each sentence, using the possessive form of the underlined noun.

17. This children book tells of Johnny Appleseed.   children's

18. Was John Chapman this character real name?   character's

19. Settlers homes between the Allegheny and Wabash rivers were Johnny territory.   Settlers', Johnny's

20. Americans imaginations soar at the thought of this pioneer journeys through the frontier.   Americans', pioneer's

LESSON 4

Collective and Compound Nouns (page 74)   Write each sentence. Underline each collective noun once and each compound noun twice. Then write whether the meaning of each collective noun is **singular** or **plural.**

21. Even in his lifetime Johnny Appleseed was known for his stout-heartedness and compassion.

22. He looked a little like a scarecrow because he gave his possessions to down-and-outers.

23. The public remembers this trailblazer fondly and has turned him into a legend.   sing.

24. My club has planned a display about him at the new middle school.   sing.

LESSON 5

Appositives (page 76)   Write each sentence. Then underline the appositive and add commas where necessary.

25. In his two canoes his chief means of transportation Johnny Appleseed carried sacks of seeds.
26. These seeds the promise of new orchards were scattered from Pennsylvania to Indiana.
27. Johnny gained a constant companion a wolf when he freed it from a trap.
28. Johnny Appleseed a unique American also distributed herbs as sources of medicine.

LESSON 6

Mechanics: Forming Possessive Nouns and Contractions (page 78)   Write the possessive form of each noun.

29. Rosemary	**32.** trout	**35.** scientist
30. infants	**33.** policemen	**36.** woman
31. principals	**34.** Gomez	**37.** uncles

LESSON 7

Mechanics: Capitalizing Proper Nouns (page 80)   Write each sentence. Capitalize each proper noun.

38. If you have read the books of laura ingalls wilder, then you know the artwork of garth williams.
39. Williams lived in new jersey and canada; he later attended the westminster art school in england.
40. This american very likely sat along the thames river and sketched london bridge.
41. Back in new york during world war II, williams met the author e. b. white.

LESSON 8

Vocabulary Building: How Language Changes (page 82)   Write whether each noun is a **clipped word,** a **blend,** or a **borrowed word.** Use a dictionary to help you.

42. shawl	**45.** telethon	**48.** dumfound
43. phone	**46.** lab	**49.** fly
44. pretzel	**47.** kimono	**50.** exam

Writing Application: Noun Usage (pages 68–81)   The following paragraph contains five errors in noun usage. Write the paragraph correctly.

51.–55.   The beachs of Cape cod are some of the loveliest in the united States. They are a swimmers paradise, with sparkling water and rolling waves. Put the Cape on your familys vacation list.

Giving Proper Credit

With a partner or small group, play a game using proper nouns. First establish a category—either person, place, or thing. The first player names a proper noun in the category. The next player must name another proper noun that begins with the last letter of the noun just given. For example, if the category were *person* and the first player names *Cleopatra,* the next response might be *Antony.* The player with the most correct answers wins.

What's in a Name?

Many words in our everyday language derive from the names of actual people. For example, the sandwich is named after the 4th Earl of Sandwich, who was too busy to eat regular meals.

Match the objects shown here with the appropriate names.

Dr. Joseph Guillotin
Thomas Derrick
Etienne de Silhouette

Find, or make up, other words that come from people's names.

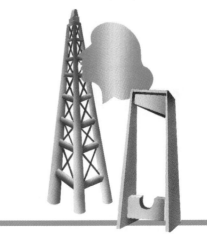

Jed's Bread

With a group of classmates write several advertisements that contain rhyming phrases. Each rhyming phrase should contain possessive nouns—common, proper, singular, or plural; for example, *Mike's bikes are best* or *Jake's cakes will sweeten your life.* Be sure to use apostrophes correctly.

CREATIVE EXPRESSION

WHO AM I?

The trees ask me,
And the sky,
And the sea asks me
> *Who am I?*

The grass asks me,
And the sand,
And the rocks ask me
> *Who I am.*

The wind tells me
At nightfall,
And the rain tells me
> *Someone small.*

Someone small
Someone small
> *But a piece*
>> *of*
>> *it*
>> *all.*

—Felice Holman

TRY IT OUT

Poets and other writers sometimes describe an object as though it were a person. Using language in this way is called **personification.** *The house shivered beneath the snow* is an example of personification. Find other examples of personification in the poem above. Then write a poem of your own and include personification.

EXTRA PRACTICE

Three levels of practice

Kinds of Nouns (page 68)

LEVEL

A. Write whether each noun is **common** or **proper**.

1. beagle
2. Snoopy
3. history
4. May Company
5. binoculars
6. galaxy
7. Green River
8. Betty
9. skyscraper
10. Brazil
11. Arizona
12. bouquet

LEVEL

B. Write each sentence. Underline each common noun once and each proper noun twice.

13. Jocelyn likes movies about the future.
14. Her friends discussed a book about a planet called Pern.
15. Another location was the land of Narnia.
16. In that world, all creatures look to Aslan, the mighty lion.
17. Mom remembers these novels from her childhood.
18. Has Yukiko read her brother and sister the first tale in this magical series?

LEVEL

C. Write each sentence, using proper nouns to replace the common nouns in parentheses. Then write whether each of the underlined nouns is **concrete** or **abstract.**

19. (name) is putting his talents to work on a tale about (a planet), where the inhabitants can fly.
20. Scientists from distant (another planet) are filled with amazement at this ability.
21. (name), the king, welcomes the visitors to his palace by the (a river).
22. He tells the history of his race; then his son shows these guests around (a city).
23. (name of son) says, "As prince, I must speak of the fear in the hearts of my people."
24. "The (name of group of people) love peace. Will you use your weapons to learn our secrets?
25. (name), the captain, discusses this difficult matter with Krogor, her lieutenant.

EXTRA PRACTICE

Three levels of practice

Singular and Plural Nouns (page 70)

LEVEL

A. Write the correct plural noun for each pair of words. Check your answers in a dictionary.

1. donkeys, donkies
2. nickels, nickeles
3. sketchs, sketches
4. sheeps, sheep

5. foxs, foxes
6. vetos, vetoes
7. pennys, pennies
8. women, womans

LEVEL

B. Write the correct plural form of each noun. Check your answers in a dictionary.

9. mystery
10. delay
11. radish
12. miss
13. deer

14. canoe
15. cameo
16. gas
17. lox
18. attorney

LEVEL

C. Write each sentence, using the plural form of each underlined noun.

19. Edison, one of the boy in my class, is reading the trilogy of different authors.
20. Your dictionary will tell you that the story in a trilogy runs through three novel.
21. In the first of the tale in this trilogy, the hero tried to explain the sound of ghostly hoof on several ranch.
22. Did those noise have anything to do with mysterious ray of light in the neighboring valley?
23. The hero played his hunch and followed the echo to a run-down shack.
24. Waiting in the bush, he finally saw two desperado and recognized them as notorious thief.
25. Although some episode read like tragedy, the hero's journey end in victory.

EXTRA PRACTICE

Three levels of practice

Possessive Nouns (page 72)

LEVEL

A. Write each sentence. Then underline each possessive noun and write whether it is **singular** or **plural**.

1. This week's story comes from Greece's ancient past.
2. Many authors' works have been drawn from this tale.
3. Atalanta's first home was in the woods.
4. She grew up to be a hunter, and her companions' envy of her was great.
5. When a hunting party was charged by a boar, a person's life was saved by Atalanta's spear.
6. According to some writers' accounts, was Atalanta seen during Ulysses's voyage?

LEVEL

B. Write the possessive form of each noun.

7. Greeks	**12.** salmon
8. athlete	**13.** Bess
9. boss	**14.** teacher
10. friend	**15.** oxen
11. women	**16.** men

LEVEL

C. Read the paragraphs and look for nouns that should be possessive. Then write the paragraphs, using the correct possessive forms.

(17.) Her parents wish was to see her marry, but Atalanta refused. **(18.)** The girls announcement was that she would marry the man who could outrun her. **(19.)** The suitors skills were no match for Atalantas ability; she won every time.

One day a new suitor appeared. **(20.)** Melanions hopes were high as he held three golden apples, **(21.)** Aphrodites gift to him. The value of the apples during the race would be great. **(22.)** At the judges signal, Atalanta shot down the track. **(23.)** Then her challengers hand moved, and an apple rolled in front of her. **(24.)** Viewers gasps filled the air as Atalanta slowed to scoop it up. He tried again; and as Atalanta reached for another apple, Melanion caught up with her. **(25.)** From this runners lips came prayers of joy as he tossed the third apple, and Atalanta stopped to take it. He crossed the finish line just seconds before his new bride.

EXTRA PRACTICE

Three levels of practice

Collective and Compound Nouns (page 74)

LEVEL

A. Write whether each word is a **collective noun** or a **compound noun.**

1. landlords
2. family
3. company
4. wheelchair
5. runner-up
6. moonlight
7. congress
8. team
9. life jacket
10. great-grandfather
11. jury
12. chorus

LEVEL

B. Write each sentence. Underline each collective noun once and each compound noun twice.

13. If you were a storyteller, what kind of tale would you write for your audience?
14. Your characters might be members of a jury, or they might live alone in a rain forest.
15. Would you set your story on a houseboat, or would you choose an exotic location, like outer space?
16. You might describe the crew of a space station.
17. Perhaps your readers would prefer reading about the give-and-take of a team of skiers.
18. When you go on tour to promote your best seller, will you speak to our club?
19. The name of our group is Bookworms.

LEVEL

C. Write each sentence. Underline each compound noun twice. Then underline each collective noun once and write whether its meaning is **singular** or **plural**.

20. A committee is evaluating this folk tale.
21. It concerns the goings-on in an unusual family.
22. The jury like the wordplay in the story.
23. The group, however, found the part about an earthquake too violent.
24. My class agrees that Rochelle's modernization of "The Three Little Pigs" should win honorable mention.
25. The committee disagree about which artwork to reward.

EXTRA PRACTICE

Three levels of practice

Appositives (page 76)

LEVEL

A. Write each sentence and underline the appositive.
1. The Brule Sioux, a people of the Midwest, offer one explanation for a mystery of nature.
2. They have a legend about how the crow, a bird with inky black feathers, became that way.
3. Crows once had white feathers, plumage like snow.
4. People relied upon one main source of food, buffalo.
5. The Sioux, hunters without horses or iron weapons, tracked buffalo with weapons of stone.
6. The white crow, the hunters' enemy, would warn the buffalo.

LEVEL

B. Write each sentence. Underline the appositive and add commas where necessary.
7. The starving people held a council a serious meeting.
8. The chief placed a buffalo skin upon the back of a young man his nephew.
9. This "buffalo" the youth in disguise moved among the herd, caught the crow, and tied its foot to a stone.
10. An angry hunter grabbed the crow and threw it into the fire a fitting punishment.
11. The fire burned through the string, and the crow flew off a released prisoner.
12. However, the fire a smoky blaze blackened the crow's feathers and forced a promise from it.
13. The crow's words an oath of silence kept the people supplied with buffalo from then on.

LEVEL

C. Write five sentences, each containing an appositive. Use the information in parentheses.
14. Mrs. LeJune (an expert about old legends)
15. these tales (wonderful adventures)
16. one story (a tale about the four seasons)
17. a talking coyote (a surprising kind of hero)
18. other animals (the coyote's friends)
19. the Kiowa (a people of the Plains)
20. "pourquoi" tales (stories that explain nature)

EXTRA PRACTICE

Three levels of practice

Mechanics: Forming Possessive Nouns and Contractions
(page 78)

LEVEL

A. Write the possessive form of each noun. The nouns in the first column are singular, and those in the second column are plural.

1. cavalry
2. climax
3. volcano
4. Chris

5. cactuses
6. adolescents
7. mice
8. birthdays

B. Write each sentence, adding apostrophes where they are needed.

9. Anne Franks family left Germany for Holland in 1933.
10. The Franks move was due to Nazi persecution of Jews.
11. Hollands invasion by the Nazis forced another move.
12. In 1942 a secret attic became the familys home.
13. A workers suspicions led to their arrest in 1944.
14. *The Diary of Anne Frank* describes Annes experiences.
15. Her diary records two years in a teenagers life.
16. The womens club in our town dramatized parts of the book.

LEVEL

C. Write each sentence, adding apostrophes where they are needed. Write **correct** if the sentence needs no correction.

17. Lorraine Hansberry won acclaim for her first play.
18. This writers play is *A Raisin in the Sun.*
19. The dramas about a black family in Chicago.
20. We see this familys struggle for a better life.
21. The play portrays peoples weaknesses and prejudices.
22. The characters actions are believable.
23. Hansberrys second play was also successful.
24. Did she write any childrens books?
25. Did she also write short stories?

PRACTICE + PLUS

Three levels of additional practice for a difficult skill

Mechanics: Forming Possessive Nouns and Contractions
(page 78)

LEVEL

A. Write the possessive form of each noun. The nouns in items 1–12 are singular, and those in items 13–24 are plural.

1. county	**9.** rhinoceros	**17.** girls
2. potato	**10.** Alex	**18.** women
3. ox	**11.** burro	**19.** boxes
4. Janis	**12.** trout	**20.** parties
5. moose	**13.** oxen	**21.** actors
6. galley	**14.** twins	**22.** armies
7. Charles	**15.** turkeys	**23.** sopranos
8. woman	**16.** mice	**24.** agencies

LEVEL

B. Write each sentence, adding apostrophes where needed.

25. Settlement houses also fulfilled the communitys educational and recreational needs.

26. A settlement houses purpose was to improve the poors living conditions.

27. Through volunteers efforts, thousands received services.

28. The founding of Toynbee Hall was made possible through university students efforts.

29. The worlds first settlement house was named after Arnold Toynbee.

30. Arnold Toynbees life was dedicated to social reform.

31. Toynbee Hall was located in Londons poor district.

32. New York Citys University Settlement was the first settlement house in the U.S.

33. The Europeans move to the U.S. was called "The Great Wave of Immigration."

34. Is this Raymonds novel about Jane Addams?

35. Janes parents settled in Illinois.

36. Her parents new home was located in Cedarville.

37. Janes birth took place there in 1860.

38. Its clear that she was a gifted child.

39. Her father sent her to a womens seminary.

40. The books theme is her intelligence and courage.

41. Her lifes struggles and triumphs make good reading.
42. Jane Addams was saddened by her fathers death.
43. The years that followed tested the womans strength.
44. The books quite detailed about her back surgery.
45. Jane Addams was bothered by her spines curvature.
46. Two surgeons efforts brought some improvement.
47. A years travel in Europe broadened her outlook.
48. Jane visited Londons famous settlement house.
49. Toynbee Halls director inspired her future work.

LEVEL
C. Write each sentence, adding apostrophes where needed. Write **correct** if the sentence needs no correction.

50. A biography's purpose is to tell a life story.
51. Jane Addamss biography dwells on her unusual career.
52. Her career involved working for peoples welfare.
53. Addams's ideas were revolutionary.
54. With Ellen Gates Starrs help, she founded Hull House.
55. Hull House became Americas most famous settlement house.
56. The settlement house tried to meet poor families needs.
57. What was the publics view of her settlement house?
58. Hull House was established for societys benefit.
59. Its success depended on the staff's dedication.
60. Hull Houses programs included cultural activities.
61. Residents of the settlement worked for the neighborhoods improvement.
62. The staffs work for better housing was successful.
63. Jane Addams's work for peace won her the Nobel Prize.
64. Her work captured the worlds attention.
65. In her generations opinion, she was a great woman.
66. Between 1830 and 1930, over 30 million immigrants settled on this country's shores.
67. Ships were the travelers usual means of transportation.
68. The Atlantic Oceans heavy seas often made the long journey uncomfortable.
69. Officials at Ellis Island's reception center processed millions of immigrants.
70. Settlement services often eased the immigrants adjustment to American life.
71. It was the travelers desire to come to a large American city.
72. A large city's job opportunities were more extensive.
73. A newcomer's skill with the English language could be developed at the settlement.
74. Children's and adults musical skills could also be improved.

EXTRA PRACTICE

Three levels of practice

Mechanics: Capitalizing Proper Nouns (page 80)

LEVEL

A. Write each proper noun, using correct capitalization.

1. empire state building
2. president chester a. arthur
3. joanna n. rose, d.d.s.
4. chicago black hawks
5. battle of the bulge
6. caspian sea
7. san franciscans
8. memorial day
9. commerce plaza
10. dominican republic

LEVEL

B. Write each sentence. Capitalize each proper noun.

11. My twin cousins, dave and derek, know a teenage genius in omaha, nebraska.
12. A student at the nebraska school for the deaf, jeff devised a way to represent music with colored light.
13. His teacher, mrs. pat moore, offered to help him.
14. In addition, judge murphy wiley agreed to help.
15. As they walked through adams park, they decided to ask audiotex, inc., to evaluate the concept.
16. Jeff chose selections by mozart and j. s. bach and then went to work on their "translation" into light.
17. On friday, may 6, elaine ray of audiotex watched the presentation in a meeting room at the red lion inn.
18. How excited the wileys were when ms. ray invited them to st. louis, missouri, to present their ideas!

LEVEL

C. Write a proper noun that fits each of the following descriptions. You may make up these words. Then write a sentence using each proper noun.

19. a street in your town that is named after a person
20. the airport that services your community
21. a professional sports team
22. a country that you would like to visit some day
23. a historical event that you have studied
24. two adult relatives
25. two federal holidays

EXTRA PRACTICE

Three levels of practice

Vocabulary Building: How Language Changes (page 82)

LEVEL

A. Match each word in the left column with its origin in the right column. Write the words and their origins; then identify each as a **clipped word**, a **blend**, or a **borrowed word**.

1. pizzeria
2. prefab
3. rodeo
4. woodchuck
5. pro
6. coupon
7. travelogue

a. from French *couper*
b. from Algonquian *otchek*
c. from *travel* and *dialogue*
d. from *pizza* and *cafeteria*
e. from *professional*
f. from Spanish *rodear*
g. from *prefabrication*

LEVEL

B. Write whether each underlined noun is a **clipped word**, a **blend**, or a **borrowed word**. Use a dictionary to help you.

8. Sherri was walking her <u>poodle</u> and thinking about a program she had seen.
9. It was a <u>sitcom</u> about a man who quit his job.
10. He went to live in a hut by a <u>lagoon</u>.
11. He did not have a <u>phone</u>, but he did have to put up with many annoying neighbors.
12. One neighbor was constantly borrowing <u>gas</u> for his snazzy new <u>motorcycle</u>.
13. This busybody even borrowed cups of <u>molasses</u>.
14. As a further distraction, he set up a <u>stereo</u> in his <u>bungalow</u>.

LEVEL

C. Use a dictionary to find the origin of each noun. Write whether it is a **clipped word**, a **blend**, or a **borrowed word**. Then write a sentence using the word.

15. motel
16. detour
17. bureaucrat
18. commando
19. cab
20. sherbet

21. smog
22. flu
23. kindergarten
24. video
25. finale

MAINTENANCE

UNIT 1: SENTENCES

Kinds of Sentences (page 2) Write each sentence, capitalizing and punctuating it correctly. Then write whether it is **declarative, interrogative, exclamatory,** or **imperative.**

1. have you ever played football
2. the game is played on a large field
3. watch the quarterback run down the field
4. how high the ball soars through the air
5. you pass the ball very well

Complete Subjects and Complete Predicates, Simple Subjects and Simple Predicates (pages 4, 6) Write each sentence. Underline the complete subject once and the complete predicate twice. Circle the simple subject and the simple predicate. If the complete subject is understood, write (*You*).

6. My cousin draws funny cartoons.
7. Have you ever seen one of them?
8. Here is one in the school newspaper.
9. Show me some more of his cartoons.
10. The young cartoonist is very talented.

Compound Subjects and Predicates, Compound Sentences (pages 8, 10) Write each sentence. Underline each complete subject once and each complete predicate twice. Then write whether the sentence has a **compound subject** or a **compound predicate** or is a **compound sentence.**

11. The ventriloquist and his dummy performed for us.
12. They talked with each other and made jokes.
13. I thought they were funny, but Cleo didn't laugh.
14. The ventriloquist made the dummy sing, and Cleo giggled in spite of herself.
15. Both the ventriloquist and the dummy bowed at the end of the show.

Correcting Fragments and Run-On Sentences (page 12) Write each group of words, correcting the sentence fragments and run-on sentences. Write *correct* next to any word group that is a sentence.

16. Many books were printed on acidic paper, they may crumble to dust soon.
17. Have grown very brittle over time.
18. Made worse by storage in unregulated temperatures.

19. The nation's librarians are worried.
20. Most books will be transferred to microfilm, this is only a partial solution.

Using Context Clues (page 16)
Write each sentence. Then write the probable meaning of each underlined word.

21. Diamond, the world's hardest substance, is a durable material.
22. X rays are not transmitted through diamonds.
23. Color, clarity, cut, and carat weight are the attributes used to judge the quality of a diamond.
24. This stone is resplendent in its jeweled setting.
25. Synthetic stones do not compare in brilliance with the natural ones.

UNIT 3: NOUNS

Kinds of Nouns (page 68)
Write each sentence. Underline each common noun once and each proper noun twice. Then label each common noun as **concrete** or **abstract**

26. Dora and Rod are interested in nutrition.
27. The cousins get fresh-milled flour from a gristmill.
28. Gristmills were once an institution in most towns in New England.
29. Chefs at some restaurants like milled flour, too.
30. The miller, Mr. Orr, sells not only flour but history.

Singular and Plural Nouns
(page 70)   Write the following words. After each word write its plural form.

31. lens   35. alley   39. self
32. proof   36. goose   40. bison
33. echo   37. lily
34. tax   38. cello

Possessive Nouns (page 72)
Write each word. After each one write its possessive form.

41. family   46. Diazes
42. airman   47. Albany
43. years   48. writers
44. hostess   49. Eskimo
45. wives   50. fox

Capitalizing Proper Nouns
(page 80)   Write each sentence. Use capital letters correctly.

51. Settlers from france founded new orleans.
52. The city lies at the mouth of the mississippi river.
53. Does galveston, texas, lie west of new orleans?
54. I believe that maria vargas, m.d., lives there.

How Language Changes (page 82)
Write whether each word is borrowed, a blend, or a clipped word.

55. fiat   58. wig
56. cab   59. smash
57. motel   60. piano

UNIT

4

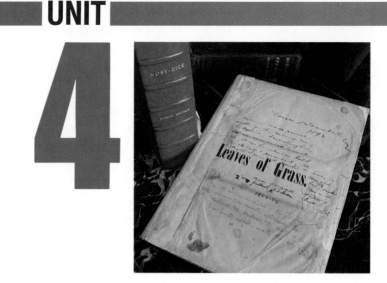

Writing Short Stories

Read the quotation and look at the picture on the opposite page. Talk about how stories become well known.

When you write a short story, it is important to keep your audience in mind. You will want your audience to think about and enjoy what you have written.

Focus A short story provides pleasure and an opportunity for reflection for an audience.

What would be a good topic for a short story? In this unit you will find a story with a surprise ending. You will see some interesting photographs, too. You can use both to find ideas for writing.

A good tale is none the worse for being twice told.
—Proverb

LITERATURE

Reading Like a Writer

Do you remember how you felt when you went off to school for the first time? Was it easy or difficult for you? How do you behave now when you are in new situations?

In "Charles," Laurie reveals almost nothing about his own experiences as he begins kindergarten. He does, however, like to tell stories about a disobedient student named Charles.

As you read, notice that the events of the story are seen through one character's eyes.

Charles

from *The Lottery and Other Stories*
BY SHIRLEY JACKSON

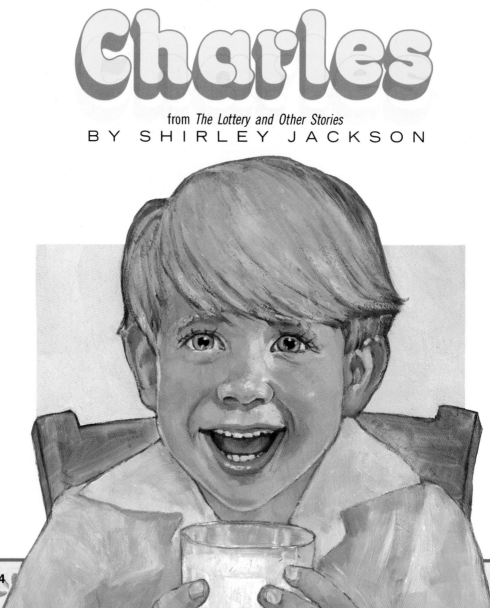

The day my son Laurie started kindergarten he renounced corduroy overalls with bibs and began wearing blue jeans with a belt; I watched him go off the first morning with the older girl next door, seeing clearly that an era of my life was ended, my sweet-voiced nursery-school tot replaced by a long-trousered, swaggering character who forgot to stop at the corner and wave good-bye to me.

He came home the same way, the front door slamming open, his cap on the floor, and the voice suddenly become raucous shouting, "Isn't anybody *here*?"[1]

At lunch he spoke insolently to his father, spilled his baby sister's milk, and remarked that his teacher said we were not to take the name of the Lord in vain.

"How *was* school today?" I asked, elaborately casual.

"All right," he said.

"Did you learn anything?" his father asked.

Laurie regarded his father coldly. "I didn't learn nothing," he said.

"Anything," I said. "Didn't learn anything."

"The teacher spanked a boy, though," Laurie said, addressing his bread and butter. "For being fresh," he added, with his mouth full.

"What did he do?" I asked. "Who was it?"

Laurie thought. "It was Charles," he said. "He was fresh. The teacher spanked him and made him stand in a corner. He was awfully fresh."

"What did he do?" I asked again, but Laurie slid off his chair, took a cookie, and left, while his father was still saying, "See here, young man."

The next day Laurie remarked at lunch, as soon as he sat down, "Well, Charles was bad again today." He grinned enormously and said, "Today Charles hit the teacher."

"Good heavens," I said, mindful of the Lord's name, "I suppose he got spanked again?"

"He sure did," Laurie said. "Look up," he said to his father.

"What?" his father said, looking up.

"Look down," Laurie said. "Look at my thumb. Gee, you're dumb." He began to laugh insanely.

"Why did Charles hit the teacher?" I asked quickly.

1. Laurie's personality traits are revealed through his actions.

"Because she tried to make him color with red crayons," Laurie said. "Charles wanted to color with green crayons so he hit the teacher and she spanked him and said nobody play with Charles but everybody did."

The third day—it was Wednesday of the first week—Charles bounced a see-saw on to the head of a little girl and made her bleed, and the teacher made him stay inside all during recess. Thursday Charles had to stand in a corner during story-time because he kept pounding his feet on the floor. Friday Charles was deprived of blackboard privileges because he threw chalk.

On Saturday I remarked to my husband, "Do you think kindergarten is too unsettling for Laurie? All this toughness, and bad grammar, and this Charles boy sounds like such a bad influence."

"It'll be all right," my husband said reassuringly. "Bound to be people like Charles in the world. Might as well meet them now as later."

On Monday Laurie came home late, full of news. "Charles," he shouted as he came up the hill; I was waiting anxiously on the front steps. "Charles," Laurie yelled all the way up the hill, "Charles was bad again."

"Come right in," I said, as soon as he came close enough. "Lunch is waiting."

"You know what Charles did?" he demanded, following me through the door. "Charles yelled so in school they sent a boy in from first grade to tell the teacher she had to make Charles

keep quiet, and so Charles had to stay after school. And so all the children stayed to watch him."[2]

"What did he do?" I asked.

"He just sat there," Laurie said, climbing into his chair at the table. "Hi, Pop, y'old dust mop."

"Charles had to stay after school today," I told my husband. "Everyone stayed with him."

"What does this Charles look like?" my husband asked Laurie. "What's his other name?"

"He's bigger than me," Laurie said. "And he doesn't have any rubbers and he doesn't ever wear a jacket."

Monday night was the first Parent-Teachers meeting, and only the fact that the baby had a cold kept me from going; I wanted passionately to meet Charles's mother. On Tuesday Laurie remarked suddenly, "Our teacher had a friend come to see her in school today."

"Charles's mother?" my husband and I asked simultaneously.

"Naah," Laurie said scornfully. "It was a man who came and made us do exercises, we had to touch our toes. Look." He climbed down from his chair and squatted down and touched his toes. "Like this," he said. He got solemnly back into his chair and said, picking up his fork, "Charles didn't even *do* exercises."

"That's fine," I said heartily. "Didn't Charles want to do exercises?"

"Naah," Laurie said. "Charles was so fresh to the teacher's friend that he wasn't *let* do exercises."

"Fresh again?" I said.

"He kicked the teacher's friend," Laurie said. "The teacher's friend told Charles to touch his toes like I just did and Charles kicked him."

"What are they going to do about Charles, do you suppose?" Laurie's father asked him.

Laurie shrugged elaborately. "Throw him out of school, I guess," he said.

Wednesday and Thursday were routine; Charles yelled during story hour and hit a boy in the stomach and made him cry. On Friday Charles stayed after school again and so did all the other children.

2. Conversations between characters reveal important events in the story.

With the third week of kindergarten Charles was an institution in our family; the baby was being a Charles when she cried all afternoon, Laurie did a Charles when he filled his wagon full of mud and pulled it through the kitchen; even my husband, when he caught his elbow in the telephone cord and pulled telephone, ashtray, and a bowl of flowers off the table, said, after the first minute, "Looks like Charles."

During the third and fourth weeks it looked like a reformation in Charles; Laurie reported grimly at lunch on Thursday of the third week, "Charles was so good today the teacher gave him an apple."

"What?" I said, and my husband added warily, "You mean Charles?"

"Charles," Laurie said. "He gave the crayons around and he picked up the books afterward and the teacher said he was her helper."

"What happened?" I asked incredulously.

"He was her helper, that's all," Laurie said, and shrugged.

"Can this be true, about Charles?" I asked my husband that night. "Can something like this happen?"

"Wait and see," my husband said cynically. "When you've got a Charles to deal with, this may mean he's only plotting."

He seemed to be wrong. For over a week Charles was the teacher's helper; each day he handed things out and he picked things up; no one had to stay after school.

"The P.T.A. meeting's next week again," I told my husband one evening. "I'm going to find Charles's mother there."

"Ask her what happened to Charles," my husband said. "I'd like to know."

"I'd like to know myself," I said.

On Friday of that week things were back to normal. "You know what Charles did today?" Laurie demanded at the lunch table, in a voice slightly awed. "He told a little girl to say a word and she said it and the teacher washed her mouth out with soap and Charles laughed."

"What word?" his father asked unwisely, and Laurie said, "I'll have to whisper it to you, it's so bad." He got down off his chair and went around to his father. His father bent his head down and Laurie whispered joyfully. His father's eyes widened.

"Did Charles tell the little girl to say *that*?" he asked respectfully.

"She said it *twice*," Laurie said. "Charles told her to say it *twice*."

"What happened to Charles?" my husband asked.

"Nothing," Laurie asked. "He was passing out the crayons."

Monday morning Charles abandoned the little girl and said the evil word himself three or four times, getting his mouth washed out with soap each time. He also threw chalk.

My husband came to the door with me that evening as I set out for the P.T.A. meeting. "Invite her over for a cup of tea after the meeting," he said. "I want to get a look at her."

"If only she's there," I said prayerfully.

"She'll be there," my husband said. "I don't see how they could hold a P.T.A. meeting without Charles's mother."

At the meeting I sat restlessly, scanning each comfortable matronly face, trying to determine which one hid the secret of Charles. None of them looked to me haggard enough. No one stood up in the meeting and apologized for the way her son had been acting. No one mentioned Charles.

After the meeting I identified and sought out Laurie's kindergarten teacher. She had a plate with a cup of tea and a piece of chocolate cake; I had a plate with a cup of tea and a piece of marshmallow cake. We maneuvered up to one another cautiously, and smiled.

"I've been so anxious to meet you," I said. "I'm Laurie's mother."

"We're all so interested in Laurie," she said.

"Well, he certainly likes kindergarten," I said. "He talks about it all the time."

"We had a little trouble adjusting the first week or so," she said primly, "but now he's a fine little helper. With occasional lapses, of course."

"Laurie usually adjusts very quickly," I said. "I suppose this time it's Charles's influence."

"Charles?"

"Yes," I said, laughing, "you must have your hands full in that kindergarten, with Charles."

"Charles?" she said. "We don't have any Charles in the kindergarten."[3]

3. The ending of the story leaves the reader with a surprise.

Thinking Like a Reader

1. Why do you think Laurie invented Charles?

2. Have you ever done something similar?

Write your responses in your journal.

Thinking Like a Writer

3. How do we know what is going on in Laurie's mind?

4. How do conversations and events help you to know him?

5. Were you surprised by the ending? Why or why not?

6. If you were writing a story about an imaginative person faced with a new situation, what might the events of the story be?

Brainstorm *Vocabulary*

In "Charles" Shirley Jackson uses carefully chosen words to describe the behavior of characters in the story; for example, *swaggering, sweet-voiced, casual, anxiously, fresh, haggard, scornfully, cautiously, respectfully,* and *grimly.* Look for other examples in the story. Then imagine characters for a story of your own. How would you describe their personalities and behavior? Perhaps your characters are based on people you know. Write down words or phrases that come to mind. Keep a personal vocabulary list in your journal. You can use these words when you write stories of your own.

Talk It Over *Act Out a Scene*

What people say and how they say it helps us to know them. Realizing this, good writers put words into their characters' mouths to give them life and personality.

In "Charles," we become acquainted with Laurie largely through his own words. Choose a scene from the story that includes Laurie's dialogue. With one or two partners, act it out. Don't just read the lines. Consider what you know about the characters. Then say the words as you think the characters themselves might say them. Vary your volume, rate, and expression according to what you think is appropriate for the characters.

Quick Write *Add an Ending*

The ending of a story is often very important. A good ending can give the reader a surprise or leave the reader with a special feeling or thought. A weak ending diminishes the power of an otherwise effective story.

The story of "Charles" ends when the teacher makes a surprising statement. The author leaves it to you to decide what that statement means and how Laurie's mother might react to it.

Add your own ending to the story. Write a few lines that tell what happens next. What does Laurie's mother say? What does she do? How does Laurie react?

Idea Corner
Start with a Setting

Stories—even very dramatic stories—do not have to take place in very dramatic places. The events in "Charles," for example, all occur at home and in school.

In your journal briefly describe a familiar place. The location might be a room in your home or a street in your neighborhood or town. Then list some dramatic events that could occur there. What might happen in your schoolyard, for instance? A cow might wander in or a helicopter might land there or perhaps a spaceship. Don't limit yourself to ordinary events—let your imagination go.

PICTURES  *SEEING LIKE A WRITER*

Finding Ideas for Writing

Look at the pictures on these pages. Think about what you see. What ideas for writing a short story do the pictures give you? Write your ideas in your journal.

1 GROUP WRITING: A SHORT STORY

COOPERATIVE
LEARNING

You know that narratives tell stories. A **short story** tells about imaginary people and events. The **purpose** of a story is to entertain an **audience**. What are the important story elements that you need to know about before you can write a good short story?

- Plot
- Characters and Setting
- Dialogue

Plot

The **plot** is the series of events that occurs in a story. Without a plot there is no story. Not every series of events makes a plot, however. Compare these two lists.

Inez was eating a sandwich.	Lee arrived home late.
The dog barked twice.	His dog Diva was not there.
Later the doorbell rang.	He searched everywhere.
A package arrived for Inez.	Two hours later a car drove up.
It was the tape she had ordered.	Diva jumped out.
She read for a half hour.	She had been looking for Lee at school.
Carla called her.	Her tag identified her.

The left-hand column contains a series of events. The right-hand column contains a plot; it tells a story. Notice that a simple series of events is not very interesting or entertaining. To become a plot, events need a **conflict**, or central problem, as in the right-hand column. The events in a plot often build to a high point, or **climax**, and end in some kind of **resolution**, or solution to the problem.

Most plots have a beginning, a middle, and an ending. The **beginning** introduces the setting, characters, and the conflict and starts the action of the plot. The **middle** develops the plot in a sequence of events. The events are usually described in chronological, or time, order. The **end-**

ing provides a climax and a resolution to the conflict. A good ending also usually leaves the reader with a feeling or idea to think about.

Guided Practice: Outlining a Plot

As a class use the list below to help you think of a plot for a story for other students your age. Then together think of ideas for the beginning, middle, and ending. Make a list of the specific events that form the plot.

mysterious package   getting lost   sports competition

Characters and Setting

The **characters** are the people in a story. Most stories contain one or two **main characters** who are involved in the central conflict of the plot. Minor characters are often introduced to help move along the events of the story.

Here are some ways to make your characters seem vivid.

1. Use specific details to describe the characters.

   Lee stood in the yard looking pale and lost, his tall, lanky body as motionless as a tree.

2. Have the characters speak.

   "I looked everywhere!" he shouted over the phone.

3. Show the characters in action.

   Lee's eyes darted everywhere, and his voice grew husky as he called and called for Diva.

4. Make statements about the personalities of the characters.

   Lee loved all kinds of dogs, but especially retrievers.

The **setting** of a story is the place and time in which the events occur. In some stories the setting is essential to the plot. In a story about space travel, for example, the setting would probably play a central part in the events. In other stories the setting simply provides a background for the events. The choice of a setting and how it is described in a story help the writer to create a **mood** or feeling.

Guided Practice: Creating Characters and Setting

Recall the plot that you created as a class. Together explore possible characters and settings for the story. Then decide on the main characters and setting that you want to use in your story.

Dialogue

Compare the following. Which one is more vivid? Why do you answer as you do?

1. Lee called his neighbor to ask if she had seen his dog anywhere recently.
2. "It's Lee, Mrs. Sims," Lee stammered over the phone, trying to keep his voice steady. "Have you seen Diva? I can't find her!"

Conversation, or **dialogue**, helps to bring the events and characters in a story to life. Make your dialogue fit the character and sound like real speech. Use specific words and phrases like *loudly, with a grin, trying to keep his voice steady* to help the reader "hear" the words of the characters.

Putting a Short Story Together

With your class you have explored ideas for a plot, characters, and a setting. On your own you have chosen your characters and setting. Now think about a beginning for your story.

One student wrote several story beginnings. Here are two.

1. When Lee came home from school, his dog wasn't there.
2. "Diva! Diva, come here!" Lee called as he entered the house. The dog always came to greet him. Where was she?

This student decided that the second beginning was more dramatic and would capture the reader's interest more effectively.

Guided Practice: Writing a Short Story

Write several beginnings for your story. Choose the one that you think will best capture the reader's interest. It should introduce the characters, the setting, and the conflict. Then follow your plot outline to complete your story. Use dialogue to bring the events to life. Supply a strong ending that leaves the reader with something to think about.

Checklist A Short Story

When you write a short story, keep a checklist of the important points that you need to remember. A sample checklist is shown below. Copy it and add any other points you want to remember. Keep it in your writing folder and refer to it as you write your story.

CHECKLIST

- Remember purpose and audience.
- Develop a plot.
  - Conflict
  - Climax
  - Resolution
- Create characters.
- Establish a setting.
- Use dialogue.
- Include effective beginning and ending.
- _____

2 THINKING AND WRITING: Understanding Point of View

Sometimes all of the events in a story are seen through the eyes of one character. In other stories, the author lets the reader see the **point of view** of several characters.

Look at the picture below. What do you see? Keep looking. Do you see something else?

What you see depends on how you look at something—or your point of view. Actually, you look at things with more than your eyes; you also "look" with your mind.

Think about a toy you loved as a child. How do you view it now? Even if the toy hasn't changed, you have. You now see the toy from a different point of view. You look at a fly and you see a buzzing nuisance; a spider looks at the same fly and may see a meal. Again, the point of view is different.

Point of view, then, refers not only to vision, but also to a state of mind.

Short stories can be written from different points of view. Here are three points of view to consider when you write.

- **First person**—The events of the story are told by one of the characters. The reader sees and knows only what that character sees and knows. **I** is used to tell the story.

- **Third person limited**—The story is told from the point of view of a character in the story; however, **he** and **she** are used.

- **Third person omniscient**—The story is told by an all-knowing narrator. The narrator knows everything about every character's thoughts.

As a writer you must decide which point of view to use in your story. One writer tried writing a part of her story two ways to help her decide which she preferred. Read both versions below.

1. As I shook Mr. Abel's hand, I felt so sad. I wanted to say something, but I didn't know if he wanted to talk. He had such a distant look on his face.
2. As Lisa shook Mr. Abel's hand, her lips moved silently. Her bright blue eyes clouded with sadness and confusion. Mr. Abel gazed into the distance, hoping that she would break the silence.

Thinking Like a Writer

- From what point of view is the first version written?
- From what point of view is the second version written?
- What are the advantages of using each point of view?

This writer chose to write her story in the first person because she wanted her readers to know only what was going on in the mind of Lisa, the main character.

When you write a story, choose a point of view that you think will help you tell your story most effectively. Then maintain the same point of view throughout your story. Shifting points of view can confuse your reader.

 THINKING APPLICATION Using Point of View

COOPERATIVE
LEARNING

The sentences below are from different stories. Identify the point of view in each sentence, and then rewrite it from a different point of view. Discuss your changes with other students. Add more sentences to each item, using the same point of view.

1. I was worried about Carlos, but I tried to hide it.
2. Ava was just five years old when she tried to ride her aunt's bicycle.
3. To his surprise, he found himself enjoying the book.
4. Yoko laughed so hard that everyone laughed, too.
5. I wanted to giggle, but I kept my mouth firmly closed.
6. Tim looked everywhere, but he could not find his cat.
7. I was out of breath after I ran up the steep hill.
8. Laura kneads the dough when she makes bread with her grandfather.

3 INDEPENDENT WRITING: A Short Story

Prewrite: Step 1

Now you can begin to plan a story of your own. You will follow a student named Julio through each step of writing a short story.

Choosing a Topic

Julio's first step was to choose a topic for his story. Julio looked through his journal for a list of experiences he had jotted down. He recorded some of those experiences and the ideas they brought to mind in a chart like the one below.

Exploring Ideas: Charting Strategy

Chart for Generating Story Ideas

Experience	Main Character(s)	Setting	Plot
Soccer game	Two players	Soccer field	Friends on opposing teams
Movie about space voyage	Captain	Spaceship	Can't return to Earth
Mystery stories	Two young people	Dark house	Frightening events

Julio did not think he could make the soccer story exciting. He really wanted to write a scary story, but he had to **narrow** his topic. What specific situation could he use? Then he remembered a recent power failure. That was it!

Once a week after school Julio and some of his friends help out in a day care center. Julio decided to write a story whose **purpose** would be to entertain an **audience** made up of the older children at the center. To explore his ideas for his story, he filled out the chart shown on the next page.

Chart for Exploring a Story Idea

Who are the main characters? What are they like?	Brother and younger sister—sister likes to act bratty sometimes, but they really care about each other.
What is the setting?	Summer cabin in the woods. House where they live—ordinary house.
What is the central problem in the plot?	Brother and sister alone in house. Power goes off. It's dark and scary. Brother sees something moving. What is it?
How is the problem resolved?	Someone or something runs off, more scared than they are? Police come, but it's only a squirrel? They hide and never find out what it was? Creature—bear? burglar?—goes after them but they escape?
How do the characters react?	Brother and sister help each other; after danger ends, they start scrapping again.

Thinking Like a Writer

- How did Julio describe the characters? the plot?
- Where did he change his mind?
- Which story outcome of his do you prefer?

YOUR TURN

Begin planning your story by choosing and exploring a topic.

JOURNAL

- List ideas you get from your journal, **Pictures,** recent experiences, books, or movies.
- Choose four or five ideas and make a story chart.
- Choose one or two of the ideas to develop in a story chart.
- Remember purpose and audience.

Write a First Draft: Step 2

To help him remember the important elements to include in his story, Julio prepared a planning checklist to use as he wrote his story.

Then Julio began to write the first draft of his story. He did not interrupt the flow of his writing by stopping to make changes. He knew he could make corrections later.

Part of Julio's First Draft

> Andrew's parents had just driven down Lincoln street into the storm when the power went out. Everything went off.
>
> Andrews' sister came creeping into his room. Pam asked him what had happened, as if it was his fault. He didn't know.
>
> Andrew managed to find two flashlights. There was a good one and a really weak one. Then he and pam just sat around being nervous. Pam remembered that their mother had a radio with batterys and went to get it.
>
> Andrew sat still. Everything looked so different in the dark. It sounded differrent too. Wait. What was that noise?
>
> "Pam? Pam! he shouted. Then he saw it.

Planning Checklist
- Remember purpose and audience.
- Make sure plot has conflict, climax, and resolution.
- Create interesting characters.
- Establish a setting.
- Use dialogue.
- Include effective beginning and ending.

YOUR TURN

Write the first draft of your story. As you write, ask yourself the following questions.

- What does my audience need to know for me to accomplish my purpose?
- What kind of a beginning would be most effective?
- What details about my characters should I add?
- Does my plot contain an interesting conflict? How will my plot build to a climax?

TIME-OUT You might want to take some time out before you revise. That way you will be able to revise your writing with a fresh eye.

Revise: Step 3

When Julio finished writing his first draft, he read it carefully to himself and made a few changes he thought would improve it. Then he asked one of his friends to read over the draft. She might be able to suggest other ways to make it a better story.

The kids will like your story. At the beginning, though, you don't tell much about where Pam and Andrew are.

Hmm. Maybe I can add some details about the house. Thanks.

After Julio had spoken with his friend, he next looked back at his planning checklist. He realized that there was something else he could improve. He placed a check mark next to the point about dialogue to remind himself that he should include more of the characters' actual words.

At this stage Julio concentrated on the important points that he had written on his checklist. Did the events of the plot follow one another clearly? Could he improve the beginning or ending? Did he need to add specific details about his characters? He did not worry about correcting errors in spelling or punctuation just yet. He would be able to fix those later.

Julio also thought more about the **purpose** and **audience** for his short story. He read his draft over to himself and asked if the events he had described would be entertaining to an audience of young children. With this in mind, he decided that the ending of his story needed to be both simpler and more suspenseful.

Julio's revisions changed his first draft. Read his revised draft on the next page.

Revising Checklist
- Remember purpose and audience.
- Make sure plot has conflict, climax, and resolution.
- Create interesting characters.
- Establish a setting.
- ✔ Use dialogue.
- ✔ Include effective beginning and ending.

Part of Julio's Revised Draft

> *Andrew couldn't believe it. His*
> ∧ ~~Andrew's~~ parents had just driven down Lincoln
>
> street into the storm when the power went out. Every-
> thing went off ∧ *in the house – the lights, the television, and*
> *the electric fan.*
>
> Andrews' sister came creeping into his room. ~~Pam~~
> *"What happened!" Pam demanded,*
> ∧ ~~asked him what had happened,~~ as if it was his fault. ~~He~~
> *"How do I know," he shot back.*
> ∧ ~~didn't know.~~
>
> Andrew managed to find two flashlights ∧ ~~There was~~
>
> a good one and a really weak one. Then he and pam just
> *After a while*
> sat around being nervous. ∧ Pam remembered that their
>
> mother had a radio with batterys and went to get it.
>
> Andrew sat still. Everything looked so different in
>
> the dark. It sounded differrent too. Wait. What was that
> *howl*
> ~~noise~~?
> *He turned on the flashlight.*
> "Pam? Pam! he shouted. ∧ Then he saw it.

Thinking Like a Writer

WISE
WORD
CHOICE

- How did Julio revise the beginning? Why?
- What did he add to the second sentence? Why?
- Where did he add dialogue? Why?
- Which sentences did he combine?

YOUR TURN

Read over your first draft. Ask yourself these questions.

- What parts can I eliminate because they do not move along the action of the plot?
- How can I improve the beginning? the ending?
- Do I need to add details to make my characters or setting more vivid for the reader?
- What sentences can I combine to improve my writing?

If you wish, ask a classmate to read your revised draft and make suggestions for improvements. Then revise your story.

Proofread: Step 4

Now that Julio has revised his draft, he is ready to proofread to check for errors in spelling, punctuation, and capitalization. To help him proofread his story, he prepared a checklist and used proofreading symbols.

Part of Julio's Proofread Draft

Andrew⌢s/sister came creeping into his room. ~~Pam~~
"What happened!" Pam demanded,
∧ ~~asked him what had happened~~, as if it was his fault. ~~He~~
"How do I know." he shot back
∧ ~~didn't know.~~

Andrew managed to find two flashlights. ~~There was~~

a good one and a really weak one. Then he and pam just
after a while
sat around being nervous. ∧Pam remembered that their
batteries
mother had a radio with ⟨batterys⟩ and went to get it.

Andrew sat still. Everything looked so different in
different
the dark. It sounded ⟨differrent⟩ too. Wait. What was that
howl
~~noise?~~

He turned on the flashlight.
"Pam? Pam!" he shouted. ∧ Then he saw it.

YOUR TURN

Proofreading Practice

Find the errors below. Then write the passage correctly.

Ramonas eyes were wide open. This was her first night in
the rain Forest of brazil, and the noises amazed her. It
seemed that when human's went to bed, every jungel
creeture woke up.

Wait. Did someone just say "Ramona"?

"Ramona, are you awake"? came a whisper through
the tent.

"That depends" she answered. "Who's there?

Proofreading Checklist
■ Did I indent each paragraph?
■ Are all words spelled correctly?
■ Did I use capital letters in proper nouns correctly?
■ Did I use punctuation marks correctly—including end marks, commas, apostrophes, and quotation marks?

Applying Your Proofreading Skills

Proofread your story. Review your proofreading checklist, as well as **The Grammar Connection** and **The Mechanics Connection** below. Use the proofreading symbols below.

THE GRAMMAR CONNECTION

Remember these rules about forming possessive nouns.

- Add an apostrophe and *s* (**'s**) to singular nouns and to plural nouns that do not end in *s*.
- Add an apostrophe (') to plural nouns that end in *s*.

  The mother**'s** scarf matched her children**'s** ribbons.
  The two girls' hair ribbons were bright green.

Proofreading Marks

Indent ⌐¶

Add ∧

Add a comma ∧

Add quotation marks ⍀ ⍀

Add a period ⊙

Take out ⌐

Capitalize ≡

Lower-case letter /

Reverse the order ∩

THE MECHANICS CONNECTION

Remember these rules about using quotation marks when you write the dialogue for a story.

- Use quotation marks before and after a direct quotation.
- Use a comma to separate a phrase such as *he said* from the quotation.
- Place commas and periods inside closing quotation marks.
- Place question marks and exclamation marks inside quotation marks only when they belong to the quotation.
- Begin a new paragraph when a new speaker is quoted.

  "I'm hungry," he said. "Do you want to eat lunch now?"
  Did Janet really say, "I know the whole story"?

Publish: Step 5

When Julio had finished proofreading his story, he copied it over. He wrote in large, neat letters so that the older children at the day care center would be able to read it. Then he got two sheets of colored paper to make a cover and wrote the story title and his name on one of the sheets. He punched holes through the cover and through the story pages, and he ran a piece of colored yarn through the holes.

Julio thought he might ask the children to take turns reading parts of the story aloud to one another.

YOUR TURN

Make a final copy of your short story, writing as neatly as you can. Use a typewriter or computer, if they are available. Decide on a good way to share your story. The **Sharing Suggestions** box below may give you some ideas.

SHARING SUGGESTIONS

Submit your story to a magazine for young people.	Have a storytelling session with some friends and read your story.	Put your class's stories together in a book. Add illustrations and display it in the school library.

---

4 SPEAKING AND LISTENING: Having a Class Discussion

Before people knew how to write stories, they told them. Before they knew how to share their thoughts in writing, they discussed them.

As you studied narrative writing, you in fact engaged in discussions when you explored writing ideas with your classmates. Those discussions were informal. Formal discussions that involve several people, however, generally are more productive if they follow certain rules.

Suppose you are a drama club member, and at the next meeting the club will discuss dramatizing a short story. To prepare yourself, you might think about the issues, review some stories, and go to the meeting with notes like these:

NOTES FOR DRAMA CLUB MEETING—MARCH 18

Which story to dramatize?

Things to consider: plot—simple but interesting
characters—only a few
settings—easy to portray on stage
dialogue—should have plenty, easier
to dramatize

Stories to consider: "Charles" by Shirley Jackson
"After Twenty Years" by O. Henry

Formal discussions are much more successful if each participant follows certain rules. Use the guidelines below when you lead or participate in a group discussion.

- Why does a group discussion need a leader?
- Why is it important to speak only when recognized?

SPEAKING APPLICATION A Discussion

Choose a group of four or five classmates with whom you would like to hold a discussion in class. The topic might be outstanding authors for young people, or any other topic you agree on. Prepare a note card for your meeting. Then select a leader and hold your discussion. The rest of the class will listen to determine how effectively you hold the group discussion.

WRITING

EXTENSION

THE CURRICULUM CONNECTION

Writing About Literature

Good books shouldn't be kept a secret. One way you can share your enjoyment of a good book with friends is to write a book report. Writing a book report can also add to your own enjoyment. It may help you remember the book for a long time.

Read the following book report.

<table>
<tr><td>

INTRODUCTION

title

author

setting

</td><td>

<u>The Call of the Wild</u>

Have you ever wondered what life is like in a harsh environment such as the wintry landscape of Alaska? <u>The Call of the Wild</u> is an exciting adventure novel written by Jack London. It takes place in Alaska at the time of the Klondike gold rush.

</td></tr>
<tr><td>

BODY

main characters

plot

</td><td>

The main characters in <u>The Call of the Wild</u> are a dog named Buck and his master, John Thornton. Buck, half Saint Bernard and half Scottish shepherd, is kidnapped from his comfortable home in California to be a sled dog in Alaska. John Thornton is a gold prospector who saves Buck from his cruel owner in Alaska. The story begins when Buck is kidnapped and goes on to describe his life as a sled dog. In Alaska Buck is beaten, starved, and forced to work until he almost dies of exhaustion. He becomes a fierce fighter and battles his way to the position of lead dog. After he is rescued by John Thornton, Buck's life improves.

</td></tr>
<tr><td>

CONCLUSION

your opinion

reasons

</td><td>

I enjoyed <u>The Call of the Wild</u> for three reasons. First, Jack London describes the setting so realistically that I could actually see the frozen wastelands and primitive Alaskan mining town. Second, the author makes the reader think of Buck as a person. Finally, the story is filled with adventure.

</td></tr>
</table>

Writing a Book Report

A book report should contain the following information.

1. The **title and the author**
2. The **introduction** should include
   - whether the book is fiction or nonfiction
   - an opening sentence that will capture your reader's attention
3. The **body of the report** should include
   - information about the setting and main characters
   - a summary of the plot that informs your reader about the problems the characters face, but without revealing the whole story
4. The **conclusion** should include
   - your opinion of the book—what you liked about it and what you did not like about it
   - reasons for your opinion
   - your recommendation to others whether to read the book

ACTIVITIES

Write a Book Report

Choose a book that you have read and enjoyed. Use the outline above to make notes about the book. Then write a book report. In your introductory paragraph, include a "hook" that will catch the reader's interest. In your conclusion, make sure that you do not give away the ending of the book. If you do, you may spoil the surprise for others who might read the book.

Create a Book Jacket

Make a book jacket for a book you have read. The front cover should include the title and author. Write a brief summary of the plot for the inside flap of the book jacket. Identify important characters and their roles in the story. On the back flap write a brief paragraph that describes the author's life, other books by the author, and the importance of the book. On the back cover write statements that review the book; give your own and other people's opinions of the book and reasons why the book held their interest. Display your book jacket for others to enjoy.

UNIT CHECKUP

LESSON 1

Group Writing: A Short Story (page 114)   On a separate piece of paper, rewrite the following story part, using dialogue where appropriate. Use quotation marks correctly. Then briefly explain why adding dialogue helps to improve the passage.

The flashlight trembling in his hand, Andrew anxiously called to Pam. At first his voice was hoarse, but it grew stronger as he crept forward. At last, with great relief, he heard an answer. Breathless, his sister said she was all right but very scared and afraid to budge. She told Andrew she had seen something moving through the house. She asked if he had seen it too and if he knew what it could be.

LESSON 2

Thinking: Understanding Point of View (page 118)   Rewrite the following passage, using the first-person point of view. Use pronouns carefully.

Andrew kept moving slowly toward Pam's voice. It wasn't hard to maneuver around all the familiar things, even in the dark. It was the unfamiliar things he was worried about! Then, as if he didn't have enough to be concerned about, he noticed that the already weak flashlight beam was growing even weaker. His heart started pounding so loudly he could hardly hear Pam's voice. If only he could get to her before his light gave out! She had a stronger flashlight—he hoped.

LESSON 3

Writing a Short Story (page 120)   Write a short story in which the main character has a wish that comes true—with surprising consequences. Have the character learn something important about himself or herself.

Use the steps of the writing process to write your story. Write a beginning that captures the reader's interest and in-troduces the main character. Establish a clear setting for the events of the story. Make sure that you include a resolution for the conflict developed in your plot. Add dialogue to bring your characters to life. Revise and proofread your story carefully before you share it with your audience.

LESSON 4

Speaking and Listening: A Class Discussion (page 128)   In a paragraph summarize the guidelines for leading and partici-pating in a group discussion.

THEME PROJECT PHOTO GALLERY

Stories are expressions of writers' imaginations, as well as of their personal thoughts and feelings about their own lives and the world around them. Language is the writer's means of expression.

Words, however, are not the only way that people communicate ideas and emotions to each other. Pictures, in the form of photographs, paintings, cartoons, drawings, and movies, are also used to express thoughts and feelings.

Discuss with your classmates your interpretations of this photo. What does it express to you? What thoughts does it bring to mind? What story does it tell? If you were putting together a photography exhibit that included this photograph, what caption would you write?

- From old magazines cut out three or four photographs that you find interesting, or select examples of your own photography, drawings, or paintings.
- Arrange your pictures for an exhibit. Paste each one on a piece of cardboard.
- Supply a caption for each picture. Each caption might tell a story, express a thought, or offer an interpretation.

UNIT

5

Verbs

In Unit 5 you will learn about verbs. A verb, which is the main word in the predicate of a sentence, often has a special relationship with other words in the predicate.

Discuss Read the lines of poetry on the opposite page. How do they capture the movement of the sea?

Creative Expression The unit theme is *Crosscurrents*. How do the ocean tides affect the seashore? Imagine that you set up your camping tent on the beach during low tide and then woke up to find yourself surrounded by water. In your journal write a story to describe this experience.

JOURNAL

THEME: *CROSSCURRENTS*

The sea is a wilderness of waves,
A desert of water.
We dip and dive,

Rise and roil,
Hide and are hidden
On the sea.

—Langston Hughes, from "Long Trip"

1 ACTION VERBS

An action verb is a word that expresses action.

Some movies are filled with nonstop action. The action in movies can be expressed by **verbs.** Verbs that express what someone or something does are called **action verbs.** The main word in the predicate of a sentence is a verb. Notice the action verbs in the sentences below.

Amanda **runs** along the beach.
Her feet **pound** the damp sand.
Taffy and Jet, her dogs, **race** by her side.
Earlier that morning, Amanda **swam** for twenty minutes.

Some action verbs express physical actions.

explore	travel	soar	speak
discuss	dive	return	observe
taste	sleep	compose	construct

Other action verbs express mental or emotional activities.

remember	enjoy	need	learn
hope	think	expect	forget
love	appreciate	imagine	attempt

Guided Practice

Name the action verb or verbs in each sentence and tell whether they describe a physical or a mental action.

Example: Waves crash on the beach.
    crash   physical

1. Amanda sits on a large piece of driftwood.
2. Taffy and Jet chase each other through the surf and the rocks on the beach.
3. The sun scatters the last traces of fog.
4. Amanda recalls her first visit to the shore.
5. Amanda and her family moved to the Oregon coast and like their new home very much.

THINK

■ How can I tell which word in the predicate of a sentence is an action verb?

REMEMBER

■ An **action verb** is a word that expresses action.

More Practice

A. Write the action verb or verbs in each sentence and whether it expresses a **physical** or **mental** action.

Example: Sunlight sparkled on the water.
> sparkled   physical

6. Amanda walked along the shore for several hours.
7. She watched the sky and sea for signs of life.
8. Suddenly a head sprang from the water and a sea lion returned her gaze.
9. Then it disappeared without a ripple.
10. Amanda smiled and thought about her next stop.
11. Three sandpipers scurried out of her way.
12. She enjoys the beauty of the coastline and studies the behavior of the marine life.

B. Write each sentence, using an action verb or verbs to complete it. Write whether each verb expresses a **physical** or **mental** action.

Example: Who ____ that beach ball?
> tossed   physical

13. Amanda finally ____ at the tidepool.
14. Patches ____ farther on, but Amanda ____ her pet.
15. King ____ by Amanda's side and ____.
16. In the tidepool a hermit crab ____ over the rocks.
17. Sea weeds ____ in the clear water like snakes.
18. Slowly a whelk ____ toward a bed of mussels.
19. Amanda ____ drawings of these creatures and ____ them in a notebook.
20. ____ the forms of life in a tidepool; each organism ____ an important role.

Extra Practice, page 168

WRITING APPLICATION A Poster

With a small group, make a poster that describes the kinds of recreational activities a beach, lake, pool, or park in your town offers. Then exchange papers with a classmate and identify the action verbs in each other's work.

COOPERATIVE
LEARNING

---

2 VERBS WITH DIRECT OBJECTS

You know that the main word in the predicate of a sentence is a verb. Sometimes the verb is the only word in the predicate.

Divers **explore.**

Often, however, someone or something named in the predicate receives the action of the verb.

Divers **explore** the ocean **floor.**
The captain **instructed** the **divers.**

A word that receives the action of a verb is called a **direct object.** A direct object is a noun or pronoun that answers the question *whom?* or *what?* after an action verb.

Some sentences have a compound direct object, that is, more than one direct object.

A diver informed the **captain** and the **crew.**

A verb that has a direct object is called a **transitive verb.** A verb that does not have a direct object is called an **intransitive verb.** Many verbs can be either transitive or intransitive.

The divers **searched** the sunken **ship.**   (transitive)
The divers **searched** thoroughly.   (intransitive)

Guided Practice

Name the action verb in each sentence. Then name the direct object, if the sentence contains one.

Example: Searchers sometimes discover treasures.
            discover   treasures

1. An ancient ship sank near Turkey.
2. Explorers found the wreck.
3. The excavation team worked hard.
4. First they built a camp.
5. They kept their boat over the wreck.

?! THINK

■ How can I tell whether an action verb is transitive or intransitive?

REMEMBER

- A **direct object** is a noun or pronoun in the predicate that receives the action of the verb.
- A **transitive verb** has a direct object. An **intransitive verb** does not have a direct object.

More Practice

A. Write the verb in each sentence. Then write the direct object, if the sentence contains one.

Example: Inez read a book about sea treasures.

      read   book

6. We saw a film about the Turkish wreck.
7. The ancient ship sank around 1400 B.C.
8. Divers worked at a depth of 140 to 170 feet.
9. This old shipwreck held great treasures.
10. Excavators found supplies and royal cargo.
11. Eventually some six tons of copper appeared.
12. The ship carried ivory and amber.

B. Write each sentence. Then draw one line under the verb and two lines under any direct object. Label the verb **transitive** or **intransitive.**

Example: The class discussed the discovery.   *transitive*

13. One jar held eighteen pieces of pottery.
14. The blue glass gleamed.
15. The team later uncovered Egyptian jewels.
16. Experts interpreted the ancient writings.
17. Divers also uncovered silver bracelets.
18. The ship traveled throughout the area.
19. What interesting information this shipwreck reveals!
20. The sea conceals many treasures.

Extra Practice, page 169

WRITING APPLICATION A Diary Entry

Imagine that you are part of a deep-sea exploration team. Write a diary entry about a busy day underwater. Then share your work with classmates. Identify the direct objects in each other's work.

GRAMMAR

3 VERBS WITH INDIRECT OBJECTS

Many of the sentences you use have a direct object. Some sentences have two kinds of objects, a direct and an indirect object. An **indirect object** tells to whom or to what an action is done.

direct object

Julie likes **stories** about the sea.

indirect object   direct object

Art gave **Julie MacArthur** a **book** by Homer.

indirect object   direct object

Julie told the **class** some interesting **facts** about Greek myths.

A sentence may contain a compound indirect object, that is, an indirect object with two or more parts.

indirect object   indirect object

Julie shows the **class** and the **teacher** the book.

Only sentences with a direct object can have an indirect object. One way to tell direct and indirect objects apart is to remember that the indirect object always comes before the direct object.

Guided Practice

Name the direct object and the indirect object in each sentence.

Example: Myths offered people explanations.

explanations   direct object
people   indirect object

1. Julie read Dale passages from the *Odyssey*.
2. Odysseus won his people a great victory.
3. The voyage brought Odysseus many troubles.
4. Odysseus found his shipmates a safe harbor.
5. Homer gave the natives a strange name.

?! THINK

- How do I know if a word is a direct object or an indirect object in a sentence?

REMEMBER

- An **indirect object** is a noun or pronoun in the predicate that answers the question *to whom? for whom? to what?* or *for what?* after an action verb.

More Practice

A. Write the direct object and the indirect object in each sentence.

Example: Robert told the class a story.

         story   direct object   class   indirect object

6. The Lotus-eaters offered the crew strange food.
7. This food caused the travelers a loss of memory.
8. Odysseus showed the natives great resistance.
9. The clever hero won his friends their freedom.
10. Fate handed Odysseus and his shipmates more surprises.
11. The goddess Circe gave the crew a great banquet.
12. Then she struck her foolish guests a blow.
13. The god of travelers spared Odysseus that evil.

B. Rewrite each sentence so that the underlined phrase becomes an indirect object. Then identify each direct and indirect object.

Example: Robert showed the illustrations <u>to Ellen</u>.

        Robert showed Ellen the illustrations. illustrations   direct object   Ellen   indirect object

14. Hermes offered <u>assistance to Odysseus</u>.
15. Odysseus brought <u>victory to his crew</u>.
16. They showed <u>thanks to their leader</u>.
17. Circe gave <u>a warning to the wayfarers</u>.
18. Creatures nearby caused <u>harm to seafarers</u>.
19. The Sirens sang <u>beautiful songs for sailors</u>.
20. At sea Odysseus gave <u>wax earplugs to his shipmates</u>.

Extra Practice, page 170

WRITING APPLICATION Instructions

Write a set of instructions that tells how to get to a remote island. Working with a partner, write your instructions in a paragraph. Then identify any indirect objects in your work.

4 LINKING VERBS

When you want to tell what someone or something is or is like, you often use a linking verb. Linking verbs do not express actions.

> Jamie **is** a young scientist.
> Whales **are** his favorite animals.

A **linking verb** connects the subject with a noun or an adjective in the predicate. Linking verbs tell what the subject of a sentence is or is like. A noun that follows a linking verb and tells more about the subject is called a **predicate noun.**

> Jaime is an **expert** on whales.   (predicate noun)

An adjective that follows a linking verb is called a **predicate adjective.**

> Most whales are **enormous.**   (predicate adjective)

The forms of the verb *be* are linking verbs. The verbs *seem, appear, look, become, taste, feel, smell,* and *grow* are often used as linking verbs. Many of these verbs may also be used as action verbs. They are action verbs when the subject of the sentence is performing an action.

> Jaime **feels** the water.   (action verb, action performed)
> The water **feels** cold.   (linking verb, no action performed)

Guided Practice

Tell whether each verb is an action verb or a linking verb.

Example: Whales are mammals.
>   *are   linking verb*

1. Jaime is knowledgeable about whales.
2. I am also a student of sea life.
3. We both visited the aquarium last week.
4. A display about whales was fascinating.
5. A model of a fin whale looked impressive.

THINK

- How can I tell whether a verb like *taste* is being used as an action verb or a linking verb?

REMEMBER

- A **linking verb** connects the subject of a sentence with a predicate noun or predicate adjective.
- A **predicate noun** renames or identifies the subject. A **predicate adjective** describes the subject.

More Practice

A. Write the linking verb and whether it is followed by a **predicate noun** or a **predicate adjective.**

Example: Whales are mammals.   *are   predicate noun*

6. The blue whale is the largest animal on earth.
7. Both its size and weight sound incredible.
8. Shrimp-like krill are its diet.
9. Whales were sometimes dangerous to seafarers.
10. Most people feel amazed in the whale's presence.
11. I am a collector of whale lore.

B. Write each sentence. Draw one line under a linking verb and two lines under an action verb. Write and label each **predicate noun** or **predicate adjective.**

Example: Harpoons were useful.   *Harpoons were useful.*
           useful   predicate adjective

12. The class grew curious about the whaling industry.
13. I appear tiny beside a whale.
14. White-patched flippers are the mark of minke whales.
15. These animals grow very strong.
16. Young whales quickly become hearty eaters.
17. We felt the flippers of a model whale.
18. The songs of the humpback whale sound beautiful.
19. Its long flippers are equally remarkable.
20. Humpback whales appear in all oceans.

Extra Practice, page 171

WRITING APPLICATION A Pamphlet

A blue whale measures 100 feet in length and weighs 150 tons. How could you help a child to understand these statistics? With a partner write a paragraph for a pamphlet that explains these facts. Then identify the linking verbs, predicate nouns, and predicate adjectives in your work.

5 PRESENT, PAST, AND FUTURE TENSES

Verbs help you tell the reader when an action takes place. The **tense** of the verb shows when the action occurs. Verbs can have many different tenses.

Use the **present tense** of a verb to express an action that is happening now or that happens repeatedly.

Use the **past tense** of a verb to express an action that happened in the past. Add **ed** to many verbs to form the past tense.

Use the **future tense** of a verb to express an action that will happen in the future. Use the helping verb *will* or *shall* with the verb to form the future tense.

	Singular	Plural
Present Tense	I look. You look. He, she, it looks.	We look. You look. They look.
Past Tense	I looked. You looked. He, she, it looked.	We looked. You looked. They looked.
Future Tense	I will (shall) look. You will look. He, she, it will look.	We will (shall) look. You will look. They will look.

Guided Practice

Tell the **present**, **past**, and **future tenses** of each verb. Use the subject *she*.

Example: return   *returns, returned, will return*

1. sail
2. lift
3. dry
4. live

5. remember
6. clean
7. wish
8. enter

?! THINK

■ How do I change a verb to show different tenses?

REMEMBER

- The **present tense** of a verb tells that something is happening now or happens repeatedly.
- The **past tense** of a verb shows an action that has already happened.
- The **future tense** of a verb shows an action that will take place in the future.

More Practice

A. Write the verb and its tense.

Example: This scientist studies minerals.
studies   present tense

  9. Last week Mr. Dawkins assigned a project.
 10. Lisa will report on mineral deposits in the sea.
 11. Scientists noted mineral masses in the Pacific Ocean.
 12. These minerals pave the floor of the sea.
 13. Lisa realizes the value of this discovery.
 14. Companies recently started recovery programs.

B. Write each sentence, using the correct tense of the verb in parentheses. Then write whether the verb is in the **present tense, past tense,** or **future tense.**

Example: Tomorrow the class (watch) a film.
Tomorrow the class will watch a film.
future tense

 15. Yesterday Lisa (research) her paper.
 16. She often (learn) interesting new facts.
 17. The world's first offshore sulfur mine (open) in 1960.
 18. A company often (dredge) for minerals.
 19. Salt (remain) an economical resource today.
 20. Perhaps companies in the near future (gather) the iron deposits in Central America.

Extra Practice, page 172

WRITING APPLICATION An Explanation

Imagine that you are an inventor. Write a brief paragraph explaining one of your inventions, including how you created it and what it will do. Exchange papers with a classmate and identify the past, present, and future tenses of verbs.

6 VERB PHRASES

Verbs have four basic forms called **principal parts.** All tenses of a verb can be formed from these principal parts.

Present	Present Participle	Past	Past Participle
talk	talking	talked	talked

Often a principal part of a verb is combined with a **helping verb** to form a **verb phrase.** In a verb phrase the word that names the main action is called the **main verb.**

helping main
verb verb

Dr. Evans *can* **explain** much about marine life.
The class *may* **ask** questions later.

The forms of the verbs *be, do,* and *have* can be used either as main verbs or helping verbs.

Is that clear?   Who **did** that?
Joe **is** speaking.   We **did** remember.

Sometimes a verb phrase is interrupted by other words.

Does Dr. Evans **study** ocean currents?
She **has** recently **studied** the Pacific Ocean.
Haven't you ever **wondered** about the tides?

Guided Practice

Name the verb phrase in each sentence. Then identify the main verb and the helping verb.

Example: Two students were studying dolphins.
            studying   main verb   were   helping verb

1. Dr. Evans was working in the Caribbean Sea.
2. The sea had fascinated her since childhood.
3. Has she photographed exotic creatures?
4. A friend of hers is collecting these pictures.
5. He will probably publish them in a book.

 THINK

- How do I know which word in a verb phrase is the main verb?

REMEMBER

- Every verb has four **principal parts.**
- A **verb phrase** consists of a main verb and all of its helping verbs.
- A **helping verb** helps the main verb to show an action or make a statement.

More Practice

Write the verb phrase in each sentence. Then identify the main verb and the helping verb.

Example: Have you played this game?

      played   main verb   *have   helping verb*

  6. Our class has invented a game about sea life.

  7. Has our teacher approved it?

  8. We were playing it just yesterday.

  9. Had the winner studied for a long time?

10. Each winner would earn extra credit in science.

11. Two students have already mastered the game.

12. May the new players ask them questions?

13. Tony has just started in the game.

14. My friend and I should coach him.

15. Can you explain the rules to me?

16. Each player must answer questions about sea life.

17. Could Tony triumph over his challengers?

18. He is always studying his textbook.

19. Must Tony review the chapter on sea animals?

20. Aren't facts about porpoises listed there?

21. Marcy has researched some facts.

22. She will read an article tonight.

23. The author had explored the sea.

24. Her discoveries have made her famous.

25. Do you know her name?

Extra Practice, page 173

WRITING APPLICATION A News Article

Imagine that the editor of your school newspaper wants you to write an article about a recent event at your school. Write one or two paragraphs for the article. Identify verb phrases and helping verbs in your work.

7 PRESENT PROGRESSIVE AND PAST PROGRESSIVE FORMS

You know that the present tense of a verb expresses an action that happens now. The past tense of a verb expresses an action that already happened.

> My brother **likes** ships.   (present tense)
> He **collected** twelve model ships.   (past tense)

Notice the verb phrases in the sentences below.

> Gregory **is collecting** ships in bottles.
> His friends **were helping** him.

The verb phrases above show verbs in the progressive form. **Progressive forms** of verbs express action in progress. They can express actions continuing in the present or the past. The progressive forms are made up of a form of the verb *be* used as helping verb and the present participle. The helping verb shows the tense.

	Singular	Plural
Present Progressive Form	I am looking. You are looking. He, she, it is looking.	We are looking. You are looking. They are looking.
Past Progressive Form	I was looking. You were looking. He, she, it was looking.	We were looking. You were looking. They were looking.

Guided Practice

Name the verb in each sentence. Tell whether each verb is in the present tense, past tense, present progressive, or past progressive form.

Example: She sings.   *sings   present tense*

1. We are visiting.
2. They visit.
3. He was helping.
4. It is raining.
5. She was laughing.
6. We are leaving.
7. You swim.
8. I am trying.
9. They like fish.

 THINK

■ How do I decide if a verb is in the progressive form?

REMEMBER

- The **present progressive** form of a verb expresses action that is continuing now.
- The **past progressive** form of a verb expresses action that continued for some time in the past.
- Progressive forms are made up of a form of *be* and the present participle.

More Practice

A. Write the verb or verb phrase in each sentence. Then write whether it is in the **present progressive** or **past progressive** form.

Example: Jon was reading the program.
　　　　　was reading   past progressive

10. The Newtown Gallery is showing marine art.
11. The gallery is presenting a new exhibit.
12. Yesterday Jon's classmates were viewing it.
13. They are studying paintings of ships.
14. Was their teacher expecting such enthusiasm?
15. Marine sculptures also were attracting attention.

B. Write each sentence, using the form of the verb shown in parentheses.

Example: The artist (sketch) a scene.   (past progressive)
　　　　　The artist was sketching a scene.

16. The guide (explain) a series of oil paintings.   (past progressive)
17. The guide (talk) continuously.   (past progressive)
18. The class (plan) a show also.   (present progressive)
19. Class artists (contribute) art.   (present progressive)
20. A professional artist (judge) the show.   (present progressive)

Extra Practice, page 174

WRITING APPLICATION A Comparison

Think about an important change that has happened in the world in the last fifty years. In a paragraph that compares the past with the present, explain the difference this change has made. Then exchange papers with a classmate and identify the progressive forms of verbs in each other's paragraphs.

COOPERATIVE LEARNING

8 PERFECT TENSES

The **perfect tenses** of a verb are made up of a form of *have* used as a helping verb and the past participle form of the main verb.

The **present perfect tense** of a verb names an action that happened at an indefinite time in the past. It also names an action that started in the past and is still happening.

> Meg **has collected** books about sharks for years.

The **past perfect tense** of a verb names an action that has happened before another past action or event.

> Meg **had feared** sharks before she studied them.

The **future perfect tense** of a verb names an action that will be completed before another action or event in the future.

> Meg **will have completed** her report by Friday.

Guided Practice

Tell the **present perfect, past perfect,** and **future perfect tenses** for each verb. Use *I* as the subject.

Example: open *have opened, had opened, will have opened*

1. wait	**4.** end	**7.** return	**10.** survey
2. jump	**5.** listen	**8.** pass	**11.** recognize
3. seem	**6.** match	**9.** agree	**12.** demand

 THINK

■ How do I know if a verb is in a perfect tense?

REMEMBER

- The **present perfect tense** of a verb expresses an action that happened at an indefinite time in the past or that started in the past and is still happening in the present.
- The **past perfect tense** expresses an action that was completed before another past action.
- The **future perfect tense** expresses an action that will be completed in the future before some other future event.

More Practice

A. Underline the verb in each sentence and tell its tense.

Example: I have gathered some facts.
        have gathered present perfect

13. Meg has followed the work of Dr. Eugenie Clark.
14. Marine life had fascinated Dr. Clark in her childhood.
15. Before long she had learned folk tales about the sea.
16. Dr. Clark has revealed the facts behind shark mythology.
17. By graduation, Meg will have carefully considered zoology as a career.

B. Write each sentence, using the tense of the verb shown in parentheses.

Example: A student (interview) Dr. Clark.   (past perfect)
        A student had interviewed Dr. Clark.

18. Meg (watch) many programs about sharks.   (present perfect)
19. Before last week she never (encounter) the name of Dr. Clark. (past perfect)
20. For a long time Meg (consider) all sharks to be vicious killers.   (past perfect)
21. By the end of this year, people (kill) an enormous number of sharks for food.   (future perfect)
22. Since sharks rarely harm people, perhaps these fish (receive) an unfair reputation.   (present perfect)

Extra Practice, page 175

WRITING APPLICATION A Letter

    Imagine that you are visiting a place by the sea. Write a letter to a friend describing what you have done since you arrived. Share your writing with a classmate and identify verbs in the perfect tenses in each other's letters.

9 IRREGULAR VERBS I

For **regular verbs** you add *ed* or *d* to form the past and the past participle. The past and past participle of **irregular verbs** are formed in a variety of ways.

Verb	Past	Past Participle
be	was, were	(have, has, had) been
do	did	(have, has, had) done
have	had	(have, has, had) had
come	came	(have, has, had) come
run	ran	(have, has, had) run
drink	drank	(have, has, had) drunk
sing	sang	(have, has, had) sung
spring	sprang	(have, has, had) sprung
swim	swam	(have, has, had) swum
bring	brought	(have, has, had) brought
buy	bought	(have, has, had) bought
catch	caught	(have, has, had) caught
feel	felt	(have, has, had) felt
hold	held	(have, has, had) held
leave	left	(have, has, had) left
lend	lent	(have, has, had) lent
make	made	(have, has, had) made
say	said	(have, has, had) said
sit	sat	(have, has, had) sat
swing	swung	(have, has, had) swung
teach	taught	(have, has, had) taught
think	thought	(have, has, had) thought

Guided Practice

Tell the past and the past participle for each verb.

Example: run   *ran, run*

1. say   **3.** drink   **5.** think   **7.** sing

2. swing   **4.** make   **6.** do   **8.** leave

?! THINK

■ How can I remember the principal parts of irregular verbs?

REMEMBER

- The past and past participle forms of **irregular verbs** do not end in *ed.*

More Practice

A. Write each sentence, using the past or past participle form of the verb in parentheses.

Example: A frog (spring) from the water.
A frog sprang from the water.

 9. Have you ever (think) about salt marshes?
10. The animal life there has (bring) me pleasure.
11. These marshes have (teach) me about nature.
12. Last week I (feel) a need for exploration.
13. Dad had (lend) me his binoculars.
14. He has (have) them for years.
15. By noon I had (be) up for several hours.
16. Finally I (come) to my observation point.

B. Write each sentence, using the correct form of the verb in parentheses. Write whether you have used the **past** or the **past participle.**

Example: Have you (swim) in a marsh?
Have you swum in a marsh?   past participle

17. In salt marshes, land and sea have (come) together.
18. The tides had (leave) traces of their flow.
19. I (feel) the patterns in the sand.
20. A mullet (swim) around in a shallow pond.
21. A raccoon (hold) a mud crab between its paws.
22. Then the crab (run) away.
23. The raccoon's first prey had (spring) from its grasp.
24. Has that blackbird (catch) a grasshopper?
25. What has the town (do) to reduce pollution?

Extra Practice, page 176

WRITING APPLICATION A Biographical Sketch

Write a paragraph that summarizes the life and accomplishments of someone you know personally or someone you have studied. Then exchange papers with a classmate. Check each other's work for the correct use of irregular verbs.

# IRREGULAR VERBS II

Below is a list of the past and past participles of some additional irregular verbs. Study their forms carefully.

Verb	Past	Past Participle
burst	burst	(have, has, had) burst
set	set	(have, has, had) set
blow	blew	(have, has, had) blown
break	broke	(have, has, had) broken
choose	chose	(have, has, had) chosen
draw	drew	(have, has, had) drawn
drive	drove	(have, has, had) driven
eat	ate	(have, has, had) eaten
fly	flew	(have, has, had) flown
freeze	froze	(have, has, had) frozen
give	gave	(have, has, had) given
go	went	(have, has, had) gone
grow	grew	(have, has, had) grown
know	knew	(have, has, had) known
ride	rode	(have, has, had) ridden
see	saw	(have, has, had) seen
speak	spoke	(have, has, had) spoken
take	took	(have, has, had) taken
tear	tore	(have, has, had) torn
throw	threw	(have, has, had) thrown
wear	wore	(have, has, had) worn
write	wrote	(have, has, had) written

Guided Practice

Use the past or the past participle of the verb in parentheses.

Example: They had (ride).   *ridden*

1. We have (eat).
2. She has (go).
3. The wind (blow).
4. Mick had (take) it.
5. He (wear) a hat.
6. The dam has (burst).

THINK

- How do I decide whether to use the past or the past participle of a verb?

REMEMBER

■ The principal parts of **irregular verbs** are formed in various ways. To learn the forms, you must memorize them.

More Practice

A. Write the correct form of the verb in parentheses for each sentence.

Example: Have you (went, gone) to a poetry reading at the student center?   *gone*

7. Nancy (saw, seen) a poster for a poetry contest.
8. She (chose, chosen) the topic of islands for her poem.
9. For two hours she had (wrote, written) the first draft of her new poem.
10. The ending (gave, given) her the most trouble.
11. Nancy (knew, known) about the formation of islands from a book she had read.
12. She had (saw, seen) a film about them last week.
13. Her teacher has (spoke, spoken) about the islands.

B. Write each sentence, using the past or the past participle of the verb in parentheses.

Example: I have (choose) a topic.
   I have chosen a topic

14. Nancy had (go) to the library for some articles.
15. She (take) out several science magazines.
16. One article had (draw) her attention.
17. A volcano has (burst) forth in the sea.
18. Lava had (fly) across the waves.
19. Then, the waters (grow) peaceful.
20. Had people (see) the formation of islands?

Extra Practice, page 177

WRITING APPLICATION A Speech

Imagine that you are running for mayor of your town. Write a short speech in which you explain why your past accomplishments qualify you for the job. Then exchange papers with a classmate. Check each other's work to make sure that irregular verbs have been used correctly.

11 SUBJECT-VERB AGREEMENT

You know that verbs change form to show tense. Verbs can also change depending on whether the subject is singular or plural.

A verb must always agree in number with its subject. If the subject is singular, use the singular form of the verb. If the subject is plural, use the plural form of the verb.

SINGULAR	PLURAL
A *scientist* **studies** oceans.	*Scientists* **study** oceans.
She **is** an oceanographer.	*They* **are** oceanographers.
The *ocean* **has** mysteries.	*Oceans* **have** mysteries.

Sometimes a helping verb comes before the subject, or the verb is separated from the subject. You must still be sure that the verb agrees with the subject.

interrogative sentences	**Does** the *ocean* **interest** you?
	Do *oceans* **interest** you?
sentences beginning with *There is/are*	There **is** an *aquarium* at the museum.
	There **are** enormous *lobsters* in it.
intervening phrases	The *man* on the stairs **is** a scientist.
	The *men* in the car **are** scientists.

Guided Practice

Choose the correct verb for each sentence.

Example: (Does, Do) our ship stop in Honolulu?   *Does*

1. Mai (prepare, prepares) a class report about Hawaii.
2. The youngest state in the union (is, are) Hawaii.
3. There (is, are) 132 islands in this state.
4. The islands (forms, form) a chain in the ocean.
5. (Does, Do) this chain extend for over one thousand miles?

?! THINK

- How can I decide whether to use the plural form or the singular form of a verb?

REMEMBER

- A verb must agree in number with its subject. Use a singular verb with a singular subject and a plural verb with a plural subject.
- A verb must agree with its subject even if the verb comes before the subject or the verb is separated from the subject.

More Practice

A. Write each sentence, using the correct form of the verb.

Example: There (is, are) beautiful beaches in Hawaii.   *are*

6. In her research Mai (finds, find) some surprises.
7. There (is, are) only eight main islands in Hawaii.
8. Most of the people (lives, live) on seven islands.
9. The island of Oahu (has, have) the largest population.
10. (Is, Are) the state capital Honolulu?
11. There (is, are) a natural harbor on Oahu.
12. (Does, Do) you know the history of Pearl Harbor?

B. Write each sentence, using the correct form of the verb, and tell if it is singular or plural.

Example: (Is, Are) the nights warm also?
       Are the nights warm also?   plural

13. Mai's report on Hawaii (pleases, please) the class.
14. The largest island in the state (is, are) Hawaii.
15. (Does, Do) it cover over 4,000 square miles?
16. There (is, are) two active volcanoes on Hawaii.
17. The volcano Kilauea (erupts, erupt) occasionally.
18. There (is, are) a highway near the crater's edge.
19. How (does, do) people describe the volcano?
20. They (calls, call) it a "drive-in volcano."
21. Thousands of tourists (visits, visit) the crater.
22. (Is, Are) there lava in the crater?
23. People also (sees, see) fire inside.
24. Lava (flows, flow) from the volcano Mauna Loa.
25. Streams of lava (runs, run) down to the ocean.

Extra Practice, Practice Plus, pages 178–179

WRITING APPLICATION A Description

Write a paragraph that describes a violent natural phenomenon. Then exchange papers with a partner and check each other's work for subject-verb agreement.

12 MECHANICS: Using Commas to Separate Parts of a Sentence

A comma signals a pause in a sentence. Some uses for commas are listed below.

Uses for Commas	Examples
to separate three or more items in a series	Gulls, pelicans, and penguins are kinds of seabirds. Seabirds dive, swim, or float.
to show a pause after an introductory word or expression	Yes, most pelicans have nearly white feathers. Of course, the brown pelican is an exception.
to set off a noun of direct address	Dr. Lane, where do pelicans build their nests? Pelicans, Daniel, build their nests near water.
to set off a phrase that interrupts the flow of thought	The brown pelican, I believe, is the only pelican that dives underwater.

Guided Practice

Tell where a comma or commas should be used in each sentence.

Example: Seabirds fascinate me Jamie.
comma before Jamie

1. Alison tell us about that bright-beaked bird.
2. Well that strange bird is a puffin.
3. Did you know that the puffin is a powerful diver swimmer and flyer.
4. This bird I must say is a funny-looking runner.
5. This photograph shows that the puffin has red yellow and black plates on its bill.

 THINK

- How do I know when to use commas to set off words or expressions in a sentence?

REMEMBER

- Use commas to separate three or more items in a series.
- Use a comma after an introductory word or expression.
- Use commas to set off a word or phrase that interrupts the flow of thought.
- Use commas to set off a noun of direct address.

More Practice

A. Write each sentence. If commas are used correctly, write **correct.** If a comma or commas are missing, write the sentence, adding commas where they are needed.

Example: Len what is an auk?   *Len, what is an auk?*

6. Seabirds range, I believe, from waders along the shore to truly seabound birds.
7. Cormorants auks and penguins chase fish.
8. Some birds Isabel live almost entirely in the water.
9. Well does the emperor penguin ever come ashore?
10. No it spends its life in the sea or on the ice.
11. This bird eats sleeps and breeds far from land.

B. Write each sentence. Add commas where they are needed. Explain your answer.

Example: Are penguins intelligent Janet?
       Are penguins intelligent, Janet?   direct address

12. Terns gulls and gannets seek food from the air.
13. Becky their colors are a kind of camouflage.
14. Yes the Arctic tern is a clever hunter.
15. It is also in my opinion a very beautiful bird.
16. Many seabirds fly almost constantly over the waves through salty spray and along the coastline.
17. Ocean pollution on the other hand still threatens seabirds.
18. Well Jaime this plan for a seabird sanctuary is practical.
19. However you need the support of the citizens of your town.
20. They must commit money time and effort to the plan.

Extra Practice, page 180

WRITING APPLICATION A Dialogue

With a partner, write a conversation between a person and an animal. Check to make sure you have used commas correctly.

13 VOCABULARY BUILDING: Word Choice

Words can have similar meanings but convey different thoughts or feelings about the subject being described. Compare these paragraphs.

> The *brilliant* sun *gleamed* on the water. Waves *washed* onto the beach, *scattering* their *cool* spray across the *pebbles*. Children *skipped* through the *surf*, *shouting* and *laughing* as they *glanced* down at an *unusual* sea *animal*.

> The *blinding* sun *glared* on the water. Waves *crashed* onto the beach, *flinging* their *chilly* spray across the *rocks*. Children *trudged* through the *currents*, *screeching* and *howling* as they *stared* down at an *eerie* sea *creature*.

The first paragraph conveys a generally positive impression, but the second paragraph expresses a negative feeling. Nevertheless, if you were to compare the dictionary definitions of the highlighted words, you would find their meanings to be quite similar.

The exact meaning of a word is its **denotation.** The impression a word conveys is its **connotation.** Both kinds of meanings are important. When you write and speak, choose words that express both the meaning and the impression you wish to communicate.

Guided Practice

Tell whether the connotation of each word is positive or negative.

Example: puny   *negative*

1. strong   3. stun   5. calm   7. tricky
2. aggressive   4. surprise   6. unexcited   8. clever

THINK

- How can I tell the difference between the denotation and the connotation of a word?

REMEMBER

- The **denotation** of a word is its exact definition.
- The **connotation** of a word is the positive or negative impression that it conveys.

More Practice

A. Write the word in parentheses that has a negative connotation.

Example: The trip was (relaxing, uneventful).
        uneventful

 9. The car arrived at the (busy, crowded) lake.
10. Leon glared and (stormed, stepped) from the car.
11. He gave his towel a (vigorous, violent) shake.
12. His body had felt (toasty, sweaty) during the drive.
13. Leon saw a friend (charging, sprinting) toward him across the parking lot.

B. Write each sentence, using one of the words in parentheses. Then write whether the word has a **positive** or a **negative** connotation.

Example: "Hurry up!" Leon (snapped, piped).
        "Hurry up!" Leon piped.   positive

14. After a (quick, hasty) swim the boys had lunch.
15. (Greedy, Hungry) seagulls ate the leftovers.
16. Leon waved to his (younger, childish) brother.
17. The boy (smiled, smirked) back at him.
18. On the horizon thick clouds (loomed, rose).
19. Before long the air felt (cool, clammy).
20. (Worried, Concerned) faces turned toward the sky, which was growing darker.

Extra Practice, page 181

WRITING APPLICATION A Descriptive Paragraph

Write a paragraph that describes some activity in a large city. First decide whether you want to suggest a positive or negative feeling. Choose words that will convey your feeling. Then exchange papers with a classmate. Look for words with positive or negative connotations in each other's work.

Using Active and Passive Voices

When you write explanations, use words in the active voice to make your writing strong and direct. A verb is in the **active voice** when the subject of a sentence performs the action. Verbs in the active voice may or may not have a direct object.

> Jacques Cousteau **developed** the aqualung.
> Emile Gagnan **helped.**

When the subject receives the action of the verb, the verb is in the **passive voice.** Verbs in the passive voice do not have a direct object. A verb in the passive voice points the action back to the subject.

> The aqualung **was developed** by Cousteau.
> He **was helped** by Emile Gagnan.
> The two men **were praised.**

Using verbs in the active voice makes your writing stronger. Use verbs in the passive voice sparingly.

Working Together

COOPERATIVE
LEARNING

Tell how you would change each sentence so that the verb is in the active voice.

Example: Questions about Cousteau were asked by students.
Students asked questions about Cousteau.

1. Divers are helped by aqualungs.
2. Cylinders of air are carried by the diver.
3. Safety measures were created by experts.
4. Air is exhaled by swimmers into the water.
5. Air can also be recycled by them.
6. An expedition was organized by scientists in 1872.
7. The ship *Challenger* was launched by the British.

Revising Sentences

Lee wrote the following sentences for a composition. Help her revise her sentences by changing each verb from the passive to the active voice. Write each new sentence.

WRITER AT WORK

8. The ship was equipped for exploration by experts.
9. The expedition was supported by the government.
10. For three years the seas were explored by the team.
11. Specimens were collected by researchers.
12. Information was also gathered by them.
13. The *Challenger Reports* were written by specialists.
14. Today the seas are studied by oceanographers.
15. Over 70 percent of the earth is covered by oceans.
16. All forms of life are affected by the sea.
17. The effects on air are examined by researchers.
18. Sources of fuel are investigated by them.
19. Currents are also observed by scientists.
20. Chemicals in sea water are analyzed by chemists.

Think about the theme of the sea that you read about in Unit 5. Then write a paragraph explaining how to perform an activity relating to the sea. For example, you might explain how to snorkel, how to treat a sunburn, or how to use seashells creatively.

When you revise, work with a partner to look for sentences that would be stronger if the verbs were in the active voice.

UNIT CHECKUP

LESSONS
1-2

Action Verbs (page 136); **Verbs with Direct Objects** (page 138)   Write each sentence. Underline the action verb and write whether it is transitive or intransitive. If it is transitive, draw two lines under the direct object.

1. Russ and Kari fed the seal at noon.
2. They expected a warm reception from Nigel.
3. Sure enough, Nigel barked happily.
4. The youngsters fed another seal and a walrus.
5. Kari wanted a job at the aquarium.

LESSONS
3-4

Verbs with Indirect Objects (page 140); **Linking Verbs** (page 142)   Write each sentence. Underline the verb twice and write whether it is an action verb or a linking verb. Then write whether each underlined word below is an indirect object, direct object, predicate noun, or predicate adjective.

6. Kari felt <u>nervous</u> about her interview.
7. Russ wished <u>Kari</u> success.
8. She told the <u>director</u> her plans for a career.
9. The director was a sympathetic <u>listener</u>.
10. After the interview Kari received the <u>job</u>.

LESSON
5

Present, Past, and Future Tenses (page 144)   For each sentence write the verb and its tense.

11. A scuba diver receives careful training.
12. Ellen purchased her equipment last month.
13. A teacher will instruct her each week.
14. One diver assists Ellen during her tests.
15. The class studied their instruction manuals.

LESSONS
6-8

Verb Phrases (page 146); **Present and Past Progressive Forms** (page 148); **Perfect Tenses** (page 150)   Write each verb phrase. Write whether the verb is in the present or past progressive, present perfect, past perfect, or future perfect tense.

16. The canoe has provided transportation for centuries.
17. People are using canoes for enjoyment as well.
18. These boats had carried explorers along streams.
19. By tonight we will have bought our new canoe.
20. Were contestants registering for the event?

LESSONS Irregular Verbs I (page 152);   Irregular Verbs II (page 154)

9-10 Write the past and past participle for each verb.

21. swim	**27.** sit
22. break	**28.** take
23. catch	**29.** ride
24. see	**30.** write
25. do	**31.** be
26. set	**32.** feel

LESSON 11 **Subject-Verb Agreement** (page 156)   Write each sentence, using the correct verb form.

33. (Have, Has) you swum in the town pool?
34. There (was, were) petitions for its construction.
35. The rules of conduct (is, are) on a roster.
36. (Have, Has) any lifeguards applied for the job?
37. The girls in that line (look, looks) like applicants.

LESSON 12 **Mechanics: Commas to Separate Parts of a Sentence** (page 158)   Write each sentence. Add commas where necessary.

38. What do you know about monk seals Russ?
39. Well they are gray and white in color.
40. Monk seals I think live in the Black Sea.
41. Has Lisa Alex or Juan heard of monk seals?
42. Yes Ms. Green I showed them this article.

LESSON 13 **Vocabulary Building: Word Choice** (page 160)   Write each pair of words. Write whether each word has a positive or negative connotation.

43. gaudy, brilliant
44. loiter, relax
45. stroll, pace
46. converse, bicker
47. drudgery, achievement

Writing Application: Verb Usage (pages 136–157)   The following passage contains 5 errors in verb usage. Rewrite the passage correctly.

48.–52.   I have saw a game of handball recently. Has you ever watched one? One player had already broke the old record for high score. There was dramatic moments in the game. The walls of the court was shaking with cheers.

Imagine that while you are on a camping trip you become lost in a forest. In an abandoned cabin you discover an old radio that works. Send an urgent message explaining your dilemma and need for help. Write at least five sentences for your message. Make sure each sentence contains a direct object or an indirect object. Identify each object. Example: I need some <u>water</u> immediately! *direct object.*

The Object Is Survival

Good Fortune

Imagine you work for the Good Fortune Cookie Company. Prepare slips that tell good fortunes to distribute among your classmates. Use and identify as many different verb tenses as possible.

For example: *At school you will pass your next science test* (future) or *You have made many long-lasting friendships* (present perfect). All the messages should be placed in a hat for random drawings.

Science and Social Studies
TIMES

HEADLINE HIGHLIGHTS

As headline writer for the *Science and Social Studies Times*, pick five scientific, historical, or current events and write headlines that contain colorful action verbs. For example, *Edison Illuminates World* or *Magellan Circumnavigates Globe!*

CREATIVE EXPRESSION

**Stopping by Woods
on a Snowy Evening**

Whose woods these are I think I know.
His house is in the village though;
He will not see me stopping here
To watch his woods fill up with snow.

My little horse must think it queer
To stop without a farmhouse near
Between the woods and frozen lake
The darkest evening of the year.

He gives his harness bells a shake
To ask if there is some mistake.
The only other sound's the sweep
Of easy wind and downy flake.

The woods are lovely, dark and deep,
But I have promises to keep,
And miles to go before I sleep.
And miles to go before I sleep.

—Robert Frost

TRY IT OUT
Both rhyme and rhythm help to unify the lines of a poem. The systematic
pattern of beats in a poem is called **meter.** Write a short poem of your own.
Try to include rhyme and rhythm.

EXTRA PRACTICE

Three levels of practice

Action Verbs (page 136)

LEVEL

A. Write the action verb in each sentence.

1. I own a book on waterfalls of the world.
2. Waterfalls thrill people of all ages.
3. Niagara Falls attracts visitors from around the world.
4. The Niagara River plunges into a deep gorge.
5. Boats carry visitors close to the falls.
6. The massive sight frightens some tourists.
7. The waterfall sprays continually.
8. Industrial pollution endangers this scenic area.

LEVEL

B. Write the action verb in each sentence. Then write whether the verb expresses a physical or a mental action.

9. Many species of fish live in the Caribbean Sea.
10. Tropical fish delight most sightseers.
11. The coral reefs protect animal life.
12. Marc watched a film about this environment.
13. An eel swam in a cove.
14. These creatures attack nearby fish.
15. Their razor-sharp teeth frighten their prey.
16. Caribbean divers recognize these dangers.

LEVEL

C. Write a sentence for each action verb.

17. explore
18. believe
19. observe
20. create
21. remove
22. understand
23. drive
24. assist
25. maintain

EXTRA PRACTICE

Three levels of practice

Verbs with Direct Objects (page 138)

LEVEL
A. Write the direct object in each sentence.
1. Alberto found some crabs along the shore.
2. The creatures aroused his curiosity.
3. A book described their features.
4. Several thousand species of crabs roam the earth.
5. Their front legs have pincers.
6. Some crabs carry objects on their backs.
7. Their pincers usually discourage attackers.
8. Some people eat crabs.

LEVEL
B. Write each sentence. Then underline each action verb once and each direct object twice. Label each verb **transitive** or **intransitive.**

9. Crabs sometimes cause quite a nuisance.
10. On Christmas Island they migrate in huge numbers.
11. Every spring millions of red crabs leave the rain forest on this island near Java.
12. They ignore highways and other obstacles.
13. Homeowners and merchants wait anxiously.
14. The red-crab migration astonishes most visitors.
15. This event disturbs many residents.
16. Nature sometimes works in strange ways.

LEVEL
C. Complete each sentence so that it contains a direct object.

17. In a pond Betsy found ____.
18. A frog made ____.
19. The sun warmed ____.
20. Betsy collected ____.
21. Then she threw ____.
22. Two ducks followed ____.
23. A snake swallowed ____.
24. The day satisfied ____.
25. Betsy saw ____.

EXTRA PRACTICE

Three levels of practice

Verbs with Indirect Objects (page 140)

LEVEL

A. Write whether the underlined word in each sentence is a **direct object** or an **indirect object.**

1. Rachel gave Eric a book about legendary places.
2. Eric immediately found a chapter on Atlantis.
3. He told the class facts about this place.
4. A philosopher first recorded information about Atlantis.
5. Plato taught his students the legend.
6. Perhaps Socrates told Plato the myth.
7. These scholars shared their knowledge.
8. They offered the world facts and theories.
9. Myths often teach people moral lessons.

LEVEL

B. Write each sentence. Then underline each direct object once and each indirect object twice.

10. The story of Atlantis excited Eric.
11. Eric read his sister a chapter from the book.
12. Plato told the Greeks the story of Atlantis.
13. The island lent the Atlantic Ocean its name.
14. Atlantis showed the Greeks a vision of happiness.
15. This kingdom offered adults and children a life of luxury.
16. The people of Atlantis wished the world their happiness.
17. The rulers gave the people wise laws.
18. Atlantis would teach the Greeks their values.
19. Eric wrote his friend a letter about Atlantis.

LEVEL

C. Rewrite the paragraph by making each underlined group of words an indirect object.

Atlantis was a place of abundance. **(20.)** It offered colorful flowers and sweet fruits to its inhabitants. **(21.)** The land gave gold, silver, and copper to the Atlanteans. **(22.)** Poets taught the legend of this kingdom to the world. Sadly, the Atlanteans lost their appreciation of their blessings. **(23.)** Then Zeus sent a punishment to the people. **(24.)** He brought a destructive end to their island, and Atlantis sank beneath the waves. **(25.)** The story offers a wise lesson to the readers.

EXTRA PRACTICE

Three levels of practice

Linking Verbs (page 142)

LEVEL

A. Write the linking verb in each sentence. Then write whether the underlined word is a predicate noun or a predicate adjective.

1. Tom seemed <u>curious</u> about the old diving bell.
2. Its surface felt <u>rough</u>.
3. The craft still looked <u>functional</u> to Tom.
4. The bell was an important marine <u>invention</u>.
5. This invention became a useful <u>tool</u> for exploration.
6. Some bells were large <u>vessels</u>.
7. Are these objects still <u>useful</u>?
8. Tom is <u>unsure</u>.

LEVEL

B. Write the linking verb in each sentence. Then identify the predicate noun or predicate adjective.

9. Tom is a tireless fact finder.
10. Years ago he became a student of the sea.
11. Underwater exploration was once a dream.
12. A submersible craft seemed almost impossible.
13. According to some legends Alexander the Great became the operator of the first diving bell.
14. The attempt seemed a brave deed for this diver.
15. Was David Bushnell the developer of a bell?
16. His submersible of 1776 looked promising.

LEVEL

C. Write a sentence for each verb. Identify any predicate nouns or predicate adjectives in your sentences.

17. be
18. appear
19. become
20. seem
21. feel   (linking verb)
22. feel   (action verb)
23. grow   (linking verb)
24. grow   (action verb)
25. taste

EXTRA PRACTICE

Three levels of practice

Present, Past, and Future Tenses (page 144)

LEVEL

A. Write whether the verb in each sentence is in the present, past, or future tense.

1. Andy likes sailboats.
2. He sailed a small one last week.
3. The boat nearly capsized once.
4. Andy's friends join him sometimes.
5. Karen will sail with Andy tomorrow.
6. She helps him with the ropes.
7. They painted the boat last week.
8. Andy will invite Robert soon.

LEVEL

B. Complete each sentence by writing the tense of the verb shown in parentheses.

9. Laura (visit) the aquarium tomorrow.   (future)
10. She (make) an excursion there every year.   (present)
11. Sherene (discover) several kinds of fish.   (past)
12. Now she eagerly (anticipate) new discoveries.   (present)
13. Laura (call) for information about hours.   (present)
14. The friends (travel) there with their cousin.   (future)
15. Carl (accompany) his parents to the aquarium.   (past)
16. They (subscribe) to its monthly magazine.   (past)

LEVEL

C. Write each sentence, using the correct tense of the verb in parentheses. Then write whether the verb is in the **present tense, past tense,** or **future tense.**

17. Last week Laura and Sherene (enjoy) their trip to the aquarium.
18. Even now they (discuss) their adventure.
19. At the aquarium an electric eel literally (crackle) with energy.
20. Laura (purchase) a souvenir banner.
21. Sherene (select) a variety of unusual shells.
22. Sherene (display) the shells to the class tomorrow.
23. Laura (talk) about the shark exhibit after Sherene's presentation.
24. Every day the aquarium (offer) lower fees for students.
25. Next weekend it (charge) only $1.50.

EXTRA PRACTICE

Three levels of practice

Verb Phrases (page 146)

LEVEL

A. Write the verb phrase in each sentence.

  1. Jerry is reading a book about life on a submarine.
  2. He has enjoyed it all afternoon.
  3. Did you read the same story?
  4. The characters must spend several weeks underwater.
  5. One crew member does not obey orders.
  6. This character is always getting into trouble.
  7. The author has even lived on a submarine himself.
  8. Ann has also borrowed the book from Jerry.

LEVEL

B. Write the verb phrase in each sentence. Underline the main verb once and the helping verb twice.

  9. Tanya and Sonia are starting an aquarium.
10. They had shared this interest for months.
11. Should Sonia read any books about tropical fish?
12. Tanya has already selected a tank.
13. Their parents may accompany them to the pet store.
14. Mr. McKenzie, the owner, had first interested Sonia and
        Tanya in this hobby.
15. He could now offer them his help in the choice of fish.
16. Doesn't Mr. McKenzie know a lot about pets?

LEVEL

C. Complete each sentence. Then underline each verb phrase and circle the main verb.

17. By this morning Tanya had ____.
18. She has now ____.
19. Sonia and Tanya were ____.
20. Have they just ____?
21. Haven't they ____?
22. Is Sonia now ____?
23. She will be ____.
24. Aren't they ____?
25. Their parents had ____.

EXTRA PRACTICE

Three levels of practice

Present and Past Progressive Forms (page 148)

LEVEL

A. Write the progressive form of the verb in each sentence.

1. Our class was studying the longest river in the world.
2. We were discussing the Nile River last week.
3. Phil is writing a report on the subject.
4. Some students are drawing maps of Egypt.
5. I am preparing a talk on the Aswan High Dam.
6. The dam is providing water for irrigation.
7. Water from the Nile was depositing fertile soil in the river valley for centuries.
8. Two students were reading an article about the Nile delta.

LEVEL

B. Write the progressive form of the verb in each sentence. Then write whether the verb is the **present progressive** form or the **past progressive** form.

9. Lonnie and I are leaning on the rail of a boat.
10. Three porpoises were escorting the boat.
11. Now the ferry is docking at Sapelo Island.
12. Both of us were expecting Phil.
13. Now he is waving from the shore.
14. We are touring the island on foot with him today.
15. Phil was working at the Marine Institute on the island.
16. I am gathering information about the Institute.

LEVEL

C. Write each sentence, using the form of the verb shown in parentheses.

17. We (stroll) along the water's edge.   (present progressive)
18. Phil (point) at some shells in the mud.   (present progressive)
19. Oysters (strain) the seawater.   (past progressive)
20. They (feast) on plankton.   (past progressive)
21. A fiddler crab (scoop) mud into its mouth.   (present progressive)
22. Sea oats (sway) gracefully in the waves.   (past progressive)
23. Now an egret (hunt) for fish.   (present progressive)
24. Katydids (buzz) in the nearby trees.   (present progressive)
25. Gulls (fly) in the sky above.   (past progressive)

EXTRA PRACTICE

Three levels of practice

Perfect Tenses (page 150)

LEVEL

A. Write the perfect-tense verb in each sentence.

1. Kim has finished a book about the Loch Ness monster.
2. Dennis had recommended it to her.
3. This Scottish mystery has fascinated people around the world.
4. Sightseers have flocked to Loch Ness for decades.
5. By the 1940s sightings of the monster had increased.
6. A British engineer has filmed a dark shape in the water.
7. Scientific expeditions have investigated the controversy.
8. By the end of this century, perhaps scientists will have confirmed the existence of "Nessie."

LEVEL

B. Write the verb in each sentence. Then write whether the verb is in the **present perfect, past perfect,** or **future perfect** tense.

9. Undersea forests of kelp have flourished for ages.
10. They had existed long before the arrival of settlers.
11. Nutrient-rich water has supported the kelp forests.
12. Scientists have measured the growth rate of kelp.
13. Lois has discovered a piece of kelp near the shore.
14. It had floated because of its air-filled bladders.
15. In the sea the kelp had once served as home for many animals.
16. When Lois returns to the beach, she will have learned more about the importance of kelp.
17. The encyclopedia will have provided her with much more information.

LEVEL

C. Write a sentence, using each verb below. Use the tense shown in parentheses.

18. consider   (past perfect)
19. use   (present perfect)
20. hunt   (future perfect)
21. realize   (present perfect)
22. earn   (future perfect)
23. taste   (past perfect)
24. explore   (present perfect)
25. discuss   (past perfect)

EXTRA PRACTICE

Three levels of practice

Irregular Verbs I (page 152)

LEVEL

A. Write the past and the past participle for each verb.

1. sink	**7.** buy
2. drink	**8.** lend
3. say	**9.** leave
4. come	**10.** have
5. be	**11.** hold
6. run	**12.** make

LEVEL

B. Complete each sentence correctly by writing the past or the past participle of the verb shown in parentheses.

13. I (swing).	**19.** John has (sing).
14. You had (swing).	**20.** She (sing).
15. Jo has (lend).	**21.** Mail (come).
16. They (lend).	**22.** News had (come).
17. It (spring).	**23.** I (do).
18. They had (spring).	**24.** You have (do).

LEVEL

C. Write the following poem, using the tense of the verb shown in parentheses.

An albacore **(25.)** (*sit*, past) on the sand
And **(26.)** (*sing*, past) with her undersea band.
   The squid who **(27.)** (*catch*, past perfect)
   Her song all **(28.)** (*bring*, past perfect)
Their friends. How they gave her a hand!

A shark then **(29.)** (*come*, past) in from afar.
He **(30.)** (*say*, past) "I **(31.)** (*make*, future) you a star!"
   Fish who **(32.)** (*sing*, present) as you **(33.)** (*do*, present)

   (34.) (*Have*, present perfect) fame—fortune, too
When I **(35.)** (*teach*, past) them to be popular.
The singer **(36.)** (*spring*, past) up with a screech.
She **(37.)** (*swim*, past) straight to the shark with this speech:
   "Tina Tuna's my name;
   I **(38.)** (*think*, present perfect) of acclaim,
But happy I **(39.)** (*be*, present) with my beach!"

EXTRA PRACTICE

Three levels of practice

Irregular Verbs II (page 154)

LEVEL

A. Write the past and the past participle of each verb.

1. throw
2. wear
3. freeze
4. break
5. eat

6. burst
7. ride
8. draw
9. tear
10. write

LEVEL

B. Complete each sentence correctly by writing the past or the past participle of the verb shown in parentheses.

11. Alex (grow).
12. He has (grow) tall.
13. A bird has (fly).
14. It (fly).
15. We have (drive).

16. Arlene (drive).
17. I (choose).
18. You have (choose).
19. My hands (freeze).
20. My feet also (freeze).

LEVEL

C. Write each sentence using the tense of the verb shown in parentheses.

21. Jean (see) some colored signal flags on a ship.   (present perfect)
22. The flags (fly) high above the deck.   (past)
23. A wind (blow) and snapped the flags.   (past)
24. Her family (drive) to the dock.   (past perfect)
25. They (go) last Memorial Day weekend.   (past)
26. Jean (choose) a book about signal flags from the library.   (past)
27. Her brother (give) her a poster showing flag signals.   (present perfect)
28. Then she (draw) some of the designs.   (past)
29. Now she (grow) more interested in flag codes.   (present perfect)
30. She even (write) a composition explaining these codes.   (past)

EXTRA PRACTICE

Three levels of practice

Subject-Verb Agreement (page 156)

LEVEL

A. Write whether the verb form in each sentence is **correct** or **incorrect.**

1. We finally arrives at Woods Hole, Massachusetts.
2. There are a marine research center on Cape Cod.
3. The oceanographic institution in Woods Hole is famous.
4. The woman with the documents are Dr. Ruiz.
5. Does you know about her career?
6. Yes, she have been a well-known marine biologist for years.
7. Don't Dr. Ruiz explore the ocean?
8. There is books by her at the library.

LEVEL

B. Write the correct verb form for each sentence.

9. (Does, Do) you help Dr. Ruiz with her research?
10. Yes, there (is, are) a major project under way.
11. The assistants on this project (is, are) students.
12. (Does, Do) your research involve plant life?
13. No, our project (focuses, focus) on sea urchins.
14. There (is, are) many articles on these spiny animals.
15. Some chemicals in sea urchins (interests, interest) us.
16. Tomorrow our search for sea urchins (begins, begin).

LEVEL

C. Revise each sentence to make the verb agree with its subject.

17. The research ship slowly leave Woods Hole.
18. The assistants on board checks Dr. Ruiz's equipment.
19. There is also two photographers on the ship.
20. Don't Dr. Ruiz dive into the water?
21. The photographers on the boat scans the water.
22. Does they find any sea urchins?
23. Near a rock there are a large sea urchin.
24. The spines on this creature feels quite sharp.
25. Sea urchins eats seaweed and other sea matter.

PRACTICE + PLUS

Three levels of additional practice for a difficult skill

Subject-Verb Agreement (page 156)

LEVEL

A. Write whether the verb form in each sentence is **correct** or **incorrect.**

1. I be a champion swimmer.
2. Do you belong to the American Olympic team?
3. Right now I swims with my school team.
4. The members of my team wins many medals.
5. Does the swimmers have a good team spirit?
6. There is many practice days every month.
7. Success in this sport require much hard work.
8. The efforts of our coach means a great deal to us.

LEVEL

B. Write the correct verb form for each sentence.

9. (Have, Has) you seen the boat show?
10. There (is, are) hundreds of boats at the show.
11. The smallest boats in the exhibit (is, are) canoes.
12. Motorboats on display (measures, measure) 100 feet.
13. (Does, Do) boats interest you?
14. Boats of all kinds (appeals, appeal) to me.
15. My favorite type of boat (is, are) the sailboat.
16. (Does, Do) your sister admire sailboats, too?

LEVEL

C. Revise each sentence to make the verb agree with its subject.

17. There is some beautiful beaches near my home.
18. The lifeguards at one beach is my friends.
19. Does you work there, Eric?
20. There is two positions available.
21. Do the sun sometimes bother you?
22. Sunglasses is necessary on most days.
23. The lifeguards on duty uses a strong sunscreen, too.
24. Some people on the beach avoids the midday sun.
25. Gloria prefer speedboats.

EXTRA PRACTICE

Three levels of practice

Mechanics: Using Commas to Separate Parts of a Sentence (page 158)

LEVEL

A. Write each sentence, using commas correctly.

1. Fiona are you doing research for your science project?
2. Yes I have chosen my topic.
3. It is about the layers of the ocean Scott.
4. Each layer you see has less light than the one above it.
5. Scott Angela and Bert can tell us about sea life.
6. The top layer of course is the most familiar one.
7. Mrs. Amberton can you recommend a good science magazine?
8. A good one Fiona is called *Scientific American.*

LEVEL

B. Write each sentence, adding commas where they are needed. Explain your responses.

9. Fiona will you tell me more about this subject?
10. Yes I will start with the top layer.
11. The sunlit zone as you can imagine reaches to an average depth of 650 feet.
12. Most fish mammals and reptiles live in this zone.
13. Scientists have seen some of these creatures at lower depths Scott.
14. Such cases are quite unusual you know.
15. No I do not know many facts about sea life.
16. Birds on the other hand have always fascinated me.

LEVEL

C. Add an introductory word, a noun of direct address, or an interrupting phrase to each sentence. Add commas where they are needed.

17. What is the next layer of the ocean?
18. It is the twilight zone of the sea.
19. The twilight zone has a depth of about two-thirds of a mile.
20. Fish in this layer are marked by darker colors and larger eyes.
21. The bottom zone contains very strange-looking fish.
22. In this cold layer live very strange creatures.
23. The vampire squid is one of its inhabitants.
24. Would you like to explore these dark depths?
25. People study the ocean for many reasons.

EXTRA PRACTICE

Three levels of practice

Vocabulary Building: Word Choice (page 160)

LEVEL

A. Divide your paper in half. In the first column write the word in each pair that has a positive connotation. In the second column write the word with a negative connotation.

1. flimsy, delicate
2. strong-willed, stubborn
3. economical, stingy
4. bossiness, leadership
5. snooping, inquisitive
6. childish, youthful
7. inventive, untruthful
8. fragrance, odor
9. glare, shine

LEVEL

B. Write each sentence, using one of the words in parentheses. Then write whether the word you selected has a **positive** or a **negative** connotation.

10. Sam (paced, strolled) across the yard.
11. Then he spoke with (nervousness, anticipation).
12. "Where are JoAnn and her father?" Sam (whined, piped).
13. "Perhaps the sights (attracted, distracted) them."
14. Soon JoAnn was (cackling, giggling) and waving at them from the front seat.
15. Mr. Martinez got out and (bellowed, encouraged), "Come on; we don't want to miss the boat!"
16. Soon Sam was (trudging, skipping) off to the waiting car.
17. They climbed (eagerly, anxiously) into the car.

LEVEL

C. The following paragraph gives a generally negative impression. Rewrite the paragraph, replacing each underlined word with a word that has a positive connotation.

The **(18.)** monstrous boat left the dock and **(19.)** lumbered into the bay. Overhead gulls **(20.)** shrieked and dove for food. In the distance **(21.)** garish buildings glittered along the skyline. Vanessa **(22.)** grimaced and put on her sunglasses. She **(23.)** plodded along the deck of the boat as she **(24.)** worried about the journey ahead of her. A **(25.)** raw wind blew across her face.

UNIT

6

Writing Explanations

Read the quotation and look at the picture on the opposite page. Talk about actions you can take to learn more about the world.

Explanatory writing benefits an audience. When you write an explanation, you will want to help your audience learn about something.

Focus An explanation provides information for an audience by presenting facts clearly.

On what subject would you like to write an explanation? In this unit you will find an article about sea and space, and some interesting photographs. You can use them to find ideas for writing.

THEME: *CROSSCURRENTS*

*One should lie empty, open, choiceless as a beach—
waiting for a gift from the sea.*

—Anne Morrow Lindbergh

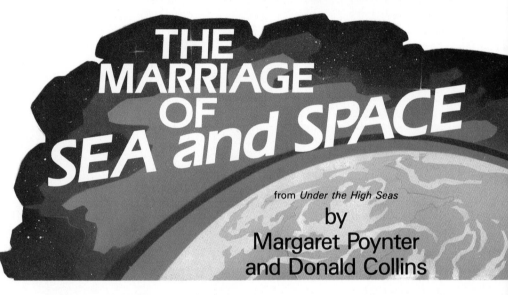

Have you ever explored an unfamiliar place? How did you plan your exploration? What skills did you need?

Exciting new inventions have made it possible for people to explore what lies deep under the ocean's surface and far into outer space. The work is challenging, and sometimes dangerous.

As you read the selection below, look for the ways the authors explain the similarities between exploring the sea and space.

THE MARRIAGE OF SEA and SPACE

from *Under the High Seas*

by
Margaret Poynter
and Donald Collins

Sea and space have often been closely connected in the minds of imaginative people.[1] In 1865, Jules Verne sparked an interest in space travel by writing about a fictional journey to the moon. Four years later, he wrote *Twenty Thousand Leagues Under the Sea* and set up waves of speculation about the conditions and creatures that exist in the depths of the world ocean.

In 1969, humans finally took that trip into space. In preparation for the venture, the moon had been thoroughly studied and probed by telescopes and other earthbound instruments. It had also been observed by unmanned spacecraft. Neil Armstrong and his fellow astronauts had a good idea of what was facing them at the end of their 214,000–mile flight.

1. The beginning sentence introduces the two subjects that will be compared.

While humans were taking giant leaps into space, Verne's other visionary adventure had already come true. Auguste Piccard, who in the 1930s had sent balloons into the stratosphere, had gone on to design a submersible called the *Trieste*. It's an elongated vessel that works like a balloon filled with air. Its striped float contains aviation gasoline that provides buoyancy. Below hangs the cabin, which is a seven-foot steel sphere.

In 1960, Auguste's son, Jacques, and Naval Lieutenant Don Walsh set a still unbeaten record by using the *Trieste* to descend seven miles into the Pacific Ocean's Mariana Trench. The two men had to have as much courage to make their short journey as the astronauts had to have to take their long one. At that time, only the shallow parts of the continental shelves had been viewed by man. There were no telescopes by which anyone could peer into the ocean's depths. In many ways, the environment of the sea floor was still less familiar to us than the craters of the moon.

The *Trieste* made a perfect landing on an ivory-colored carpet of ooze that had been lain down during the course of thousands of years. Jellyfish, crabs, and worms floated past the windows of the submersible. Within a few moments, a foot-long fish joined them. The sight answered the long-standing question about whether or not a true fish could exist in the deepest parts of the ocean.

Manned submersibles usually are built to descend to depths of two or three miles. To go deeper, they would have to be much more resistant to pressure and have other features that would make them very expensive. At this time, with no danger to people, remote instruments can be used to do whatever jobs are necessary in the deeper parts of the ocean.

Meanwhile, in these submersibles, such as *Alvin*, which is laden with instruments and remote control samplers, scientists are able to climb underwater cliffs as people scale continental mountains. They're able to look around and see the texture of the rocks, ignore the poor samples, and ask the pilot to take only the more valuable specimens. They can view the marine creatures in their natural environment and take extensive pictures and notes. The time spent in a submersible is expensive, so geologists and biologists must make every minute count.

In 1966, *Alvin* played a big part in retrieving a hydrogen bomb that had fallen into the sea off the Spanish coast. Again and again, it carried a team of men into the ocean. The search was exhausting and dangerous.

"It was like flying a helicopter in the Rocky Mountains on a dark night," said one team member. "A mud slide coming down a slope could have given us a very bad time."

Days passed before the men spotted the track that the bomb had made as it slid down a hill. Before they could find the bomb itself, *Alvin's* batteries almost died, and they had to surface. Later, with the help of CURV, a leashed robot, the bomb was pulled from its precarious perch on the edge of a crevasse.

As in space, the senses and minds of human beings can play a vital part in the exploration of the sea. Walking in space and experiments with living and working underwater have proved that humans are the most adaptable of all of earth's creatures. They can cope with garbled speech, nausea, fatigue, disorientation, weightlessness, and pressure and still perform their scheduled tasks and suffer no long-lasting ill effects.[2]

Nevertheless, most of the exploration of space and sea will continue to be done by unmanned or remote instruments and devices. Their "eyes," "ears," and "hands" can work tirelessly,

2. The writers make specific comparisons between the exploration of the sea and space.

and those that function underwater need none of the time-consuming decompression that prevents pressure sickness or death in humans. *Gloria* and *Deep Tow* are two of the "seeing ears" that use sonar to explore the structures on the ocean bottom. Robots can build and repair submarine installations and lay pipelines and cables, leaving human beings to do less dangerous work. Someday robots will be used to build offshore airports, loading docks, and power plants. They may even help to construct small communities on the surface of the ocean. Plans for an Aquapolis or a Triton City envision a doughnut-shaped apartment and shopping complex atop a circle of long columns rising from the sea.

Some remote instruments work twenty-four hours a day, all year long. They are buoys that bob about on the ocean's surface and collect information about weather conditions, surface currents and waves, and the temperature and composition of the water. A newly-designed monster buoy can take one hundred different air and water measurements while continuing to function in winds up to 160 miles per hour and in seas sixty feet high.

The data that's gathered by buoys is often transmitted to the most spectacular of all remote instruments—the earth orbiting oceanographic satellites. The first of these—*Seasat I*—was launched in 1978. From its 500-mile high vantage point, *Seasat* could scan about ninety-five percent of the world ocean every thirty-six hours. The *Nimbus I* is another such satellite. It carries a special instrument that accurately measures the distribution of color on the ocean's surface. This color shows the location of oil slicks, the presence of marine life, the meanderings of currents, and the areas where rivers spread their sediment and pollution into the sea.

Plans are being made for the launching of other oceanographic satellites. TOPEX will measure ocean currents more accurately than has ever been done before.

With robots prowling the ocean and satellites keeping a tireless vigil from space, it may sometimes seem that human beings are being pushed to the sidelines in the exploration of the world ocean. The opposite is true. Only humans have the ability to make quick decisions and to direct these remote instruments. Only humans have the ability to analyze the data and apply the results to the needs of fishers, merchants, and sailors. Only humans have the curiosity to keep on with their explorations and their probing of the unknown. Most of our discoveries have been made by oceanographers going out on small ships again and again. They have been the ones who have mapped the ocean floor and discovered the mountain ranges, the trenches, the rifts, and the volcanoes.

When a scientist is at sea, he or she faces the same inconveniences and dangers that any sailor faces on a small vessel. Doing research under such conditions can be very satisfying. It can also be very frustrating. Measurements are hard to take because the ship is always moving. The sea floor seems to gobble up cameras and other expensive equipment. If the instruments aren't lost, they often become damaged. If there are no replacements on board, one or more experiments may have to be postponed.

Anything that's placed on a bench or tabletop will slide off unless it's lashed, nailed, screwed, or taped into place. All small items must go into boxes that are secured to the walls. When scientists are looking at the recordings of an instrument, they may have to wedge their chair into place and hold onto a solid object to keep from being thrown into the knobs and dials and smashing them.

Dredging and coring is done from the fantail of the ship. The crew must work only a few feet above water, so the equipment can be raised and lowered with the least chance of damaging it. Getting soaked in the tropics isn't so bad. It's not so pleasant in the Arctic Ocean.

Accidents can happen no matter how careful everyone is. Two oceanographers were once leaning against the rail of their research vessel. They were directly on a line between the dredge on the deck and the sheave, or pulley, on the end of a boom through which the dredging wire led to the winch. One of the men grew uneasy. He knew there was little chance of the winch starting up, but nevertheless he took his companion's arm and they moved to another location.

Moments later, for no apparent reason, the winch started to haul in the line. In response, the dredge moved across the deck and tore away the railing against which the men had been leaning a short while earlier.

All oceanographers eventually have some close calls. They all experience the discomforts that occur when a ship is rolling and pitching under their feet. And they all think that their work is well worth it. "I've never lost the wonder and excitement of the sea," said one man. He went on to tell of his first trip in a submersible. "The whole scene could best be pictured by imagining a series of steep rocky alpines dusted by freshly fallen powder snow and bathed in green moonlight."

Oceanographers aren't working only to satisfy their unending curiosity. They know that their discoveries benefit people. In just one area—that of weather prediction—they may soon be able to save thousands of lives by issuing long-term predictions about floods and droughts.

A few climatologists are currently keeping a close eye on the polar icecaps. They claim that the ice is melting because of a "greenhouse effect" in which heat radiating from the earth is trapped under a thickening layer of carbon dioxide. The melting is causing the sea level to increase slightly. If that increase were to speed up, it could destroy the massive unstable ice sheet in western Antarctica. The oceans could then rise and inundate the coastal regions of the world. Such massive flooding could occur within the next fifty to two hundred years. By monitoring the melting of the icecaps, oceanographers could give plenty of advance warning to people who live in Gulf Coast cities, such as Galveston and New Orleans, plus Savannah, Charleston, New York City, and Boston and other towns and cities all along our Eastern seaboard.

While some oceanographers are keeping an eye out for potential disasters, others are working on improving the lives of human beings. They are constantly seeking new ways to use the resources that the sea holds in such abundance. One enthusiastic researcher said, "Someday we'll be using everything in the ocean except the roar of the surf."

Perhaps considering our current technology, he was exaggerating. Perhaps not. When we finally harness the power of tides and waves, we may someday be using everything in the ocean *including* the roar of the surf.

Lyndon Johnson once said, "The depth of the sea is a new environment for man's exploration and development, just as crossing the western plains was a challenge to centuries past. We shall encounter that environment with the same conviction and pioneering spirit that propelled ships from the Old to the New World."

Every oceanographer and space explorer knows that the age of discovery is far from over. In a few years, we may be touching the surface of the abyssal plain as we have touched the surface of the moon.[3]

3. A main idea is stated in the concluding paragraph.

Thinking Like a Reader

1. What benefits are there to the exploration of sea and space?
2. Has your life been affected by these benefits? How?

Write your responses in your journal.

Thinking Like a Writer

3. How do the authors show that exploring space and sea are very similar?
4. Which similarities do you think are strongest?
5. If you were going to write about the sea or space, what topics would you want to investigate?

Write your responses in your journal.

Brainstorm *Vocabulary*

New words related to the sea come into existence as new marine discoveries and technological advances are made. "The Marriage of Sea and Space" contains many words related to the sea, for example, *submersible, buoys*, and *oceanographers*. Find other similar terms and look up their meanings in a dictionary if they are unfamiliar to you.

What aspects of the sea or outer space interest you? Think about the words and terms that are used in connection with the area you choose. Write these words and phrases in your journal. Create a personal vocabulary list. You can use these words in your writing.

Talk It Over

An Interview

Imagine that you are appearing in a talk show on television. Have a classmate conduct an interview with you in which you explain how to do something you know well. You might explain how to set up a tent, scuba dive, or create jewelry. Present your interview before the class. Keep in mind that your audience may not be familiar with the process that you are explaining.

Now change roles with your partner and become the interviewer. Prepare questions on the topic you have selected with your partner and decide on an order in which to ask the questions.

Quick Write *How to Survive*

Write survival tips for life on a deserted island. Your tips can be serious or funny. Explain how someone might confront the problems of finding food, shelter, and transportation. How can a person avoid danger in such an environment? You might include a map of the place you are describing.

If you wish, use the following list of items for other points to consider.

water
clothing
fuel
communication
amusement
medical treatment

Idea Corner *Explanations*

Science often explains how something works. "The Marriage of Sea and Space" tells how scientists explore the oceans and outer space both to investigate their mysteries and to obtain useful information. In your journal write down your thoughts about topics related to the sea or space. Some possible topics are listed below. Talk with your classmates, friends, or family members to find other ideas. Keep your notes for possible composition topics.

shipbuilding
space stations
language of dolphins
constellations

PICTURES

SEEING LIKE A WRITER

Finding Ideas for Writing

Look at the pictures on these pages. Think about what you see. What ideas for writing an explanation do the pictures give you? Write your ideas in your journal.

Dolphin trainer at Miami Seaquarium

Submersible exploration vessel

Surfer riding wave in Hawaii

Diver examining spider crab in the Caribbean Sea

PICTURES: Ideas for Explanatory Writing

1 GROUP WRITING: AN EXPLANATORY PARAGRAPH

COOPERATIVE
LEARNING

Explanations present facts to inform an **audience.** The **purpose** of explanatory writing can be to tell how something works or how to do something. A good explanation contains several elements that help the audience understand the facts clearly.

- Topic Sentence
- Order of Supporting Details
- Transition Words
- Concluding Sentence

Topic Sentence

The selection below explains how ocean currents have been charted. As you read the explanation, notice the underlined sentence.

> Early explorers and scholars discovered several reliable ways to map the ocean and its currents. In 1663, for example, a Dutch scholar named Isaac Vossius was able to map the great clockwise flow of currents in the North Atlantic Ocean by collecting information from the logs of generations of sea captains. Sixteen years later, Count Luigi Marsili mapped the currents between the Mediterranean Sea and the Black Sea. He constructed a model that showed that differences in water density can cause the movement of currents. In addition, an explorer named William Dampier charted the different tides and currents after he returned home in 1691 from his voyages through the Atlantic and Pacific oceans. Although many others have added to our knowledge of the oceans, these three people established the main ways to chart ocean currents.

The underlined sentence contains the main idea or topic of the paragraph. This kind of a sentence is called the **topic sentence** of the paragraph. The topic sentence often comes at the beginning of a paragraph, but it may also appear in the middle or at the end.

Guided Practice: Writing a Topic Sentence

As a class, choose one of the topics from the list below, or think of one that everyone agrees on. You may wish to look through your writer's journal for ideas that the photographs or literature selection in this unit may have given you. Narrow the topic, if necessary, and explore your ideas with your classmates. Then write a good topic sentence that you could use for an explanation. Identify your purpose and audience. Save your notes.

how to set up a tent	how to care for house plants
whales	nutrition
how to treat a sunburn	how a class election works

Supporting Details and Transition Words

The **supporting details** in an explanation provide information that develops or supports the topic sentence in the paragraph. Supporting details in explanatory writing may be facts, examples, reasons, or steps in a process.

The supporting details in explanations are arranged in a logical order. Information can be given in **chronological,** or time order, as in the sample paragraph above. Facts may also be presented in **order of importance** or arranged to show a **comparison.** For a paragraph that explains how to do something or how something works, however, chronological order is the most clear and direct, and easiest for the reader to follow.

Transition words and phrases help to show readers how ideas in an explanation are connected. In the sample paragraph above, the transition words are *for example*, *later*, and *in addition*. Some other transition words that you might use in an explanation are listed below.

first	eventually	at the same time
finally	in contrast	in the end
then	similarly	at last

Guided Practice: Listing Details

With your classmates, list supporting details that explain the topic sentence you have already composed together. Arrange the details in chronological order. Make sure you have not left out any important facts that your audience will need to know in order to understand your explanation.

Concluding Sentence

An explanatory paragraph often has a **concluding sentence.** The concluding sentence may:

1. summarize the information given in the paragraph;
2. restate the topic sentence in different words; or
3. leave the audience with an important point to consider.

In the explanatory paragraph above, the concluding sentence both summarizes the information and restates the main idea presented in the topic sentence.

Guided Practice: Writing a Concluding Sentence

As a class, decide on an effective concluding sentence for the explanation you are composing. Discuss several possible concluding sentences before you agree on the one that you think is the most effective. If you restate the topic sentence, use different words to avoid sounding repetitious.

Putting an Explanatory Paragraph Together

With your class you have explored ideas for an explanation, written a topic sentence, listed supporting details, and arranged the details in a logical order. You have also thought about appropriate transition words and a concluding sentence for your explanation.

Guided Practice: Writing an Explanation

Now write your explanation. Look at your topic sentence to make sure that it states the main idea of your explanation. Add any missing details that you think your audience will need to know to understand your explanation. Eliminate facts that do not support your topic. Add transition words to connect your ideas. Write a concluding sentence.

Share your explanation with a friend. Ask if he or she was able to follow your explanation and found it informative.

Checklist An Explanation

When you write an explanation, keep a checklist of the important points that you need to remember. A sample checklist is shown below. Copy it and add any other points you want to remember. Keep it in your writing folder and refer to it as you write your explanation.

> **CHECKLIST**
>
> - Remember purpose and audience.
> - Include a topic sentence.
> - Provide supporting details.
> - Arrange details in a logical order.
> - Use transition words.
> - End with a concluding sentence.
> - _____

2 THINKING AND WRITING: Comparing and Contrasting

Explanations can tell how something works or how to do something. Sometimes you can explain something more clearly by comparing and contrasting it with a related subject. When you **compare** two subjects, you show their similarities. When you **contrast** two things, you point out their differences.

One student was interested in how mining in the sea is done. He decided to write an explanation showing the similarities and differences between mining on land and in the sea. After brainstorming for ideas, he organized the information in a three-column chart.

	Similarities	Differences
Purpose	to obtain valuable metals	
Method		ocean—hosing or netting land —blasting
Equipment	enormous	
Cost		ocean—more expensive land —less expensive
Other issues		ocean—there is question of ownership of metals land —no question of ownership

Thinking Like a Writer

- What similarities are listed? What differences?
- Why would making a chart like this be helpful?

When you compare and contrast in an explanation, there are different ways you can arrange your information. You can present all the details about one subject first and then give all the facts about the other subject. Another way is to explain the similarities or differences point by point, alternating between the two subjects. Notice how the writer used the point-by-point method in the following explanation.

Mining in the ground and in the sea are similar processes with several important differences. The purpose of both is to obtain valuable metals, mineral ores, and other materials. Like mining in the earth, ocean mining uses large machines to gather and load the ore. Their methods, however, are very different. Ore is blasted out of the ground. A huge hose or net, on the other hand, is used to collect materials from the bottom of the sea, which is a more expensive procedure than blasting. Finally, arguments over who owns the precious metals on the floor of the sea make ocean mining a more complicated process than its counterpart. Although similar in purpose, mining in the sea and earth offer miners very different challenges.

THINKING APPLICATION Comparing and Contrasting

COOPERATIVE LEARNING

You know that comparing is finding similarities and contrasting is finding differences.

1. Decide which pairs of topics listed below would be appropriate to compare and contrast in an explanation. You may wish to discuss your ideas with a group of classmates.
   a. marine life at the North Pole and South Pole
   b. penguins and polar bears
   c. two early maps of the world
   d. scuba diving and snorkeling
   e. Niagara Falls and the Mississippi River
   f. water and ice
   g. the planets in our solar system
   h. zebras and giraffes
2. Choose which sentences below could be used in an explanation that *compares*.
   a. Ice-skating is a winter sport, while swimming is a summer sport.
   b. Skating and swimming are both individual sports.
   c. Swimming and skating each require good coordination.
   d. Both skating and swimming provide opportunities for team participation.
   e. Skating requires special equipment; swimming does not.
   f. Swimming and skating both provide good exercise.

3 INDEPENDENT WRITING: An Explanation

Prewrite: Step 1

You have learned the basic elements for writing effective explanations. Now you are ready to choose a topic for writing an explanation of your own. Jill, a student your age, chose a topic in this way.

Choosing a Topic

Jill's first step was to make a list of subjects that interested her and for which she wanted to write an explanation. She looked through her journal for ideas.

Jill liked the last item on her list best. But she needed to narrow her topic; so she decided to compare and contrast two kinds of seals. She thought that the members of her science club would make a good **audience**. Her **purpose** would be to present a clear and informative explanation.

kinds of clouds
types of computers
styles of clothing
marine life

Jill then went to the library and did some research on her subject. She made the following notes.

Crabeater seal	Elephant seal
—most beautiful seal	—lives in Arctic and Antarctic
—graceful, playful swimmer	—over 6,000 pounds
—lives only in Antarctic	—inflates nose, howls
—friendly looking	—largest seal in world
—gray-white pelt, brown eyes	—clumsy looking, even in water
—whiskers	—most terrifying seal

Exploring Ideas: Charting Strategy

Jill thought that she had some good ideas but needed to organize her information. She made the following chart.

	Similarities	Differences
Type:	both hair seals, not fur seals	
Habitat:	both Antarctic	elephant seal —also Arctic
Appearance:		crabeater seal—most beautiful seal, gray-white pelt, soft brown eyes, whiskers, my favorite elephant seal —most terrifying seal, largest seal, 6,000 pounds
Behavior:		crabeater seal—graceful, playful elephant seal —clumsy, inflates nose, howls

Thinking Like a Writer

- How did Jill organize her notes?
- What similarities does she list? What differences?
- What detail did she eliminate? Why?

YOUR TURN

Think of two subjects to compare and contrast in an explanation. Use **Pictures** or your journal for ideas.

JOURNAL

- Write a list of ideas.
- Choose two subjects that can be compared and contrasted in a brief explanation.
- Narrow your topic, if necessary.
- Think about your purpose and audience.

Explore your ideas in a comparison and contrast chart. You can add to or delete from your chart at any time.

Write a First Draft: Step 2

Jill prepared a planning checklist to use as she wrote her explanation. Then she began to think about how she could use her comparison and contrast chart to arrange details logically in her writing. She decided to explain the similarities and differences between her two subjects on a point-by-point basis, alternating between the two subjects.

After she thought about the important parts of a comparison and contrast piece of writing, Jill began to write her first draft. While writing her first draft, she did not interrupt the flow of her ideas by stopping to correct errors. She knew she could make corrections and changes later.

Jill's First Draft

> The crabeater seal and the elephant seal are both hair seals, as opposed to fur seals. Both types of seals have a pelt that is stiff coarse and protective against cold water. the crabeater seal, however, is a playful swimmer, whereas the elephant seal is awkword and clumsy looking. It is clumsy looking even swiming in water. Crabeater seals are quite lovely, with their grayish white pelt and soft, brown eyes. The 6,000–pound elephant seal on the other hand looks weird, especially when it inflated its snout and howls!

Planning Checklist
- Remember purpose and audience.
- Include a topic sentence.
- Provide supporting details.
- Arrange details in a logical order.
- Use transition words.
- End with a concluding sentence.

YOUR TURN

Write the first draft of your explanation. As you write, ask yourself the following questions.
- What does my audience need to know for me to accomplish my purpose?
- How does my topic sentence state my main idea? Is the topic sentence clear?
- How can I best organize the details in my explanation? Should I use the point-by-point method?

TIME-OUT You might want to take some time out before you revise. In that way you will be able to revise your writing with a fresh eye.

Revise: Step 3

After Jill finished writing her first draft, she read it over to herself to see if there were any improvements she wanted to make. Then she shared her draft with a classmate and asked how she might make it a better explanation.

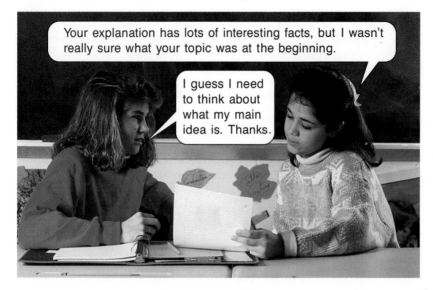

Your explanation has lots of interesting facts, but I wasn't really sure what your topic was at the beginning.

I guess I need to think about what my main idea is. Thanks.

After Jill met with her friend, she looked once again at her planning checklist. She realized that she forgot to include one other important part in her explanation. She placed a check mark next to both points to remind herself to make the changes on her first draft.

Then Jill began revising her first draft. Besides making the changes she marked on her checklist, she thought about other possible improvements. What details could she add to make her explanation clearer? What words could she change to be more precise? Did she arrange details in a logical order and did she include transition words?

As she revised her draft, Jill thought more about her **purpose** and **audience.** She asked herself how much background information they would need to understand the comparisons and contrasts she was making. She also decided to keep her language nontechnical so that her audience would not need to look up any words.

Jill made all her changes on the first draft, crossing out some words and adding sentences. Look at how her corrections changed her first draft.

Revising Checklist
- Remember purpose and audience
- ✔ Include a topic sentence.
- Provide supporting details.
- Arrange details in a logical order.
- Use transition words.
- ✔ End with a concluding sentence.

Jill's Revised Draft

Although all seals share certain features, the differences between some types of seals can be striking.
The crabeater seal and the elephant seal are both hair

seals, as opposed to fur seals. Both types of seals have a

pelt that is stiff coarse and protective against cold water.
graceful
the ^ crabeater seal, however, is a playful swimmer, whereas

the elephant seal is awkword and clumsy looking. ~~It is~~

~~clumsy looking~~ even swiming in water. Crabeater seals

are quite lovely, with their grayish white pelt and soft,

brown eyes. The 6,000–pound elephant seal on the other
terrifying
hand looks ~~weird,~~ especially when it inflated its snout and

howls! *Even though they are members of the same species, these two types of seals hardly seem related.*

WISE
WORD
CHOICE

Thinking Like a Writer

- What did Jill add to the beginning of her explanation? Why?
- Do you think the concluding sentence she added is effective? Why?
- Why do you think she changed a word?
- What sentences did she combine? Why do you think she combined them?

YOUR TURN

Read your first draft carefully and make any necessary revisions. Ask yourself these questions.

- How will adding or changing the topic sentence improve my explanation?
- What details do I need to add or rearrange to make my writing clearer?
- How can I improve my concluding sentence?
- What sentences can I combine to avoid repeating words?

If you wish, ask a friend or classmate to read your paragraph and make suggestions for improvements. Then revise your writing.

Proofread: Step 4

After Jill revised her first draft, she proofread her writing. She used a checklist and proofreading marks to make corrections.

Part of Jill's Proofread Draft

> <u>*graceful*</u>
> the crabeater seal, however, is a playful swimmer, whereas
> *awkward*
> the elephant seal is (awkword) and clumsy looking. ~~It is~~
> *swimming*
> ~~clumsy looking~~ even (swiming) in water. Crabeater seals
>
> are quite lovely, with their grayish white pelt and soft,
>
> brown eyes. The 6,000—pound elephant seal, on the other
> *terrifying* *inflates*
> hand, looks ~~weird,~~ especially when it ~~inflated~~ its snout and
> *Even though they are members of the same species,*
> howls! *these two types of seals hardly seem related.*

Thinking Like a Writer

- What punctuation marks did Jill add? Why?
- What word did she capitalize? Why?
- What spelling correction did she make?

YOUR TURN

Proofreading Practice

Proofread the following paragraph. Then write the paragraph, making all the necessary corrections.

> How do today's Lighthouses compare with those of the past. Lighthouses formerly had candles and oil lanterns that guided ships past danger. Today in contrast automatic beacons have replaced candles and lanterns. Whereas the lighthouse keeper once rung a bell by hand, now flashing buoys fog sirens and radio signals warn ships of approaching dangers.

Proofreading Checklist
- Did I indent each paragraph?
- Are all words spelled correctly?
- Did I use capital letters correctly?
- Did I use commas and other punctuation marks correctly?
- Did I use verbs and other parts of speech correctly?

THE WRITING PROCESS: Proofreading **205**

Applying Your Proofreading Skills

Proofread the explanation you have written. Review your proofreading checklist and **The Grammar Connection** and **The Mechanics Connection** below. Use the proofreading marks to make changes.

THE GRAMMAR CONNECTION

Remember these rules about using verbs correctly.

- Use verb tenses consistently. Avoid shifting between past, present, and future tenses.
- Use the past-tense form and past participle of irregular verbs carefully. A helping verb comes before the past participle to express action in the past, but it is not used before the past tense.

The elephant seal **looks** terrifying when it **inflates** its snout. The class **had seen** a film. We **saw** some seals.

Check your explanation. Have you used verb forms correctly?

THE MECHANICS CONNECTION

Remember these rules about using commas.

- Use commas to separate words in a series.
- Use commas to set off introductory words, nouns of direct address, and interrupting words.

Do hair seals have pelts that are coarse, stiff, and protective? Yes, they do, Manuel. Fur seals, in contrast, have soft pelts.

Review your writing. Have you used commas correctly?

Proofreading Marks
Indent ¶
Add ∧
Add a comma ∧
Add quotation marks ⱽ ⱽ
Add a period ⊙
Take out ℐ
Capitalize ≡
Lower-case letter /
Reverse the order ∩

Publish: Step 5

Jill used her mother's typewriter to make a neat, final copy of her writing. Then she used the photocopier at the library to make a copy for each member of her science club. At the next meeting of the club, she distributed the copies. She also placed a copy of her work in a notebook of articles and information that the science club kept.

After reading her composition about seals, several members of her science club decided they wanted to visit the city aquarium to examine seals for themselves.

YOUR TURN

Make a final copy of your explanation. Write as neatly as you can, or use a typewriter or computer. Then decide on a good way to share your writing. The **Sharing Suggestions** box below may give you some ideas.

SHARING SUGGESTIONS

Illustrate your explanation with drawings, diagrams, or photographs and share it with your friends and family.	With your classmates use your explanations to create a notebook of information called "Facts on File."	Give an oral presentation of your writing to your class or another class.

4 SPEAKING AND LISTENING: Giving Instructions

Explanations can give facts by telling how something works or by comparing and contrasting two subjects. Explanations can also give instructions or directions about how to do something. Perhaps you have had to give someone directions for reaching a certain location or for playing a certain sport. You may have tried to teach someone how to create something. Writing instructions and giving them orally involve many of the same steps.

First you must consider your purpose and the audience who will be listening to your instructions. Think about the information they will need to know to follow your instructions. Then review the steps involved in your instructions. Be sure that you include each step and arrange the steps in a logical order. You may wish to write down notes to make sure you have included all the necessary information. One student's notes are shown below.

Topic: How to collect salt from sea water

Audience: Group of fourth graders
— Set clear, shallow bowl in sunny window.
— Leave bowl uncovered.
— First fill bowl with sea water.
— Water evaporates.
— Bowl will look filmy—— salt and ocean chemicals.
— To get more salt, keep adding sea water.

- Why is it important to arrange the steps in a set of instructions in the right order?
- How will the writer have to rearrange the notes that are shown above?

When you give instructions orally, keep the following guidelines in mind. They will help you plan and deliver your instructions effectively.

SPEAKING GUIDELINES: Giving Instructions

1. Remember your purpose is to give clear information.
2. State your topic in the first sentence.
3. Consider what your specific audience will need to know.
4. Plan the steps in your instructions. Arrange the steps in the right order. Be sure they are complete. Practice your talk.
5. Speak in a clear, audible voice. Look at your listeners.

One student organized her notes and gave the following instructions to a group of fourth-grade students.

How to Collect Salt from Seawater

You can collect salt from ocean water by doing a simple experiment. First fill a jar with seawater. Then pour some of the water into a clear bowl. Now set the bowl in a sunny window. Each day you will see that the water level is a little lower. This is because water evaporates into the air. When all the water is gone from the bowl, the glass will look unclear. The film on the glass comes from the chemicals that were in the water. Most of the leftover chemical film is made up of salt. To get more salt, keep adding ocean water to the bowl as the water evaporates. As more water evaporates, more salt gathers in the bowl.

 SPEAKING APPLICATION Giving Instructions

Using your classmates as an audience, prepare a set of instructions about how to do or make something. Use the Speaking Guidelines above to help you. Your classmates will be using the guidelines below as they listen.

LISTENING GUIDELINES: Instructions

1. Listen for each step in the instructions.
2. Listen for the order of each step.
3. Take notes to remember information.
4. Repeat the instructions to yourself or to the speaker to make sure you have understood them.

Writing About Science

Scientists are people who seek explanations and want to know how things work. As a matter of fact, the word "science" comes from a Latin word meaning "to know." Sometimes scientists explain things by comparing and contrasting new discoveries to something more familiar. For example, when scientists first found the platypus, a strange, furry, duckbilled creature, they compared it to a duck to figure out what it could be.

Modern science is divided into two categories, "pure" and "applied." People who study the "pure" sciences try to explain how something works; people who study the "applied" sciences apply those theories to daily life. Working together, scientists have been able to make many important and useful discoveries.

ACTIVITIES

Make a Catalog

You may have seen expensive, oddly shaped yellow bath sponges in the stores. These are natural sponges that come from the sea. Sponges are animals that "breathe" water containing air and food through little holes, called pores, in their bodies. Only a few kinds are useful as bath sponges. Divers collect sponges from the sea bed. Living sponges are grayish and slimy. They are washed and stamped on, or beaten, to clean them. The clean, yellow part of the sponge that we use is its skeleton. The skeletons are trimmed to make nice shapes and sent all over the world.

Make or collect pictures that show useful items that come directly from nature. Label the source and use of each item.

Create an Invention

Imagine that you have just created an invention that is going to replace a well-known device. First explain how to use your invention. Then show how your invention is similar but different from the product that is now available. What makes yours so much better? Make a diagram or model of your invention and explain it.

Respond to Literature

Some myths, like this African folk tale, give imaginative explanations of various aspects of nature.

Where the Stars Came From

It was evening time, but Effion at once called the townspeople together and said, "I have a thing here which is worth a great price."

They cried, "Let us see it."

He brought the cap outside and opened it before them. All the shining things fell out. As they fell, a strong breeze came and caught them and blew them all over the town. They lay on the roads and on the floors of the compounds, each like a little star.

All the children came round and began picking them up. They gathered and gathered. In the daytime they could not see them, but every night they went out and sought for the shining things. All that they picked up they put in a box. At length many had been gathered together and they shone like a little sun in the box. At the end of about a month nearly all had been collected. They could not shut down the lid, however, because the box was too full, so when a great breeze came by it blew all the shining things about again. That is why sometimes we have a small moon and plenty of stars shining around it, while sometimes we have a big moon and hardly any stars are to be seen. The children take a month to fill the box again.

Write a response to the folk tale. You might write a continuation of the story or a scientific explanation of a related topic.

UNIT CHECKUP

Group Writing: An Explanatory Paragraph (page 194)
Imagine that you are planning to explain how to tap the ocean's energy. You wish to explain that the ocean has un-limited energy but that it is very difficult and expensive to harness. Write a topic sentence. Then decide which of the following details you would use in your explanation. Write those details on a separate piece of paper.

1. energy spread through huge volumes of water
2. heat in Gulf of Mexico could produce 30% of electricity used in U.S.
3. waves striking 60-mile coastline could power a million homes
4. 100 pounds of seaweed yields one pound methane gas
5. solar energy can also be harnessed   not related

Thinking: Comparing and Contrasting (page 198)   Write a paragraph comparing apples and pears. Use the notes below and add your own.

Similarities

Excellent low calorie snack foods; 100 calories per piece.

Both have yellow and red varieties.

Grow on trees about 40–50 feet high.

Have white blossoms on trees in the spring.

Writing an Explanatory Paragraph (page 200)   Compare and contrast two related sports or two similar games that you enjoy. Explore the topic and organize your notes. Be sure to write a topic sentence that states your main idea. Use logical transition words to connect your ideas. Write a concluding sentence that summarizes your main idea. Revise and proof-read your work carefully.

Speaking and Listening: Giving Instructions (page 208)   In a paragraph summarize the important points to remember for giving oral instructions effectively.

THEME PROJECT

SEA STORIES

The sea has challenged many scientists to explain its mysteries. The sea has also played a part in many stories, poems, and plays throughout history. Read the following poem about the sea.

All Day I Hear

All day I hear the noise of waters
   Making moan,
Sad as the sea-bird is, when going
   Forth alone,
He hears the wind cry to the waters'
   Monotone.

The grey winds, the cold winds are blowing
   Where I go.
I hear the noise of many waters
   Far below.
All day, all night I hear them flowing
   To and fro.

—James Joyce

With your classmates, discuss your favorite stories, poems, movies, or songs that have portrayed the sea. Compare and contrast the thoughts and feelings that these works express.

Choose one of the projects below, or create one of your own.

- Make a collection of stories, poems, or song lyrics about the sea. Include an introduction that explains their histories.
- Write a sea tale about a ghost ship or sunken treasure.
- Explain the rules for safe conduct at a beach. Make a poster.

UNIT

7

Pronouns

In this unit you will learn about pronouns. Since pronouns function as nouns in sentences, they can be used in your writing when you want to avoid repeating nouns.

Discuss Read the poem on the opposite page. Why are dreams so important to success?

Creative Expression The unit theme is *Challenges*. Think about your friends and your family. What challenges have they faced? Whom do you admire the most? In your journal explain why you admire this person.

JOURNAL

Gold Medalist

*In all my endeavor
I wish to be ever
A straight arrow spearing
Just past the possible.*

—Lillian Morrison

1 PERSONAL PRONOUNS

A pronoun is a word that takes the place of one or more nouns and the words that go with the nouns.

To avoid repeating words in your sentences, you can sometimes replace nouns with pronouns. A **pronoun** is a word that can take the place of one or more nouns. Personal pronouns are pronouns that refer primarily to persons.

> Rita likes books. **She** collects biographies.
> Tim and Sue bought a new book. **They** read often.

Some personal pronouns are used as the subjects of sentences. These are called **subject pronouns.**

> Tim owns several dictionaries. **He** enjoys words.

Other personal pronouns are used as objects of verbs or as the objects of prepositions. These are called **object pronouns.**

> Al has a book of poems. Lila gave **it** to **him.**

Subject Pronouns		Object Pronouns	
Singular	Plural	Singular	Plural
I	we	me	us
you	you	you	you
he, she, it	they	him, her, it	them

Guided Practice

Name a personal pronoun to use in place of the underlined word or words.

Example: <u>Mr. Phelps</u> is our drama coach.   *He*

1. <u>Sarah Bernhardt</u> was a world-famous actress.
2. A few early recordings by <u>Sarah Bernhardt</u> exist.
3. The "divine" Sarah played <u>many roles</u> on stage.
4. Her portrayal of <u>Hamlet</u> astonished the critics.
5. <u>Such performances</u> brought her international fame.

?! THINK

- How do I know whether to use a subject pronoun or an object pronoun?

REMEMBER

- A **pronoun** takes the place of one or more nouns and the words that go with them.
- Use a **subject pronoun** as the subject of a sentence. Use an **object pronoun** as the object of a verb or preposition.

More Practice

A. Write what pronoun you could use in place of the underlined words in each sentence.

Example: <u>Sarah Bernhardt</u> was born Rosine Bernhard. *She*

 6. <u>Thomas Edison</u> recorded the voice of Bernhardt.
 7. <u>These recordings</u> are rare collectors' items.
 8. Many photographs of <u>Sarah Bernhardt</u> exist.
 9. The photographs show <u>the leading lady</u> in costume.
10. <u>Ellen Terry and Eleanora Duse</u> were rivals of Sarah's.
11. <u>Sarah Bernhardt</u> was friends with <u>Ellen Terry</u>.
12. <u>Sarah's biographers</u> praise the <u>actress</u>.

B. Write each sentence, replacing the underlined word or words with the correct pronoun. Label each pronoun **subject** pronoun or **object** pronoun.

Example: The acting coach told <u>Tim and me</u> about Bernhardt. *us object pronoun*

13. <u>Today's actors</u> are great admirers of Bernhardt and her acting powers.
14. Elena read an article by <u>John Gielgud</u>.
15. <u>Elena</u> must find other articles for a class report.
16. <u>Steven</u> is Elena's partner on this project.
17. <u>The two</u> have become very curious about <u>Bernhardt</u>.
18. <u>Elena and Steven</u> were amazed by her early debut.
19. <u>The young girl</u> acted on <u>the French stage</u> at fourteen.
20. Fifty years later <u>audiences</u> still cheered and admired <u>Bernhardt</u>.

Extra Practice, page 242

WRITING APPLICATION A Summary

Write a summary of a scene from a movie or play in which you would like to star. Then share your summary with a classmate and identify the personal pronouns in each other's work.

2 PRONOUNS AND ANTECEDENTS

Pronouns help you refer back to nouns in other sentences. The noun that a pronoun refers to is called the **antecedent** of the pronoun. The antecedent includes any words that go with the noun.

ANTECEDENTS	PRONOUNS
The book lists inventors.	**It** is fascinating.
Robert Fulton was included.	**He** invented the steamboat.
Fulton and Bell changed America.	**They** were geniuses.

A pronoun must agree with its antecedent in number and gender. A pronoun may be singular or plural in **number** and masculine (male), feminine (female), or neuter (referring to things) in **gender.**

> **Mrs. Peters** is a librarian. **She** recommends books.
> I like reading about **inventors. They** inspire me to think creatively.

When you use pronouns, make sure that their antecedents are clear.

Guided Practice

Complete the second sentence in each pair by giving the correct personal pronoun.

Example: Janet is interested in science. ____ knows all about inventors.   *She*

1. Alexander Graham Bell was a tireless inventor. ____ invented more than just the telephone.
2. Bell also did research on other machines. ____ included the airplane and the phonograph.
3. In addition, Bell worked on a hydrofoil. ____ was not a success.
4. Maria is reading a biography of Bell. ____ will lend it to me next week.

 THINK

■ How do I choose a pronoun that refers clearly back to its antecedent?

REMEMBER

- An **antecedent** is a word or group of words to which a pronoun refers.
- A pronoun must always agree with its antecedent in number and gender.

More Practice

A. Complete the second sentence in each pair by writing the correct pronoun or pronouns.

Example: Bell married Mabel Hubbard. ___ lost her hearing from scarlet fever. *She*

5. Alexander Graham Bell was also a teacher of the deaf. ___ married a deaf woman.
6. Bell's wife had been one of his students. ___ assisted Bell in his work with the deaf.
7. Helen Keller and Bell were friends. ___ snared an interest.
8. Keller gave Bell special insight. ___ learned from ___.

B. Write the sentences. Complete the second sentence of each pair with a pronoun, underlining its antecedent.

Example: Bell's <u>mother</u> was an accomplished musician. ___ was also an artist. *She*

9. Bell made a great deal of money. For ___ money provided opportunity.
10. He funded magazines like *Science* and *National Geographic*. ___ would not have survived otherwise.
11. Charles Babbage built an early computing machine. ___ was called a "difference engine."
12. Babbage was English. ___ was born in 1791.
13. Ada Lovelace was the daughter of the poet Lord Byron. ___ was as gifted a mathematician as ___ was a writer.
14. There was no program for Babbage's machine. Ada Lovelace helped ___ by writing one.

Extra Practice, page 243

WRITING APPLICATION An Explanation

Explain the purpose of a recent invention in a brief paragraph. Ask a classmate to help you make sure that all pronouns agree with their antecedents.

3 USING PRONOUNS CORRECTLY

You have learned that subject pronouns are used as subjects of sentences and that object pronouns are used as objects of verbs and of prepositions. This is still true even when the subjects or objects are compound.

> Beth and **he** took speech class together.
> Bob and **she** are on the same debate team.
> The school reporter commended Laura and **him.**
> Their points were convincing to the judges and **us.**

If you are not sure which pronoun to use, say the sentence to yourself with only the subject pronoun or object pronoun. Your ear may help you decide which form is correct.

If the pronoun *I* or *me* is part of a compound subject or object, it is polite to put it last.

> David and **I** will represent our school.
> Will you listen to David and **me?**

In formal writing use a subject pronoun after a linking verb.

> My opponent was **she.**
> The last judges were **they.**

Guided Practice

Choose the correct pronoun or pronouns for each sentence listed below.

Example: Margaret and (her, she) competed. *she*

  1. My brother and (I, me) are interested in chess and play together quite often.
  2. (He and I, I and he) play chess together, like young Bobby Fischer and his sister.
  3. Bobby's teacher was (she, her).
  4. Bobby Fischer is a hero to my brother and (I, me).
  5. His championship play amazed his rivals and (we, us).

?! THINK

- How do I decide which pronoun to use in a compound subject or object?

REMEMBER

- If a pronoun is part of a compound subject, use a subject pronoun.
- If a pronoun is part of a compound object, use an object pronoun.
- Use the pronoun *I* or *me* last in a compound subject or object.

More Practice

A. Write the correct pronoun or pronouns for each sentence.

Example: Tony and (her, <u>she</u>) hope to become athletes.

6. My class and (I, me) are studying sports heroes.
7. (Elena and I, I and Elena) began with tennis.
8. Both Guillermo Villas and (she, her) are Argentines.
9. Golfing is also intriguing to (she, her).
10. The teacher asked Ed and (she, her) about golf pros.
11. The choice for a report was between (they, them) and amateurs.
12. The best researcher in class is (her, she).

B. Write each sentence, using the correct pronouns. Label your choice **subject pronoun** or **object pronoun.**

Example: Sally and (me, <u>I</u>) used to root for baseball player Ray Knight. *subject pronoun*

13. Nancy Lopez interested (her and me, she and I).
14. Ed talked about (she, her) in class.
15. Jim and (I, me) knew all about their careers.
16. Clyde and (they, them) chose versatile Herschel Walker.
17. I became interested in (he, him) and his sister.
18. Like my brother and (I, me), Veronica Walker was a runner.
19. Both Herschel and (she, her) won amateur titles.
20. In 1982 the college athlete who won the 50-meter dash was (he, him).
21. The teacher praised (me and them, them and I, them and me) for our reports.

Extra Practice, Practice Plus, pages 244–245

WRITING APPLICATION A Narrative

Think of a time when you worked with others to achieve a goal. Write about your experience in a narrative. Ask a classmate to check your use of pronouns in compounds.

4 POSSESSIVE PRONOUNS

Pronouns that show who or what has or owns something are called **possessive pronouns.** A possessive pronoun can take the place of a possessive noun.

POSSESSIVE NOUN	POSSESSIVE PRONOUN
Lincoln's speech is famous.	**His** speech is famous.
This pen is **Ramona's.**	This pen is **hers.**

Possessive pronouns have two forms. One is used before a noun. The other form is used alone.

Possessive Pronouns			
Used Before Nouns		**Stand Alone**	
my	our	mine	ours
your	your	yours	yours
his, her, its	their	his, hers, its	theirs

Possessive pronouns never have apostrophes, as possessive nouns do. Do not confuse pronoun contractions, such as *it's* and *you're*, with possessive pronouns.

> Read **Irene's** report on Nat Turner.   (possessive noun)
> **Its** subject is not widely known.   (possessive pronoun)
> **It's** very informative.   (contraction of *It is*)

Guided Practice

Name the possessive pronoun in each sentence. Tell whether it comes before a noun or stands alone.

Example: Who is your favorite figure in history?
your   before a noun

1. Her name is Sojourner Truth and she had a mission.
2. Few people have possessed courage like hers.
3. She told Americans a truth about their country.
4. Ours is a history of individual struggle.

 THINK

- How can I tell the difference between a possessive pronoun and a contraction?

REMEMBER

- A **possessive pronoun** shows who or what owns something.
- Possessive pronouns can come before a noun or stand alone.
- Possessive pronouns never have apostrophes.

More Practice

A. Write the possessive pronoun in each sentence. Tell whether it comes before a noun or stands alone.

Example: Her real name was Isabella Baumfree.
     her before a noun

5. My oral report is about Sojourner Truth.
6. Her mission was the abolition of slavery.
7. Hers was a life of toil and achievement.
8. A victim of slavery, she denounced its evil effects.
9. Frederick Douglass was a friend of hers.
10. His valuable work affected many blacks.
11. The abolitionists welcomed her voice among them.
12. It's the aim of this report to convey her powerful presence.

B. Write each sentence, replacing each underlined possessive noun with the correct possessive pronoun.

Example: Truth helped to improve the blacks' living conditions. *their*

13. The other class completed written reports; this class's reports are oral.
14. Sojourner's eloquence, wit, and energy were remarkable.
15. Sojourner moved audiences; they became Sojourner's.
16. Slaveholders defended slaveholders' views.
17. Leon's report discusses the Dred Scott case.
18. Dred Scott was suing for Scott's right to be free.
19. That case's effect was to uphold slaveholders' rights.
20. When all the students had given the students' reports, I said to Leon, "I especially enjoyed hearing Leon's."

Extra Practice, page 246

WRITING APPLICATION A Speech

Research the achievement of a historical figure and write a brief speech explaining why this person should be remembered. Ask a partner to check your work for the correct use of possessive pronouns.

5 INDEFINITE PRONOUNS

Most of the pronouns you use refer to specific antecedents. An **indefinite pronoun** does not refer to a particular
person, place, or thing.

	Indefinite Pronouns				
Singular	another anybody anyone	each either everyone	everything much neither	nobody no one nothing	one someone something
Plural	both	few	many	others	several
Singular or Plural	all	any	most	none	some

Some indefinite pronouns can be singular or plural, depending on the phrase that follows the pronoun.

Most of Gandhi's life is well known.   *singular*
Most of his listeners were inspired.   *plural*

Whenever you use possessive pronouns with indefinite
pronouns, you must make sure they agree with their antecedents in number and gender.

Many read **their** reports aloud.   *plural*
Each reads **his** or **her** report.   *masculine or feminine*
Each of the girls raised **her** hand.   *feminine*

Guided Practice

Name each singular and plural indefinite pronoun.

Example: Few missed the speech.   *few   plural*

1. Many have devoted their lives to Gandhi's ideals.
2. No one has dedicated his or her life as totally as he did.
3. Most of his followers have their own religions.
4. Everybody has an interpretation of his words.

?! THINK

■ How do I decide which possessive pronoun to use with an
indefinite pronoun?

REMEMBER

- An **indefinite pronoun** does not refer to a particular person, place, or thing.
- Any possessive pronouns used with an indefinite pronoun must agree with it in number and gender.

More Practice

A. Write the indefinite pronoun in each sentence. Then write whether it is **singular** or **plural.**

Example: You cannot learn everything in one year.
$\qquad$ *everything   singular*

5. Everybody needs role models.
6. Few can live without heroes or leaders.
7. Some of my friends look up to politicians.
8. Others find their inspiration in literature.
9. Everyone can embrace a religion.
10. Each can also search his or her own conscience.
11. All of the true seekers have found unique answers.
12. Any of the great philosophers offer wisdom.

B. Write each sentence, completing it with the correct possessive pronoun or pronouns. Then underline the indefinite pronoun and write whether it is **singular** or **plural.**

Example: Each must examine _____ beliefs.
$\qquad$ *his or her   singular*

13. Several of the world's leaders have left ____ mark on masses of people.
14. Others leave behind only ____ names.
15. Everyone must concentrate on ____ own purpose in life.
16. No one is free from the effects of ____ actions.
17. Few can afford to ignore ____ futures.
18. Some of my friends discuss ____ favorite presidents.
19. Most of the world's leaders uphold ____ responsibility.
20. None of them will be judged on ____ words alone.

Extra Practice, page 247

WRITING APPLICATION An Interview

With a partner, write an imaginary interview with a person you admire. Check to make sure you have used indefinite pronouns correctly. Present your interview orally.

COOPERATIVE
LEARNING

6 SUBJECT-VERB AGREEMENT WITH INDEFINITE PRONOUNS

You have learned that every verb must agree with its subject. When the subject is an indefinite pronoun, the verb must agree with it. Singular indefinite pronouns take singular verbs. Plural indefinite pronouns take plural verbs. Some indefinite pronouns can be singular or plural, depending on the phrase that follows them.

> **Each** of the stories *has* a good plot.
> **All** of them *deserve* to be read.

	Indefinite Pronouns
Singular	**Everyone** *likes* a good story. **Each** of the girls *has* her favorite **Nothing** *entertains* me more.
Plural	**Many** *tell* memorable tales. **Others** *listen* well. **Few** *write* down their stories.
Singular or Plural	**All** of this book *is* well written. (*singular*) **All** of these writers *are* wonderful. (*plural*) **Some** of the plot *was* confusing. (*singular*) **Some** of the characters *surprise* the reader. (*plural*)

Guided Practice

Tell which verb is correct in each sentence.

Example: Many (like, likes) English class.   *like*

1. Most of the students (take, takes) history class.
2. Some of American history (fascinate, fascinates) me and the other members of my class.
3. Each of the early patriots (has, have) a story.
4. Few (knows, know) many facts about those who wrote the Constitution.

 THINK

- How do I decide whether to use a singular or plural verb with an indefinite pronoun?

REMEMBER

- Use a singular verb with a singular indefinite pronoun.
- Use a plural verb with a plural indefinite pronoun.
- With indefinite pronouns that can be singular or plural, look at the phrase that follows the pronoun to decide whether to use a singular or plural verb.

More Practice

A. Write the correct form of the verb for each sentence.

Example: Someone (<u>was</u>, were) blocking our view.

5. None of the students (knows, know) all 39 signers of the Constitution.
6. Everybody (name, names) Jefferson and Washington.
7. Both (is, are) well-known founding fathers.
8. Most of my classmates also (mentions, mention) Hamilton.
9. Many (suggest, suggests) Benjamin Franklin.
10. Few (remembers, remember) James Madison of Virginia.
11. Neither of these two states (were, was) represented.
12. All of the other signers (is, are) unnamed, and some of those named (was, were) not actually signers.

B. Write each sentence, using the correct form of the verb. Explain your answer.

Example: Many (<u>know</u>, knows) about Patrick Henry.

13. Some of the facts about Patrick Henry (was, were) known.
14. Several (think, thinks) about his situation.
15. No one (understand, understands) Henry's opinions.
16. Perhaps none of Henry's distrust (was, were) realistic.
17. Some of the delegates (does, do) not sign.
18. One of the nonsigners (was, were) Edmund Randolph.
19. Most of his reluctance (was, were) just caution.
20. None of his fears (prove, proves) necessary.

Extra Practice, page 248

WRITING APPLICATION An Editorial

Imagine that you are participating in an important historical event. Write a newspaper editorial telling your thoughts on this occasion. Exchange papers with a classmate and check each other's work to make sure each verb agrees with its subject.

7 REFLEXIVE AND INTENSIVE PRONOUNS

Some pronouns are like mirrors. They reflect the action of the verb back to the subject. These pronouns are called **reflexive pronouns.**

> Karl reminded **himself** about the party.

Reflexive Pronouns	
Singular	**Plural**
myself	ourselves
yourself	yourselves
himself, herself, itself	themselves

Avoid using *hisself* for *himself* and *theirselves* for *themselves.*

The pronouns in the chart above may also be used to intensify a statement. An **intensive pronoun** adds emphasis to a noun or pronoun already named.

> The students **themselves** organized the assembly.

Do not use a reflexive or intensive pronoun where a subject or an object pronoun belongs.

> CORRECT: Al and **I** sang.
> Show Al and **me.**
> INCORRECT: Al and myself sang.
> Show Al and myself.

Guided Practice

Name the correct pronoun for each sentence.

Example: Wildlife interests Ann and (myself, me).   *me*

1. I treated (me, myself) to a book on Joy Adamson.
2. My friends and (I, myself) found her story exciting.
3. Adamson (her, herself) wrote a book.
4. Her descriptions gave (us, ourselves) pleasure.

THINK

- How can I tell whether a pronoun in a sentence is being used as a reflexive pronoun or an intensive pronoun?

REMEMBER

- A **reflexive pronoun** directs the action of the verb back to the subject.
- An **intensive pronoun** adds emphasis to a noun or pronoun already named.

More Practice

A. Write the correct pronoun for each sentence.

Example: We (us, <u>ourselves</u>) liked this biography best.

5. Joy found (her, herself) bored at home in Vienna.
6. (She, Herself) had studied Africa in books.
7. Now she set out for the wilds of Africa (it, itself).
8. George Adamson asked (her, herself) for her hand in marriage.
9. Joy and (he, himself) made Kenya their home.
10. George Adamson (hisself, himself) was a botanist.
11. The game preserves (themselves, theirselves) were an entire world.
12. George (he, himself) asked Joy to raise the lion cub, Elsa.

B. Write each sentence, using the correct pronoun. Label each as a **reflexive, intensive, subject,** or **object** pronoun.

Example: We tired (us, <u>ourselves</u>) setting up the campsite. _reflexive_

13. At first (you, yourself) may doubt the story about Elsa.
14. Several of (us, ourselves) saw the movie _Born Free._
15. The movie (it, itself) shows how the bond developed.
16. Joy (her, herself) returned Elsa to the wild.
17. Elsa later brought (her, herself) back to the camp.
18. (She, Herself) and her cubs became regular visitors.
19. Rita and (I, myself) became very interested in the cubs.
20. After all, they were being reared by Elsa (her, herself), a lion raised in captivity.

Extra Practice, page 249

WRITING APPLICATION A Story

Imagine that you owned a magic mirror that could predict the future of whomever looked into it. With a group of classmates write a brief story in which several characters use the mirror. Check your work to make sure you have used reflexive pronouns correctly.

COOPERATIVE
LEARNING

8 INTERROGATIVE AND DEMONSTRATIVE PRONOUNS

Sometimes you use pronouns to help you ask questions. An **interrogative pronoun** is a pronoun that introduces an interrogative sentence.

Who owns the pen?   **Whose** is the paper?
Whom did you call?   **Which** is yours?
For **whom** did you ask?   **What** is it?

Be careful when you use *who* and *whom*. Use *who* as the subject of a sentence. Use *whom* as the object of a verb or the object of a preposition.

Do not confuse the interrogative pronoun *whose* with *who's*, which is the contraction of *who is*.

Whose is this jacket? **Who's** the girl in red?

Demonstrative pronouns point out things. *This* (singular) and *these* (plural) point out something nearby. *That* (singular) and *those* (plural) point out something at a distance.

This is a good apple.   **That** is a new chair.
These are good apples.   **Those** are new chairs.

If *this, that, these,* or *those* is used directly before a noun rather than in place of a noun, it is functioning as an adjective rather than as a pronoun.

This is a huge building.   (*demonstrative pronoun*)
This building is huge.   (*demonstrative adjective*)

Guided Practice

Identify the interrogative pronoun or demonstrative pronoun in each sentence.

Example: Whom did Sheila call?   *whom*   *interrogative*

1. Who wrote the first American speller?
2. Whose is the name on many dictionaries?
3. These are interesting questions.
4. What was Noah Webster's lifelong ambition?

?! THINK

- How can I tell if a pronoun is an interrogative pronoun or a demonstrative pronoun?

 REMEMBER

- An **interrogative pronoun** is a pronoun that introduces an interrogative sentence.
- A **demonstrative pronoun** points out something and stands alone in a sentence.

More Practice

A. Write the correct word for each sentence.

Example: To (who, whom) did you give the dictionary?

whom

5. (Who's, Whose) Noah Webster and when did he live?
6. (Who, Whom) wrote a report about him?
7. (This, These) are a few facts about Webster.
8. (That, Those) was the best biography of him.
9. To (who, whom) did you give the dictionary?
10. (Who's, Whose) copy is this?
11. (Who, Whom) wrote the first dictionary?
12. From (who, whom) did you get that fact?

B. Write each sentence, choosing the correct word. Then write whether your choice is an **interrogative pronoun, contraction,** or **demonstrative pronoun.**

Example: (Whose, <u>Who's</u>) that author? *contraction*

13. (Who, Whom) are the experts on American English?
14. (These, What) is the origin of many place-names?
15. From (who, whom) did we get names for some of the most common plants?
16. (This, These) were Native American names.
17. (Which, Who's) culture contributed the words *adobe* and *patio*?
18. (That, Those) words come from Spanish.
19. (Who's, Whose) shaping American English today?
20. (Whose, Who's) influences are the strongest?

Extra Practice, page 250

WRITING APPLICATION An Interview

Imagine that you will interview a person whose achievements have changed society. Write a series of questions that you would ask in the interview. Ask a classmate to check your work for the correct use of interrogative and demonstrative pronouns.

9 MECHANICS: Using Abbreviations

An **abbreviation** is the shortened form of a word.

Many abbreviations begin with a capital letter and end with a period.

Titles	**M**s. Vivian Huang **D**r. Carl Baird
	Mr. Donald Newell, **Jr.** **M**rs. Elias
Days	**S**un. **M**on. **T**ues. **W**ed. **T**hurs.
Months	**J**an. **A**pr. **O**ct. **N**ov. **D**ec.
Streets	**S**t. **A**ve. **D**r. **B**lvd. **R**d.
Businesses	**I**nc. **C**orp. **C**o.

Some abbreviations use capital letters and periods.

Titles	Nora Brown, **M.D.** Donald Lam, **R.N.**
Times	8:45 **A.M.** 6:30 **P.M.** 30 **B.C.** **A.D.** 476

Other abbreviations use capital letters and no periods.

Agencies and Organizations	**CORE** (**C**ongress **o**f **R**acial **E**quality)
	CBS (**C**olumbia **B**roadcasting **S**ystem)
States	**TX** (Texas) **CA** (California) **OH** (Ohio)

Abbreviations for many units of measure begin with a small letter and end with a period, as in **ft.** (for *foot* or *feet*), **qt.** (for *quart* or *quarts*), and **lb.** (for *pound* or *pounds*).

Guided Practice

Name the word that can be abbreviated in each item. Then tell the abbreviation for the word.

Example: Doctor Janeth Rouzer   *Dr.*

1. October 23, 1990
2. El Paso, Texas
3. 23 Elm Street
4. Anthony White, Junior

 THINK

■ How do I write abbreviations of certain words?

REMEMBER

- An **abbreviation** is the shortened form of a word.
- Many abbreviations begin with a capital letter and end with a period. If necessary, check a dictionary for abbreviations.

More Practice

A. Find the word or words that can be abbreviated in each item. Then write the abbreviation.

Example: the Wright brothers   *bros.*

5. one pound
6. three feet
7. Toledo, Ohio
8. 7:15 in the morning
9. Hudson Boulevard
10. Wednesday meeting
11. Mister Simon Wood

12. Shamrock Corporation
13. 5:30 in the evening
14. Mark Bloom, Registered Nurse
15. Actors and Writers, Incorporated
16. Columbia Broadcasting System.
17. the year 100 after Christ's birth
18. the year 39 before Christ's birth

B. Find the word or words in each sentence that can be abbreviated. Then write the abbreviation.

Example: Captain Linda Andrews is a helicopter pilot.   *Capt.*

19. Doctor Ann Mack started work on a new project today.
20. Ann and Al Lon, Junior, will study vitamins.
21. They will conduct research for Good Health Company.
22. Rick Funes, Medical Doctor, is the project director.
23. He is a member of the American Medical Association.
24. On Monday Rick ordered vitamins.
25. Fifty quarts of supplies will arrive.

Extra Practice, page 251

 WRITING APPLICATION A Chart

Look at the front page of a newspaper. With a partner, make a chart that shows the abbreviations of words you find there. Use categories such as *Titles* and *Days* in your chart. If necessary, use a dictionary to help you write abbreviations correctly.

10 BUILDING VOCABULARY: Homophones and Homographs

You have learned that words like *who's* and *whose* and *it's* and *its* are often confused because they sound alike but have different meanings. Words like these are called **homophones.**

stair—a step	one—a single unit
stare—to look at intently	won—gained a victory
road—street	
rode—was carried by a vehicle	
rowed—propelled a boat by using oars	

Other words cause confusion because they are spelled exactly alike but have different meanings. These words are called **homographs.** Some homographs also have different pronunciations.

hide—to shelter	bear—a furry animal
hide—an animal skin	bear—to endure
tire—a wheel	bow—to bend forward
tire—to become weary	bow—a weapon for shooting arrows

To understand the correct meaning of a homograph, you must study the context in which it appears.

I could not **bear** another moment of delay.
The **bear** was growling near the campsite.

Guided Practice

Tell which word in parentheses correctly completes each sentence.

Example: Did the thief (flea, flee)? *flee*

1. Our school's (principal, principle) set up a special project for the seventh-grade classes.
2. (Its, It's) purpose was to honor Martin Luther King, Jr.
3. We could choose our own (way, weigh) of taking part.
4. (Their, There) were many reports and speeches.

THINK

■ How can I decide which spelling of a homophone is correct in a sentence?

REMEMBER

- **Homophones** are words that sound alike but have different spellings and different meanings.
- **Homographs** are words that are spelled the same but have different meanings and sometimes different pronunciations.

More Practice

A. Write each sentence, choosing the correct word in parentheses. Use a dictionary to help you.

Example: (They're, <u>There</u>) is no milk left.

5. Rob (red, read) passages from King's speeches.
6. It was difficult to choose one (feet, feat) among so many fine achievements.
7. Which one does (you're, your) report cover?
8. (Sum, Some) students discussed the boycotts and marches.
9. These were (cymbals, symbols) of future events.
10. King served (wear, where) he was needed.
11. This man appealed to (hour, our) national conscience.
12. (Who's, Whose) lives were influenced by him?
13. You can (here, hear) his voice on recordings.
14. His message was one of (peace, piece) and justice.
15. It was a message for the (hole, whole) world.

B. For every homograph, write two sentences, each sentence illustrating a different meaning of the homograph. Use a dictionary if necessary.

Example: hide

Where did she hide? Is that the hide of a cow?

16. board
17. fair
18. wind
19. stable
20. bow

21. plane
22. note
23. pound
24. yard
25. count

Extra Practice, page 252

WRITING APPLICATION Sentences

Choose several pairs of homophones from this lesson, or think of some others. For each pair write a sentence that contains both words. Then exchange papers with a class-mate. Identify and define the homophones in each other's sentences.

Right margin: G R A M M A R

GRAMMAR
—AND
WRITING
CONNECTION

Combining Sentences

When you write facts about people, sometimes you can show a clearer connection between your ideas by combining information from two sentences. You can use *that, which,* or *who* when you add details to a sentence.

> **SEPARATE:** This author wrote a book.
> The book won a Pulitzer Prize.
>
> **COMBINED:** This author wrote a book **that won a Pulitzer Prize.**

Use *that* to add information that is essential to the sentence. Do not use commas to set off essential information. Use *which* to add information that is not essential to the sentence. Use commas to set off information that is not essential.

> **SEPARATE:** This copy belongs to Jeff.
> The copy looks well read.
>
> **COMBINED:** This copy, **which looks well read,** belongs to Jeff.

The word *who* may introduce information that is either essential or not essential. Use *who* when you are referring to people.

> Sophie reads about women **who have met challenges.**

Working Together

COOPERATIVE LEARNING

Combine each pair of sentences by using **that, which,** or **who.**

1. Clara Barton organized the American Red Cross.
   She did volunteer work during wartime.
2. Eleanor Roosevelt sat on a panel.
   The panel spoke out for human rights.
3. Dorothea Lange took this magnificent photograph.
   The photograph was shown at the Museum of Modern Art.

Revising Sentences

Combine each pair of sentences using **that, which,** or **who.** Add commas where they are needed.

4. Phoebe Butler was a sharpshooting star in the Wild West.
Phoebe Butler was known as Annie Oakley.

5. Leontyne Price sang an aria.
The aria won tremendous applause at the opera house.

6. Ida Tarbell was a reporter.
The reporter exposed corruption in industry.

7. *The Fannie Farmer Cookbook* helped thousands of people with their cooking.
The book first used standardized measurements in recipes.

8. Grandma Moses sold her first painting at 78.
Grandma Moses created colorful landscapes.

9. Wilma Rudolph won three Olympic gold medals.
The medals established her fame.

10. Georgia O'Keeffe painted pictures.
The pictures captured the starkness of the desert.

Think about some of the famous people that you have read about in this unit. What are the challenges that they encountered? Choose the one that interests you most and write a paragraph about that person.

When you revise your work, look for sentences that you can improve by combining them with *that, which,* or *who.* Be sure to add commas where they are needed.

UNIT CHECKUP

Personal Pronouns (page 216)   Write each sentence, replacing the underlined word with the correct pronoun.

1. Do you know about <u>any Indian tribes</u>?
2. <u>Sarah Winnemucca</u> was of the Southern Paiute tribe.
3. <u>Many tribes</u> lived in what is now Nevada.
4. A settler family gave <u>Sarah</u> a first name.
5. <u>Winnemucca</u> was her grandfather and head of the tribe.

2

Pronouns and Antecedents (page 218)   Fill in the blank with the correct pronoun. Underline its antecedent.

6. Sarah also had an Indian name. ____ was called Thocmetony.
7. At first, Chief Winnemucca was friendly with newcomers. chief invited ____ onto his land.
8. Winnemucca even accompanied Captain John Frémont on an expedition. ____ was an early explorer of California.
9. Sarah learned English. This helped ____.

3

Using Pronouns Correctly (page 220)   Choose the correct pronoun. Then write whether it is a **subject** or an **object pronoun.**

10. My sister and (I, me) are reading about the Paiutes.
11. (They, Them) and other tribes were sent to reservations.
12. Agents cheated the Northern Paiutes and (they, them).
13. Arthur and (we, us) are disturbed by this fact.
14. One of the protesters was (she, her).

4

Possessive Pronouns (page 222)   Replace each underlined possessive noun with the correct possessive pronoun.

15. <u>Sarah's</u> competence was a great benefit to the Paiutes.
16. She was able to speak up for the <u>people's</u> rights.
17. The <u>Paiutes'</u> was a difficult position for a small group.
18. The <u>protest's</u> immediate effect, however, was disastrous.

Indefinite Pronouns and Subject-Verb Agreement (pages 224, 226)   Write each sentence with the correct word. Underline each indefinite pronoun.

19. No one (was, were) surprised by the outbreak of war.
20. Most of her people had lost (his, their) patience.
21. A few of her tribe (was, were) still in favor of peace.
22. Everyone had (his or her, their) point of view.

Reflexive and Intensive Pronouns (page 228)   Write each sentence, using the correct pronoun. Write whether your choice is a **reflexive, intensive, subject,** or **object** pronoun.

23. Sarah found (her, herself) in need of General Howard.
24. General Howard and (she, herself) trusted each other.
25. Northern Paiutes had kidnapped the chief (hisself, himself).
26. (They, Themselves) had joined the Bannock uprising.
27. Would the soldiers (themselves, theirselves) free the chief?

Interrogative and Demonstrative Pronouns (page 230)   Choose the correct pronoun. Write whether your choice is an **interrogative** or **demonstrative** pronoun.

28. (Who, Whom) rescued Winnemucca?
29. (This, These) is the exciting part of the story.
30. (Who, What) can compare to a trek in the wilderness?
31. (Who, Whom) are we discussing?
32. (That, Those) were dangerous territories.

Mechanics: Abbreviations (page 232)   Find the word or words that can be abbreviated. Write the abbreviation.

33. Dallas, Texas
34. Friday, August 21
35. The Penny Company
36. Mister Sam Chen, Junior
37. 301 Evergreen Drive
38. 9:00 in the morning
39. 1 pound
40. Columbus, Ohio

Homophones and Homographs (page 234)   Choose the correct homophone. Write the meaning of the word you choose.

41. Sarah could not (bare, bear) the thought of being discovered.
42. She climbed cliffs with her (bear, bare) hands.
43. Fortunately for her this was not (bare, bear) country.
44. You will be happy to (here, hear) that she escaped.

Writing Application: Pronoun Usage (pages 216–231)
   The following paragraph contains 6 errors with pronouns. Rewrite the paragraph correctly.

45.–50.   The museum director hisself gave a lecture on the peaceful Paiute tribe. He said they're houses were cone-shaped. Members of the tribe hunted game and collected berries for theirself. I and Manuel imagined life in the Old West to be enchanting. "What you're forgetting is that the Paiutes' environment was very harsh," said the director to we and the audience. Most of the listeners was impressed.

PRONOUNS FIRST AND LAST

Have a pronouns sports match with a partner. One player makes a statement about sports or games. The statement must begin with a subject pronoun. The other player must then make a statement that ends with the object pronoun that corresponds with the subject pronoun.

For example: *I* like tennis. Football bores *me*.

Hunting Antecedents

Identifying pronoun antecedents in reading material can sometimes be tricky. Find a complicated newspaper article, editorial, or poem. Underline each pronoun in the selection and then circle its antecedent. Share your work with a partner to see if he or she agrees with your choices.

What's the Question?

Play this game with a partner. Choose a subject area such as social studies or science and have your textbook handy for use. One player makes a statement with an important fact missing, for example, *He invented the light bulb.* The other player must answer with a question, as in *Who is Thomas Edison?* Use subject, object, interrogative, and demonstrative pronouns correctly. The player who supplies the most correct questions wins.

WHO'S ON FIRST

Have you ever heard the Bud Abbott and Lou Costello comedy routine "Who's On First"? The whole joke is that the players in a baseball game are named *Who*, *What*, and so on.

Make up a comedy routine between two people. In it, make the joke revolve around a sports team made up of players who are named *Me*, *You*, *He*, *She*, *It*, and *They*. Here is an example of how you might begin the comedy routine:

Comedian One: Who is that player on second base?

Comedian Two: She is on second.

Comedian One: No, the girl is playing first base. Who is the boy playing second?

Comedian Two: I told you. She is.

Reflexive Ads

One of the most common uses for reflexive and intensive pronouns is in advertising. Advertisements often say things like this:

Make yourself more popular with Tootharama Toothpaste.

"I myself always used Tootharama," says Wilbert Smiley, star of movies and television. Wilbert always treats himself to a good brushing with Tootharama before stepping in front of the camera.

Write two advertisements for made-up products. Use the techniques advertisers use to try to sell your products. Use at least two reflexive or intensive pronouns in each of your advertisements.

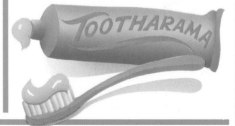

Perfect Pearl

Imagine that you are out with a friend's family celebrating the birthday of your friend's mother. Your friend's name is Lynn, and her mother's name is Mrs. Goodwin. Also at the dinner are Lynn's father and her brother, Carl. You have not brought a present for the mother. You order oysters, and one of them looks different from the others. You discover that it contains a perfect pearl. Write this event as a story. Try to use the names of all the people present. Use as many personal pronouns as possible.

EXTRA PRACTICE

Three levels of practice

Personal Pronouns (page 216)

LEVEL

A. Write the personal pronoun in each sentence.
1. She was the founder of a traveling theater company.
2. I am talking about actor-director Miriam Colon.
3. It is called The Puerto Rican Traveling Theatre.
4. Have you heard of this theater company?
5. They bring plays into New York City neighborhoods.
6. People in the city appreciate her.
7. Theater does not often come to them.
8. Almost any show thrills me.

LEVEL

B. Write the personal pronoun in each sentence. Then write whether the pronoun is a **subject** or **object** pronoun.

9. Miriam Colon has interested me for several years.
10. She was born in Puerto Rico and moved to New York.
11. At first, acting gave her complete satisfaction.
12. Later, the limited roles for Hispanics frustrated her.
13. There were not enough parts for them at the time.
14. It was a problem that cried out for an answer.
15. You know about Colon's solution.
16. The Traveling Theatre provided important work for her and many others.

LEVEL

C. Write each sentence, replacing the underlined word or words with the correct pronoun. Write whether you use a **subject** or **object** pronoun.

17. Miriam Colon also wanted to expose Hispanic culture to a wider audience.
18. The writers were waiting for this opportunity.
19. Plays by these authors needed an outlet.
20. The audience was found in the local schools and parks.
21. The success of the productions deeply gratified Miriam Colon.
22. Colon and her company really filled the needs of the audiences.
23. The Puerto Rican Traveling Theatre is just one of many successful community theaters.
24. Many small dance companies have formed across the country.
25. My sister recently joined a local company.

EXTRA PRACTICE

Three levels of practice

Pronouns and Antecedents (page 218)

LEVEL

A. Write the antecedent of the underlined pronoun.

1. Benjamin Franklin attended the Constitutional Convention of 1787. <u>He</u> was the oldest delegate.
2. The convention was held in Philadelphia. <u>It</u> is the city Americans associate with Franklin.
3. The delegates had an important matter to settle. The political future was up to <u>them</u>.
4. Jefferson and Washington were much younger than Franklin. <u>They</u> would live to govern the nation.
5. The new country needed leaders. <u>It</u> found <u>them</u> in these men.

LEVEL

B. Write each personal pronoun and its antecedent.

6. My classmates admired much about Franklin. They were amazed at his achievements.
7. Benjamin Franklin was not really a politician. He was a philosopher, diplomat, and man of letters.
8. The younger men saw Franklin as their representative statesman. They wanted Franklin to endorse the new Constitution.
9. Franklin spoke with the arguing delegates. To him the success of the Constitution depended on an agreement of minds.
10. The new Constitution caused a great deal of controversy. Of course, it continues to do so today.

LEVEL

C. Write the following sentences, filling the blanks with the correct pronouns. Then write the antecedent of each pronoun you supply.

11. From 1775 to 1785 Franklin was a commissioner to the French court. The French greatly approved of ____.
12. In 1778 John Adams was appointed as a second commissioner to the French. ____ was not liked as well by ____.
13. John Adams wrote to Abigail Adams about the manners of the French. Later ____ joined ____ in Paris.
14. Abigail Adams learned to respect a people very foreign to ____. ____ proved capable of adapting to changes.
15. The students presented a scene from the colonial period. ____ used costumes and props.

Three levels of practice

Using Pronouns Correctly (page 220)

LEVEL

A. Write the correct pronoun or pronouns.

1. Laura and (I, me) are birdwatchers.
2. (I and she, She and I) go out birding on weekends.
3. At first, the expert was (she, her).
4. Now I rarely rely on (she, her) or other birders.
5. Laura and (they, them) are good company, however.
6. My parents and (we, us) share a love of the outdoors.
7. Mom and Dad often hike along with Laura and (I, me).
8. They and (we, us) learn much on our hikes.

LEVEL

B. Write the correct pronoun for each sentence. Then write whether your choice is a **subject** or **object** pronoun.

9. Mom and (me, I) are interested in insects.
10. Dad talks to (me and her, her and me) about butterfly collecting.
11. Mom and (he, him) have quite a large collection.
12. For my friends and (I, me) conservation is very important.
13. (They and I, Me and them) are unsure about collecting.
14. Dad agrees with my friends and (I, me) about hunting.
15. Dad and (we, us) worry about saving wildlife.
16. The most politically active member of our family is (he, him).

LEVEL

C. Rewrite each sentence by replacing the underlined word or words with a pronoun. Then write whether each pronoun you supply is a **subject** or **object** pronoun.

17. My sister and brother enjoy mountain climbing.
18. An expert assured my parents and me of the sport's safety.
19. Sometimes my parents still worry about Lisa and James.
20. Lisa explained the concept of climbing teams to my parents and me.
21. My friends and Lisa often climb together and always use the best equipment.
22. A climb often consists of experts and beginners like my brother and sister.
23. Unfortunately my parents and I are afraid of heights.
24. Lisa and my friends are fearless.
25. No trail frightens that group of adventurers.

PRACTICE + PLUS

Three levels of additional practice for a difficult skill

Using Pronouns Correctly (page 220)

LEVEL

A. Write the correct pronoun for each sentence.

1. My family and (I, me) often read stories aloud.
2. Dad entertains my sister and (I, me) with mysteries.
3. For (he, him) Sherlock Holmes is a great character.
4. According to Dad, the best detective is (he, him).
5. Ann says these stories are too complicated for (she, her).
6. Dad and (her, she) also read poetry to the family.
7. Robert Frost interests Laura and (I, me).
8. Emily Dickinson and (he, him) are my favorite poets.

LEVEL

B. Write each sentence, using the correct pronoun or pronouns. Then write whether your choice is a **subject pronoun** or an **object pronoun.**

9. My sisters and (me, I) love adventure stories.
10. I like reading Mark Twain's stories to (they, them).
11. The twins and (me, I) appreciate Twain's humor.
12. One day Mom asked my sister and (I, me) a question.
13. Would animal stories be of interest to (she and I, her and me)?
14. Dad bought a volume of Aesop's fables for (we, us).
15. Mom and (we, us) chose our favorite fables.
16. Both Dad and (her, she) enjoyed our readings.

LEVEL

C. Rewrite each sentence by replacing the underlined word or words with a pronoun. Then write whether each pronoun you supply is a **subject pronoun** or **object pronoun.**

17. Yesterday Aunt Sue and Uncle Jim visited us.
18. My brother and I always enjoy these visits.
19. Uncle Jim and Aunt Sue take many sea cruises to distant lands.
20. My uncle tells my brother and me wonderful sea stories.
21. He describes what happened to my uncle at sea.
22. These adventures also entertain my father and mother.
23. To my brother and me, a sea cruise to a tropical island would be a dream come true.
24. Uncle Jim learned to sail when he was six years old.
25. To my brother and me, that seemed very young.

EXTRA PRACTICE

Three levels of practice

Possessive Pronouns (page 222)

LEVEL

A. Write the possessive pronoun in each sentence.

1. Louise Nevelson emigrated from Russia with her mother.
2. They left their home and joined Louise's father in Maine.
3. Theirs was a long and difficult journey by boat.
4. Isaac Berliawsky awaited his family in Rockland, Maine.
5. There have been many uprooted families like his.
6. Jews in Russia often fled their country.
7. Our country has welcomed many immigrant families.
8. Immigrants helped give American art its variety.

LEVEL

B. Write the possessive pronoun. Then write whether the possessive pronoun stands alone or comes before a noun.

9. Even during her childhold Louise was interested in art.
10. Her drawing teacher, Miss Cleveland, encouraged her.
11. Louise's parents believed in education for all their children.
12. In the past, talent like hers had been ignored in women.
13. Her dream was to study art at Pratt Institute in New York.
14. Charles Nevelson also made his home in that city.
15. Theirs was a marriage that seemed to offer everything.
16. The excitement of a great city was hers.

LEVEL

C. Write each sentence, replacing each underlined possessive noun with the correct possessive pronoun.

17. Louise Nevelson's development as an artist continued at the Art Students League.
18. In the League's studios she met artists with new ideas.
19. These artists' commitment encouraged her to strengthen Louise's.
20. Two of Louise's friends were Diego Rivera and Rivera's wife.
21. Rivera's murals helped awaken Mexicans to the Mexicans' glorious Indian past.
22. Louise's most original mode of expression became sculpture.
23. Sculpture's versatility inspired her, and now Louise's works are exhibited all over the world.
24. Nevelson's is an art of box-like forms.
25. The forms' shapes became imaginary structures in the artist's mind.

EXTRA PRACTICE

Three levels of practice

Indefinite Pronouns (page 224)

LEVEL

A. Write the indefinite pronoun in each sentence. Then write whether the pronoun is **singular** or **plural.**

1. Has anyone in class attended a writer's workshop?
2. Many have found these workshops very helpful.
3. All of the participants are eager writers.
4. None of their work is criticized harshly.
5. Most of the workshop consists of conferences.
6. Each of the groups has a similar purpose.
7. Everybody participates in the revision process.
8. Most of the people write very well.

LEVEL

B. Write the correct possessive pronoun or pronouns for each sentence. Then write the indefinite pronoun.

9. Most of us enjoyed (ours, our) work.
10. Many in my class finished (his, their) assignments.
11. No one has turned in (his or her, their) paper yet.
12. All of us want to do (their, his) best.
13. Some of the students formed (his or her, their) own editing teams.
14. None of the girls refused to share (her, their) ideas.
15. Everyone did (his or her, their) share of the work.
16. Several completed (his or her, their) revisions.
17. Few could judge (his or her, their) own work.

LEVEL

C. Write each sentence, filling in the blank with the correct possessive pronoun or pronouns. Underline the indefinite pronoun and write whether it is **singular** or **plural.**

18. Most of the great writers have revised ____ work.
19. None of them produced ____ best work the first time.
20. Everyone can benefit from reworking ____ first efforts.
21. No one should expect ____ first draft to be perfect.
22. Several of the literary greats have actually thrown out ____ manuscripts.
23. Some writers never finish ____ revisions.
24. Everything, however, must have ____ limits, including revising.
25. Each must decide on ____ own standards.

EXTRA PRACTICE

Three levels of practice

Subject-Verb Agreement with Indefinite Pronouns (page 226)

LEVEL

A. Write each sentence. Draw one line under the indefinite pronoun and two lines under the verb. Write whether the verb is **singular** or **plural.**

1. Few think of spring without a sense of joy.
2. All of my favorite poets have praised the spring.
3. Everyone is happy with the longer days.
4. Many of the animals are emerging from winter homes.
5. Each of the trees begins to bud.
6. Most of the woodland is covered with wildflowers.
7. A few of the flowers bloom very early.
8. All of the bulbs have sprouted tender green shoots.

LEVEL

B. Write each sentence, using the correct verb. Underline the indefinite pronoun.

9. Few (is, are) sorry about the departure of winter.
10. Some of my friends (enjoys, enjoy) spring most of all.
11. One of my favorite activities (is, are) observing nature.
12. Many of the willow twigs (has, have) budded.
13. Most of the skunk cabbage (is, are) already visible.
14. Everyone (looks, look) for shoots in the crocus bed.
15. Another of the signs (is, are) the chattering of birds.
16. Much of the new growth (happen, happens) invisibly.

LEVEL

C. Write each sentence. If the verb agrees with its subject, write **correct.** Correct any verb that does not agree with its subject.

17. In spring much of the sap rises in the trees.
18. Most of the bird species prepares for nesting or migration.
19. Few of the children comes indoors willingly.
20. Everyone head for the park on the first warm day.
21. Some of the girls brings lilacs to the teacher.
22. Most of the students want a day of celebration.
23. No one knows the exact cause of "spring fever."
24. Many of the activities of spring is delightful.
25. Some of the weather is windy and wet.

EXTRA PRACTICE

Three levels of practice

Reflexive and Intensive Pronouns (page 228)

LEVEL

A. Write the reflexive or intensive pronoun in each sentence. Then write which kind it is.

1. I have given myself the task of studying the life of Alexander Hamilton.
2. Alexander Hamilton himself was aware of his genius.
3. I myself knew little about his achievements.
4. Jefferson himself was a rival of Hamilton.
5. The rivalry itself is an interesting subject.
6. The American political parties themselves reflect these early divisions.
7. We Americans should acquaint ourselves with this story.

B. Write the correct word for each sentence.

8. Hamilton found (him, himself) among many admirers.
9. To (themselves, them), Hamilton was brilliant, polished, and persuasive.
10. He could count George Washington (hisself, himself) among his friends.
11. Even his marriage offered (him, himself) advantages.
12. His wife (her, herself) was the daughter of a general.
13. The Hamiltons placed (theirselves, themselves) at the top of New York society.
14. Perhaps Hamilton's importance is unclear to (you, yourself).

LEVEL

C. Write each sentence using the correct pronoun. Write whether your choice is a **reflexive, intensive, subject,** or **object** pronoun.

15. Hamilton (he, himself) believed in central authority.
16. Jefferson and (he, himself) held very different views.
17. Some friends quizzed John and (myself, me) about these men's ideas.
18. The citizens (themselves, theirselves) were unsure of the best form of government.
19. Jefferson committed (hisself, himself) to a particular form of democracy.
20. The rivalry between (them, themselves) ended abruptly.

EXTRA PRACTICE

Three levels of practice

Interrogative and Demonstrative Pronouns (page 230)

LEVEL

A. Write the interrogative pronoun or demonstrative pronoun in each sentence. Then write which kind it is.

1. Who coined the largest number of English words?
2. This is an intriguing question.
3. What do you know about Shakespeare's vocabulary?
4. To whom does the term "Elizabethan" refer?
5. Whose is the largest literary vocabulary in English?
6. That is another achievement of Shakespeare.
7. Whom do you choose as the greatest writer?
8. What plays did Christopher Marlowe write?

LEVEL

B. Write each sentence, using the correct word.

9. (Who, Whom) spoke Elizabethan English?
10. (Whose, Who's) is this report on American dialects?
11. (Who's, Whose) an expert on word origins?
12. (This, These) are difficult questions to answer.
13. (Who, Whom) do you read most often?
14. (Whom, Who) was Geoffrey Chaucer?
15. (This, These) is one of his books.
16. (Whom, Whose) book can we borrow?

LEVEL

C. Write each sentence, using the correct word. Then write whether your choice is an **interrogative pronoun, contraction,** or **demonstrative pronoun.**

17. (Who's, Whose) a recent inventor of English words?
18. (This, These) come to mind: Ogden Nash and Lewis Carroll.
19. (Whom, Who) wrote *Alice in Wonderland*?
20. (Who's, Whose) is this copy of the novel?
21. (That, Those) are unusual words.
22. (Who, Whom) have you selected as a subject for a biographical sketch?
23. (That, These) is an interesting choice.
24. To (whom, whose) sketch will we give a prize?
25. To (who, whom) should we give the prize?

EXTRA PRACTICE

Three levels of practice

Mechanics: Using Abbreviations (page 232)

LEVEL
A. Write the abbreviation for each word or group of words.

1. Tuesday
2. Mister
3. California
4. Drive
5. Corporation

6. January
7. pound
8. before noon
9. 6:00 in the evening
10. 536 before Christ's birth

LEVEL
B. Find the word or words that can be abbreviated in each sentence. Write the word and the abbreviation.

11. It is a steamy Sunday.
12. It is only March, but it feels like August.
13. We are driving along the gulf in Galveston, Texas.
14. Our car overheats near Bay Avenue.
15. Dad pours a quart of water into the radiator.
16. My father is Doctor José Gonzales.
17. I am José Gonzales, Junior.
18. We are invited to a barbecue at 6:30 in the evening.
19. Luckily, a telephone is only several feet away.
20. Dad calls our hostess, Eve Stein, Medical Doctor.
21. Carla Stein, Registered Nurse, answers the phone.
22. Carla works for the Columbia Broadcasting System.

LEVEL
C. Find the word or words that can be abbreviated. Write the word and the abbreviation.

(23.) Senator Donna Perez
(24.) 404 White Avenue
(25.) Sacramento, California 95814
(26.) Dear Senator Perez:

I am a middle school student. **(27.)** My father is Doctor Jason Cole. **(28.)** He is on the board of the National Association for the Advancement of Colored People. **(29.)** When Dad and I visited Houston, Texas, last week for a convention, we heard you speak at the local university. Your speech about the importance of a good education really impressed us. **(30.)** Would you be able to speak at my school, Emerson Junior High School, sometime next spring?

EXTRA PRACTICE

Three levels of practice

Homophones and Homographs (page 234)

LEVEL
A. Match each homophone in the left column with its correct meaning in the right column.

1. pail		a.	belonging to you
2. your		b.	achievement
3. feet		c.	lacking color
4. right		d.	put words on paper
5. write		e.	correct
6. feat		f.	body parts
7. you're		g.	contraction for *you are*
8. pale		h.	bucket

LEVEL
B. Write each sentence, using the correct word. Use a dictionary if necessary.

9. (Whose, Who's) is this watercolor on the wall?

10. Is that (won, one) of your pictures?

11. (Your, You're) quite accomplished with a brush.

12. I have designed my own (stationery, stationary).

13. (There, Their) are some samples of my calligraphy.

14. I take great (pried, pride) in my work.

15. Of (course, coarse), painting requires a great deal of patience.

16. These pictures give me a (sense, cents) of freedom and movement.

LEVEL
C. Each word below is a homograph. For each word write two sentences that reflect the different meanings of the word. Use a dictionary if necessary.

17. draft

18. fair

19. wind

20. game

21. pound

22. arm

23. state

24. board

25. hound

MAINTENANCE

UNIT 1: SENTENCES

Complete Subjects and Complete Predicates, Simple Subjects and Simple Predicates (pages 4, 6)   Write each sentence. Underline the complete subject once and the complete predicate twice. Circle the simple subject and the simple predicate.

1. Several actors entered the theater.
2. The watchman greeted each one.
3. The director of the play called for attention.
4. All the actors took their places on the stage.
5. The rehearsal of the play began.

Correcting Fragments and Run-On Sentences (page 12) Write each group of words, correcting the sentence fragments and run-on sentences. Write **correct** next to any word group that is a sentence.

6. All of the lions in the zoo.
7. The monkey house was empty, the monkeys had been rented by a movie studio.
8. Bounds around the enclosure swiftly and gracefully.
9. The giraffe ate some acacia leaves, acacia trees grow very tall.
10. The zookeeper is closing the gate for the night.

UNIT 3: NOUNS

Possessive Nouns (page 72) Write each word. After each one write its possessive form.

11. geese
12. Ellis
13. soldier
14. men
15. soprano
16. skaters
17. parents
18. ladies
19. Katzee
20. day

UNIT 5: VERBS

Action Verbs (page 136) Write each action verb. Then write whether the verb expresses a **physical** or a **mental** action.

21. Cindy rides her horse daily.
22. The horse gallops over the open countryside.
23. A tiny stream runs through the wide green fields.
24. Cindy enjoys the scenery.
25. The horse jumps over hedges smoothly and easily.

Verbs with Direct Objects (page 138)   Write each sentence. Draw one line under each verb and two lines under each direct object, predicate noun, or predicate adjective. Label each verb as **transitive, intransitive** or **linking.**

26. The chef prepares a barbecue sauce.
27. His sauce is spicy and aromatic.

28. People discuss his dishes with admiration.

29. The chef adds some more hot pepper.

30. The chef is the winner of a prize for great sauces.

Verbs with Indirect Objects

(page 140)   Write each sentence. Then underline each direct object once and each indirect object twice.

31. Mr. Ruiz handed the archaeologist a dinosaur egg.

32. The archaeologist offered Mr. Ruiz a payment.

33. Mr. Ruiz made the archaeologist a present of the egg.

34. The archaeological team sent the museum a notice about the egg.

35. The museum gave the archaeological team a high commendation.

Present, Past, and Future Tenses; Verb Phrases; Perfect Tenses

(pages 144, 146, 150) Write each sentence. Underline the verb or main verb once and the helping verb (if any) twice. Then tell the principal part from which the verb or main verb was formed.

36. Passenger trains are returning to popularity.

37. Rail service had deteriorated before Amtrak took over.

38. Next year over 21 million people will travel by train.

39. Business travelers in the East appreciate efficient trains.

40. People have rediscovered scenic beauty and the friendliness of people on trains.

Irregular Verbs I, Irregular Verbs II

(pages 152, 154)   Write each sentence, using the correct form of the verb shown in parentheses. Then write whether the verb is in the **past** or **past participle** form.

41. The flying doctor had (come) yesterday to our wilderness outpost.

42. He has (fly) here every year.

43. He looked at our throats and (take) our temperatures.

44. He (teach) us ways to keep healthy.

45. The children have all (grow) a lot this year.

Subject-Verb Agreement

(page 156)   Rewrite the sentences so that all verbs agree with their subjects.

46. Most ski resort areas is open daily.

47. Has you studied the trail map yet?

48. On this mountain is several trails.

49. Over there is the trail-marking symbols for the easy slopes.

50. A danger to skiers are closed trails.

Using Commas to Separate Parts of a Sentence

(page 158) Rewrite each sentence by adding a comma or commas where needed.

51. Did you go to the folk art show Jim?

52. Yes I saw some fascinating things there.

53. The weather vanes scrimshaw and trade signs interested me most.

54. Dale did you notice the wood carving of Liberty?

55. No I was too busy looking at the coverlets painted firemen's hats and an old money box.

UNIT 7: PRONOUNS

Personal Pronouns (page 216) Write each sentence, replacing the underlined word or words with the correct pronoun. Label each pronoun **subject pronoun** or **object pronoun**.

56. The tennis pro gives lessons at the health club.

57. Lisa and Tom are his newest pupils.

58. Lisa skillfully serves the ball to Tom.

59. Unfortunately, the ball goes out of bounds.

60. Tom slams the next serve back to Lisa.

Pronouns and Antecedents

(page 218)   Write each pair of sentences, filling the blank in the second sentence with the correct pronoun. Label the antecedent of each pronoun you supply.

61. Robin Hood lived in Sherwood Forest. ____ was a skilled archer and legendary outlaw.

62. Little John was a big, stalwart man. ____ tumbled Robin into a brook.

63. The Sheriff of Nottingham and Guy of Gisborne were the enemies of Robin Hood. ____ both received justice at Robin's hand.

64. Friar Tuck was fat and jovial. ____ was the chaplain of Robin Hood's band.

65. Maid Marian was a latecomer to the Robin Hood legend. ____ originated as Queen of the English May festivals.

Using Pronouns Correctly

(page 220)   Write each sentence, choosing the correct pronoun or pronouns in parentheses.

66. Gena, Rob, and (I, me) study the bassoon.

67. (She, Her) and Larry think the instrument is funny.

68. The teacher asked (Don and he, Don and him) to stop laughing.

69. (She, Her) gave us the instruments.

70. At least (him and I) (he and I) don't study the contrabassoon!

Homophones and Homographs (page 234)   Write a pair of sentences for each pair of homophones.

71. plain, plane
72. groan, grown
73. break, brake
74. flower, flour
75. steel, steal

UNIT 8

Writing Biographical Sketches

Read the quotation and look at the picture on the opposite page. Talk about characteristics and values that make someone heroic.

When you write a biographical sketch, you will want to summarize the achievements of a particular person. You will want your audience to understand the ways in which this person has inspired others.

Focus A biographical sketch presents information about the life of a person.

Whom do you feel would make a good subject for a biographical sketch? On the following pages you will find a biography of a famous person—Stevie Wonder. You will also find photographs of other people. Perhaps they will give you some ideas for writing.

Whoever I write about, I try very hard to make that person seem like a real person, with troubles as well as triumphs. . . .

—James Haskins

LITERATURE

Reading Like a Writer

AWARD WINNING SELECTION

Have you ever wanted to learn more about the lives and careers of people you admire? Have you wondered who influenced them and what obstacles they had to overcome?

The following selection is from a biography of Stevie Wonder. It describes Stevie's early life as a blind child and the beginnings of his interest in music.

As you read the selection, notice that the writer focuses on the important events that helped shape Stevie Wonder's development as a musician.

from The Story of Stevie Wonder

by James Haskins

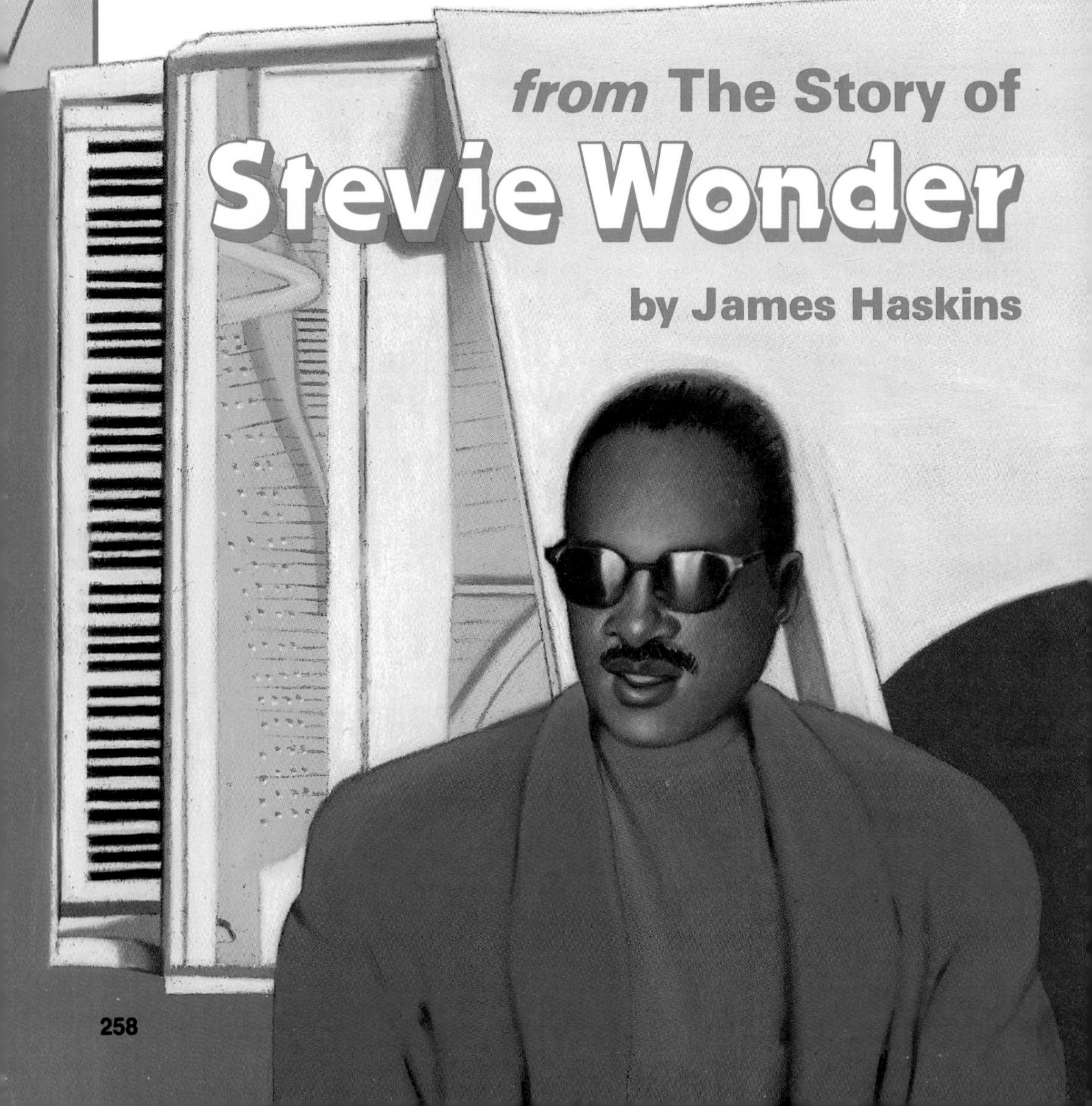

Stevie Wonder says, "There's one thing to remember about sound—sound happens all the time, all the time. If you put your hands right up to your ears, if you close your eyes and move your hands back and forth, you can hear the sound getting closer and farther away . . . . Sound bounces off everything, there's always something happening."

Stevie Wonder was born Steveland Morris on May 13, 1950, in Saginaw, Michigan. He was the third boy in a family that would eventually include five boys and one girl. All except Stevie were born without handicaps. He was born prematurely, and his early birth led to his total blindness.[1]

"When I was young," he says, "my mother taught me never to feel sorry for myself, because handicaps are really things to be used, another way to benefit yourself and others in the long run." This was the best possible advice Stevie's mother could have given. He learned to regard his blindness in more than one way. It could be a hindrance, but it could also be a special gift. He was able to accept this idea, sometimes better than his mother could.

"I know it used to worry my mother," Stevie recalls, "and I know she prayed for me to have sight someday, and so finally I just told her that I was *happy* being blind, and I thought it was a gift from God, and I think she felt better after that."

Stevie was a lucky child in many ways. He was lucky to have two brothers close enough to him in age not to understand at first about his blindness and to expect him to do many of the things they did. He was also lucky to have a mother and a father, and occasionally an uncle, who understood how important sound was to him, and how important it was for him to learn to identify things he could not see by their sound. He recalls:

"I remember people dropping money on the table and saying, "What's that, Steve?" That's a dime—buh-duh-duh-da; that's a quarter—buh-duh-duh-duh-da; that's a nickel. I could almost always get it right except a penny and a nickel confused me.

"I don't really feel my hearing is any better than yours," Stevie says now; "we all have the same abilities, you know. The only difference is how much you use it." Encouraged by his

---

1. A major event in the subject's life is stated at the beginning.

family, Stevie used his hearing more and more as he grew older. He learned how to tell birds apart by their call, and tell trees apart by the sound their leaves made as they rustled in the wind.

He also spent a lot of time beating on things, to make sounds and to make music. Although his mother was a gospel singer, the family was not especially musical. But Stevie had shown musical interest and ability very young. By the time he was two years old his favorite toys were two spoons, with which he would beat rhythmically on pans and tabletops and anything else his mother would let him beat on. When she began to worry about her furniture, she bought him cardboard drums from the dime store. None of them lasted very long. "I'd beat 'em to death," Stevie says with a chuckle. But there would always be a new drum, and there were other toy instruments as well.

"One day someone gave me a harmonica to put on my key chain, a little four-hole harmonica," Stevie recalls. He managed to get a remarkable range of sounds from that toy instrument.

"Then one day my mother took me to a picnic and someone sat me behind my first set of drums. They put my foot on the pedal and I played. They gave me a quarter. I liked the sound of quarters."[2]

At a very early age, too, Stevie began to sing. All voices were very important to him, for they brought him closer to the world around him, a world he could not see. As he grew older, his own voice became particularly important to him, especially at night when the rest of the house was silent. He learned the endless possibilities of the human voice by experimenting with his own, and by mimicking others'.

Music itself, not necessarily made by him, became very important to him. He loved to listen to the radio; his earliest memory is of hearing Johnny Ace singing "Pledging My Love" on the radio. Shortly before he entered school he was given a small transistor radio for his very own. From then on, that radio

2. To describe important events, the writer uses the subject's actual words.

was his constant companion. He even slept with it under his pillow at night. It played softly, providing sounds for him in an otherwise silent apartment. When he started school, he insisted on taking it to school with him.

Stevie was enrolled in special classes for the blind in the Detroit public school system. A special bus picked him up every morning and brought him back every afternoon. Stevie wished he could walk to school as his brothers did, and go to their neighborhood school. But he was learning to adjust to the fact that he must lead a different life, and in his special classes he was taught many things that would help him lead as normal a life as possible.

Sighted children attended the same school, and they often whispered about "the blind kids" as they passed by. Adults did the same thing. Somehow, normal people have the idea that blind people cannot hear them. It was hard to deal in an honest way with sighted people or even with his partially sighted classmates.

Stevie had an additional problem in getting along with other children. Not only was he blind; he was also black. At first it might seem that the idea of skin color should not be very important to a child who has never seen color. But blackness is not just skin color; it is a culture, a way of looking at things. People divide themselves into "Us" and "Them" because of skin color, but that is not the only division; it just would not be on the basis of appearance.

At home, Stevie heard his brothers and their friends talk about the white kids they knew. Before long, even though Stevie could not himself see color, he was very aware of skin color, and in addition to being self-conscious because of his blindness he was a little bit ashamed of being black.

"I remember when I was little," says Stevie, "I used to listen to this black radio station in Detroit on my way to school. Like I

261

was the only black kid on the bus, and I would always turn the radio down, because I felt ashamed to let them hear me listening to B.B. King. But I *loved* B.B. King. Yet I felt ashamed because—because I was *different* enough to want to hear him and because I had never heard him anywhere else."

Stevie was not about to stop listening to B.B. King; he simply played his radio softly in situations where he felt uncomfortable. That radio meant more to him than just about anything else in the world.

"I spent a lot of time listening to the radio," Stevie recalls, "and I was able to relate to the different instruments and know what they were. I began to know them by name."

He would sing the words of the songs quietly to himself. He would hum the tunes. He would tap out the beats on his toy drums and try to play the melodies on his four-note harmonica. It frustrated him not to have real, grown-up instruments to play on, and it was hard for him to accept the fact that his mother just did not have enough money to buy real instruments for him. But luck soon proved to be with Stevie. Within the space of about a year and a half, he managed to acquire not one but *three*, real instruments.

Every year the Detroit Lions Club gave a Christmas party for blind children, and at Christmas-time during his first-grade year at school Stevie went to one. Each child received a gift, and someone must have told the Detroit Lions about Stevie's interest in music, for his gift—he could hardly believe it—was a set of real drums! Stevie sat down and began to pound on them right then and there.

Later a neighborhood barber gave Stevie a harmonica—a real one. He practiced and practiced until he had mastered that.

Then, when he was seven, Stevie became the proud owner of a real piano. A neighbor was moving out of the housing project, and she really did not want to take her piano. Knowing how much Stevie loved music, she decided to give it to him. Stevie remembers, "I kept asking, 'When they gonna bring the piano over, Mamma?' I never realized how important that was going to be to me." When the piano finally arrived, it was like all the birthdays Stevie could remember all rolled into one. He ran his hands along the smooth wooden top, down the sides and around the back, down the slim legs, around to the cold metal of the pedals, and back up to the keys, some flat, some raised. He asked his mother to open the top of the piano, so he could feel the strings inside. He asked her what color they were. They were kind of gold, and the small wooden blocks between them were light brown. What color was the piano? A dark brown. From that moment on, dark brown, although he had not ever seen it and would never see it, meant something nice to Stevie. And since, he had been told, his skin was a sort of dark brown, too, he began to feel much better about his skin color.

By the time he was nine or ten Stevie was a very popular member of the neighborhood. He was certainly the most gifted musically, and he spent many Saturdays and after-school hours on the front of neighbors' houses on Horton Street. By this time Stevie had a set of bongo drums, which he had mastered as he had every other instrument to which he had been exposed. Often he would play his bongos; sometimes it would be the harmonica. Everyone would join in the singing, but Stevie's clear, strong voice always took the lead. Without exception the music was rhythm and blues, the kind the people listened to on WCHB.[3]

One of his favorite singing partners was a boy about his age named John Glover. John Glover had a grown-up cousin named

3. Events in the subject's life are related in chronological order.

Ronnie White, who lived in another part of the city. Ronnie White was a member of the singing group the Miracles, which had enjoyed great success recording with a company named Hitsville USA.

White arranged with the president of Hitsville USA, Berry Gordy, to take Stevie to the company's recording studio and to give him an audition, and one exciting afternoon Stevie was taken to the place that would be like a second home to him for the next ten years.

Stevie will never forget that afternoon. White took him around the studio, helping him to the different instruments and sound equipment, letting him touch them. It seemed to Stevie that every wonderful instrument in the world was right there in that sound studio, and he never wanted to leave it. Then he was introduced to Berry Gordy. Gordy listened to him sing, and play the harmonica and drums, and hired him on the spot, which says a lot for Gordy. Few, if any, other record company owners would have taken such a chance back in 1960.

Of course, Stevie's mother actually signed Stevie's contract with Hitsville, for he was under age. There was little talk of money or other conditions. Stevie's family was so excited, so grateful for this opportunity for him, that they would have agreed to anything!

Thinking Like a Reader

1. How does Stevie Wonder feel about his blindness?
2. How has it affected his life?
3. How would you adjust to a condition such as blindness?

Write your responses in your journal.

Thinking Like a Writer

4. How does the author help you to understand Stevie Wonder's development as a person and as a musician?
5. How do you think the author decided which experiences to relate, and in what order to relate them?
6. Which experiences seemed most important and interesting to you? Why?
7. If you were going to write about a famous entertainer, who would you choose? Why?

Write your responses in your journal.

Brainstorm *Vocabulary*

"The Story of Stevie Wonder" describes many of the early influences on Stevie's life and career, such as the following:

culture
religion
economic class
skin color
education

If you were writing about either your own life or a famous person who interests you, what other terms might be important to give the reader an accurate picture? Write down some words and phrases that come to mind. Keep a personal list of vocabulary words in your journal. You can use them in your own writing.

Talk It Over
Conduct an Interview

Interview a friend, relative, or any other person you know. Ask the person this question: Who or what has been the most important influence in your life? Prepare a list of other questions that are related to this question. Take notes. Use a tape recorder if one is available. If you wish, write the interview on paper and share it with other people who might be interested.

Quick Write
Write an Autobiographical Note

Imagine that you are appearing in a class play. Write a brief note about yourself for the program guide. List information in chronological order.

> Michael Garcia is a seventh grader at Three Rivers Junior High. He has been taking singing lessons since the age of 9. At school he has been a member of the Drama Club and Glee Club for two years. Earlier this year he made his first appearance with the New Community Players as a member of the chorus in *The Music Man.* Michael, who looks forward to a career in the theater, hopes to attend the Young Actors' Workshop.

Idea Corner *Topics*

The person who wrote "The Story of Stevie Wonder" chose a famous and influential person to write about. Whom would you choose if you were writing a biographical sketch? Would it be someone famous or a person in your life? In your journal write down a list of places where you have seen biographical notes; for example, book jackets, record albums, and magazines. Who might like to read your biographical composition?

PICTURES  *SEEING LIKE A WRITER*

Finding Ideas for Writing

Look at the pictures. Think about what you see.
What ideas for writing a biographical sketch do the pictures
give you? Write your ideas in your journal.

Mountain climber in Rocky Mountains

Kevin Gormley, magician

Andre Agassi, tennis player

Sally Ride, astronaut

267

1 GROUP WRITING: A BIOGRAPHICAL SKETCH

COOPERATIVE LEARNING

A **biographical sketch** provides factual information about the life of a person. The **purpose** of a biographical sketch is to inform an **audience** about the person's most important life experiences and achievements. You can write an effective biographical sketch with the following parts.

- Introduction
- Body
- Conclusion

The Introduction

Read this introductory paragraph from a sketch.

> Louis Kane remembers the exact day he decided to become a magician. It was the day he turned six years old. For his birthday party Louis's mother hired The Amazing Waldo to entertain the children with magic tricks. He seemed to be able to read minds and see through walls. By the time the party was over, Louis had turned into a boy with a dream. He would be a magician.

This paragraph introduces the subject of the biographical sketch. It also tells the reader what is important or interesting about the subject. This writer decided to begin with a specific, dramatic event in the magician's life.

Guided Practice: Writing an Introduction

As a class, decide on a subject for a biographical sketch. The subject might be an athlete, a teacher, a popular singer, a national political figure, or a subject from history. Find out about the life and achievements of the person. Then write a brief introduction.

The Body

The **body** of a biographical sketch tells the important events and experiences in the person's life. These are usually related in the order in which they occurred, that is, in **chronological order**. **Transition words** such as *after, later,* and *during* help the reader see a sequence of events in time order. Below is the body of a biographical sketch.

> Louis began performing magic tricks in elementary school. By the time he was 16 he had created an act that could be booked for local parties. Later, in high school, Louis discovered the second great passion of his life—chemistry. He began to incorporate chemical magic into his act. Now there were transformations and explosions. When Louis's parents advised him to prepare himself for a career in the regular work-a-day world, Louis chose to study chemistry at State College. During the summer, however, he studied with a retired stage magician. After graduation, Louis worked for a time as a research chemist and then embarked on a full-time career as a stage magician.

- In what kind of order are the events arranged?
- What transition words help you to understand the order of events in time?

Guided Practice: Using Chronological Order

As a class you have written an introduction for a biographical sketch. Now list the important events in your subject's life and think about what you should include in the body of the composition. Choose the information that is most significant. Eliminate minor details. Arrange the events in chronological order. Use transition words to make clear when each event happened in time.

The Conclusion

A biographical sketch ends with a **conclusion** that says something about the significance of the subject's life. The final paragraph may sum up the person's accomplishments or personality, or both. Read the following conclusion of a biographical sketch.

Today Louis Kane is a full-time magician with more engagements than he can easily handle. "I have not yet mastered the trick of being in two cities at once," he says. Nevertheless Louis has toured the United States and Canada, as well as Great Britain and Latin America. If the responses of audiences are any indication, Louis Kane has already won a place in the history of stage magic.

Guided Practice: Writing a Conclusion

As a class, decide what you should put in the concluding paragraph of the biographical sketch you have been composing. Discuss different conclusions and write down notes for a conclusion that you think would be most effective.

Putting a Biographical Sketch Together

With your classmates you have selected a subject for a biographical sketch and have written an introduction. You have listed the important events and experiences in the person's life and arranged the information in chronological order. You used transition words for clarity.

Guided Practice: Writing a Biographical Sketch

Now write your biographical sketch. Use the introduction you have already prepared. In the body, include only the most important facts about the person's life. Eliminate unnecessary information. Be sure to use transition words to help the reader understand when events occurred. Finally, write a conclusion that sums up the person's accomplishments and personality.

Share your biographical sketch with a friend. Ask your friend if he or she thought that the time order of events in the person's life was clear.

Checklist A Biographical Sketch

When you write a biographical sketch, you will want to keep some important points in mind. To help you remember them, you can make a checklist.

First, remember that the **purpose** of a biographical sketch is to inform your **audience** about the important events and experiences in the life of your subject. Begin with an introduction that will capture the reader's interest and provide a focus for your sketch. Include the significant facts from the person's life, and arrange them in chronological order. Include a strong conclusion.

Below is a checklist for writing a biographical sketch. Make a copy of it and add any other points that you want to remember. Keep the checklist in your writing folder. You can refer to it when you write a biographical sketch.

> **CHECKLIST**
>
> - Remember purpose and audience.
> - Begin with an introduction.
> - Write the body.
> - Include important events.
> - Arrange details in chronological order.
> - Use transition words.
> - Add a conclusion.
> - _____

2 THINKING AND WRITING: Understanding Sequence

Think about what you have learned about writing a biographical sketch. You know that the writer can help the reader understand a person's life story by arranging the events in chronological order. By describing a logical **sequence** of events in time order, the writer can show a pattern of development in the subject's life.

When writing the body of a biographical sketch, a writer usually begins with the birth and childhood of the subject and ends with the last or most recent events and accomplishments in the person's life.

Look at this page from a writer's journal. The writer plans to write a biographical sketch about Elizabeth Cady Stanton.

> - born in Johnstown, New York, in 1815
> - during 1830s became interested in women's rights
> - organized first women's rights convention in U. S. in 1848
> - became interested in abolition of slavery in 1830s
> - during the 1850s and the Civil War, worked for women's rights and abolition
> - founded National Woman Suffrage Association with Susan B. Anthony in 1869
> - in 1840 married Henry B. Stanton, an abolitionist

Thinking Like a Writer

■ How should the notes be arranged to show time sequence?

The writer needs to arrange the events in chronological order before he begins writing his biographical sketch. By organizing the details in a logical sequence in time, the writer will be able to show the reader how one event in the person's life leads to another.

When you write a biographical sketch, arrange the facts about your subject's life in a clear sequence of events.

THINKING APPLICATION Sequencing

Each of the writers named below is planning to write a biographical sketch. Help each writer arrange information in a time sequence. Write your notes on a separate paper. You may wish to discuss your thinking with your classmates.

1. Joy's biographical sketch is about a young local artist.

> — studied at College of Art
> — won first prize at this year's outdoor Art Fair
> — influenced by high school art teacher
> — several exhibitions during college
> — her father sketched with her when she was child
> — upcoming one-woman show at Fine Arts Museum
> — raised in El Paso, Texas

2. Felipe is writing about the writer Henry David Thoreau for his book discussion club.

> — 1846 spent night in jail for refusing to pay taxes to government that supported slavery
> — born in Concord, Massachusetts, in 1817
> — entered Harvard College in 1833; began to keep journal
> — as a boy loved nature
> — 1845 built cabin by Walden Pond; studied nature

3. Andrew is writing a biographical sketch about his grandmother for her birthday gift.

> — planning to take her grandson cross-country skiing this winter
> — came to this country when she was three
> — will be sixty-eight tomorrow
> — born in Greece
> — learned how to ski when she was a young girl
> — on the ski team in college

3 INDEPENDENT WRITING: A Biographical Sketch

Prewrite: Step 1

By now you are familiar with the structure and main elements of a biographical sketch. You are ready to choose a subject to write about. Karen, a student your age, chose a topic in the following way.

Choosing a Topic

Karen talked with a classmate about possible subjects for a biographical sketch. They had read an interesting story by Isaac Bashevis Singer in their English class. The class had enjoyed the story very much. Karen thought that her class-mates would enjoy learning more information about the author's life. She had now selected her subject, **purpose**, and **audience**.

Exploring Ideas: Making a Time Line

After selecting her topic, Karen read information about Singer. At the library she found information in the encyclo-pedia and in biographies of Singer. Then, she made a list of important events and experiences in his life which she could use in her biographical sketch.

> – won Nobel Prize for Literature in 1978
> – born in Poland in 1904
> – worked as a journalist during the 1920s
> – during 1940s career as writer blossomed
> – as a child, greatest joy was listening to mother's stories
> – in 1966 published his first children's book
> – family was poor
> – his story "Yentl" made into movie in 1983

After reviewing her notes, Karen decided that the focus of her biographical sketch would be the development of Singer as a storyteller.

Karen had not written her notes in chronological order. To keep the order of events clear in her mind, she decided to arrange her information in the form of a **time line**. A time line shows events in chronological order. Then she consulted one other book about the life of Singer and added other important facts to her time line.

born in Poland · joy in mother's stories · worked as journalist · moved to U.S. · career as writer develops · published his first children's book · Nobel Prize for Literature · "Yentl" made into movie

(1904) (1920s) (1925) (1940s) (1966) (1978) (1983)

Thinking Like a Writer

- How did Karen organize her information?
- What information did Karen add to her time line?
- How would making a time line help you to write a biographical sketch?

YOUR TURN

Begin planning a biographical sketch by choosing a topic and explaining it. Use **Pictures** or your journal for ideas. Follow these steps.

JOURNAL

- Write a list of ideas.
- Choose a subject that would be of interest to you and an audience.
- Gather information and arrange it in a time line, or use any other method of organizing your facts.
- Add more facts to your time line or cross out unnecessary details at any time.
- Remember your purpose and audience.

Write a First Draft: Step 2

Karen reviewed what she knew about writing a biographical sketch and prepared a planning checklist. She included points about her introduction, body, and conclusion.

Then Karen wrote her first draft. She did not interrupt the flow of her ideas by correcting her work. She knew she could make changes later. Read the first draft of the introduction and body of her biographical sketch.

Part of Karen's First Draft

Isaac Bashevis Singer is one of the best-known storytellers in the world. Readers of all ages have enjoyed his legendary tales of imps and demons. His Jewish education forms the basis of his writing. His Polish background also does.

Singer was born in 1904 in a small town in Poland. Him and his brothers and sisters had few toys because the family was very poor. Isaac's greatest joy was listening to his Mother's stories. When he was twenty-one he went to New York. As a teenager he worked as a proofreader for a Yiddish magazine. In the 1940s his carreer as a writer developed, and he published novels and short stories. His stories began to be translated from Yiddish into English. In 1978 he was awarded the Nobel Prize for Literature. In 1983 "Yentl," one of Mr Singer's stories, was made into a movie.

Planning Checklist
- Remember purpose and audience.
- Begin with an introduction.
- Write the body.
- Arrange events in chronological order.
- Use transition words.
- Add a conclusion.

YOUR TURN

Write the first draft of your biographical sketch. As you write, ask yourself these questions.

- What does my audience need to know for me to achieve my purpose?
- What information should go in the introduction? the body?
- Are events arranged in chronological order?

TIME-OUT You might want to take some time out before you revise. That way you will be able to revise your writing with a fresh eye.

Revise: Step 3

After she had finished writing her first draft, Karen read it over to herself and made some changes that she thought would improve it. Then, since she was writing her biographical sketch for the students in her English class, she asked one of them to read her draft. She asked him if there were any changes she should make.

You've included lots of interesting facts about Singer's life, but some of the events don't seem to be in order.

Thanks for the reminder, Greg.

Karen also looked at her planning checklist to see if she had included the necessary parts in her draft. She realized there was one more point she had missed. She noticed that she had not included transition words to help make the connection between her ideas clearer. Karen put a check mark next to both points to remind herself to fix her draft.

As Karen revised her first draft, she paid special attention to the points on her checklist. Could she improve the introduction or conclusion? Did she leave out any important information in the body of her composition? Were events arranged in chronological order? She would wait until later to check for errors in spelling and punctuation.

Karen thought more about the **purpose** and **audience** for her writing. She asked herself what would be of greatest interest about Singer's life for her readers. She hoped her audience would become interested enough to read more of Singer's works.

Look at Karen's revised draft on the next page.

Revising Checklist
- Remember purpose and audience.
- Begin with an introduction.
- Write the body.
- ✔ Arrange events in chronological order.
- ✔ Use transition words.
- Add a conclusion.

THE WRITING PROCESS: Revising   **277**

WRITING PROCESS

Isaac Bashevis Singer is one of the best-known storytellers in the world. Readers of all ages have enjoyed his legendary tales of imps and demons. His Jewish education *and Polish background* forms the basis of his writing. ~~His Polish background also does.~~

Singer was born in 1904 in a small town in Poland. Him and his brothers and sisters had few toys because the family was very poor. Isaac's greatest joy was listening to his Mother's stories. *Then* When he was twenty-one he went to New York. As a teenager he worked as a proofreader for a Yiddish magazine. In the 1940s his carreer as a writer developed, and he published novels and short stories. *Soon* His stories began to be translated from Yiddish into English. *Then* In 1978 he was awarded the Nobel Prize for Literature. *Shortly afterward* In 1983 "Yentl," one of Mr Singer's stories, was made into a movie.

Thinking Like a Writer

WISE
WORD
CHOICE

- Why did Karen move a sentence?
- What words did she add? Why did she add them?
- What sentences did she combine? Why?

YOUR TURN

Read over your first draft. Ask yourself the questions below.

- How can I improve the introduction?
- What events need to be rearranged in time order?
- How can I make my conclusion stronger?

Now revise your biographical sketch. If you wish, share your writing with a classmate and ask for suggestions.

Proofread: Step 4

Karen knew that after she revised her draft, she had to proofread her work for errors in spelling, punctuation, grammar, and capitalization. She used proofreading marks to make corrections in her work.

Part of Karen's Proofread Draft

Singer was born in 1904 in a small town in Poland. ~~Him~~ He and his brothers and sisters had few toys because the family was very poor. Isaac's greatest joy was listening to his mother's stories. Then When he was twenty-one, he went to New York. As a teenager he worked as a proofreader for a Yiddish magazine. In the 1940s his ~~carreer~~ career as a writer developed, and he published novels and short stories. Soon His stories began to be translated from Yiddish into English. Then In 1978 he was awarded the Nobel Prize for Literature. Shortly afterward In 1983 "Yentl," one of Mr. Singer's stories, was made into a movie.

YOUR TURN

Proofreading Practice

See Teacher's Edition for proofreading corrections.

Find the errors. Write the paragraph correctly on a separate piece of paper.

Barbara and her sisters remember the rural Town where they grew up Their wanderings often took their friends and they through woods and fields. barbara recalls the many animals that she cared for and fed. Her and her sisters grew to enjoy the world of animals and had many pets of their own.

Proofreading Checklist

■ Did I indent each paragraph?

■ Did I spell each word correctly?

■ What errors in punctuation do I need to correct?

■ What errors in capitalization do I need to correct?

■ What errors in pronoun usage do I need to correct?

Applying Your Proofreading Skills

Now proofread your biographical sketch. Review your checklist and **The Grammar Connection** and **The Mechanics Connection** below. Use the proofreading marks.

THE GRAMMAR CONNECTION

Remember these rules about using pronouns correctly.

- Use a **subject pronoun** when the pronoun is the subject of a sentence.

  She and her sisters remembered the town.

- Use an **object pronoun** when the pronoun is the object of a verb or the object of a preposition.

  The people of the town missed Arlene and **her**.
  The girls' memories were important to **them**.

Check your writing. Have you used pronouns correctly?

THE MECHANICS CONNECTION

Remember these rules about writing abbreviations correctly.

- Many abbreviations begin with a capital letter and end with a period.

  Dr. Laurie Kranz introduced **Mr.** Paul Saks, **Sr.**, to us.

- Some abbreviations use capital letters and no periods.

  He spoke about how **UNICEF** began.

Review your writing. Have you used abbreviations correctly?

Proofreading Marks
Indent ¶
Add ∧
Add a comma ∧
Add quotation marks ѱ ѱ
Add a period ⊙
Take out ℘
Capitalize ≡
Lower-case letter /
Reverse the order ∩

Publish: Step 5

Karen made a final copy of her biographical sketch, using her best handwriting. Then she found a photograph of Isaac Bashevis Singer in a biography about him. She made a photocopy of the photograph and attached it to a sheet of paper to use as a cover for her writing. Her English teacher suggested that she display her work in the class library at the back of the room. Several of Karen's classmates asked her questions about Isaac Bashevis Singer's life and writing.

YOUR TURN

Make a final copy of your biographical sketch. Use your best handwriting, a typewriter, or a computer. Think of a way to share your biographical sketch. You may find some ideas in the **Sharing Suggestions** box below.

SHARING SUGGESTIONS

Make a tape recording of your biographical sketch. Share it with your family and friends.	Read your sketch to the class. Use a costume or other props to help bring your subject to life.	Mail a copy of your writing to someone you think might be interested in the subject of your biographical sketch.

4 SPEAKING AND LISTENING: Conducting an Interview

To write a biographical sketch, you may find information in books and articles. Another way to gather information is to **interview** the person if he or she is available.

You may ask for an interview either by telephone or by letter. State the purpose of the interview and suggest a time and location.

You should have enough knowledge about the topic so that your questions are sensible and meaningful. Base your questions on the 5 W's: *who, what, when, where,* and *why.* Prepare your questions in advance. You may want to give a list of the questions to the person before the interview. One student prepared the questions below for an interview with a research scientist.

1. What has been the most important achievement or event in your scientific career?
2. What is the most rewarding part of your job?
3. Who or what in your childhood influenced you to choose this kind of work?
4. What are your goals for the future?
5. What advice do you have for young people interested in a scientific career?

When you conduct an interview, keep the following guidelines in mind.

> **SPEAKING GUIDELINES: An Interview**
>
> 1. Be sure the person knows in advance the purpose of your interview.
> 2. Plan questions that reflect your purpose.
> 3. Make notes of important information or ask the person if you may tape record the interview.
> 4. Be attentive. Ask politely for more details when necessary.
> 5. Be courteous. Tactfully conclude the interview when the allotted time has been reached. Thank the person for the interview.

- Why is it important to tell the person you are interviewing your purpose in advance?
- Why is it helpful to prepare a list of questions before the interview?

If you are using the information from your interview in a biographical sketch, review your notes. Select and arrange the information that is most important. Do not change the meaning of what the person said. When you want to tell your audience the exact words of your subject, use quotation marks around the passage.

 SPEAKING APPLICATION An Interview

Interview your favorite teacher, a relative, or another adult whose work interests you. Focus on a purpose and prepare questions for your interview. Use the Listening Guidelines below. If possible, tape record the interview and share it with the class.

> **LISTENING GUIDELINES: An Interview**
>
> 1. Listen for the key phrases and ideas mentioned in the interview. Take notes on important points.
> 2. Listen for unexpected information. Adjust some of your questions, if necessary.
> 3. Be polite. Allow the speaker to answer your questions without interrupting him or her.

THE CURRICULUM CONNECTION

Writing About Health

A visit to the doctor is like being interviewed. Questions are asked and personal information is supplied. The purpose: your health.

Health is a state of well-being that involves many aspects of life—physical, mental, and social. Elements of physical health include proper nutrition, exercise, and medical and dental care. But emotional development and good social relationships are equally important in maintaining good health. Health is not only a physical condition, but also a state of mind.

Doctors, medical researchers, and other health professionals all rely on personal information about people for their work. They use case studies and the medical histories of their patients to help people achieve and keep good health. It is possible that the knowledge a doctor gains from your visit can end up benefiting not only you, but others as well!

ACTIVITIES

Be a Cartoonist

Create a comic strip that features a character called the Health Nut, a talking peanut that works for the cause of better health. Create a humorous situation in which this character raises a health issue that is important to you. Have your comic strip offer your readers an actual health tip. With your classmates, collect your comic strips into a volume called "Health Humor."

Interview a Health Professional

Interview a doctor, nurse, physical therapist, dentist, or medical assistant. As the basis for your interview, you may want to use the question "What is the most important health issue for young people today?" Tape record your interview, if possible. Then write it and share your work with an audience. You may wish to send your interview to the editor of your school or local newspaper.

Respond to Literature

Recent medical breakthroughs have produced amazing results in the lives of people whose bodies have been seriously injured in accidents. After reading the selection below, write a response to it in the form of an essay, story, or article.

One Step at a Time

The night after she graduated from high school in June, 1978, Nan Davis was driving through the country with her boyfriend. Suddenly, he lost control on a curve. The car skidded off the road and into a ditch.

Lying in the wreck, Nan was aware that her legs were limp. In the hospital, Nan found out she had broken her back and neck. Her spinal cord was damaged, and she was paralyzed in both legs. Doctors told eighteen-year-old Nan that she would never walk again.

But on November 10, 1982, Nan entered Dr. Jerrold Petrofsky's laboratory. Electronic sensors, wired to a computer, were taped to her leg muscles.*

Holding onto handrails, Nan rose from her wheelchair. "Right leg coming up," said Dr. Petrofsky, using the computer to control the electric sensors. Nan's right leg bent, rose, and moved forward a step. "Left leg coming up," Dr. Petrofsky said. Her left leg moved forward.

For the first time in four years, Nan Davis was walking.

* Since Nan Davis's first walk at Wright State University, the system has been improved and made portable.

UNIT CHECKUP

LESSON 1
Group Writing: A Biographical Sketch (page 268)   Read the paragraph below. On a separate sheet of paper copy the paragraph, adding transition words to help the reader tell the order in which events occurred.

   Marc preferred swimming to all other sports. He won several swimming competitions. He was on the swim team and became its captain. Marc realized that he wanted to develop other interests. He took courses in psychology, health, and education. Marc teaches physical education at the Community College, where he is also coach for the swim team. He is Water Sports Director at a camp for disabled children.

LESSON 2
Thinking: Understanding Sequence (page 272)   Rewrite the paragraph below. Arrange all the sentences in chronological order. Do not change the position of the first sentence of the paragraph.

   Six students at Mayfair School have won an award for brightening their neighborhood. After getting buckets, brushes, and paint, the youngsters chose work areas. The students finished their project yesterday. Afterward several local merchants offered the students summer jobs. The students first suggested the idea a month ago.

LESSON 3
Writing a Biographical Sketch (page 274)   Write a biographical sketch for a new teenagers' magazine called *People Parade*. Your subject can be a famous person from history, an interesting relative, or a member of your community. If possible, interview the person. Remember to include an introduction, a body, and conclusion in your sketch. Use chronological order and transition words to help readers follow the sequence of events in your subject's life. Revise and proofread your work carefully. Then share it with friends, classmates, or family members.

LESSON 4
Speaking and Listening: Conducting an Interview (page 282) In a paragraph summarize the guidelines for conducting an effective interview. Be sure to include points for both speaking and listening effectively in an interview.

THEME PROJECT CHARACTERS

The stories of people's lives often include how they have met certain types of challenges. Achieving goals sometimes involves overcoming obstacles. The challenges in people's lives can be physical, mental, or emotional. The achievements may be in the world or within oneself.

Look at the pictures below. Use the pictures as the basis for a class discussion about the different types of challenges in people's lives. Talk about the challenges that you have faced in your own life, as well.

Create a character for a play.

- Summarize the life of the character, including an important challenge that he or she has met.
- Then write a scene for the play, with dialogue for two characters.
- If you wish, present your character summary and scene to the class.

UNIT

Adjectives and Adverbs

In this unit you will learn about adjectives and adverbs. These words add to the framework of a sentence by adding details.

Discuss Read the poem on the opposite page. What is the poet describing?

Creative Expression The unit theme is *Visions*. Reflect on sights you see every day. What beauty can you see in ordinary things? Write a description of something you would normally overlook as if you are seeing it for the first time. Write your description in your journal.

THEME: *VISIONS*

Beyond the dark trees
lightning flashes on water,
bright, like a vision.

—Shiki

1 ADJECTIVES

An adjective is a word that modifies, or describes, a noun or pronoun.

When you describe people, places, and things, you use words that tell about their size, shape, color, number, or other qualities. Words that describe nouns or pronouns are called **adjectives.**

> **One nervous** actor forgot Juliet's **last** name.

A **predicate adjective** is an adjective that follows a linking verb and describes the subject of the sentence.

> The director is **imaginative** and **bold.**

Present and past participles may be used as adjectives and predicate adjectives.

> The **angered** families have a meeting.
> *Romeo and Juliet* is **exciting** and **touching.**

Guided Practice

Identify the adjectives and predicate adjectives. Then name the words they modify.

Example: The actors were professional.
professional actors

1. We watched a moving performance of *Romeo and Juliet*.
2. The play tells the tragic story of two young lovers.
3. The unhappy teenagers meet with tragedy.
4. The play teaches important lessons about the ancient conflict between generations.
5. The dialogue in the play is rich and poetic.
6. Two families, the Capulets and Montagues, are bitter enemies.
7. A noble prince forbids the two groups to fight.
8. The wealthy Capulets give a festive banquet.
9. An uninvited Romeo arrives in a clever disguise.

 THINK

- How can I use adjectives to make my writing more vivid?

REMEMBER

- An **adjective** modifies a noun or a pronoun.
- A **predicate adjective** follows a linking verb and describes the subject.

More Practice

A. Write each adjective or predicate adjective and the word that it modifies or describes.

Example: Romeo and Juliet live in an ancient city.
    ancient city

10. The annoyed Capulets recognize Romeo.
11. They are furious about his trick.
12. Wise old Capulet does not confront Romeo.
13. Later Juliet voices her distress from a high window.
14. The waiting Romeo responds with words of love.
15. Is the play admired by your classmates?

B. Write each sentence. Fill in each blank with a suitable adjective. Then underline the word it modifies.

Example: Shakespeare's ____ plays appeal to
    many people.
    Shakespeare's timeless <u>plays</u>
    appeal to many people.

16. The actors presented a ____ production.
17. Many people filled the ____ theater.
18. The curtain rose for the ____ act.
19. One actress wore a ____ dress.
20. Romeo's costume was ____ .
21. The most ____ scene was Romeo and Juliet's funeral.
22. The performances by the players were ____ .
23. The audience responded with ____ applause.
24. The cast received a ____ bouquet of flowers.
25. The actors' ____ smiles showed they were ____.

Extra Practice, page 318

WRITING APPLICATION A Review

Write a brief review of a play or concert you have attended. Then, exchange papers with a classmate and identify the adjectives in each other's work.

2 ARTICLES AND PROPER ADJECTIVES

You know that an adjective is a word that modifies, or describes, a noun or pronoun. *A, an,* and *the* are special kinds of adjectives called **articles.**

A and *an* are called **indefinite articles** because they refer to one of a group of people, places, things, or ideas.

a carrot	**an** apple pie
a ripe tomato	**an** hour
a lobster	**an** orange

Use *a* before words beginning with a consonant sound; use *an* before words beginning with a vowel sound.

The is called a **definite article** because it identifies a specific person, place, thing, or idea.

the answer	**the** skateboard

Another kind of adjective is formed from a proper noun. This type of adjective is called a **proper adjective.** A proper adjective is capitalized.

Canadian bacon	**New England** clam chowder
German noodles	**Idaho** potatoes

Sometimes a proper adjective has the same spelling as its related proper noun. More often, however, the proper adjective and noun are spelled differently.

Guided Practice

Tell which word should be capitalized in each pair of words. Then, add the correct indefinite article before each pair.

Example: Maine lobster

a Maine

1. italian movie
2. hawaiian pineapple
3. french cheese
4. american tourist
5. california raisin
6. norwegian salmon

 THINK

■ How do I know if a word is a proper adjective?

REMEMBER

- **Articles** are special kinds of adjectives. *The* is a **definite article.** *A* and *an* are **indefinite articles.**
- A **proper adjective** is formed from a proper noun and begins with a capital letter.

More Practice

A. Write each pair of words. Add the correct indefinite article, and capitalize each proper adjective.

Example: arabian horse   *an Arabian horse*

7. greek salad
8. english tea
9. new york steak
10. honest effect
11. chinese chopstick
12. italian sausage
13. japanese restaurant
14. russian accent
15. mexican taco
16. irish stew
17. canadian flag
18. egg sandwich
19. rome apple
20. nicaraguan banana
21. florida orange
22. honorable intention

B. Write each sentence. Underline and capitalize each proper adjective. Identify any definite or indefinite articles in the sentence.

Example: A <u>siamese</u> cat lapped some cool milk.
   Siamese   a, indefinite article

23. The waiter brought a long loaf of italian bread to the table.
24. We enjoyed the fresh fruit and swiss cheese.
25. The new zealand lamb is fresh and tasty.
26. My father enjoys the taste of indian food.
27. Many people believe korean ginseng aids digestion.
28. A chef adds brazil nuts to the salad.
29. Would you like an english muffin for breakfast?

Extra Practice, page 319

WRITING APPLICATION A Menu

Imagine that you own a restaurant that serves many international dishes. Create a menu for your restaurant that includes a description of each dish. Then, exchange menus with a classmate and identify the proper adjectives in each other's work.

3 COMPARATIVE AND SUPERLATIVE ADJECTIVES I

Sometimes you use adjectives to compare two or more persons or things.

Use the **comparative form** of an adjective to compare two persons or things. You often add *er* to an adjective to form the comparative.

Use the **superlative form** of an adjective to compare more than two persons or things. You often add *est* to an adjective to form the superlative.

Adjective	Comparative	Superlative
tall	tall**er**	tall**est**
big	bigg**er**	bigg**est**
smart	smart**er**	smart**est**

Some adjectives are irregular. Their comparative and superlative forms are not made by adding *er* or *est*.

Adjective	Comparative	Superlative
good, well	better	best
bad	worse	worst
many, much	more	most

Guided Practice

Choose the correct form of each adjective.

Example: Who is (taller, tallest), Amy or Jess? *taller*

1. Which state is ____, Idaho or Wyoming? (bigger, biggest)
2. Yellowstone is the nation's ____ national park. (larger, largest)
3. Its ____ mountain is Electric Peak. (higher, highest)
4. Is Yellowstone ____ than Yosemite? (better, best)
5. Yellowstone has the ____ number of hot springs of any park in the world. (greater, greatest)

?! THINK

- How do I decide whether to use the comparative or the superlative form of an adjective?

G R A M M A R

REMEMBER

- The **comparative form** of an adjective compares *two* nouns. Add *er* to many adjectives to form the comparative.
- The **superlative form** of an adjective compares more than two nouns. Add *est* to many adjectives to form the superlative.

More Practice

A. Write the correct form of each adjective.

Example: The campers chose the <u>steepest</u> of three trails to climb. (steeper, steepest)

6. Some hot springs have brilliant colors; others have ____ colors. (duller, dullest)

7. The color of Emerald Spring is ____ than that of any other spring. (richer, richest)

8. Old Faithful is ____ than another giant geyser we visited. (smaller, smallest)

9. The students chose the ____ campsite of all. (better, best)

10. Yellowstone Lake has a ____ altitude than Lake Superior. (higher, highest)

B. Write each sentence, using the correct comparative or superlative form of the adjective in parentheses.

Example: Is it <u>warmer</u> today than yesterday? (warm)

11. The ____ spot in the United States is Death Valley. (low)

12. During the Ice Age the climate there was ____ than it is now. (wet)

13. Is Death Valley the ____ place on earth? (hot)

14. This is the ____ beautiful part of the valley. (much)

15. The north rim is ____ than the south rim. (high)

16. Is the climate ____ in winter than in summer? (good)

17. We developed a ____ knowledge of trees. (deep)

18. The redwood is ____ than most other trees. (big)

19. The ____ redwood tree of all is enormous. (large)

20. It is ____ than many apartment buildings. (tall)

Extra Practice, page 320

WRITING APPLICATION A Travel Brochure

Write sentences for a travel brochure in which you compare different vacation spots. Check to make sure you have used the correct adjective forms.

4 COMPARATIVE AND SUPERLATIVE ADJECTIVES II

You know that you add *er* to form the comparative and *est* to form the superlative of many adjectives. The comparative and superlative forms of other adjectives, however, are made by using the words *more* and *most*, or *less* and *least*, before the adjective.

Adjective	Comparative	Superlative
fascinating	more fascinating	most fascinating
active	more active	most active

1. For most one-syllable adjectives add *er* or *est*.   tall, tall**er**, tall**est**
2. For two-syllable adjectives add *er* or *est*, or use the words *more* and *most* or *less* and *least*.   lovely, loveli**er**, loveli**est**; honest, **more** honest, **most** honest
3. For adjectives with three or more syllables, use the words *more* and *most* or *less* and *least*.   difficult, **more** difficult, **most** difficult
4. Do not use *more* and *most* or *less* and *least* with adjectives ending in *er* and *est*.   This error is called a **double comparative,** as in *Today is more warmer than yesterday.*

Guided Practice

Choose the correct comparative or superlative form.

Example: Joe is ___ than I am.   (more musical, musicaler)
          more musical

1. We attended the winter season's ___ concert.   (most exciting, excitingest)
2. The hall looked ___ than a ballroom.   (more grander, grander)
3. I had been ___ than Susan to hear the concert.   (least patient, less patient)
4. The magnificent stage was even ___ than the hall was.   (beautifuller, more beautiful)

 THINK

- How can I avoid using a double comparison?

REMEMBER

- To form the comparative or superlative of some two-syllable adjectives, add *er* or *est*; for others use *more* or *most*.
- Use *more* or *most* with three-syllable adjectives.
- Do not use *more* and *most* with adjectives ending in *er* or *est*.

More Practice

A. Write the correct form of the comparative or superlative adjective for each sentence.

Example: The musicians were taught at the <u>most respected</u> school in the state.   (more respected, most respected)

  5. The conductor was ____ from Joe's seat than from mine.   (visibler, more visible)

  6. The orchestra began with its ____ piece.   (more popular, most popular)

  7. The flutes played the ____ parts.   (best, most best)

  8. The string solos were ____ than the brass solos.   (least dramatic, less dramatic)

  9. The trumpets played the ____ melodies.   (most stirring, stirringest)

B. Write each sentence, filling in the blank with a comparative or superlative form of an adjective.

Example: The concert selections were <u>more melodic</u> than last season's choice.

 10. The first piece was ____ than the one that followed it.

 11. The conductor made ____ gestures in the quiet sections.

 12. He used a ____ stroke to accent the louder beats.

 13. The pianist seemed ____ than the conductor.

 14. The soprano's voice was the ____ of all.

 15. The applause was the ____ for the ____ performance.

Extra Practice, page 321

WRITING APPLICATION A Comparison

COOPERATIVE LEARNING

Write a descriptive paragraph comparing two types of music, books, or movies that you enjoy. Then, exchange papers with a classmate and check to make sure that comparative and superlative adjectives have been used correctly. Check the rules in this lesson.

5 DEMONSTRATIVE ADJECTIVES

Demonstrative adjectives point out people, places, and things. *This, that, these,* and *those* are demonstrative adjectives. *This* and *these* point out nearby people, places, and things. *That* and *those* point out people, places, and things that are farther away.

> **This** flower is an orchid.
> **Those** blossoms are unique.

When you use a demonstrative adjective, do not add the word *here* or *there* after it.

> CORRECT: **That** beautiful rose has thorns.
> INCORRECT: That there beautiful rose has thorns.

Do not use the pronoun *them* in place of *those.*

> CORRECT: **Those** buds are delicate.
> INCORRECT: Them buds are delicate.

When *this, that, these,* and *those* take the place of nouns and stand alone in a sentence, they are **demonstrative pronouns.**

> **These** are prettier than **those.**
> **That** is a lovely blossom.

Guided Practice

Identify the demonstrative adjective or demonstrative pronoun in each sentence.

Example: That garden is lovely.
> *That demonstrative adjective*

1. This class went to the botanical garden.
2. These are biology students.
3. The teacher showed them this exotic plant.
4. These lovely blossoms grow in the West Indies.
5. Are those very rare?

?! THINK

- How can I tell the difference between a demonstrative adjective and a demonstrative pronoun?

REMEMBER

- A **demonstrative adjective** points out something and describes nouns by answering the question *which one?* or *which ones?*
- A **demonstrative pronoun** points out specific persons, places, or things and stands alone in a sentence.

More Practice

A. Write and label the **demonstrative adjective** or **demonstrative pronoun** in each sentence.

Example: That is the entrance. *That   demonstrative pronoun*

6. The students noticed those tiny violets.
7. These created a blanket on the shady forest floor.
8. That golden flower has large, pale leaves.
9. What kind of flower is this?
10. Those have clusters of yellow flowers.
11. That darkly colored flower is called a bloodroot.
12. Large, flat leaves support that water lily.

B. Write each sentence, using an appropriate demonstrative word. Write whether you used a **demonstrative adjective** or a **demonstrative pronoun.**

Example: <u>Those</u> are the bluest cornflowers I have ever seen. *demonstrative pronoun*

13. ____ lilies drift in the murky water.
14. What is the name of ____ fuzzy-petaled flower?
15. ____ resemble lotuses.
16. The brilliant color of ____ rose will attract bees.
17. Have you ever visited ____ garden before?
18. ____ is my first time here.
19. The fragrance of ____ roses is glorious.
20. Are ____ orchids?

Extra Practice, page 322

WRITING APPLICATION A Dialogue

Work with a partner to write a dialogue between two people who are touring a landmark in your town or in a famous city. Check your work to make sure that you have used demonstrative adjectives and demonstrative pronouns correctly.

6 ADVERBS

An adverb is a word that modifies a verb, an adjective, or another adverb.

You know that adjectives describe nouns. Adverbs are another kind of modifier. An **adverb** describes a verb, an adjective, or another adverb.

Adverbs modify words in a number of ways. They usually answer the question *how? when? where?* or *to what extent?*

Kinds of Adverbs			
How	**When**	**Where**	**To What Extent**
quickly	tonight	here	extremely
softly	before	forward	very
reasonably	first	anywhere	quite

Athletes **vigorously** train for the Olympic Games.
(*Train* is a verb.)

A **very** large crowd watched the skiing event.
(*Large* is an adjective.)

We had waited **quite** patiently for the race to begin.
(*Patiently* is an adverb.)

Guided Practice

Name each adverb and the word it modifies.

Example: A skier fell suddenly.
suddenly fell

1. Many fans eagerly watched the Winter Olympics.
2. Some spectators had traveled far.
3. The mountain winds were quite strong.
4. Skiers sped skillfully through the powdery snow.
5. The crowd cheered very enthusiastically.

 THINK

■ How can I tell if a word in a sentence is an adverb or an adjective?

REMEMBER

- An **adverb** is a word that modifies a verb, an adjective, or another adverb.

- Adverbs answer the questions *how? when? where?* or *to what extent?*

More Practice

A. Write each adverb and the word its modifies.

Example: The spectators wildly cheered our skating
team. *wildly cheered*

6. Skaters competed daily in the large stadium.
7. A worker had smoothed the ice very carefully.
8. The wet ice glittered brightly under the lights.
9. Nervously, the young skaters prepared for the race.
10. Their gleaming skates were extremely sharp.
11. Two American racers competed first.
12. The winner quite happily accepted the medal.
13. Triumphantly, she waved a very beautiful bouquet of roses.

B. Write each adverb and the word it modifies. Then write whether the modified word is a **verb,** an **adjective,** or an **adverb.**

Example: A very experienced announcer explained
each maneuver.
very experienced   adjective

14. Two young skaters quietly waited on a bench.
15. Their shiny costumes sparkled quite brilliantly.
16. The skaters glided gracefully on the empty ice.
17. One moved through a somewhat difficult routine.
18. The other danced rhythmically to a tango beat.
19. His fluid movements were almost perfect.
20. When the skater suddenly fell, he became very pale.

Extra Practice, page 323

WRITING APPLICATION A Newscast

Imagine that you are a reporter at the Olympic Games. In a paragraph, describe one of the events for a radio broadcast. Then, exchange papers with a classmate and identify the adverbs in each other's description.

7 COMPARATIVE AND SUPERLATIVE ADVERBS

The **comparative** form of an adverb compares two actions. The **superlative** form of an adverb compares more than two actions.

1. Add er or est to all adverbs with one syllable and to a few adverbs with two syllables.   fast, fast**er**, fast**est**; early, earli**er**, earli**est**
2. For most adverbs with two syllables and all adverbs with more than two syllables, use more or most.   quickly, **more** quickly, **most** quickly; cheerfully, **more** cheerfully, **most** cheerfully
3. Use less or least to form negative comparisons. **less** often, **least** often
4. Do not use er with more or est with most.

Some adverbs have irregular comparative and superlative forms. See the chart below.

Adverb	Comparative	Superlative
badly	worse	worst
well	better	best
far (distance)	farther	farthest
far (degree)	further	furthest
little	less	least

Guided Practice

Choose the correct word or words for each sentence.

Example: Rain fell (harder, more harder).   *harder*

1. The wind blew (more, most) strongly today than yesterday.
2. The sky turned dark (earlier, more earlier) than usual.
3. The river flooded (worse, worst) than the pond.
4. Weather forecasters predicted heavy rain (more later, later).
5. Waves crashed (worse, worst) near the capital than farther south.

?! THINK

- How do I decide whether to use er or more to form a comparative adverb?

REMEMBER

- The **comparative** form of an adverb compares two actions. Add *er* or use *more* with the adverb.
- The **superlative** form of an adverb compares more than two actions. Add *est* or use *most* with the adverb.
- Do not use *er* with *more* or *est* with *most*.

More Practice

A. Write the correct word or words for each sentence.

Example: The (poorer, poorest) visibility in the state was reported on the coast.   *poorest*

6. Rain fell (more, most) heavily at night than during the day.
7. The storm traveled (farther, more farther) than expected.
8. June glanced out the window (more, most) often than I did.
9. Lightning flashed (less, least) frequently during this storm than during the last one.
10. Traffic was affected (seriouslier, more seriously) along the coast than in town.

B. Write each sentence, using the correct comparative or superlative form of the adverb in parentheses.

Example: One rescue team worked <u>most courageously</u> of all. (courageously)

11. The violent storm struck our town ____ than it struck the capital.   (badly)
12. Low-lying homes were damaged ____ than those in the hills.   (severely)
13. The storm passed through the town ____ than we had hoped.   (slowly)
14. Of all the buildings in town, the town hall has been struck ____ by lightning.   (frequently)
15. Unfortunately, we prepared ____ for this storm than for the last one.   (little)

Extra Practice, page 324

WRITING APPLICATION A Descriptive Paragraph

Compare life in your town with what you imagine life might be like in a foreign country that interests you. Then, exchange papers with a partner and check each other's work to make sure that you have used comparative and superlative adverbs correctly.

8 AVOIDING DOUBLE NEGATIVES

You have already studied several kinds of adverbs. The word *not* is also an adverb. It is a negative word that is often part of a contraction.

> The singer did **not** perform often.
> The singer **didn't** perform often.

Here are some other negative words with their positive forms.

hardly . . . almost	nowhere . . . anywhere
nothing . . . anything	never . . . ever
nobody . . . anybody	none . . . any
no . . . any	no one . . . anyone

Use only one negative word to convey a negative meaning. The incorrect use of two negative words is called a *double negative*. Notice that there are two ways you can correct a sentence that has a double negative.

> **INCORRECT:** The singer didn't use no microphone.
> **CORRECT:** The singer didn't use a microphone.
> **CORRECT:** The singer used no microphone.

Guided Practice

Choose the correct word for each sentence below.

Example: Haven't you (never, ever) heard her before?   *ever*

1. The Yellow Star Cabaret (has, hasn't) hardly been open a year.
2. The cozy little club doesn't charge (no, any) admission.
3. Nobody (never, ever) waits long for a table.
4. You won't see such talented performers (nowhere, anywhere) else.

 THINK

- How can I avoid using a double negative?

REMEMBER

- A **double negative** is the incorrect use of two negative words to convey a negative meaning.
- Avoid double negatives by using only one negative word to convey a negative meaning.

More Practice

A. Write the correct word or words for each sentence.

Example: The pianist could not find his sheet music (nowhere, anywhere).   *anywhere*

5. There (was, wasn't) hardly room for the performer on the stage.
6. No one had (never, ever) heard the young singer.
7. She didn't sing (no, any) songs that we knew.
8. The spotlight didn't shine on (no one, anyone) but her.
9. The singer (couldn't, could) hardly see anything because of the dazzling lights.
10. During the first act there (was, wasn't) hardly a sound in the audience.

B. Write each sentence correctly.

Example: She was not planning to sing neither ballad.   *She was not planning to sing either ballad.*

11. We hadn't never heard a better performer.
12. Didn't no one notice the pianist?
13. The musician hardly never made a mistake.
14. He didn't never look flustered when he played.
15. There wasn't no note that sounded wrong.
16. Hardly no one left the room during the intermission.
17. The singer and musician had never performed together nowhere before.
18. There wasn't nobody as impressed with them as I was.
19. Wasn't there nothing about the performance in the newspaper?
20. I didn't see no announcement about the next show.

Extra Practice, page 325

WRITING APPLICATION A Story

COOPERATIVE
LEARNING

Imagine that you are participating in a stage performance in which everything goes wrong. With a small group of classmates, write a brief story describing the events. Check to make sure that you have not used any double negatives.

9 USING ADJECTIVES AND ADVERBS

You have learned that both adjectives and adverbs describe other kinds of words. Adjectives describe nouns or pronouns. Adverbs modify verbs, adjectives, or other adverbs.

> The **cheerful** tourist arrived in London.   (adjective)
> The tourist drove **cheerfully** through London.   (adverb)

Many adverbs are formed by adding *ly* to an adjective.

ADJECTIVES: serious   careful   sad   childish
ADVERBS: seriously   carefully   sadly   childishly

Some adjectives and adverbs are often confused with each other.

ADJECTIVES: bad   good   real
ADVERBS: badly   well   really

Although *well* is usually an adverb, it is an adjective when it refers to someone's health.

> The tourist met a **real** prince.   (adjective)
> The tourist **really** met a prince.   (adverb)
>
> He had a **bad** subway ride.   (adjective)
> The train shook **badly.**   (adverb)
>
> The tourist had a **good** time in London.   (adjective)
> He used his time **well.**   (adverb)
> Did he feel **well** yesterday?   (adjective)

Guided Practice

Choose the correct word in parentheses for each sentence.

Example: We took photographs (frequent, frequently).
                frequently

1. The bus moved (slow, slowly) through London.
2. We peered (eager, eagerly) out the window.
3. It rained (bad, badly) on several days.
4. Each day we waited (patient, patiently) for the sun.

 THINK

- How can I tell if a word is an adjective or an adverb?

REMEMBER

- Use adjectives, including *bad, good,* and *real,* to describe nouns or pronouns.
- Use adverbs, including *badly, well,* and *really,* to modify verbs, adjectives, or other adverbs.
- You can also use *well* as an adjective when referring to someone's health.

More Practice

A. Write the correct word for each sentence.

Example: We (excited, excitedly) boarded the jumbo jet for our flight.   *excitedly*

5. Each member of our group felt (good, well) during the trip.
6. A tour guide spoke to us (enthusiastic, enthusiastically) about the Tower of London.
7. The jewels sparkled (brilliant, brilliantly) behind the glass.
8. The tower cells were (real, really) small.
9. We strolled (happy, happily) along the Thames River.
10. The English tend their gardens very (good, well).

B. Write each sentence, using the correct word. Then write whether the word is an **adjective** or an **adverb.** Underline the word it modifies.

Example: The bus <u>stopped</u> (abrupt, <u>abruptly</u>) in heavy traffic.   *adverb*

11. We waited (patient, patiently) for the portrait gallery to open.
12. The royal portraits had (magnificent, magnificently) gold frames.
13. One painting of the queen was extremely (well, good).
14. The guide knew his subject very (well, good).
15. We spent a (real, really) long time wandering (slow, slowly) through charming streets back to the hotel.

Extra Practice, Practice Plus, pages 326–327

WRITING APPLICATION A Summary

Write a brief summary of a movie, book, or television show set in a foreign locale. Then, exchange papers with a partner and check to make sure that adjectives and adverbs have been used correctly in each other's work.

10 MECHANICS: Commas with Dates, Addresses, and Names

Remember the following rules for using commas when you write dates, addresses, the titles of people, and letters.

Use a comma before and after the year when you include both the month and the day. Do not use a comma if you use only the month and the year.

> Radio station WXXX began operating on
> June 14, 1954, in Montpelier.
> Its first full month of operation was July 1954.

Use a comma before and after the name of a state or a country when you write it with the name of a city. Do not use a comma after the name of a state if you include the ZIP code.

> Guests from Rutland, Vermont, and other towns spoke
> during the first broadcast.
> You can write to the station at 12 Green Street,
> Montpelier, VT 05602.

Use commas to set off an abbreviated title or degree following a person's name.

> Sarah Collins, M.D., has a radio program on WXXX.

Use a comma after the salutation of a friendly letter and after the closing of both a friendly and a business letter.

> Dear Jim,   Your friend,   Sincerely yours,

Guided Practice

Tell where a comma or commas are needed.

Example: Is Roger Brown Jr. an announcer?
       commas before and after Jr.

1. We visited a radio station near Albany New York.
2. May 1 1990 was a breezy spring day.
3. The bus stopped at 60 Weil Drive Chazy New York.
4. Janice Reddington Ph.D. led the tour of the station.
5. In the cramped newsroom sat Rich Granger M.D.

THINK

- How do I use commas when writing dates and addresses?

REMEMBER

- Use commas to separate the parts of dates and addresses.
- Use commas to set off titles and degrees.
- Use a comma after the closing of a letter and after the salutation of a friendly letter.

More Practice

A. Write these sentences, adding commas where needed.

Example: Send your vote to Deejay Lou Monte Jr. by April 7.
Send your vote to Deejay Lou Monte, Jr., by April 7.

6. Henry Tilson Jr. writes radio scripts.
7. His most popular series is called "Tara Douglas M.D."
8. On June 7 1990 Henry received a fan letter.
9. The envelope read: 13 Dean Drive Bakersfield California.
10. Frank Hopkins Ph.D. was the grateful fan.
11. Hopkins lived at 7 Park Lane Warren Vermont 05674.

B. Write the following letter, adding commas where needed.

                                890 Beadsley Place
                    (12.) Englewood New Jersey 07631
                    (13.) June 30 199_

(14.) George Robinson Ph.D.
         WHLZ
(15.) Newark New Jersey 07619

(16.) Dear George

    Thank you for your extremely entertaining program. **(17.)** I particularly enjoyed the show featuring health issues that aired on June 1 1988. **(18.)** Bill Henderson M.D. was a fascinating guest. Keep up the good work! **(19.)** I look forward to the broadcast you will be doing from Princeton New Jersey next month.

                            (20.) Very truly yours
                            (21.) Doris Grady R.N.

Extra Practice, page 328

WRITING APPLICATION A Letter

Write a letter to your local radio station asking what kinds of programs are offered for young people. Check to make sure you have used commas correctly in dates, addresses, and in the closing.

11 VOCABULARY BUILDING: Synonyms and Antonyms

Using exact language helps you to express your ideas with color and precision. Using synonyms and antonyms can help you to make your writing clearer and more descriptive.

A **synonym** is a word that has the same or nearly the same meaning as another word. Sometimes you can replace a vague or general word in a sentence with a synonym that is more precise.

> The tennis player felt **fine** when the match was over.
> The tennis player felt **exhilarated** when the match was over.

You can also contrast ideas in your writing by using antonyms. **Antonyms** are words with opposite meanings.

> The challenger played **cautiously** at first, but then she **aggressively** fought back to win the match.
> Although Tom **lost** the first set, he **triumphed** in the second set.

When you use an antonym, choose one that is precise. Precision makes contrast sharp and clear.

Guided Practice

Choose the word in parentheses that is more precise.

Example: The weather was (bad, stormy) this morning.
　　　　　　stormy

1. Many young players find the game of tennis (fun, challenging).
2. The bright sun did not distract the (good, skillful) players.
3. The sun-tanned athletes looked (happy, eager).
4. The summer morning was quite (clear, nice).
5. A (small, sparse) group of spectators watched the match.

?! **THINK**
　■ How can using synonyms and antonyms improve my writing?

REMEMBER

- A synonym has the same or almost the same meaning as another word. Antonyms have opposite meanings.
- You can use synonyms and antonyms to make your writing clearer and more precise.

More Practice

A. For each sentence write the word that is more precise.

Example: The match between the eager amateurs (pleased, thrilled) the crowd. *thrilled*

6. An excited audience filled the (big, gigantic) stadium.
7. Each player (longed, wanted) to win the valuable trophy.
8. The competitors (looked, squinted) at each other.
9. Then the young amateur (held, gripped) the racket.
10. The other player's face (showed, expressed) determination.
11. She (slammed, hit) the ball with great strength.
12. The ball (sailed, flew) swiftly through the air.
13. Her opponent (leaped, jumped) to reach the ball.

B. Write each sentence, replacing each underlined word with its antonym. Consult a dictionary, if necessary.

Example: His movements on the court were clumsy. (awkward, graceful) *graceful*

14. Jan appeared serious at first. (solemn, jovial)
15. Then she gave a brief smile. (prolonged, momentary)
16. Jan was confident that she would win the match. (uncertain, positive)
17. She had a strong forehand stroke. (energetic, feeble)
18. The audience gave Jan a loud cheer. (inaudible, deafening)
19. She felt tired after the two-hour match. (listless, vigorous)
20. Yet she walked off the court looking very enthusiastic. (excited, defeated)

Extra Practice, page 329

WRITING APPLICATION Revise a Composition

Find a composition that you have already written and read it over carefully. Revise any sentences that could be made clearer by replacing words with synonyms that are more colorful or precise. Where it is possible, use antonyms to contrast ideas sharply.

GRAMMAR —AND WRITING CONNECTION

Combining Sentences

When you describe persons, places, or things in your writing, you can sometimes connect your ideas better by combining details from two different sentences. To combine sentences you may use descriptive words that end in *ing* or *ed*.

SEPARATE: The coach talked with the players.
The coach stood smiling.
COMBINED: The smiling coach talked with the players.

SEPARATE: One player glanced around nervously.
The player was worried.
COMBINED: One worried player glanced around nervously.

Sometimes the word ending in *ing* or *ed* is part of a group of words.

SEPARATE: Beth saw the volleyball.
She saw it spinning on the ground.
COMBINED: Beth saw the volleyball spinning on the ground.

SEPARATE: The team noticed the spectators.
The spectators were seated in the bleachers.
COMBINED: The team noticed the spectators seated in the bleachers.

Working Together

COOPERATIVE
LEARNING

Work with your classmates to combine each pair of sentences. Use words ending in *ing* or *ed*.

Example: The players shook hands. The players were competing.
The competing players shook hands.

1. One player wiped her brow. Her brow was dripping with sweat.
2. The referee checked the score. The score seemed confusing.
3. A change was made on the scoreboard.
The scoreboard was situated near the court.

Revising Sentences

Yoko wrote the following sentences in her journal when she was planning a composition. Help her revise her notes by combining sentences. Use words ending in *ing* or *ed* to combine each pair of sentences.

4. The fans heard a plane.
   They heard it flying overhead.
5. The crowd scowled toward the sky.
   The crowd was annoyed.
6. Soon the plane passed by.
   The plane was soaring.
7. Now the audience concentrated on the players.
   The audience watched the players maneuvering on the court.
8. Some fans peered through binoculars.
   The binoculars were rented.
9. One player succumbed to the heat.
   The heat was sweltering.
10. The game was played on a new court.
    The court was designed for frequent use.
11. A reporter spoke with some players.
    The reporter found them waiting on a bench.
12. The reporter was interviewing young people.
    The reporter knew they were interested in sports careers.

Think about the sights, sounds, people, and places described in this unit. Choose one of these subjects or a topic of your own and write a descriptive paragraph that lets the reader share your view of your subject.

When you revise your paragraph, work with a partner to find pairs of related sentences that you could improve by combining them. Use words ending in *ing* or *ed* to help when you combine sentences.

UNIT CHECKUP

LESSON 1

Adjectives (page 290)   For each sentence write the adjectives and the words they describe. Label each **predicate adjective.**

1. The ancient people of Egypt built enormous pyramids.
2. The magnificient structures look gigantic on the horizon.
3. Many people have traveled to the pyramids since early times.
4. Lovely works of art decorate the pyramids' inner walls.

LESSON 2

Articles and Proper Adjectives (page 292)   Capitalize each proper adjective. Add the correct indefinite article.

5. old canadian city
6. early egyptian vase
7. juicy florida orange
8. portuguese tourist
9. delicious french meal
10. unusual chinese temple

LESSONS 3-4

Comparative and Superlative Adjectives (pages 294, 296)   Write each sentence, using the correct form of the comparative or superlative adjective given in parentheses.

11. At one time the Empire State Building was the ____ building in the world.   (most tallest, tallest)
12. Is it ____ than before?   (more popular, most popular)
13. The shape of the Eiffel Tower is ____ than the shape of the Leaning Tower of Pisa.   (unusualler, more unusual)
14. Who designed the world's ____ stadium?   (most largest, largest)

LESSON 5

Demonstrative Adjectives (page 298)   Write each sentence, using the correct word or words in parentheses.

15. Louis Sullivan created ____ designs.   (those, them)
16. ____ building, like most of his work, has a distinctive style.   (This here, This)
17. Is ____ drawing one of Sullivan's plans?   (that, that there)
18. The style of ____ office buildings was influenced by one of ____ early designs by Sullivan.   (these, these here) (them, those)

LESSON 6

Adverbs (page 300)   Write each adverb. Then write whether it modifies a **verb,** an **adverb,** or an **adjective.**

19. Architects work carefully on their plans for buildings.
20. Groups of architects very often create a single new plan.
21. They work together toward a satisfactory building design.
22. A good building meets the needs of its owner completely.
23. Especially ambitious architects create really exciting styles.

LESSON

7

Comparative and Superlative Adverbs (page 302)   Write the
comparative and superlative forms of each adverb. See Teacher's
Edition for

24. proudly
25. far (distance)
26. little

27. slowly
28. intensely
29. well

30. fast answers.
31. effectively
32. friendly

LESSONS

8-9

Avoiding Double Negatives (page 304); **Using Adjectives and
Adverbs** (page 306)   Write each sentence, using the correct
word.

33. Hardly ____ country has more cathedrals than France. (any, no)
34. Gothic cathedrals rise ____ toward the sky. (majestically,
majestic)
35. The world hadn't ____ seen such lofty architecture. (never, ever)
36. Their stained glass windows can be ____ dazzling. (real, really)

LESSON

10

Mechanics: Commas (page 308)   Write each sentence, using
commas where they are needed.

37. On May 4,1989,the antipollution project began.
38. Speakers came from Phoenix,Arizona,and Paris,France.
39. Ana Fujita,Ph.D.,spoke about air pollution.
40. Write to me at 12 Ridge Road,Orange,CT 06477.

LESSON

11

Vocabulary Building: Synonyms and Antonyms (page
310)   Write each sentence, replacing each underlined word
with a more precise synonym. Then write an antonym for
each word you use.   Answers may vary.

41. Last month our class took an <u>interesting</u> trip to New York City.
42. A guide conducted a <u>nice</u> bus tour of many of the city's most
famous sights.
43. We <u>went</u> down Fifth Avenue and saw towering skyscrapers and
famous department stores.
44. Everyone in the group was <u>sad</u> when we had to return home.

Writing Application: Using Adjectives and Adverbs (pages
290–307)   The following paragraph contains 10 errors with
adjectives and adverbs. Rewrite the paragraph correctly. See Teacher's
Edition for

45.–50.   The tourists exhibited their vacation photos <u>proud</u> and <u>eager</u>. answers.
Brian enjoyed Maria's <u>eerily</u> shot of the moonlit pyramids. Sally
laughed <u>merry</u> at the photo of Howard wearing a floppy <u>french</u>
chef's hat. Betty wished she could see how <u>majestically</u> the Eiffel
Tower looked at sunrise.

All-Purpose Adjectives

Imagine that you are an ad writer for an all-purpose department store. Using each letter of the alphabet, write pairs of adjectives and nouns describing items sold at the store. For example, *admirable armchairs, beautiful bowling balls, clever computers.* Share your work with classmates.

YOU DON'T SAY

Play a guessing game with a partner or small group of players. One player thinks of an object, person, or place; he or she then supplies a sentence that contains an adjective or a comparative or superlative adjective describing the subject. Other players take turns trying to identify the mystery topic.

Tom Swifties

Tom Swift was the hero of a popular series of boys' books published over fifty years ago. Today, people still enjoy a word game called *Tom Swifties.* These are puns, or plays on words, that involve adverbs. Some examples of Tom Swifties are: "Where is the sandpaper?" asked Tom roughly. "Let's get this corn shucked," said Tom huskily. "I'm going to the racetrack," said Tom hoarsely. How many Tom Swifties can you create? Here are some ideas to get you started: . . . said Tom chirpingly . . . said Tom gravely . . . said Tom weakly . . . said Tom brightly.

AROUND THE WORLD

Find a map, atlas, or globe. Write a list of proper adjectives that are formed from the names of at least ten places around the world. Then, use your list to write a brief story about a hotel that attracts tourists from many nations.

The Best Destination

Think of a place you would love to visit. Try to persuade a classmate to travel there with you. Use comparative and superlative adverbs and adjectives to help you convince your friend that he or she should join you on a trip.

A Message from Outer Space

Every night astronomers in observatories all over the world listen for a message originating from a life form in another solar system. Imagine that tonight is the night and you are the lucky scientist to be on duty when the message describing life on another planet is received. Share the message with a classmate. Use vivid adjectives and adverbs to communicate what life is like in outer space.

EXTRA PRACTICE

Three levels of practice

Adjectives (page 290)

LEVEL

A. Write the adjective or adjectives in each sentence.

1. Last week, our class went on an exciting trip.
2. We saw a fine play by Tennessee Williams.
3. A theatrical company performed the emotional drama.
4. The simple set resembled an average home.
5. Dim lights hung from the high ceiling.
6. In one scene Amanda appears in a frilly dress.
7. Her daughter keeps a collection of delicate glass.
8. The tiny animals are precious to Laura.

LEVEL

B. Write each adjective or predicate adjective and the word it describes.

9. Our production of *West Side Story* was very colorful.
10. The lively action of the play takes place on the streets.
11. Several energetic actors portrayed the teenagers.
12. They snapped their fingers to a rhythmic beat.
13. The music is essential to the play.
14. One young actress sang beautifully.
15. Many characters meet for a fight.
16. The tragic scene takes place in a playground.

LEVEL

C. Write each sentence, using an appropriate adjective to complete it. Then underline the word the adjective describes.

17. Kim attended a ____ production of *As You Like It*.
18. The ____ Shakespeare play was performed outdoors.
19. The ____ trees and plants provided the setting.
20. The ____ audience sat comfortably on the grass.
21. The performers looked ____ in their costumes.
22. During the intermission, we strolled around the ____ theater.
23. After the ____ act, raindrops began to fall.
24. Workers covered the ____ stage with plastic.
25. The play continued when the sky looked ____.

EXTRA PRACTICE

Three levels of practice

Articles and Proper Adjectives (page 292)

LEVEL

A. Write each group of words. Underline and capitalize each proper adjective. Add the article *a* or *an*.

1. italian pizza
2. chinese egg roll
3. french soufflé
4. greek spinach pie
5. polish ham
6. african mask
7. spanish omelet
8. hungarian goulash
9. new england lobster
10. alaskan crab

LEVEL

B. Write each sentence. Underline and capitalize each proper adjective. Add an indefinite article in the blank.

11. ＿＿ english restaurant usually serves scones with tea.
12. The cook prepared ＿＿ bowl of spicy mexican chili.
13. ＿＿ israeli falafel is a special sandwich.
14. Bob made the thin pastry for ＿＿ german strudel.
15. The guests enjoyed ＿＿ creamy yorkshire pudding.
16. The fragrant sauce contained ＿＿ jamaican spice.
17. ＿＿ scottish haggis is a flavorful boiled pudding.

LEVEL

C. Change each group of words into a phrase that contains a proper adjective. Then, write a sentence for each phrase that contains the indefinite article *a* or *an* before the phrase.

18. furniture set from Sweden
19. automobile from Japan
20. wool from England
21. perfume from France
22. chef from Italy
23. singer from Brazil
24. movie from Australia
25. prince from Spain

EXTRA PRACTICE

Three levels of practice

Comparative and Superlative Adjectives I (page 294)

A. Write and label the comparative adjective or superlative adjective in each sentence.

1. The group on this trip was bigger than the last group.
2. The greatest thrill was the huge skyscrapers.
3. What city could be noisier?
4. The traffic was worst in the downtown section.
5. The neon signs seemed brighter at night than during the day.
6. We thought it was the best trip we have taken.
7. The city was busiest during rush hour.

LEVEL

B. Write the correct comparative or superlative adjective for each sentence.

8. The subway was much (faster, fastest) than the bus.
9. The peaceful ferry boat ride was the (quieter, quietest) of all.
10. A ride in the fancy horse-drawn carriage was (bumpier, bumpiest) than the bus.
11. The winding path through the park was a (slower, slowest) route than some others.
12. The park was the (prettier, prettiest) spot of all.
13. The students spent a (longer, longest) time in the park than they had expected.

LEVEL

C. Write each sentence, using the correct superlative or comparative form of the adjective in parentheses.

14. The graceful Empire State Building was once the ____ building in the world. (tall)
15. The World Trade Center is even ____. (high)
16. The view of the impressive city was ____ of all from the observation deck on the top floor. (good)
17. Everything looked ____ from that level than from the lower level. (little)
18. The majestic Statue of Liberty seemed ____ than a toy model. (short)
19. The ____ problem was deciding which landmarks to skip. (bad)
20. The ____ part of the entire visit was telling stories of a million encounters. (good)

EXTRA PRACTICE

Three levels of practice

Comparative and Superlative Adjectives II (page 296)

LEVEL

A. Write the comparative or superlative adjective.

1. The museum is the most beautiful place in town.
2. The plaza fountain looked more exquisite at night than during the day.
3. The plaza was less busy late at night.
4. Last night's performance was more impressive than today's.
5. The most magnificent building of all is the opera house.

LEVEL

B. Write the correct comparative or superlative adjective.

6. The lobby of the spacious opera house is the (more interesting, most interesting) area of all.
7. We took a tour to get a (closer, more closer) look at the luxurious building.
8. The fascinating tour was (less crowded, least crowded) than we had expected it to be.
9. The (most intriguing, intriguingest) room is the well-kept art gallery downstairs.
10. The (most loveliest, loveliest) part is the chandeliers.
11. They were suspended in the (cleverer, cleverest) way.
12. When they dimmed, they also glided upward with the (smoother, smoothest) motion.
13. This was probably a (greater, greatest) surprise to us than to the others.

LEVEL

C. Write each sentence, using the correct comparative or superlative form of the adjective in parentheses.

14. The lighting controls were the ____ I have ever seen. (intricate)
15. The busy scenery shop was filled with the ____ equipment imaginable. (advanced)
16. The scenery for the next play seemed ____ than that for the last production. (realistic)
17. The dressing room was ____ than others I had seen. (crowded)
18. The seats in the expensive family circle were the ____ of all. (luxurious)
19. The decorations were ____ than we had expected. (dazzling)
20. The auditorium was the ____ when the curtain rose. (hushed)

EXTRA PRACTICE

Three levels of practice

Demonstrative Adjectives (page 298)

LEVEL

A. Write the demonstrative adjective in each sentence.

1. This biology class studies many trees.
2. These evergreen leaves are long and sharp.
3. That thick outer bark helps to protect the tree.
4. Do you know the height of those trees?
5. Silvery colored bark covers these beech trees.
6. This berry-shaped cone is smaller than those.
7. Take a picture of that stately blue spruce.

LEVEL

B. Write each sentence. Draw one line under each demonstrative adjective and two lines under the word it describes.

8. Look at these towering trees.
9. This velvety flower grows on a magnolia tree.
10. In the fall these leaves turn brilliant red.
11. Those light, dry pods come from the maple tree.
12. The roots of this old tree are thick and gnarled.
13. That tree does not belong to this species.
14. Which tree produces these exotic fruits?

LEVEL

C. Write each sentence, using the correct demonstrative adjective in parentheses. Then underline the word the adjective describes.

15. The giant redwood tree produces ____ yellow-green needles, which stay on the tree for years.   (these, this)
16. ____ gigantic trees impressed everyone.   (Those, Them)
17. A huge forest of ____ redwoods looks dark and crowded.   (these, this)
18. The tough texture of ____ species helps to protect it from fire.   (that, that there)
19. ____ lumpy growth on the tree trunk is called a burl.   (This, This here)
20. People value ____ burls for their decorative grain.   (these, them)

EXTRA PRACTICE

Three levels of practice

Adverbs (page 300)

LEVEL

A. Write the adverb or adverbs in each sentence. Then write the word that each adverb modifies.

1. Many fans cheer loudly during baseball games.
2. Players train daily during the spring.
3. The new catcher reacts quickly.
4. Each batter watches the ball very intently.
5. If you swing the bat wildly, you may miss.
6. These batters hit the ball accurately.
7. A swift runner sometimes slides on the ground.
8. The tall outfielder patiently waits in the field.

LEVEL

B. For each sentence write the adverb or adverbs and the words they modify. Then write whether each modified word is a **verb,** an **adjective,** or an **adverb.**

9. The huge stadium quickly filled with fans.
10. Vendors sold very inexpensive baseball caps.
11. Jonathan sat nervously in the steep bleachers.
12. The enthusiastic crowd shouted noisily for their team.
13. The players respectfully saluted the flag.
14. The bright sun shone directly in the pitcher's eyes.
15. He squinted quite badly from the glare.
16. A thick, dark cloud soon covered the sun.
17. Immediately, the famous pitcher threw the ball.

LEVEL

C. Write each sentence, using a suitable adverb. Then underline the word modified by the adverb and write whether it is a **verb,** an **adjective,** or an **adverb.**

18. Players filed ____ across the field.
19. The catcher waited ____ behind home plate.
20. He reached ____ toward the speeding ball.
21. ____, he threw the ball to the expectant pitcher.
22. The umpire ____ examined the muddy ball.
23. Karen's fingers gripped the wooden bat ____ tightly.
24. The catcher ____ adjusted his metal face mask.
25. Karen looked ____ joyful as she reached home base.

EXTRA PRACTICE

Three levels of practice

Comparative and Superlative Adverbs (page 302)

A. Write each sentence, using the correct comparative or superlative adverb in parentheses.

1. Betty arrived at the apartment ____ than I did.   (earlier, earliest)
2. Many guests came in ____ than we did.   (later, more later)
3. One singer was dressed ____ of all.   (more elegantly, most elegantly)
4. She waited ____ than I did.   (most calmly, more calmly)
5. The voice teacher spoke ____ than she usually spoke. (more nervously, most nervously)
6. The vocal concert started ____ than anyone had expected. (sooner, more sooner)

B. Write each sentence, using the correct comparative or superlative form of the adverb in parentheses.

7. The host paced ____ than the pianist did. (anxiously)
8. The first singer performed ____ than the second. (confidently)
9. An inexperienced young man sang ____ than we thought he would. (well)
10. After the song he bowed ____ than was necessary. (often)
11. The curly-haired soprano stood ____ than a queen. (proudly)
12. She sang the delicate high notes ____ of all. (beautifully)

C. Write each sentence. Correct each mistake in the use of comparative or superlative adverbs.

13. Rita sings more better than that performer.
14. The pianist played the last number more beautifully of all.
15. He performed more better during this recital than the last.
16. I enjoy recitals least than Laura.
17. Of all the seasons, this duo performs more frequently during the winter.
18. The audience was more noisier during the first intermission than the second.
19. One person coughed most loudest than anyone we had ever heard.
20. Someone complained even politely than we did.

EXTRA PRACTICE

Three levels of practice

Avoiding Double Negatives (page 304)

LEVEL

A. Write each sentence, using the correct word or words in parentheses.

1. The film crew hadn't (never, ever) worked at this location.
2. The quiet director hardly said (anything, nothing) to the actors.
3. The crew didn't waste (no, any) time constructing the sets.
4. The first set didn't satisfy (nobody, anybody).
5. There wasn't (nothing, anything) original about it.
6. Didn't the set designer (never, ever) approve the final plan?
7. She couldn't find (anyone, no one) to supervise the crew.

LEVEL

B. Rewrite each sentence by replacing each underlined negative word with a positive word.

8. There wasn't <u>no</u> room in the crowded screening room.   any
9. No one knew <u>nothing</u> about the new film.   anything
10. We didn't see <u>no one</u> familiar in the audience.   anyone
11. Haven't you <u>never</u> seen a preview before?   ever
12. The ending of the film didn't make <u>no</u> sense.   any
13. This film isn't playing <u>nowhere</u> else.   anywhere
14. Hasn't <u>no one</u> heard of this director?   anyone

LEVEL

C. Write each sentence correctly.   Answers may vary

15. Hardly <u>no one</u> had seen the new set.   anyone
16. There wasn't a larger prop <u>nowhere</u> at the movie studio.   anywhere
17. Unfortunately, the crane couldn't lift <u>no</u> heavy equipment.   any
18. Didn't the director do <u>nothing</u> about the problem?   anything
19. The young director never hired <u>nobody</u> unprofessional.   anybody
20. She didn't want <u>none</u> of the actors to be amateurs.   any

EXTRA PRACTICE

Three levels of practice

Using Adjectives and Adverbs (page 306)

LEVEL
A. Write the correct word for each sentence.
1. Ramon thought (cheery, cheerily) about his backpacking trip.
2. He ran (quick, quickly) down the train station stairs.
3. The huge train clanked (bad, badly) as it began to move.
4. Ramon gazed (curious, curiously) through the window at the lush green landscape.
5. He could observe much of the scenery quite (good, well) from his seat.

LEVEL
B. Write each sentence, using the correct word in parentheses. Then write whether the word is an **adjective** or an **adverb.**
6. The inhabitants of the village greeted Ramon (charming, charmingly).
7. His helpful map was drawn very (clear, clearly).
8. Ramon walked (casual, casually) down the narrow dirt path that led to the sea.
9. High in the midday sky, the sun was (intense, intensely).
10. He was (real, really) glad when he finally reached the beautiful ocean.

LEVEL
C. Write each sentence, using a suitable adjective or adverb to complete it. Write whether the word you add is an **adjective** or an **adverb.**

11. Ramon gazed ____ across the beach.
12. The waves crashed ____ against the rocks.
13. He felt ____ beside the sea.
14. The sunset was ____ in the western sky.
15. Ramon walked ____ along the beach.
16. He thought ____ about the problem.
17. The problem was ____.
18. The solution was simply ____.
19. ____ he stopped.
20. The answer flashed through his mind like a ____.

PRACTICE + PLUS

Three levels of additional practice for a difficult skill

Using Adjectives and Adverbs (page 306)

LEVEL

A. Write the correct word for each sentence.

1. Rosa's art class decided (recent, recently) on a class trip.
2. They made their choice (easy, easily).
3. A nearby museum was (particular, particularly) interesting.
4. It had an (unusual, unusually) collection of American art.
5. Rosa waited (impatient, impatiently) for the day of the trip.
6. The day arrived (final, finally).
7. Rosa's class (quiet, quietly) entered the museum.

LEVEL

B. Write each sentence, using the correct word in parentheses. Then write whether the word is an **adjective** or an **adverb.**

8. Rosa was (eager, eagerly) to see the new American art exhibit.
9. The artists used colors (good, well).
10. They painted their subjects (bold, boldly).
11. Rosa liked the (dramatic, dramatically) interpretations.
12. Her teacher spoke (brief, briefly) about the various styles.
13. Some of the artists relied (heavy, heavily) on a wide range of colors.
14. Other artists (rare, rarely) used bright colors.

LEVEL

C. Complete each sentence with an appropriate adjective or adverb. Write whether the word you add is an **adjective** or an **adverb.**

15. Later the students spoke ____ about the trip.
16. Some students praised the ____ American sculpture.
17. Rosa liked the mobiles ____ of all.
18. She admired the ____ designs.
19. George wrote ____ about the paintings he saw.
20. All the students had ____ ideas for their own art work.

G
R
A
M
M
A
R

EXTRA PRACTICE

Three levels of practice

Mechanics: Using Commas with Dates,

Addresses, and Names (page 308)

LEVEL
A. Decide whether commas are used correctly or incorrectly in each sentence. Write **correct** or **incorrect.**

1. On April 3 1990 Doris received an invitation.
2. She was invited to speak at the Bonner Museum in June 1990.
3. The letter was sent from Bangor Maine.
4. Frances Keiler, Sr. drove Doris to the building.
5. The address was 78 Grady Street, Bath Maine 04530.
6. Gordon Franklin, M.D., accompanied Doris.
7. Helen Troiami Ph.D. opened the huge museum doors.
8. The large, old art museum was founded on June 6, 1897.

LEVEL
B. Write each sentence, adding commas where they are needed.

9. Many beautiful paintings arrived from Rome Italy.
10. George Peters Jr. donated many heavy golden frames.
11. This modern portrait arrived on July 12 1989.
12. The artist lives at 98 Rock Road Augusta Maine 04330.
13. This small stone sculpture came from Cairo Egypt last week.
14. The large, colorful painting was dated August 1 1790.
15. The director of the museum is Robert Taylor Ph.D.
16. He held a small, floral etching dated June 1954.
17. We soon drove back to 43 Gare Street Troy New York.

LEVEL
C. Write the following letter. Add commas were they are needed.

(18.) Sharon Tiley M.D.
432 Thorton Circle

(19.) Fort Collins Colorado 80523

(20.) Dear Sharon

(21.) Thomas Richards Ph.D. will arrive in our town in June 1990. (22.) We are most honored to welcome him at our museum in Memphis Tennessee 37501. (23.) We would like you to join us at 980 Frewer Street Memphis Tennessee 37501.

(24.) Sincerely

(25.) Vera Lancaster Ph.D.

EXTRA PRACTICE

Three levels of practice

Vocabulary Building: Synonyms and Antonyms (page 310)

LEVEL

A. For each sentence write the word that is more precise.

1. The instructors at the health club are (nice, friendly).
2. One instructor gave Helen a (good, detailed) tour.
3. The two of them even (went, jogged) around the track once.
4. The training rooms were (airy, big).
5. Helen also (saw, inspected) the pool.
6. The instructor spoke (knowledgeably, well) about the importance of fitness.
7. The membership fee was (inexpensive, good).

LEVEL

B. Write each sentence, replacing the underlined word with its antonym. Use one of the words in parentheses.

8. The music sounded <u>cheerful</u> to Helen. (lively, uninspiring)
9. The exercise class began at a <u>quick</u> pace. (hasty, leisurely)
10. Helen's <u>stylish</u> sneakers pounded the wooden floor. (unfashionable, attractive)
11. The instructions for each exercise were <u>simple</u>. (concise, elaborate)
12. The <u>noisy</u> room shook with music and motion. (tranquil, boisterous)
13. Some students arrived <u>late</u>. (tardily, promptly)

LEVEL

C. Write each sentence, replacing each underlined word with a more precise synonym.

14. We have <u>good</u> physical education facilities at our school.
15. The swimming pool is <u>big</u>.
16. My gym teacher is <u>nice</u>.
17. The basketball players <u>moved</u> across the court.
18. Amanda <u>put</u> the ball through the net.
19. The spectators <u>said</u> different cheers.
20. The losing team felt <u>sad</u>.

UNIT

10

Writing Descriptions

Read the quotation and look at the picture on the opposite page. Talk about how a writer paints a picture with words.

When you write a descriptive paragraph, you will want to construct a vivid image for your audience. You will want to create a mood for the paragraph and provide enough details to help your audience see the picture in their minds.

Focus Descriptive writing presents an overall impression and includes sensory details that create a clear picture of a person, place, or thing.

What would you like to describe? On the following pages you will find a story filled with description. You will see some photographs, too. You can use them to find ideas for writing.

THEME: *VISIONS*

*We can see the world through books, and
the books will be our tents.*

—M. B. Goffstein

AWARD
WINNING
SELECTION

Have you ever owned a pet? How did you get it? What funny or dangerous situations did your pet get into?

Helvi is the daughter of Finnish people who have set up a farm in the Canadian wilderness. Her parents speak no English. She is starved for companionship—until one day she notices a limp, furry creature clinging to life by the riverbank.

As you read about Helvi's adventures, notice the details that the author describes to help you share her experiences.

from The Incredible Journey

BY SHEILA BURNFORD

Many miles downstream on the side to which the dogs had crossed, a small cabin stood near the bank of the river, surrounded by three or four acres of cleared land, its solid, uncompromising appearance lightened only by the scarlet geraniums at the window sills and a bright blue door. A log barn stood back from it, and a steam-bath house at the side nearer the river. The patch of vegetable garden, the young orchard and the neatly fenced fields, each with their piles of cleared boulders and stumps, were small orderly miracles of victory won from the dark encroaching forest that surrounded them.[1]

Reino Nurmi and his wife lived here, as sturdy and uncompromising as the cabin they had built with their own hand-hewn logs, their lives as frugal and orderly as the fields they had

1. A main impression of orderliness is expressed at the beginning.

wrested from the wilderness. They had tamed the bush, and in return it yielded them their food and their scant living from trap lines and a wood lot, but the struggle to keep it in subjection was endless. They had retained their Finnish identity complete when they left their homeland, exchanging only one country's set of solitudes and vast lonely forests for another's, and as yet their only real contact with the new world that lay beyond their property line was through their ten-year-old daughter Helvi, who knew no other homeland. Helvi walked the lonely miles to the waiting school bus each day, and through her they strengthened their roots in the security of the New World, and were content meanwhile with horizons limited by their labor.

On the Sunday afternoon that the beaver dam broke, a day of some relaxation, Helvi was down by the river, skipping flat stones across the water, and wishing that she had a companion; for she found it difficult to be entirely fair in a competition always held against herself. The riverbank was steep and high here, so she was quite safe when a rushing torrent of water, heralded by a great curling wave, swept past. She stood watching it, fascinated by the spectacle, thinking that she must go and tell her father, when her eye was caught by a piece of debris that had been whirling around in a back eddy and was now caught on some boulders at the edge of the bank. She could see what looked like a small, limp body on the surface. She ran along by the boiling water to investigate, scrambling down the bank, to stand looking pityingly at the wet, bedraggled body, wondering what it was, for she had never seen anything like it before. She dragged the mass of twigs and branches further up on land, then ran to call her mother.

Mrs. Nurmi was out in the yard by an old wood stove which she still used for boiling the vegetable dyes for her weaving, or peelings and scraps for the hens. She followed Helvi, calling out to her husband to come and see this strange animal washed up by an unfamiliar, swift-surging river.

He came, with his unhurried countryman's walk and quiet thoughtful face, and joined the others to look down in silence at the small limp body, the darkly plastered fur betraying its slightness, the frail skull bones and thin crooked tail mercilessly exposed. Suddenly he bent down and pulled back the skin above and below one eye and looked more closely. He turned and saw Helvi's anxious, questioning face close to his own and beyond that her mother's. "Is a drowned *cat* worth trying to save?" he asked them, and when her mother nodded, before Helvi's pleading eyes, he said no more, but scooped the soaking bundle up and walked back to the cabin, telling Helvi to run ahead and bring some dry sacks.

He laid the cat down in a sunny patch by the wood stove and rubbed it vigorously with sacking, turning the body from side to side until the fur stood out in every direction and it looked like some disheveled old scarf. Then, as he wrapped the sacking firmly around and her mother pried the clenched teeth open, Helvi poured a little warm milk and precious brandy down the pale cold throat.[2]

She watched as a spasm ran through the body, followed by a faint cough, then held her breath in sympathy as the cat retched and choked convulsively, a thin dribble of milk appearing at the side of its mouth. Reino laid the straining body over his knee and pressed gently over the ribcage. The cat choked and struggled for breath, until at last a sudden gush of water streamed out, and it lay relaxed. Reino gave a slow smile of satisfaction and handed the bundle of sacking to Helvi, telling her to keep it warm and quiet for a while—if she was sure that she still wanted a cat.

She felt the oven, still warm though the fire had long died out, then placed the cat on a tray inside, leaving the door open. When her mother went into the cabin to prepare supper and Reino left to milk the cow, Helvi sat cross-legged on the ground by the stove, anxiously chewing the end of one fair braid, watching and waiting. Every now and then she would put her hand into the oven to touch the cat, to loosen the sacking or to stroke the soft fur, which was beginning to pulsate with life under her fingers.

After half an hour she was rewarded: the cat opened his eyes. She leaned over and looked closely into them—their blackness now contracted, slowly, to pinpoints, and a pair of astonishingly vivid blue eyes looked up instead. Presently, under her gentle stroking, she felt a throaty vibration, then heard a rusty, feeble purring. Wildly excited, she called to her parents.

Within another half hour the little Finnish girl held in her lap a sleek, purring, Siamese cat, who had already finished two

2. The writer uses details that refer to several of the senses.

saucers of milk (which normally he detested, drinking only water) and who had groomed himself from head to foot. By the time the Nurmi family were eating their supper around the scrubbed pine table, he had finished a bowl of chopped meat, and was weaving his way around the table legs, begging in his plaintive, odd voice for more food, his eyes crossed intently, his kinked tail held straight in the air like a banner. Helvi was fascinated by him, and by his gentleness when she picked him up.

That night the Nurmis were having fresh pickerel, cooked in the old-country way with the head still on and surrounded by potatoes. Helvi ladled the head with some broth and potatoes into a saucer and put it on the floor. Soon the fishhead had disappeared to the accompaniment of pleased rumbling growls. The potatoes followed; then, holding down the plate with his paw, the cat polished it clean. Satisfied at last, he stretched superbly, his front paws extended so that he looked like a heraldic lion, then jumped onto Helvi's lap, curled himself around and purred loudly.

The parents' acceptance was completed by his action, though there had never before been a time or place in the economy of their lives for an animal which did not earn its keep, or lived anywhere else except the barn or kennel. For the first time in her life Helvi had a pet.

Helvi carried the cat up to bed with her, and he draped himself with familiar ease over her shoulder as she climbed the steep ladder stairs leading up to her little room in the eaves. She tucked him tenderly into an old wooden cradle, and he lay in sleepy contentment, his dark face incongruous against a doll's pillow.

Late in the night she woke to a loud purring in her ear, and felt him treading a circle at her back. The wind blew a gust of cold rain across her face and she leaned over to shut the window, hearing far away, so faint that it died in the second of windborn sound, the thin, high keening of a wolf. She shivered as she lay down, then drew the new comforting warmth of the cat closely to her.

When Helvi left in the morning for the long walk and ride to the distant school the cat lay curled on the window sill among the geraniums. He had eaten a large plate of oatmeal, and his coat shone in the sun as he licked it sleepily, his eyes following Mrs. Nurmi as she moved about the cabin. But when she went outside with a basket of washing she looked back to see him standing on his hind legs peering after, his soundless mouth opening and shutting behind the window. She hurried back, fearful of her geraniums, and opened the door—at which he was already scratching—half expecting him to run. Instead he followed her to the washing line and sat by the basket, purring. He followed her back and forth between the cabin and the wood stove, the henhouse and the stable. When she shut him out once by mistake he wailed pitifully.

This was the pattern of his behavior all day—he shadowed the Nurmis as they went about their chores, appearing silently on some point of vantage—the seat of the harrow, a sack of potatoes, the manger or the well platform—his eyes on them constantly. Mrs. Nurmi was touched by his apparent need for companionship: that his behavior was unlike that of any other cat she attributed to his foreign appearance. But her husband was not so easily deceived—he had noticed the unusual intensity in the blue eyes. When a passing raven mocked the cat's voice and he did not look up, then later sat unheeding in the stable to a quick rustle in the straw behind, Reino knew then that the cat was deaf.

Carrying her schoolbooks and lunch pail, Helvi ran most of the way home across the fields and picked up the cat as well when he came to meet her. He clung to her shoulder, balancing easily, while she performed the routine evening chores that awaited her. Undeterred by his weight she fed the hens, gathered eggs, fetched water, then sat at the table stringing dried mushrooms. When she put him down before supper she saw that her father was right—the pointed ears did not respond to any sound, though she noticed that he started and turned his head at the vibration if she clapped her hands or dropped even a small pebble on the bare floor.

She had brought home two books from the traveling library, and after the supper dishes had been cleared away her parents sat by the stove in the short interval before bed while she read aloud to them, translating as she went. They sat, in their moment of rare relaxation, with the cat stretched out on his back at their feet, and the child's soft voice, flowing through the dark austerity of the cabin, carried them beyond the circle of light from the oil lamp to the warmth and brightness of strange lands . . .

They heard of seafaring Siamese cats who worked their passages the world over, their small hammocks made and slung by their human messmates, who held them second to none as ship's cats; and of the great proud Siamese Ratting Corps who patrolled the dockyards of Le Havre with unceasing vigilance; they saw, with eyes withdrawn and dreaming, the palace watch-cats of long-ago Siam, walking delicately on long simian legs around the fountained courtyards, their softly padding feet polishing the mosaics to a lustered path of centuries. And at last they learned how these nobly born Siamese acquired the kink at the end of their tails and bequeathed it to all their descendants.

And as they listened, they looked down in wonder, for there on the rag rug lay one of these, stretched out flat on his royal back, his illustrious tail twitching idly, and his jeweled eyes on their daughter's hand as she turned the pages that spoke of his ancestors—the guardian cats of the Siamese princesses. Each princess, when she came down to bathe in the palace lake, would slip her rings for safekeeping on the tail of her attendant cat. So zealous in their charge were those proud cats that they bent the last joint sideways for safer custody, and in time the faithful tails became crooked forever, and their children's and their children's children's . . .

One after another the Nurmis passed their hands admiringly down the tail before them to feel the truth in its bent bony tip; then Helvi gave him a bowl of milk, which he drank with regal condescension before she carried him up the ladder to bed.

That night, and for one more, the cat lay curled peacefully in Helvi's arms, and in the daytime during her absence he followed her parents everywhere. He trailed through the bush after her mother as she searched for late mushrooms, then sat on the cabin steps and patted the dropped corn kernels as she shucked a stack of cobs. He followed Reino and his work horse across the fields to the wood lot and perched on a newly felled pungent stump, his head following their every movement, and he curled by the door of the stable and watched the man mending harness and oiling traps. And in the late afternoons when Helvi returned he was there waiting for her, a rare and beautiful enigma in the certain routine of the day. He was one of them.

But on the fourth night he was restless, shaking his head and pawing his ears, his voice distressed at her back. At last he lay down, purring loudly, and pushed his head into her hand—the fur below his ears was soaking. She saw their sharp black triangles outlined against the little square of window and watched them flicker and quiver in response to every small night sound. Glad for him in his new-found hearing, she fell asleep.

When she woke, later in the night, aware of a lost warmth, she saw him crouched at the open window, looking out over the pale fields and the tall, dark trees below. His long sinuous tail thrashed to and fro as he measured the distance to the ground. Even as her hand moved out impulsively towards him he sprang, landing with a soft thud.

She looked down and saw his head turn for the first time to her voice, his eyes like glowing rubies as they caught the moonlight, then turn away—and with sudden desolate knowledge she knew that he had no further need of her. Through a blur of tears, she watched him go, stealing like a wraith in the night towards the river that had brought him. Soon the low swiftly running form was lost among the shadows.[3]

3. The writer makes comparisons to describe things, such as "eyes glowing like rubies."

Thinking Like a Reader

1. How does Helvi feel about the cat?
2. What do her parents think?
3. What would you do if you had found a helpless animal?

Write your responses in your journal.

Thinking Like a Writer

4. How does the author let you know what Helvi and her parents feel about the cat?
5. What specific details does the author describe?
6. What descriptions in the selection do you think are best?
7. If you were writing about a pet or some other special possession, what specific details would you mention?

Brainstorm *Vocabulary*

In "The Incredible Journey," Sheila Burnford paints a vivid word picture of the cat. For example, when she describes the cat begging for food, she speaks of its "plaintive, odd voice" and its "kinked tail held straight in the air like a banner." Think of a person or animal whose actions you have observed or feel you know well. In your journal, write down words and images that occur to you as you imagine your subject. Keep a personal vocabulary list of words and phrases. You can use these words and phrases in your writing. Remember the following kinds of figurative language that create vivid images.

A *metaphor* states a comparison: The snow was a white blanket spread throughout the forest. A *simile* uses *like* or *as* to make a comparison: His voice was like a trumpet calling us to attention.

Talk It Over

Describe a Scene

Think of a scene from a movie, play, or television show. Use the scene as the basis for a brief movie review to tell a friend or classmate. Include specific details that describe the sights and sounds in the scene you have chosen. You might also want to include comparisons that will make your images clearer to your listener, as when Sheila Burnford compares the cat to a "heraldic lion."

Quick Write

Write a Pamphlet

Imagine that you work for a zoo. Write a brief description of an animal that could be used in a pamphlet for visitors to the zoo. For example, if you were describing a leopard, you might write the following paragraph.

> The leopard's colorful spotted coat helps it to blend into its shadowy jungle home. Its sleek but muscular legs allow it to fly like an arrow through the thick underbrush. Even the boldest animal is no match for its gleaming, razor-sharp fangs.

You may describe an animal that is exotic or very familiar. If you wish, describe your own pet.

Idea Corner *Think of Topics*

Descriptions can tell about people or places, animals or landscapes, imaginary things or objects you see every day. You have begun gathering ideas for writing a description of your own. Use your journal as a place to jot down additional topics you might like to use as the subject for a description. Write down some of the words, images, and comparisons you could use when you write your description. Decide which subject you would most like to share with readers.

PICTURES  *SEEING LIKE A WRITER*

Finding Ideas for Writing

Look at the pictures on these pages. Think about what you see. What ideas for writing a description do the pictures give you? Write your ideas in your journal.

Buttes in Monument Valley, Arizona

1 GROUP WRITING: A DESCRIPTION

COOPERATIVE
LEARNING

The **purpose** of descriptive writing is to create a clear and vivid picture of a person, place, or thing. A good description has several elements that help to make the subject clear and vivid for your **audience**. These elements are:

- Overall Impression
- Sensory Details
- Ordering of Details

Overall Impression

The **overall impression** in a description is the general idea or feeling about your subject that you want to express to your reader. Notice the underlined sentence in the following paragraph.

> In the distance, at a bend in the road, the dark, abandoned house looked as solitary as a lost person. The shabby shutters of the house hung limply at the sides of the broken windows. The boards that had been carelessly hammered over the front door resembled fingers covering a mouth with many stories to tell. Tall yellow weeds reached up to the railing of the sagging front porch, and the branches of the scrawny tree in the front yard drooped low, as if in mourning.

The first sentence establishes the mood of the paragraph. The overall impression, which might be expressed as sadness or loneliness, is supported by the details of the paragraph.

Guided Practice: Stating an Overall Impression

As a class, think of a sentence that gives an overall impression of each place named below, or choose your own topic.

Example: The town square looked like a silent white ghost town after the big snowstorm.

a city street	a schoolyard	a cemetery
a zoo	a beach	a sporting event

Sensory Details

The details that develop the overall impression in a description are often **sensory details**; that is, they refer to one or more of the five senses—sight, hearing, touch, taste, or smell.

Look back at the paragraph about the abandoned house. Notice that sensory details are described to help you see what the house looks like.

- What specific words in the paragraph help to develop the overall impression?
- What details could you add that develop the overall impression and appeal to other senses?

Guided Practice: Charting Sensory Details

Choose one of the topics for which you wrote an overall impression. Then copy the following chart. Working as a class, think of sensory details to describe your subject and write them in the chart. Use words that are as specific as possible: for example, *tattered* is a more specific detail than *old*.

Sight	Hearing	Smell	Taste	Touch

Ordering of Details

Another element that adds to the clarity of a description is the logical ordering of the sensory details. Just as a house is built according to a logical plan, a good description has a clear organization.

Look once more at the sample paragraph. Notice that the scene is described from far to near. Other ways of arranging details in a description are from top to bottom, side to side, or inside to outside. Choose a method of organization that is best suited to your subject and which will help your reader see your subject most clearly.

Putting a Description Together

As a group, you and your classmates have selected a topic for a description and written a sentence that states an overall impression of your subject. You have also chosen a variety of sensory details that describe your topic. Now it is time to make some important decisions.

First, you must decide which sensory details you listed contribute to the overall impression you wish to convey. Below is one student's chart of sensory details. The sentence above the chart states the overall impression. Notice that the student has crossed out details that do not support the main impression.

MAIN IMPRESSION:
The outdoor market was alive with cheerful activity.

Hearing	Sight	Smell/Taste	Touch
buzz of conversation	colorful fruits, vegetables	varieties of flowers	firm vegetables
vendors calling out prices	white canopies	~~rotten fruit~~ sausage sandwiches	mild breeze gravel on ground
~~fire engine~~			

Using metaphors and similes can help your readers form images of your subject. A **metaphor** compares two subjects in a direct way, as in "The sun was an open eye." A **simile** uses *like* or *as* to make a comparison, as in "The house stood like a lost person."

Guided Practice: Writing a Description

As a class, add more sensory details to each category of the chart you have already made. Eliminate any details that do not contribute to the overall impression. Then write supporting sentences that use the details from your chart. Use an ordering method that works best for your subject.

Checklist A Description

To keep the important parts of a description in your mind, you can make a checklist.

Below is a checklist for writing a description. Copy it and add any other points to it that you wish to remember when you are writing a description. Keep the checklist in your writing folder and use it when you write.

CHECKLIST

- Remember purpose and audience.
- Include an overall impression.
- Use sensory details.
  - Sight
  - Sound
  - Smell
  - Touch
  - Taste
- Order details logically.
- _____

2 THINKING AND WRITING: Classifying

When you select sensory details for a description, you classify them according to one of the five senses. **Classifying** is grouping items that have features in common. For example, a pile of different kinds of apples could be classified according to type, size, weight, color, or age.

Look at the illustration below. How many different classes or groups can you name for the items shown?

You could classify the ducks according to size, shape, general color, color of tails, color of necks, and so on.

Classifying can help you understand or use things more efficiently. Books at the library are classified so that you can find them more easily. Animals are classified as vertebrate or invertebrate so that you can understand the basic forms of life more clearly.

When you write a description, classifying can help you select details for each of the five senses. You also classify when you choose details that develop a particular overall impression. For example, in a description of the sea, a detail about the quiet lapping of gentle waves contributes to an overall impression of peacefulness. A detail about noisy swimmers would not be classified in the same way.

Thinking Like a Writer

■ How can classifying sensory details help you to write an effective description?

THINKING APPLICATION Classifying Descriptive Details

You know that classifying sensory details can help you write an effective description.

A. Read the following sentences that describe a lake at daybreak. Work with a classmate to classify each detail mentioned according to one or more of the five senses—sight, hearing, smell, taste, or touch.

1. The mountains in the distance made a jagged purple line against the pale sky.
2. The cheery twittering of birds broke the stillness.
3. Blue smoke from the campfire pointed the way to hot, fragrant coffee and crisp, sizzling bacon.
4. A thick, moist blanket of pine-scented mist hung like a canopy over the silent forest.
5. The gurgling of a thin, ice-blue stream could be heard over the crackle of the burning hickory wood.

B. The following sensory details describe a pet dog. Classify each detail according to one of the senses.

1. sniffles while he sleeps
2. patches of brown on white
3. tail like limp rope
4. quivers when petted
5. a pushed-in nose

C. Read the following chart that a student made for writing a description of a place she loves to visit—the beach. Choose the details that contribute to an overall impression of peacefulness and enjoyment.

Sight	Hearing	Taste/Smell	Touch
bright sunshine	gentle waves	coconut suntan oil	warm sand
blue water	loud music from radio	salty air	frigid water
blinding sand	laughter	gasoline in parking lot	cool breeze

Then think of a favorite place of yours. Make a chart with details that show why you like this setting. Share your chart with another student.

3 INDEPENDENT WRITING: A Description

Prewrite: Step 1

By now you have learned the important elements of a good description and are ready to choose a topic of your own. Troy, a student your age, chose his topic in this way.

Choosing a Topic

As Troy began thinking about a good topic, he also decided that the audience for his writing would be his classmates. His purpose would be to create a clear and vivid picture of his subject in the minds of his readers.

Then he jotted down possible topics for a description.

> fishing   snowstorm
> music concert   baseball

Troy liked the last topic best; but he knew that it was too broad to describe in one paragraph and needed to narrow it. Since he had recently attended a baseball game, he decided to write about the activity in the stadium before the game.

Exploring Ideas: Clustering Strategy

Troy explored his topic by making a cluster. He wrote his topic at the center and wrote down his ideas around it as they came into his head.

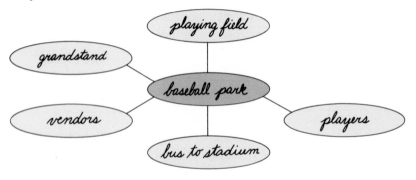

To remember more clearly the game he had attended, Troy closed his eyes and thought about the activity at the stadium. The overall impression he had of the ballpark was one of excitement and anticipation. Then he looked at his cluster again. He added sensory details and eliminated one idea that did not relate closely enough to his topic. Notice how he changed his cluster.

- green grass
- noise of fans
- playing field
- red uniforms
- grandstand
- baseball park
- players
- mountain of people
- ~~bus to stadium~~
- thump of ball
- popcorn
- vendors
- crack of bat
- calling

Thinking Like a Writer
- What did Troy add?
- What senses do the details refer to?
- What did he eliminate? Why?

YOUR TURN

Think of a topic that you would like to describe. Follow these steps.

JOURNAL

- Make a list of topics. Use **Pictures** or your journal to find ideas.
- Choose one topic you like best. If necessary, narrow the topic.
- Think of an overall impression.
- Remember your purpose and audience.

Now make a cluster to explore your topic. Remember that you can add to or eliminate from your cluster at any time during the writing process.

Write a First Draft: Step 2

To help him remember the important parts of an effective description, Troy had made a planning checklist. On his checklist he included points about purpose, audience, overall impression, sensory details, and logical order. He took out his checklist and used it as he wrote the first draft of his description.

Then Troy wrote his first draft. He did not stop to make corrections in his work. At this point he was more concerned with putting his ideas on paper while they were fresh in his mind. He knew he could read over his work later and then make any needed changes.

Troy's First Draft

> On this warm summer day memorial stadium was busy. At the back of the field, players were warming up by exercising on the grass. Other players lined up for batting practice. They were in bright red uniforms. The sounds of the crack of the bat and the thump of the ball rose from the field. The Grandstand was a mountain of people, their voices humming and buzzing eager. Drifting through the crowd were the aromas of popcorn and french fries from the vendors in the isles. However, the calls of the vendors were practically lost in the waves of anticipation passing through the noisy spectators. Three hours later the game would finally be over.

Planning Checklist
- Remember purpose and audience.
- Include an overall impression.
- Use sensory details.
- Sight
- Sound
- Smell
- Touch
- Taste
- Order details logically.

YOUR TURN

Write the first draft of your description. As you write, ask yourself these questions.

- What does my audience need to know to form a clear picture of my subject?
- What overall impression do I want to give?
- How can I best arrange the details?

TIME-OUT You might want to take some time out before you revise. That way you will be able to revise your writing with a fresh eye.

Revise: Step 3

After he finished writing his first draft, Troy looked his work over carefully and decided he needed to make a few improvements. He also asked a classmate to read his first draft and make suggestions for changes.

I like your description, Troy, but the beginning doesn't really give me a strong feeling about the ballpark.

You're right. Thanks for the pointer, Debbie.

Troy wanted to be sure to use Debbie's comment when he revised his description. To help him remember, he took out his planning checklist and put a check mark next to the point about including an overall impression. Troy now had a checklist to use as he revised.

As Troy revised his first draft, he referred to his checklist and asked himself several questions. Did he need to add sensory details? Was his overall impression clear? Were the details arranged logically? Did information need to be eliminated? He didn't stop to correct each error in his first draft. He waited until later to check for errors in spelling, capitalization, and grammar.

As he revised his description, Troy also thought more about the **purpose** and **audience** for his writing. He wanted to make sure that he had achieved his purpose of creating a clear picture of his subject in the minds of his readers. He read over his draft one more time as if he were a person reading the description for the first time.

Read Troy's revised draft on the next page.

Revising Checklist
- Remember purpose and audience.
- ✔ Include an overall impression.
- Use sensory details.
- Sight
- Sound
- Smell
- Touch
- Taste
- Order details logically.

Troy's Revised Draft

> *alive with pregame anticipation and excitement*
> On this warm summer day memorial stadium was
>
> busy. At the back of the field, players were warming up by
>   *soft, green*   *in bright red uniforms*
> exercising on the grass. Other players lined up for batting
>
> practice. ~~They were in bright red uniforms.~~ The sounds of
>
> the crack of the bat and the thump of the ball rose from
>   *in front of the field*
> the field. The Grandstand was a mountain of people, their
>
> voices humming and buzzing eager. Drifting through the
>   *mouthwatering*
> crowd were the aromas of popcorn and french fries from
>   *songlike*   *near us*
> the vendors in the isles. However, the calls of the vendors
>
> were practically lost in the waves of anticipation passing
>
> through the noisy spectators. ~~Three hours later the game~~
>
> ~~would finally be over.~~

Thinking Like a Writer

- How did Troy change the first sentence. Why?
- What words did he add? Why do you think he added them?
- What sentences did he combine? Why?
- What did he eliminate? Why?

YOUR TURN

Read your first draft. Ask yourself these questions.

- How can I make my overall impression stronger?
- Do I need to add sensory details to give my audience a clearer picture of my subject?
- How could I arrange the details of my description more effectively?
- How could I improve my writing by combining sentences that have related information?

Now, revise your description. If you wish, ask a classmate to read your writing and give suggestions for improvements.

Proofread: Step 4

After Troy revised his draft, he read over his work once more to look for errors in spelling, punctuation, capitalization, and grammar. Troy used a proofreading checklist and proofreading marks to make corrections.

Troy's Proofread Draft

alive with pregame anticipation and excitement
On this warm summer day memorial stadium was
~~busy.~~ At the back of the field, players were warming up by
exercising on the *soft, green* grass. Other players *in bright red uniforms* lined up for batting
practice. ~~They were in bright red uniforms.~~ The sounds of
the crack of the bat and the thump of the ball rose from
the field. The Grandstand *in front of the field* was a mountain of people, their
voices humming and buzzing *eagerly* ~~eager.~~ Drifting through the
crowd were the *mouthwatering* aromas of popcorn and french fries from
the vendors in the (isles) *aisles*. However, the *songlike* calls of the vendors *near us*
were practically lost in the waves of anticipation passing
through the noisy spectators. ~~Three hours later the game~~
~~would finally be over.~~

YOUR TURN

Proofreading Practice

Find the errors in the paragraph below. Then write the paragraph correctly on a separate sheet of paper.

> The boston pitcher was hot and tired but stood with his feet planted firm on the mound Large beads of perspiration formed on his face and ran slow down his neck. His red sox uniform clung tight to his weary body. He looked like he had just been caught in a Rainstorm

Proofreading Checklist
- Did I indent each paragraph?
- Did I spell each word correctly?
- What errors in punctuation do I need to correct?
- What errors in capitalization do I need to correct?
- What errors in the use of adjectives and adverbs do I need to correct?

Applying Your Proofreading Skills

Now proofread your description. Review your checklist and **The Grammar Connection** and **The Mechanics Connection** below. Use the proofreading marks to make changes.

THE GRAMMAR CONNECTION

Remember these rules about using adjectives and adverbs correctly.

- Use **adjectives** to describe nouns or pronouns. *Good*, *bad*, and *real* are adjectives.

  Sam didn't get a **good** look at that **quick** ball.

- Use **adverbs** to modify verbs, adjectives, or other adverbs. *Well*, *badly*, and *really* are adverbs. *Well* is an adjective only when it refers to someone's health.

  The outfielder stumbled **badly** as the ball flew **quickly** overhead.

Review your writing. Have you used adjectives and adverbs correctly?

THE MECHANICS CONNECTION

Remember this rule about proper adjectives.

- An adjective formed from a proper noun is a **proper adjective**. Always capitalize a proper adjective.

  The **Toronto** team thrilled the **Canadian** fans.

Review your writing. Have you capitalized each proper adjective?

Proofreading Marks

Indent ⌐⌐
Add ∧
Add a comma ⋏
Add quotation marks ⋁ ⋁
Add a period ⊙
Take out ꙡ
Capitalize ≡
Lower-case letter /
Reverse the order ∩

Publish: Step 5

Troy prepared a final, neat copy of his description and thought of ways he could share his writing. He spoke with some classmates, and they decided to assemble their descriptions in a notebook. They each prepared illustrations to accompany their writing, and Troy wrote a table of contents. The students kept their notebook in the back of the classroom for the entire class to share and added to it during the year. Troy wrote two more descriptions that he decided to add to the collection.

YOUR TURN

Make a final copy of your description, using neat handwriting, a typewriter, or a computer. Then think of ways to share your writing. You might find some ideas in the **Sharing Suggestions** box below.

SHARING SUGGESTIONS

Include your description in a letter to a friend or relative.	Make a poster that illustrates your description and attach your writing to it. Hang it on the bulletin board.	Read your description aloud to your family or friends.

4 SPEAKING AND LISTENING: Listening for Details

Whether written or spoken, a good description is made up of a variety of sensory details that convey an overall impression. Through vivid details, the writer or speaker creates a clear picture of the sights, sounds, smells, and tastes connected with the subject.

An oral description, however, is only as good as its listeners. When you listen to a description, pay attention to the specific details or groups of details that develop the overall impression.

As you read the following description that a student presented orally to the class, note the important details that contribute to the overall impression.

> My favorite summer escape is a peaceful walk on the beach. The dazzling sunlight dances on the blue water, and the sand is a warm blanket underfoot. A cool breeze fans my face while my toes tingle in the chilly surf. Gentle waves lap at my feet. Opposite the refreshment stand the smell of grilling hot dogs mingles with the fragrance of coconut suntan oil. High above the splashing and laughter, a brightly colored kite sails in the cloudless sky. As I walk along, licking the salty air off my lips, I feel lighthearted and at peace.

- What details develop the overall impression in the description?
- What senses do the details appeal to?
- What comparison is used?

When you listen to information that is not descriptive, you should focus on other kinds of details. In stories, besides descriptions you should pay attention to the important events in the plot, as well as when each event happens. In explanations, instructions, and directions, the details are facts or examples or steps in a process. When you listen to a speech, focus on the reasons the speaker gives for his or her opinions.

LISTENING GUIDELINES: Listening for Details

1. Concentrate on what the speaker is saying.
2. Listen for sensory details that create the overall impression in a description.
3. Listen for the main events that develop the plot in a story.
4. Listen for important facts, examples, or steps.
5. Listen for specific reasons that support opinions given in a speech.
6. Take notes to remember important details.

LISTENING APPLICATION Taking Notes

You know that listening carefully for details can help you better understand a speaker's message.

A. Listen to a description given on a radio or television program, for example, a program about some aspect of nature. Take notes on the important details you hear. Then share your notes with a friend and see if she or he can form a clear picture of your subject based on the details that you gathered.

B. Write the title "My Listening Habits" at the top of a sheet of paper. Divide the paper into two columns with the headings "Formal Situations" and "Informal Situations." Think about a typical school day and note your listening habits in different kinds of situations. Summarize any similarities or differences regarding formal and informal situations.

THE CURRICULUM CONNECTION

Writing About Art

Just as writers share their imaginations with others by creating pictures with words, artists use paint, chalk, marble, metals, and other materials to communicate their vision. Visual imagery can sometimes more effectively express a perception or feeling than words can.

Art can take many different forms. Paintings, sculpture, and drawings are a few. Pottery, jewelry, and architecture are other kinds of art; these serve useful functions.

Art is one of the oldest forms of human expression, far older than writing. Since prehistoric times, artists have used physical materials to express their thoughts and feelings about nature, people, or their own lives. Throughout history, art has provided people with both the enjoyment of beauty and knowledge about the world. Whatever their subject matter, artists express their unique visions of life.

ACTIVITIES

Create a Collage
Think of some aspect of your life that is very important to you; it might be your family, school, traveling, or growing up. Then, create a collage of words and pictures that expresses your ideas and feelings about the theme you have selected. Cut out or make photocopies of photographs, drawings, cartoons, sentences, and individual words you find in magazines or newspapers. If you wish, make a sculpture or mobile using your materials.

Describe a Sculpture
Write a description of a sculpture you can observe in person or a picture of one in a book. Describe both what you see and the thoughts and feelings that the sculpture evokes in you. Then share your description with a friend and see if he or she is able to "see" the sculpture.

Respond to Literature

What ideas or feelings does the poem below give you? Write your response in the form of a poem, paragraph, or story.

Drawing by Ronnie C., Grade One

For the sky, blue. But the six-year-
old searching his crayon-box, finds
no blue to match that sky
framed by the window—a see-through shine
over treetops, housetops. The wax colors
hold only dead light, not this water-flash
thinning to silver
at morning's far edge.
Gray won't do, either:
gray is for rain that you make with
dark slanting lines down-paper

                                              Try orange!

—Draw a large corner circle for sun, egg-yolk solid,
with yellow strokes, leaping outward
like fire bloom—a brightness shouting
flower-shape wind-shape joy shape!

The boy sighs, with leg-twisting bliss creating . . .

It is done. The stubby crayons
(all ten of them) are stuffed back
bumpily into their box.

                                    —Ruth Lechlitner

UNIT CHECKUP

LESSON 1 **Group Writing: A Description** (page 342)   Read each of the following topics for a description. For each topic, list sensory details that might be used in a description. Then, write a sentence that conveys an overall impression of the subject.

a. a city bridge at night
b. a view from a mountaintop
c. the school cafeteria at lunch time
d. a farmyard in the morning
e. a thunderstorm

LESSON 2 **Thinking: Classifying** (page 346)   On a separate sheet of paper, make a chart with four columns labeled: *Sight, Sound, Touch, Taste/Smell*. Classify each of the following sensory details by writing its letter in the correct column. (Some of the details may be classified under more than one heading.) Then, write a sentence that expresses an overall impression of the subject.

a. Heat rose from the steaming pavement in shimmering waves.
b. The nonstop blare of car horns was like a hundred angry voices singing out of tune.
c. The shirts of some of the drivers, soaked through with perspiration, clung to their bodies.
d. The smell of gasoline fumes mixed with the odor of hot asphalt.
e. The winding line of cars up ahead was a long, glittering snake of glass and metal.
f. A sip of cool lemonade refreshed me.

LESSON 3 **Writing a Description** (page 348)   Imagine that you are an athlete competing in the Olympic Games. You are just about to have your turn in your event. Write a description of this moment. Use a variety of sensory details. Include a sentence that expresses an overall impression.

LESSON 4 **Speaking and Listening: Listening for Details** (page 356)   In a paragraph summarize the guidelines for listening for details effectively.

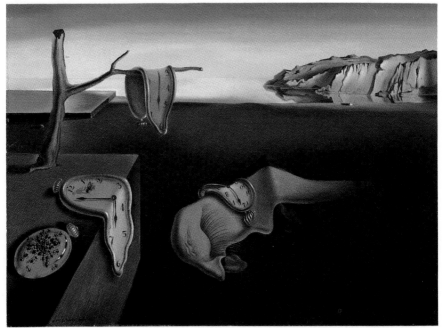
Good descriptions create clear, strong pictures in the mind of the reader or listener. Descriptions often depict persons, places, or things that are real or that resemble familiar things. The art of description can also be used to illustrate places or things that exist entirely in the realm of the imagination.

Writers and artists both have the power to invent imaginary objects and dreamlike settings and then turn them into real books or pictures that others can enjoy. Look at the strange painting below. With your classmates, discuss what you see in the painting. Decide what ideas and feelings are part of the artist's vision.

Salvador Dali, *The Persistence of Memory*, 1931, oil on canvas, 9½ × 13″. Collection, The Museum of Modern Art, New York.

Think about an unusual place you have "visited" in a dream; or close your eyes and try to imagine a world very different from your own.

- What impossible things are part of your dream landscape?
- Write a description of this place in the form of a paragraph or as part of a story or brief play.
- Make a picture or collage to accompany your description.

UNIT

11

TAKE NOTHING FROM THIS TRAIL, BUT

PHOTOGRAPHS AND MEMORIES

AND LEAVE NOTHING BUT FOOTPRINTS

Prepositions, Conjunctions, and Interjections

In this unit you will learn about prepositions and conjunctions. These words show relationships between sentences or parts of sentences. You will also learn about interjections—words or phrases used to express strong feelings.

Discuss Read the poem on the opposite page. In what ways do you change each day?

Creative Expression The unit theme is *Outlooks*. How would someone else describe you? Imagine you are your best friend. In your journal write a description of yourself through your best friend's eyes.

JOURNAL

Good
or Bad

Good or bad
By tomorrow I will have
Changed something—

Myself, perhaps.
Maybe?
No, for sure.

—Calvin O'John

1 PREPOSITIONS AND PREPOSITIONAL PHRASES

A preposition is a word that shows the relationship between a noun or a pronoun and another word in a sentence.

To describe locations you often use **prepositions.**

José placed his bag **under** his desk.

Here is a list of common prepositions. Notice that some prepositions consist of more than one word.

about	before	except	on	until
above	behind	for	out	up
across	below	from	outside	with
after	beneath	in	over	within
against	beside	inside	past	without
among	between	into	since	because of
around	by	like	through	due to
as	down	of	to	except for
at	during	off	under	on account of

A **prepositional phrase** is a group of words that begins with a preposition and ends with a noun or a pronoun. The noun or the pronoun that follows the preposition is called the **object of the preposition.**

Linda explained her ideas **to her friend.**

Guided Practice

Name the preposition and the object of the preposition in each sentence.

Example: I arrived with Tom. *with   Tom*

1. Our class will hold an election on Tuesday.
2. Irene will be running for president.
3. The former president of our class did a fine job.
4. Charles is running against Irene.
5. Whose name did you write on the ballot?

 THINK

- How can I identify a prepositional phrase?

REMEMBER

- A **preposition** relates a noun or a pronoun to another word in a sentence.
- A **prepositional phrase** is a group of words that begins with a preposition and ends with a noun or a pronoun. That noun or pronoun is called the **object of the preposition.**

More Practice

A. Write each prepositional phrase. Draw one line under the preposition and two lines under the object of the preposition.

Example: The council will meet <u>after <u><u>lunch</u></u></u>.

6. Our town council wants a stoplight at that corner.
7. The mayor does not agree with the town council.
8. The head of the council gave a long speech today.
9. Her speech was broadcast on television.
10. On account of that speech, voters may accept her proposal.
11. However, the mayor is completely against the idea.
12. He wrote an editorial about his position.
13. His editorial will be published in the town paper.
14. People will discuss this issue until the election.
15. After the election I hope they can agree!

B. Write each sentence, filling in the blank with an appropriate prepositional phrase.

Example: The team can't practice <u>without a gym</u>.

16. Do the students ___ need a new recreation center?
17. The old building has a great deal ___.
18. A new center will serve a variety ___.
19. We can hold dances ___.
20. The facility should have a field ___.

Extra Practice, page 388

WRITING APPLICATION A Persuasive Paragraph

Think of something in your school that you would like to see changed, for example, your library or cafeteria. Write a paragraph that describes the change and the reasons you support it. Then exchange papers with a classmate and identify the prepositional phrases in each other's work.

2 USING PRONOUNS IN PREPOSITIONAL PHRASES

You often use pronouns as the objects of prepositions. When the object of a preposition is a pronoun, use an object pronoun.

> Rita described the book to **me.**
> I will buy a copy for **her.**

Sometimes a preposition has a **compound object,** that is, an object consisting of two or more words. Always use object pronouns in a compound object.

> Have you spoken to Juan and **them**?
> I discussed the issue with **her and him.**

When you use the word *me* in a compound object, make sure that it always comes last.

> CORRECT: Except for **Jo and me,** no one agreed.
> INCORRECT: Except for me and Jo, no one agreed.

Avoid using a reflexive pronoun as the object of a preposition when an object pronoun is needed.

> CORRECT: Mr. Li stood between Tad and **me.**
> INCORRECT: Mr. Li stood between Tad and myself.

Guided Practice

Choose the word or words that correctly complete each sentence.

Example: Are novels of interest to you and (she, her)?   *her*

1. Are biographies of contemporary writers more appealing to Ellen and (he, him)?
2. I heard about a book from Ilene and (they, them).
3. Except for Ilene and (I, me), no one liked it.
4. Reading about the life of Jack London was a treat for (Ilene and me, me and Ilene).
5. To (myself, me), it was well written.

?! THINK

- How can I decide what pronoun to use as the object of a preposition?

REMEMBER

- When the object of a preposition is a pronoun, use an object pronoun.
- Use *me* or *us* last when it is part of a compound object of a preposition.
- Do not use a reflexive pronoun when an object pronoun is needed.

G R A M M A R

More Practice

A. Write the correct word or words for each sentence.

Example: Rosa gave the books to Jake and (them, they). *them*

6. Jake discussed *White Fang* with Rosa and (they, them).
7. Will that book appeal to Tomas and (she, her)?
8. Miriam read it to Larry and (me, I).
9. For (me and Tomas, Tomas and me), novels are more fun than biographies.
10. There are often disagreements about books between Miriam and (me, myself).
11. Except for Ty and (I, me), everyone liked the book by London.
12. Jess explained his opinion to Miriam and (he, him).

B. Write each sentence correctly.

Example: Walk in front of Charles and she.
   Walk in front of Charles and her.

13. Eric walked to the library with my sister and I.
14. The librarian had found a new book for me and him.
15. She always saves new adventure books for ourselves.
16. Without him and she, I would rarely hear about new books.
17. For people like him and I, adventure stories are most fun.
18. Science fiction novels also appeal to Eric and myself.
19. Disagreement is rare between me and him.
20. Jean asked for opinions from him and I.

Extra Practice, page 389

WRITING APPLICATION An Advertisement

COOPERATIVE LEARNING

Imagine that you are in charge of an advertising campaign for a new book. You like the book and want to convince other students to read it. Write an ad for the book. Then, exchange papers with a classmate and identify all object pronouns used in prepositional phrases.

3 PREPOSITIONAL PHRASES AS ADJECTIVES OR ADVERBS

Adjectives are words that describe nouns or pronouns. When a prepositional phrase is used to describe a noun or pronoun, it functions as an adjective.

> The books **in our library** are very old.
> Everyone **from our school** is concerned.

A prepositional phrase that is used as an adjective is called an **adjective phrase.**

Always place an adjective phrase as close as possible to the word it modifies. Otherwise, you may convey an unintended meaning.

> INCORRECT: The man explained the budget **in the blue jacket.**
>
> CORRECT: The man **in the blue jacket** explained the budget.

You have also learned that adverbs often modify verbs. A prepositional phrase that modifies a verb is called an **adverb phrase.** An adverb phrase can tell *when, where, why,* or *how* an action takes place.

> Carol went **to the library.** (*where?*)
> She investigated **until nightfall.** (*when?*)
> The librarian asked **about her purpose.** (*why?*)

Guided Practice

Identify the adjective phrase or adverb phrase.

Example: We spoke after the meeting.
> *after the meeting   adverb phrase*

1. Do you think the budget of the library is too small?
2. Who will speak at the next meeting?
3. Perhaps there will be a disagreement about this issue.
4. We should not decide until Wednesday.
5. By next week, the question will be settled.

?! THINK

- How do I know whether a prepositional phrase is an adjective phrase or an adverb phrase?

REMEMBER

- An **adjective phrase** is a prepositional phrase that modifies a noun or pronoun.
- An **adverb phrase** is a prepositional phrase that may modify a verb.

More Practice

A. Write the prepositional phrase in each sentence. Then write whether it is an **adjective phrase** or an **adverb phrase.**

Example: The library in our town is big.
　　　　　 in our town   adjective phrase

6. Have you visited the library at our school?
7. The books in its collection are too old-fashioned.
8. Leroy agrees without reservation.
9. He will explain his ideas for a solution.
10. Carol informed Leroy after her investigation.
11. A group of students approached the school librarian.
12. He has not received new books since last year.

B. Underline each prepositional phrase. Draw two lines under the word it describes. Write whether the phrase is an **adjective phrase** or an **adverb phrase.**

Example: The team <u>discussed</u> the problem <u>after school</u>.
　　　　　 adverb phrase

13. The principal told us her opinion about this matter.
14. Yesterday, we met in her office.
15. She is someone with many responsibilities.
16. Her point of view is broad.
17. Must the school choose between new books and a new pool?
18. The bottom of the pool is badly cracked.
19. Everyone on the swim team has the same idea.
20. The members of the team want a new pool.

Extra Practice, page 390

WRITING APPLICATION An Editorial

Think of an issue at your school that concerns you. Describe your opinion in an editorial. Then identify the adjective phrases and adverb phrases in your work.

4 USING VERBS AFTER PREPOSITIONAL PHRASES

You know that a verb must always agree with its subject.

The *mayor* **is** in favor of the plan.
The *ballots* **are** ready.

Sometimes a prepositional phrase comes between the subject and the verb in a sentence. When that happens, you must make sure that the verb agrees with the subject of the sentence and not with the object of the preposition.

A *decision* on these issues **is** necessary.
The *members* of the council **were** in agreement.

To help you decide whether to use a singular or plural verb in a sentence, mentally "cross out" the prepositional phrase that comes between the subject and verb.

The *plans* ~~for a new town~~ hall **are** controversial.

Guided Practice

Choose the correct verb form for each sentence.

Example: The voters in this town (is, are) active.   *are*

1. The arguments during our last meeting (was, were) brief.
2. Fortunately, the head of the council members (is, are) polite.
3. Other people in the council (is, are) less diplomatic.
4. The issue on their minds (seems, seem) crucial.

 THINK

- Which verb form do I use after a prepositional phrase?

REMEMBER

- A verb must always agree with its subject.
- Do not confuse the subject of a sentence with the object of a preposition that may follow the subject.

More Practice

A. Write the correct form of the verb for each sentence.

Example: The members of the council (has, have) arrived.
  have

5. The downtown areas of some American cities (needs, need) improvements.
6. The reports of the secretary (seems, seem) accurate.
7. His record, except for a few errors, (is, are) good.
8. Most of the committee (agree, agrees) with José.
9. The ideas of one person often (has, have) great impact.
10. Two members of the council (suspects, suspect) trouble.
11. The proposal, in their minds, (is, are) hasty.
12. The people behind the plan (does, do) not agree.

B. Write each sentence correctly. Make sure that each verb agrees with its subject. Underline the prepositional phrase that follows the subject.

Example: The mayor's point <u>about funds</u> are correct. *is*

13. An article about the disputes appear in today's newspaper.
14. Many people at City Hall has spoken their minds.
15. Which one of the plans seem most sensible?
16. One proposal by some city planners save the city much money.
17. The time since the last two meetings have gone quickly.
18. Statements by the mayor has been issued.
19. Funds for the project is available.
20. This disagreement among friends still are not settled.

Extra Practice, Practice Plus, pages 391–392

WRITING APPLICATION A Speech

With a partner, write a brief speech about a problem in your town that is of concern to both of you. In your speech, propose a solution to the problem. Check to make sure that each verb following a prepositional phrase agrees with its subject. Present your speech to an audience.

5 CONJUNCTIONS

Conjunctions connect parts of sentences. A **coordinating conjunction** may connect two subjects, two predicates, two objects of a preposition, or two simple sentences. *And, or, but, for,* and *nor* are used as coordinating conjunctions.

COMPOUND SUBJECT:	Lou **and** Ricki enjoy television.
COMPOUND PREDICATE:	The shows amuse **and** relax us.
COMPOUND OBJECT OF A PREPOSITION:	I do not agree with him **or** her.
COMPOUND SENTENCE:	They like TV, **but** I do not.

Notice that a comma is used before a conjunction that joins the two simple sentences in a compound sentence.

You can also use pairs of words called **correlative conjunctions** to connect parts of a sentence.

Common Correlative Conjunctions

both . . . and	neither . . . nor	either . . . or
not only . . . but also	whether . . . or	just as . . . so

Both Maria **and** Rosie prefer movies to television.

Guided Practice

Identify the conjunction or conjunctions in each sentence. Then tell whether the conjunction joins a compound subject, compound predicate, compound object of a preposition, or compound sentence.

Example: The screen flickered and darkened.
　　　　　and   compound predicate

1. Movies and television are entertaining.
2. Neither television nor movies can compare with a good book.
3. I read with both enthusiasm and care.
4. Not only is television often dull, but also it can be harmful.
5. Television either tires your eyes or wastes your time.

 THINK

■ How can I tell if a word in a sentence is a conjunction?

REMEMBER

- A **coordinating conjunction** connects parts of a sentence or two sentences.

- **Correlative conjunctions** are pairs of words used to connect parts of a sentence or two sentences.

More Practice

Write the coordinating or correlative conjunctions in each sentence. Then write whether the conjunction joins a **compound subject, compound predicate, compound object of a preposition,** or **compound sentence.**

Example: Either books or plays are often made into films.
either, or   compound subject

6. Many parents and teachers dislike television.
7. Others watch television and approve of most programs.
8. Sal neither approves wholly nor disapproves wholly.
9. Either he watches an educational program, or he reads.
10. He watches programs with both his parents and his sisters.
11. Not only do we learn from books, but we also learn from TV.
12. Neither I nor my friends ever miss a good nature program.
13. Does television waste too much of your time and energy?
14. I cannot often afford movies, but I don't mind.
15. Perhaps both television and movies could be improved.
16. Critics discuss and compare both forms of entertainment.
17. Gerry agrees with many critics, but I do not.
18. What would many people do without television or movies?
19. Perhaps parents and children would talk more.
20. Opinions among both my friends and my classmates vary.
21. Many of my friends either love or hate television.
22. Others do not like television but watch it anyway.
23. I enjoy television, but I cannot watch it often.
24. Either I am busy, or I would rather listen to music.
25. Both you and I must decide how to use television.

Extra Practice, page 393

WRITING APPLICATION A Dialogue

Write a dialogue between two people who hold different viewpoints about a topic such as the value of television. Then, exchange papers with a classmate and identify the conjunctions.

6 MAKING VERBS AGREE WITH COMPOUND SUBJECTS

Choosing a verb to agree with a compound subject can sometimes be tricky. A **compound subject** contains two or more simple subjects joined by a conjunction. The type of conjunction that connects the parts of a compound subject determines whether the verb that follows it should be singular or plural.

When two or more subjects are joined by *and* or by *both . . . and*, the verb is plural.

> Terry *and* I **enjoy** debates.
> *Both* Mickey *and* Roberto **agree** with our position.

When two or more subjects are joined by *or*, *nor*, *either . . . or*, or *neither . . . nor*, the verb agrees with the subject that is closest to it.

> Sue *or* Pedro **has** my notes.
> *Either* a good argument *or* strong facts **are** effective.
> *Neither* facts *nor* an argument **is** enough for Mickey!
> He *or* his brothers **argue** with me all the time.

Guided Practice

Choose the correct verb form.

Example: Either Ellen or John (take, takes) notes.   *takes*

1. Either Pedro or Sue (call, calls) the meeting to order.
2. Jo and I (like, likes) school debates.
3. A debate or argument always (interest, interests) us.
4. Both she and I often (help, helps) plan school debates.
5. This week neither she nor I (has, have) the time.

THINK

- How do I decide whether a compound subject takes a singular or plural verb?

REMEMBER

- When two or more subjects are joined by *and* or *both . . . and,* the verb is plural.
- When two or more subjects are joined by *or, nor, either . . . or,* or *neither . . . nor,* the verb agrees with the subject that is closest to it.

More Practice

Write the correct form of the verb for each sentence. Underline each conjunction.

Example: <u>Neither</u> Pedro <u>nor</u> Al (wish, wishes) to debate. *wishes*

6. John and Al (find, finds) debates challenging.
7. Either the students or a teacher (decides, decide) on the topic for the debate.
8. Neither she nor the aide (votes, vote) on the result.
9. However, she and the principal (offers, offer) ideas.
10. Either a schoolroom or the auditorium (is, are) a good location.
11. Either the moderator or a teacher (ask, asks) for silence.
12. Pedro and Liz (wants, want) to make their points.
13. Both Leo and Sally (agrees, agree) with the teacher.
14. She and they (wants, want) school to be open all year.
15. Sue or Elena (have, has) the strongest opinion.
16. Neither Sue nor her friends (hesitates, hesitate) to speak.
17. Neither my classmates nor I (has, have) made a decision.
18. Either Kay or Vernon (give, gives) us advice.
19. Neither he nor she (knows, know) the right statistics.
20. However, both Rosa and Bert (believes, believe) in a solution.
21. Bert and his friends (thinks, think) about the issue.
22. (Does, Do) he or his friends agree with the others?
23. Either statistics or a good argument (is, are) needed.
24. Neither loud words nor a quick temper (helps, help).

Extra Practice, page 394

 WRITING APPLICATION A Story

COOPERATIVE
LEARNING

With a partner or group of classmates, write a brief story about a problem that might occur in your school, for example, a power failure or the discovery of stolen goods. Make sure that each verb you use agrees with its subject.

7 INTERJECTIONS

Exclamatory sentences express strong feelings. Sometimes you may use a single word or phrase to express a strong feeling, such as surprise. These words are called **interjections.**

Common Interjections				
Ah	Gee	Gosh	Oh, my	Wow
Aha	Golly	Phew	Oh, no	Yippee
Hooray	Good heavens	Hey	Oops	Rats

Use an exclamation mark after an interjection that stands alone.

> Hey! Isn't that Jorge?
> Did you hear his last speech? Wow!

Use a comma after an interjection that is used at the beginning of a sentence.

> Gee, I wanted to run for student council myself.
> Oh, don't worry about that now.
> For goodness sake, you can always run next year!

An interjection that stands alone usually suggests a stronger feeling than an interjection that is used as part of a sentence.

Guided Practice

Name the interjection in each sentence.

Example: Phew! This room is too crowded.   *Phew*

1. Ah, that cold water tastes good!
2. Gee, my throat was so dry after my long speech.
3. Hey! What did you think of my speech?
4. Good heavens, you must have talked for an hour!
5. Oh, no! My speech lasted only about fifteen minutes.

?! THINK

■ How do I decide whether to use an exclamation mark after an interjection?

REMEMBER

- An **interjection** is a word or phrase used to express strong feeling.
- Use an exclamation mark after an interjection that stands alone. Use a comma after an interjection that comes at the beginning of a sentence.

More Practice

A. Write the interjection in each sentence.

Example: Oh, yes, we can win the debate.   *Oh*

6. Aha! I thought our opponent would bring up that point.
7. Jorge knew just how to answer him. Wow!
8. Hey, do you think we should schedule another rally?
9. Oh, no, I don't think anyone would attend.
10. Oops! I almost ruined this poster.
11. Gee, try to be a little more careful.
12. Good heavens, everyone makes mistakes!

B. Write each sentence, filling in each blank with an interjection of your choice. Add the correct punctuation.

Example: ____ Look at the number of votes we got.   *Wow!*

13. ____ we almost forgot to put up these posters.
14. Can you imagine how upset Jorge would have been? ____
15. ____ Jorge left the notes for his speech at home.
16. ____ What time is the rally, anyway?
17. ____ it is in one hour!
18. Jorge has written a whole new speech. ____
19. ____ I'm beginning to think he can do anything.
20. ____ I knew I would find you in the auditorium.
21. ____ can you help me decorate it for our celebration?
22. I think we are going to win the election. ____
23. ____ I don't know everything, you know!
24. ____ So far, our opponents are behind by two to one.
25. ____ We finally won the election!

Extra Practice, page 395

WRITING APPLICATION A Poster

Imagine that you or someone you know is running for some kind of office. Design a campaign poster. Identify any interjections that you use.

8. MECHANICS: Using Semicolons and Colons

Use a semicolon to join parts of a compound sentence when a coordinating conjunction such as *and*, *or*, or *but* is not used.

> I am concerned about the environment; it is in danger.

Use a semicolon to join parts of a compound sentence when the parts are long and subdivided by commas, even if a coordinating conjunction is used.

> Recycling paper can help the environment, save money, and protect our forests; **and** it may also become a profitable business in our community.

Use a colon to introduce a list of items that ends a sentence.

> The problems with recycling are the following: expense, noise, and possible further pollution.

Use a colon to separate the hour and the minute when you write the time of day, and after the salutation of a business letter.

> 7:15 A.M.   8:23 P.M.
> Dear Sir: Dear Mr. Delgado:

Guided Practice

Add the correct punctuation to each sentence.

Example: Mr. Phelps is an ecologist he studies the environment.   *semicolon before* he

1. The meeting begins at 730 P.M.
2. The topic concerns me and it concerns the principal, the teachers, and many of the students as well.
3. We have the following problems apathy, lack of organization, and laziness.
4. The environment is very important it needs our help.
5. Perhaps recycling is the answer perhaps it is not.

?! THINK

- How do I decide whether to use a comma or a semicolon in a compound sentence?

REMEMBER

- Use a **semicolon** to join parts of a compound sentence when a coordinating conjunction is not used, or when the sentence parts are long and contain commas.
- Use a **colon** before a list, in the time of day, and after the salutation in a business letter.

More Practice

Write each sentence. Add semicolons and colons where they are needed.

Example: Acid rain is a problem it needs our attention.
Acid rain is a problem; it needs our attention.

6. Many students do not notice the environment they are unconcerned.
7. Our club can interest them as follows by writing, by talking, and by organizing.
8. Perhaps we should call a meeting after school at 400 P.M.
9. We will invite parents, community leaders, and student groups others may also be interested.
10. Many will not respond they have other concerns.
11. We can raise their interest we only have to try!
12. We can recycle the following cans, jars, and paper.
13. Let us hold the meeting at 430 P.M. instead.
14. Football practice will be over perhaps more students will attend.
15. Three teams have practice soccer, swimming, and chess.
16. We should not meet without them it will hurt our cause.
17. Jan is organizing the meeting and she will ask whether we may use the auditorium, the gym, or a classroom.
18. She will meet with the principal by 1100 this morning.
19. A letter to the school paper cannot hurt it would probably be very useful.
20. Rita will begin the meeting she is a good speaker.

Extra Practice, page 396

WRITING APPLICATION A Journal Entry

Think of some topic related to nature or the environment about which you feel strongly. Write a journal entry describing your feelings and your thoughts about the topic. Make sure you have used semicolons and colons correctly.

9 VOCABULARY BUILDING: Prefixes

A **prefix** is a word part added to the beginning of a base word. A base word is a word to which affixes such as prefixes and suffixes can be added.

Prefix	Meaning	Example
de	from, down	**de**press
ex	out	**ex**claim
fore	before	**fore**tell
inter	between	**inter**city
post	after	**post**script
pre	before	**pre**cede
re	again, back	**re**peat
sub	under, lower	**sub**marine
bi	two	**bi**cycle
tri	three	**tri**angle
uni	one	**uni**verse
dis	opposite or lack of	**dis**approve
in*	without, not	**in**expensive
mis	wrongly, badly	**mis**behave
non	not	**non**sense
un	not, opposite of	**un**button

* becomes *il* when word begins with *l*: **il**logical;
becomes *im* when word begins with *b, m,* or *p*: **im**balance;
becomes *ir* when word begins with *r*: **ir**responsible

Guided Practice

Identify the prefix in each underlined word. Then give the meaning of the word.

1. Lila disagrees with my opinion about that movie.
2. "The plot is ridiculous," she exclaimed.
3. I told her she was illogical.
4. She said my opinion was uninteresting.

 THINK

■ How can knowing prefixes help to increase my vocabulary?

REMEMBER

- A **prefix** is a word part added to the beginning of a base word. A prefix changes the meaning of the base word to which it is added.

More Practice

A. Write each word and underline its prefix. Then write the meaning of the word and the meaning of its prefix.

Example: <u>pre</u>paid   *having received pay before*   *before*

5. unicycle
6. interrupt
7. review
8. subdue

9. foreseen
10. nonfiction
11. misunderstand
12. improper

B. Write each sentence. Replace the underlined words with a word that has a prefix. Use a dictionary to help you.

Example: I think the actor was <u>cast wrongly</u>.   *miscast*

13. They change the movies <u>twice a week</u> in our town.
14. First, they show <u>views of coming attractions</u>.
15. Some of the movies are definitely <u>below standard</u>!
16. Opinions about these shows are not <u>of one form</u>.
17. I thought one movie was <u>badly named</u>.
18. It was called *Balanced*; it was more like <u>*Not Balanced*</u>!
19. Some days they have <u>three-part</u> features.
20. They play straight through, with no <u>break in between</u>.
21. I watched the clock with <u>the opposite of belief</u>.
22. The second feature was <u>not satisfying</u>.
23. By the last feature, I was <u>not impressed</u>.
24. People who left the theater were not <u>admitted back in</u>.
25. Seeing that last movie should be <u>not legal</u>!

Extra Practice, page 397

WRITING APPLICATION An Interview

With a partner, write a list of questions you would ask in an interview with a movie or television star. In your interview try to use words containing prefixes from this lesson. Then, exchange papers with another pair of class-mates and find the prefixes in each other's work.

GRAMMAR —AND WRITING CONNECTION

Combining Sentences

Whether you are writing an editorial or a short story, you want to tell your readers all the important details about your subject. Sometimes you can combine details from two or three sentences into one sentence to avoid repeating words.

You can combine sentences by adding phrases.

> **SEPARATE:** Our class occasionally takes special trips.
> The trips are **to local museums.**
> The trips are **during the weekend.**

> **COMBINED:** Our class occasionally takes special trips **to local museums during the weekend.**

In addition to adding phrases, you can also combine sentences by moving descriptive words from one sentence to another.

> **SEPARATE:** The students waited patiently.
> The students were **enthusiastic.**
> The students waited **on the school grounds.**

> **COMBINED:** The **enthusiastic** students waited patiently **on the school grounds.**

Working Together

COOPERATIVE
LEARNING

Think about each group of sentences. Then tell how you would combine them into a single sentence.

1. The students enjoyed the trip. The trip was to the County Arts Museum. The trip was on Saturday.
2. We liked many paintings. The paintings were rustic. The paintings were in the upstairs gallery.
3. We saw some special exhibits. The exhibits were historical. The exhibits were in Smith Hall.

Revising Sentences

Louisa wanted to convince her teachers to take her classmates on more trips. Help her revise her notes by using phrases and descriptive words to combine each set of sentences.

4. Our science class took a special trip.
   The trip was to Magic Caves.
   The trip was in October.
5. We saw many rock formations.
   The rock formations were fascinating.
   The rock formations were throughout the caves.
6. Another trip was to a marine institute.
   The marine institute is famous.
   The marine institute is near our school.
7. We left the institute and walked to the beach.
   We left the institute after the tour.
   The beach was nearby.
8. Some of us spotted a whale.
   The whale was tremendous.
   The whale was on the horizon.
9. The guide presented a talk.
   The talk was informative.
   The talk was about sea creatures.
10. We learned facts about marine life.
    The facts were strange.
    The marine life is in tide pools.

Think about a class trip you would like to take. Then imagine that another student would prefer to take a different trip. Write a paragraph that gives reasons to support your opinion. Make sure that you tell the reasons why you think your suggestions would be better than the other student's. Then revise your work. Check to see if you can combine sentences by using phrases and descriptive words.

UNIT CHECKUP

LESSON 1

Prepositions and Prepositional Phrases (page 364)   Write the prepositional phrase. Then underline the preposition.

1. Pollution is a serious danger to our nation.
2. Preventing it requires the efforts of all concerned people.
3. The lakes and rivers across the country are being polluted.
4. Smog in our cities is another serious problem.
5. This has been an issue for a long time.

LESSON 2

Using Pronouns in Prepositional Phrases (page 366)   Write the correct pronoun for each sentence.

6. Between you and (I, me), I don't think we can win.
7. Lou told (he, him) and José about the problem.
8. The campaign for José and (she, her) should have started.
9. Now all the work must come from José and (me, myself).
10. It is too much work for (me and him, him and me).

LESSON 3

Prepositional Phrases as Adjectives or Adverbs (page 368) Identify the **adjective phrase** or **adverb phrase.**

11. Does the library in our school need improvements?
12. We have waited for several months to voice our concern.
13. Many students have strong opinions about this topic.
14. I expressed my views at our student council meeting.
15. The president of the council did not speak at the last meeting.

LESSON 4

Using Verbs After Prepositional Phrases (page 370)   Write the correct verb form for each sentence.

16. The problems of the downtown area (is, are) severe.
17. Visitors to our city (has, have) mentioned this.
18. The area around the big stores (needs, need) development.
19. The editorials in the newspaper (present, presents) opinions.

LESSON 5

Conjunctions (page 372)   Write each conjunction and write whether it is a **coordinating** or **correlative** conjunction.

20. Lisa and I made a bet yesterday.
21. Both she and I would try not to watch television.
22. Could we last one week, or would we give in?
23. Neither she nor I was sure what would happen.

LESSON 6

Making Verbs Agree with Compound Subjects (page 374)
Write the correct verb form for each sentence.

24. Either Sam or Elena (read, reads) the most.
25. Both Jenny and Pablo (wants, want) a new library.
26. Neither Lucy nor I (agrees, agree) with them.
27. Either you or my other friends (is, are) at the library every day.
28. My sisters or Delbert (tells, tell) me about the new novels.
29. The fiction and the nonfiction (is, are) both excellent.

LESSON 7

Interjections (page 376)   Write each sentence. Underline the interjection and punctuate it correctly.

30. Wow The campaign rally is starting really early.
31. I'm glad we weren't late. Whew
32. Hey did you hear what the candidate said?
33. Gee I don't think I agree.
34. There are too many long speeches. Ugh

LESSON 8

Mechanics: Using Semicolons and Colons (page 378)
Write each sentence by using a semicolon or a colon.

35. My friends are concerned citizens they discuss issues often.
36. Gina worries about pollution she is always involved in a cause.
37. Please bring the following posters, buttons, and crepe paper.
38. Let's begin the meeting at 8 15 this evening.
39. Francine, Joanna, and Allene are all good organizers but the one who is most enthusiastic is Gina.
40. Gina is smart and perceptive she is also quite idealistic.

LESSON 9

Vocabulary Building: Prefixes (page 380)   Replace each underlined phrase with one word that contains a prefix.

41. That new movie was badly cast.
42. I watched it with lack of belief.
43. Ira agrees with me, which is not usual.
44. Clark thinks I should evaluate again the movie.
45. Did I interpret wrongly the movie?

Writing Application: Using Prepositions and Conjunctions (pages 364–371)   The following paragraph contains 5 errors with prepositions and conjunctions. Correct the errors.

46.–50.   Clark saw a movie with Ira and I. Our opinions of the movie was rejected by Clark. Some of Clark's views seems confusing to us. However, a discussion about movies always interest me. Space movies appeal to me and Ira more than other kinds.

Zounds! It's an Old-Fashioned Melodrama!

Oh dear! For shame! Nay, nay! You are probably familiar with old-fashioned melodramas in which the hero—Dudley Doright, for example—defeats a nasty villain and saves someone from an oncoming railroad train. Write a short, old-fashioned melodrama. Use several interjections.

A HOLE IN THE BOTTOM OF THE OCEAN

With a small group of classmates, or by yourself, create sentences that contain many prepositional phrases, including the words "the hole in the bottom of the ocean." Here is an example: "There's a flea on the bump on the dog on the log in the boat from the wharf near the hole in the bottom of the ocean." Your sentences may be as nonsensical as you wish. Turn this activity into a game by assigning points for each phrase.

THE CONJUNCTION CONNECTION

With two other classmates create a group story using a coordinating conjunction in each sentence. Use *and, but,* and *or* as conjunctions in compound subjects, compound predicates, and compound sentences. If you wish, turn this activity into a game with competing teams. Each team scores a point for each conjunction used.

CREATIVE EXPRESSION

Smiling, the West Wind
  rattles the dry, falling leaves.
Why do the trees frown?
          —Anonymous

From watching the moon
  I turned and my friendly old
shadow led me home.
                    —Shiki

Where does he wander
  I wonder, my little one,
hunting dragonflies?
                —Chiyo

Try It Out

Haiku is an ancient form of Japanese poetry written in three lines. The first and third lines each contain five syllables. The second line has seven syllables. Haiku usually contain images of nature and suggest one of the four seasons. In a haiku the poet tries to convey a specific feeling or mood. Write a haiku about some aspect of nature or one of the seasons.

EXTRA PRACTICE

Three levels of practice

Prepositions and Prepositional Phrases (page 364)

LEVEL

A. Write the prepositional phrase in each sentence.

1. Yesterday our class had an argument about sports.
2. Should our school spend more money on the teams?
3. Some students get scholarships through sports.
4. On the other hand, academics are important, too.
5. Is there enough money for both areas?
6. Lately there has been a shortage of funds.
7. I will discuss this with Lillian.
8. She might have a new idea about the subject.
9. Due to Lillian, I have often changed my mind.

LEVEL

B. Write each prepositional phrase. Draw one line under each preposition and two lines under each object of the preposition.

10. Lillian has her own ideas on this subject.
11. The editor of the paper will write an article.
12. Lillian will approach the editor before Tuesday.
13. She will tell him her opinion during their talk.
14. He must decide between our two sides.
15. After last night, I am against my old position.
16. Lillian convinced me, except for one small point.
17. Since yesterday, I am basically on her side.

LEVEL

C. Write each sentence, filling in the blank with a preposition. Underline each prepositional phrase.

18. I sat ＿＿ Lillian ＿＿ the meeting.
19. She looked ＿＿ her and saw Mei ＿＿ the doorway.
20. Mei glanced ＿＿ the room and sat ＿＿ the window.
21. Was there a fight ＿＿ Lillian and Mei ＿＿ this?
22. Mei has been captain ＿＿ the tennis team ＿＿ March.
23. ＿＿ that, she is very excited ＿＿ all sports.
24. ＿＿ you and me, I like her point ＿＿ view.
25. However, I agree ＿＿ Lillian ＿＿ this case.

EXTRA PRACTICE

Three levels of practice

Using Pronouns in Prepositional Phrases (page 366)

LEVEL

A. Choose the correct word or words for each sentence.

1. Yesterday I was talking to Roy and (he, him).
2. For (Roy and I, Roy and me), the subject was familiar.
3. Jason sat between (him and me, he and I).
4. He enjoys talking with (we, us) about sports.
5. To Jason and (me, myself), tennis is the best sport.
6. Racketball also interests both (he, him) and Roy.
7. Then Linda walked past another friend and (we, us).
8. She disagrees with (me and Jason, Jason and me).
9. For (she, her) and her friends, soccer is more exciting.

LEVEL

B. If the prepositional phrase contains a pronoun error, correct it. If it is correct, write **correct.**

10. There are no secrets between her and I.
11. Alice sat down beside me and him.
12. Because of Joe and she, I began to reconsider.
13. She spoke firmly to Jason and myself.
14. Except for her, we all agreed.
15. Then she began to convince Debbie and myself.
16. Jason explained himself to her and we.
17. Like me and him, Roy listened carefully.
18. We did not want to go on without her and them.

LEVEL

C. Write each sentence. Fill in the blank with a pronoun.

19. For my sister Jan and ____, Career Day at school is exciting.
20. For ____ and me, it provides the chance to learn about careers.
21. Speakers discuss various jobs with ____.
22. They tell us about careers that might be of interest to ____.
23. Our brother Mike sits next to Jan and ____.
24. Mike says that being a police officer appeals to ____.
25. Between you and ____, my parents want him to be a doctor.

EXTRA PRACTICE

Three levels of practice

Prepositional Phrases as Adjectives or Adverbs (page 368)

LEVEL

A. Write whether the underlined prepositional phrase is an **adjective phrase** or an **adverb phrase.**

1. I love reading adventure stories about heroes.
2. Margery gave this novel to me.
3. The beginning of this book did not interest me.
4. However, the hero triumphs in the end.
5. I read that book during study periods.
6. The imagination of the author is very lively.
7. The setting of the story is ancient Greece.
8. The action occurs during the Trojan War.

LEVEL

B. Write and label the **adjective phrase** or **adverb phrase** in each sentence. Then write the word the phrase modifies.

9. Jorge peeked into the thick blue book.
10. The cover of the book looked unusual.
11. He studied its pages for a few minutes.
12. Perhaps this was a story about the future.
13. Books about space travel are his favorites.
14. I now love science fiction because of his influence.
15. I read little else during my free time.
16. The library has a whole section of it.

LEVEL

C. Write each sentence. Fill in the blank with an adjective or an adverb phrase.

17. What kind ____ do you usually read?
18. Do you like books ____?
19. The author ____ also wrote a famous novel.
20. I looked for it ____.
21. I finally found the book ____.
22. The descriptions ____ are quite vivid.
23. My friends do not agree ____.
24. They prefer books ____.
25. I usually read ____.

EXTRA PRACTICE

Three levels of practice

Using Verbs After Prepositional Phrases (page 370)

LEVEL

A. Choose the correct verb form for each sentence.

1. This article about two cities (is, are) disturbing.
2. One of the towns (wants, want) a new dump.
3. Plans for the dump (upsets, upset) the other town.
4. A meeting of councilors (has, have) been called.
5. Dates for a meeting (was, were) discussed at length.
6. A day after the holidays (seems, seem) best.
7. Supporters of the mayor (is, are) very vocal.
8. Concerns about the environment (was, were) raised.
9. A survey among the voters (shows, show) indecision.

LEVEL

B. Write each sentence, using the correct present-tense form of the verb in parentheses.

10. My own opinions about the matter (change) every day.
11. The argument between the two councilors (confuse) me.
12. Speeches during the meeting (continue) endlessly.
13. The seats within the council room (be) uncomfortable.
14. People in front of me (talk) too much.
15. The atmosphere among the listeners (be) tense.
16. A disagreement within the group (seem) serious.
17. All councilors except Mr. Lopez (be) confused.
18. Plans for the new dump (involve) his property.

LEVEL

C. Write each sentence. Correct each error in verb usage.

19. The discussion among voters are lively.
20. Their criticism of the plans are serious.
21. Pollution of waterways were an issue.
22. Disagreement among citizens are nothing new.
23. A clash of opinions sometimes result in improvements.
24. Solutions due to negotiation resolves most matters.
25. Several new locations for the dump was proposed.

PRACTICE + PLUS

Three levels of additional practice for a difficult skill

Using Verbs After Prepositional Phrases (page 370)

LEVEL

A. Choose the correct verb form for each sentence.

1. The lot between the factories (is, are) now a garden.
2. People from the nursery (provide, provides) tools and gardening tips.
3. Plants in every garden (require, requires) fertilizer and water.
4. Stakes in the ground (support, supports) the heavy tomato plants.
5. The corn in the rows (grow, grows) very high.
6. A bouquet of fragrant lilacs (scent, scents) the air.
7. The sunflowers along the fence (attract, attracts) many birds.
8. A nest of robins (live, lives) in the oak tree.

LEVEL

B. Write each sentence, using the correct present tense form of the verb in parentheses.

9. The running shoes in my locker (be) very expensive.
10. The design of the shoes (prevent) stress injuries.
11. Registration of all entrants (take) place today.
12. Runners from each club (arrive) on time.
13. The racers at the gate (wait) for the starting gun.
14. Beads of perspiration (fall) across their foreheads.
15. Volunteers along the route (give) water to the marathoners.
16. Onlookers from the stands (cheer) the runners to victory.

LEVEL

C. Write each sentence. Correct each error in verb usage.

17. The dancers from the ballet company performs each night at the theater.
18. Members of the audience whispers excitedly before the performance.
19. The prima ballerina in the white tutu dance beautifully.
20. Her performance of the roles are lovely.
21. The life of a ballet artist demand great discipline.
22. The dancers in the troupe practices long hours daily.
23. The male dancers in this company exhibits great strength.
24. Selections on the program varies each night.
25. Dances from the modern era appeals to Edward.

EXTRA PRACTICE

Three levels of practice

Conjunctions (page 372)

LEVEL

A. Write each sentence. Underline each conjunction.

1. Do you enjoy television and video games?
2. Neither one nor the other interests me.
3. Judith or Tony can tell you what I mean.
4. Video games can be fun, but most become boring.
5. Whether you believe me or not, I do not like them.
6. Either they waste my time, or they waste my money.
7. You and your friends do not agree with me.
8. Video games are stimulating to both you and Davy.

LEVEL

B. Write each sentence. Underline each conjunction and write whether it is a **coordinating conjunction** or a **correlative conjunction.**

9. Hector and I prefer playing sports to playing video games.
10. We occasionally play soccer with either Tony or Judith.
11. Neither they nor I spend time watching television.
12. I enjoy a good movie but not most television programs.
13. Both my friends and I prefer reading a good book.
14. I usually read novels, but this biography looks interesting.
15. Pat neither reads much nor plays sports.
16. He not only writes stories but also plays the piano.

LEVEL

C. Write each sentence. Underline each conjunction and write whether it links two **subjects, predicates, objects of prepositions,** or **simple sentences.**

17. Skill and accuracy are necessary in video games.
18. That is the argument of both Mary and Paolo.
19. Either Tony or Judith gives them tips.
20. Tony is an expert, but Judith plays even better.
21. Mary watches and learns from them.
22. She sometimes plays a game with Judith or Tony.
23. Not only do they like the games, but they also designed a new one.
24. Neither Mary nor Tony drew the design.
25. Judith both draws and plays well!

EXTRA PRACTICE

Three levels of practice

Making Verbs Agree with Compound Subjects (page 374)

LEVEL

A. Choose the correct form of the verb for each sentence.

1. Mrs. Phelps and Miss Rodriguez (wants, want) our attention.
2. Neither our teacher nor her aides (speaks, speak) loudly.
3. They and the principal (has, have) an announcement.
4. Either Mrs. Phelps or the principal (begins, begin) most assemblies.
5. She and he (explains, explain) the issue.
6. They and the school board (is, are) preparing a proposal.
7. The cafeteria or the sports facilities (needs, need) improvements.
8. Most students and the principal (wants, want) a new cafeteria.
9. Neither the school board nor the sports teams (agrees, agree).

LEVEL

B. Write each sentence, using the correct present tense form of the verb in parentheses.

10. The auditorium and cafeteria also (serve) as meeting rooms.
11. Parents and teachers (be) asking for better facilities.
12. Neither funds nor an architect (be) available.
13. Expansion or remodeling (require) a bigger budget.
14. Mrs. Phelps and the school board (ask) for assistance.
15. Either Miss Rodriguez or a teacher usually (close) the meetings.
16. Both the principal and Mrs. Phelps (present) their opinions.
17. Questions and answers (take) a lot of time.
18. Albert or Donna (be) writing an editorial on the issue.

LEVEL

C. Write each sentence. Where necessary, correct each error in verb use.

19. The plan and the cost is attractive to everyone.
20. Both the principal and his proposal makes a lot of sense.
21. Either his ideas or a similar plan seem possible.
22. The school board and Mrs. Phelps reviews the proposal.
23. Either the school grounds or the building are always under criticism.
24. Little or nothing is ever done.
25. Miss Rodriguez and the principal is hopeful for the future.

EXTRA PRACTICE

Three levels of practice

Interjections (page 376)

LEVEL

A. Write each interjection.

 1. Hey! Tomas is running for council president!
 2. Wow! Lydia is running against him.
 3. Well, I wonder which of them will win.
 4. Good heavens, isn't it obvious?
 5. Oh, no, I think it will be a close race.
 6. Look at that beautiful poster of Lydia's. Wow!
 7. I never saw anything so pretty. Gee!
 8. Whew, I was afraid we would be late for the rally.

LEVEL

B. Write each sentence. Underline the interjection and add the correct punctuation.

 9. Gee this meeting room is quite crowded.
10. Hey Watch where you're going!
11. That boy just stepped on my foot. Ow
12. Golly people can be rude sometimes.
13. Oh, no We forgot to remind Tony to attend.
14. Now he will not hear the speeches. Rats
15. Yippee The poll looks promising.
16. Oh it may be too late to cast a vote.
17. Look how many votes there are! Wow

LEVEL

C. Write each sentence. Add an interjection either at the beginning or the end of the sentence. Be sure to punctuate the new sentence properly.

18. Look at all those colored balloons!
19. Where did they get them all?
20. I suppose they took up a collection to raise money.
21. Why didn't we think of something like that!
22. It's too late now.
23. Wait a minute.
24. It isn't too late.
25. Let's run to the store before it closes.

EXTRA PRACTICE

Three levels of practice

Mechanics: Using Semicolons and Colons (page 378)

LEVEL
A. Use either a semicolon or a colon in the blank.

1. The problems we face are ____ smog, smoke, and garbage.
2. The dump is full ____ people in the area are worried.
3. Most concerned are the following ____ Jo, Ira, Lou, and Sal.
4. Their concerns are serious ____ I am sympathetic.
5. In addition, garbage trucks arrive at 6____15 A.M.
6. Have you ever been awakened before 7____00 in the morning?
7. Because Sal is concerned, she may investigate the matter ____ or she may write more letters.
8. Lou has already written to the following ____ the mayor, the editor of the newspaper, and the environmental agency.
9. The citizens are impatient ____ they want action.

LEVEL
B. Add a semicolon or a colon where it is needed.

10. Peter agrees with Sal he has been concerned for a while.
11. In fact, the disposal of industrial waste disturbs several students and they have formed a group.
12. This group includes the following Carmen, Kim, and Tom.
13. They meet at 8 00 P.M. every Thursday night.
14. The members discuss issues they also write articles.
15. Uncollected trash is dangerous naturally, they are upset.
16. Children may be hurt in addition, pets are getting ill.
17. The following parents help the group Mr. Jones, Mrs. Wilkins, and Mr. Chung.
18. All share the work involved they also share the rewards.

LEVEL
C. Correct the punctuation error in each sentence.

19. Perhaps we need one of the following, a petition, a meeting, or a vote.
20. Ellen will analyze the situation, her judgment is reliable.
21. The group discussed the following; air pollution, traffic control, and housing.
22. They made proposals, however, nothing has been decided.
23. Housing has become essential, little is currently available.
24. Ms. Laudato advises us; but the group is quite independent.
25. Cooperation is most important: caring and concern are, too.

EXTRA PRACTICE

Three levels of practice

Vocabulary Building: Prefixes (page 380)

LEVEL

A. Write each word and underline its prefix. Then write the meaning of the word and the prefix. Use a dictionary to help you.

1. revise
2. illegal
3. misapply
4. precook
5. bisect
6. triple
7. unify
8. interrupt
9. misplace

LEVEL

B. Write each sentence, substituting a word with a prefix for the underlined words. Check your new word in a dictionary.

10. I like reading books that are not fiction.
11. Yesterday I arranged again my bookshelves.
12. My friend Jaime and I had a lack of agreement.
13. I think he interpreted wrongly what I meant.
14. I just wanted to give him an early view of a book.
15. He said that doing so made the book not interesting.
16. He wished I had used more thought ahead of time.
17. I thought he was a little not patient.
18. His lack of satisfaction did not last, however.

LEVEL

C. Match each word in the right column with a prefix in the left column. Check a dictionary to make sure the new word exists. Then, write the definition of the word.

19. re   **a.** script
20. ir   **b.** usable
21. dis   **c.** occupy
22. post   **d.** regular
23. un   **e.** funds
24. im   **f.** perfect
25. pre   **g.** pleasure

UNIT 12

Writing Editorials

Read the quotation and look at the picture on the opposite page. Talk about ways to express your opinions in a convincing manner.

When you write an editorial, you will want to anticipate questions your audience may have, and then answer them by presenting facts and your own opinions in a persuasive manner.

Focus An editorial is a statement found in newspapers and magazines, which expresses an opinion supported by facts and strong reasons.

What opinion do you have that you could express through an editorial? In this unit you will find a story that includes persuasion. You will also see some photographs. You can use them to find ideas for writing.

THEME: *OUTLOOKS*

Look out how you use proud words. When you let proud words go, it is not easy to call them back. They wear long boots, hard boots.

—Carl Sandburg

LITERATURE

Reading Like a Writer

Have you ever changed your opinion about something? What changed your mind? Was it something that you read in a newspaper or magazine?

When Uncle Dick hired Melvin Spencer to sell his farm, he knew Melvin had a way with words. As you read the selection, look for the ways Melvin uses words to make the farm sound attractive.

THIS FARM FOR SALE

by Jesse Stuart

"This time we're goin' to sell this farm," Uncle Dick said to Aunt Emma. "I've just learned how to sell a farm. Funny, I never thought of it myself."

My cousins—Olive, Helen, Oliver, and Little Dick—all stopped eating and looked at one another and then looked at Uncle Dick and Aunt Emma. While Aunt Emma smiled, they smiled, too. Everybody seemed happy because Uncle Dick, who had just come from Blakesburg, had found a way to sell the farm. Everybody was happy but me. I was sorry Uncle Dick was going to sell the farm.

"This farm is just as good as sold!" Uncle Dick talked on. "I've got a real estate man, my old friend Melvin Spencer, coming here tomorrow to look the place over. He's goin' to sell for me."

"I'd like to get enough for it to make a big payment on a fine house in Blakesburg." Aunt Emma said, "I've got the one picked out that I want. It's the beautiful Coswell house, I understand it's up for sale now and no one's livin' in it!"

"Gee, that will be wonderful," Cousin Olive said. "Right on the street and not any mud. We wouldn't have to wear galoshes all winter if we lived there!"

"I'll say it will be wonderful," Helen said, with a smile. "Daddy, I hope Mr. Spencer can sell this place."

I wanted to tell Aunt Emma the reason why no one was living in the Coswell house. Every time Big River rose to flood stage, the water got on the first floor in the house; and this was the reason why the Coswells had built a house on higher ground outside Blakesburg and had moved to it. And this was the reason why they couldn't keep a renter any longer than it took Big River to rise to flood stage. But this wasn't my business, so I didn't say anything.[1]

"Mel Spencer will come here to look this farm over," Uncle Dick said, puffing on his cigar until he'd almost filled the dining room with smoke. "Then he'll put an ad in the *Blakesburg Gazette*."

"What will we do about the cows, horses, hogs, honeybees, hay in the barn lofts and in the stacks, and corn in the bins?" Cousin Oliver asked.

"Sell them too," Uncle Dick said. "When we sell, let's sell everything we have but our house plunder."

1. The narrator supports his opinion with specific reasons.

It was ten o'clock the next day before Melvin Spencer came. Since he couldn't drive his car all the way to Uncle Dick's farm, he rode the mail truck to Red Hot. Red Hot is a store and post office on the Tiber River. And at Red Hot, Uncle Dick met him with an extra horse and empty saddle. So Melvin Spencer came riding up with Uncle Dick. And I'll never forget the first words he said when he climbed down from the saddle.

"Richard, it's a great experience to be in the saddle again," he said, breathing deeply of the fresh air. "All this reminds me of another day and time."

Oliver, Little Dick, and I followed Melvin Spencer and Uncle Dick as they started walking toward the Tiber bottoms.

"How many acres in this farm, Richard?" Melvin Spencer asked.

"The deed calls for three hundred, more or less," Uncle Dick said.

"How many acres of bottom land?" he asked Uncle Dick.

"I'd say about sixty-five," Uncle Dick replied.

We walked down the joly-wagon road, where my cousins and I had often ridden Nell and Jerry to and from the field. "What kind of land is this?" Melvin Spencer asked. He had to look up to see the bright heads of cane.

"It's limestone land," Uncle Dick bragged. "Never had to use fertilizer. My people have farmed these bottoms for over a hundred years."

Then Uncle Dick showed Melvin Spencer the corn we had laid by. It was August, and our growing corn was maturing. Melvin Spencer looked at the big cornfield. He was very silent. We walked on to the five acres of tobacco, where the broad leaves crossed the balks and a man couldn't walk through. Then we went down to the river.

"My farm comes to this river," Uncle Dick said. "I've often thought what a difference it would be if we bridge across this river. Then I could reach the Tiber road and go east to Blakesburg and west to Darter City. But we don't have a bridge; and until we go down the river seven miles to Red Hot where we can cross to the Tiber road, we'll always be in the mud. I've heard all my life that the county would build a bridge. My father heard it, too, in his lifetime."

"You are shut in here," Melvin Spencer agreed, as he looked beyond the Tiber River at the road.

"Now, we'll go to the house and get some dinner," Uncle Dick said. "Then I'll take you up on the hill this afternoon and show you my timber and the rest of the farm."

When we reached the big house, Melvin Spencer stopped for a minute and looked at the house and yard.

"You know, when I sell a piece of property, I want to look it over," he told Uncle Dick. "I want to know all about it. How old is this house?"

"The date was cut on the chimney," Uncle Dick said.

Melvin Spencer looked over the big squat log house with the plank door, big stone steps, small windows, the moss-covered roof. Then we went inside, and he started looking again. That is, he did until Uncle Dick introduced him to Aunt Emma and Aunt Emma introduced him to a table that made him stand and look some more.

"I've never seen anything like this since I was a boy," Melvin Spencer said, showing more interest in the loaded table than he had in the farm.

"All of this came from our farm here," Uncle Dick said.

I never saw a man eat like Melvin Spencer. He ate like I did when I first came to Uncle Dick's and Aunt Emma's each spring when school was over. He tried to eat something of everything on the table, but he couldn't get around to it all.

"If I could sell this farm like you can prepare a meal, I'd get a whopping big price for it," he said with a chuckle as he looked at Aunt Emma.

"I hope you can," Aunt Emma said. "We're too far back here. Our children have to wade the winter mud to get to school. And we don't have electricity. We don't have the things that city people have. And I think every country woman wants them.''

Melvin Spencer didn't listen to all that Aunt Emma said. He was much too busy eating. And long before he had finished, Uncle Dick pulled a cigar from his inside coat pocket, struck a match under the table, lit it, and blew a big cloud of smoke toward the ceiling in evident enjoyment.

He looked at Aunt Emma and smiled.

"The old place is as good as sold, Mother," Uncle Dick said with a wink. "You're a-goin' to be out of the mud. We'll let some other woman slave around here and wear galoshes all winter. We'll be on the bright, clean streets wearin' well-shined shoes—every blessed one of us. We'll have an electric washer, a radio where we won't have to have the batteries charged, a bathroom, and an electric stove. No more of this stove-wood choppin' for the boys and me."

When Uncle Dick said this, Olive and Helen looked at Aunt Emma and smiled. I looked at Oliver and Little Dick, and they were grinning. But Melvin Spencer never looked up from his plate.

When we got up from the table, Melvin Spencer thanked Aunt Emma, Cousin Olive, and Helen for the "best dinner" he'd had since he was a young man. Then he asked Aunt Emma for a picture of the house.

Aunt Emma sent Helen to get it. "If you can, just sell this place for us," Aunt Emma said to Melvin Spencer.

"I'll do my best," he promised her. "But as you ought to know, it will be a hard place to sell, located way back here and without a road."

"Are you a-goin' to put a picture of this old house in the paper?" Uncle Dick asked, as Helen came running with the picture.

"I might," Melvin Spencer said. "I never say much in an ad, since I have to make my words count. A picture means a sale sometimes. Of course, this expense will come from the sale of the property."

He said good-by to Aunt Emma, Olive, and Helen. Little Dick, Oliver, and I followed him and Uncle Dick out of the house and up the hill where the yellow poplars and the pines grow.

"Why hasn't this timber been cut long ago?" Melvin Spencer asked, looking up at the trees.

"Not any way to haul it out," Uncle Dick told him.

"That's right," Melvin Spencer said. "I'd forgot about the road. If a body doesn't have a road to his farm, Richard, he's not got much of a place."

"These old trees get hollow and blow down in storms," Uncle Dick said. "They should have been cut down a long time ago."

"Yes, they should have," Melvin Spencer agreed, as he put his hand on the bark of a yellow poplar. "We used to have trees like this in Pike County. But not any more."

While we walked under the beech grove, we came upon a drove of slender bacon hogs eating beechnuts.

"Old Skinny bacon hogs," Uncle Dick said, as they scurried past us. "They feed on the mast of the beeches and oaks, on saw-briar, greenbriar, and pine-tree roots, and on mulberries, persimmons, and pawpaws."

When we climbed to the top of a hill, the land slanted in all directions.

"Show me from here what you own," Melvin Spencer said.

"It's very easy, Mel," Uncle Dick said. "The stream on the right and the one on the left are the left and right forks of Wolfe Creek. They are boundary lines. I own all the land between them. I own all the bottom land from where the forks join, down to that big bend in the Tiber. And I own down where the Tiber flows against those white limestone cliffs."

"You are fenced in by natural boundaries," Melvin Spencer said. "They're almost impossible to cross. This place will be hard to sell, Richard."

Then we went back down the hill, and Melvin and Uncle Dick climbed into the saddles and were off down the little narrow road toward Red Hot. Their horses went away at a gallop, because Melvin Spencer had to catch the mail truck, and he was already behind schedule.

On Saturday, Uncle Dick rode to Red Hot to get the paper. Since he didn't read very well, he asked me to read what Melvin Spencer had said about his house. When I opened the paper and turned to the picture of the house, everybody gathered around.

"Think of a picture of this old house in the paper," Aunt Emma said.

"But there are pictures of other houses for sale in the paper," Uncle Dick told her. "That's not anything to crow about."

"But it's the best-looking of the four," Cousin Olive said.

"It does look better than I thought it would," Aunt Emma sighed.

"Look, here's two columns all the way down the page," I said. "The other four places advertised here have only a paragraph about them."

"Read it," Uncle Dick said. "I'd like to know what Mel said about this place. Something good, I hope."

So I read this aloud:

Yesterday, I had a unique experience when I visited the farm of Mr. and Mrs. Richard Stone, which they have asked me to sell. I cannot write an ad about this farm. I must tell you about it.

I went up a winding road on horseback. Hazelnut bushes, with clusters of green hazelnuts bending their slender stems, swished across my face. Pawpaws, heavy with green clusters of fruit, grew along this road. Persimmons with bending boughs covered one slope below the road. Here are wild fruits and nuts of Nature's cultivation for the one who possesses land like this. Not any work but just to go out and gather the fruit. How many of you city dwellers would love this?

"What about him a-mentionin' the persimmons, pawpaws, and hazelnuts!" Uncle Dick broke in. "I'd never have thought of them. They're common things!"

When we put the horses in the big barn, Mr. Stone, his two sons, his nephew, and I walked down into his Tiber-bottom farm land. And, like the soil along the Nile River, this over-flowed land, rich with limestone, never has to be fertilized. I saw cane as high as a giraffe, and as dark green as the waves of the Atlantic. It grew in long, straight rows with brown clusters of seed that looked to be up against the blue of the sky. I have never seen such dark clouds of corn grow out of the earth. Five acres of tobacco, with leaves as broad as a mountaineer's shoulders. Pleasant meadows with giant haystacks here and there. It is a land rich with fertility and abundant with crops.[2]

"That sounds wonderful," Aunt Emma said, smiling.

This peaceful Tiber River, flowing dreamily down the valley, is a boundary to his farm. Here one can see to the bottoms of the deep holes, the water is so clear and blue. One can catch

2. Melvin uses specific facts and examples to make his writing persuasive.

fish from the river for his next meal. Elder bushes, where they gather the berries to make the finest jelly in the world, grow along this riverbank as thick as ragweeds. The Stones have farmed this land for four generations, have lived in the same house, have gathered elderberries for their jelly along the Tiber riverbanks, and fished in its sky-blue waters that long—and yet they will sell this land.

"Just a minute, Shan," Uncle Dick said as he got up from his chair. "Stop just a minute,"

Uncle Dick pulled a handkerchief from his pocket and wiped the sweat from his forehead. His face seemed a bit flushed. He walked a little circle around the living room and then sat back down in his chair. But the sweat broke out on his face again when I started reading.

The proof of what a farm produces is at the farm table. I wish that whoever reads what I have written here could have seen the table prepared by Mrs. Stone and her two daughters. Hot fluffy biscuits with light-brown tops, brown-crusted cornbread, buttermilk, sweet milk (cooled in a freestone well), wild-grape jelly, wild-crab-apple jelly, mast-fed lean bacon that melted in my mouth, fresh apple pie, wild-blackberry cobbler, honey-colored sorghum from the limestone bottoms of the Tiber, and wild honey from the beehives.

"Oh, no one ever said that about a meal I cooked before," Aunt Emma broke in.

"Just a minute, Shan," Uncle Dick said, as he got up from his chair and with his handkerchief in his hand again.

This time Uncle Dick went a bit faster as he circled the living room. He wiped sweat from his face as he walked. He had a worried look in his face. I read on:

Their house, eight rooms and two halls, would be a show place if close to some of our modern cities. The house itself would be worth the price I will later quote you on this farm.

Giant yellow poplar logs with twenty- to thirty-inch facings, hewed smooth with broadaxes by the mighty hands of Stone pioneers, make the sturdy walls in this termite-proof house. Two planks make the broad doors in this house that is one-hundred-and-six years old. This beautiful home of pioneer architecture is without modern conveniences, but since a power line will be constructed up to the Tiber River early next spring, a few modern conveniences will be possible.

"I didn't know that!" Aunt Emma was excited. "I guess it's just talk, like about the bridge across the Tiber."

After lunch I climbed a high hill to look at the rest of this farm. I walked through a valley of virgin trees, where there were yellow poplars and pine sixty feet to the first limb. Beech trees with tops big enough to shade twenty-five head of cattle. Beechnuts streaming down like golden coins, to be gathered by the bacon hogs running wild. A farm with wild game and fowl, and a river bountiful with fish! And yet, this farm is for sale!

Uncle Dick walked over beside his chair. He looked as if he were going to fall over.

Go see for yourself roads not exploited by the county or state, where the horse's shoe makes music on the clay, where apple orchards with fruit are bending down, and barns and bins are full. Go see a way of life, a richness and fulfillment that make America great, that put solid foundation stones under America! This beautiful farm, fifty head of livestock, honeybees, crops old and new, and a home for only $22,000!

"Oh!" Aunt Emma screamed. I thought she was going to faint. "Oh, he's killed it with that price. It's unheard of, Richard! You couldn't get $6,000 for it."

Uncle Dick still paced the floor.

"What's the matter, Pa?" Oliver finally asked.

"I didn't know I had so much." Uncle Dick said. "I'm a rich man and didn't know it. I'm not selling this farm!"

"Don't worry, Richard," Aunt Emma said. "You won't sell it at that price!"

I never saw such disappointed looks as there were on my cousins' faces.

"But what will you do with Mr. Spencer?" Aunt Emma asked. "You've put the farm in his hands to sell."

"Pay him for his day and what he put in the paper," Uncle Dick told her. "I know we're not goin' to sell now, for it takes two to sign the deed. I'll be willing to pay Mel Spencer a little extra because he showed me what we have."[3]

Then I laid the paper down and walked quietly from the room. Evening was coming on. I walked toward the meadows. I wanted to share the beauty of this farm with Melvin Spencer. I was never so happy.

3. Melvin has effectively used persuasive language to change Uncle Dick's mind.

Thinking Like a Reader

1. What made Uncle Dick change his mind about selling the farm?
2. What convinced Melvin Spencer of the farm's value?
3. When have you changed your opinion about an important matter? Why did you change your mind?

Write about your experience in your journal.

Thinking Like a Writer

4. What details about the farm does Melvin Spencer use to convince his readers?
5. How persuasive are these details to you?
6. If you wanted to persuade someone to buy your home, what would you say about it?

Write your responses in your journal.

Brainstorm *Vocabulary*

In "This Farm for Sale," Melvin Spencer uses colorful comparisons to describe Uncle Dick's farm. "I saw cane high as a giraffe," he writes, "and as dark green as the waves of the Atlantic." These comparisons help to create a vivid picture in the mind of a possible buyer. Think of something that you might like to sell and picture it in your mind. In your journal, write several comparisons that would help another person form a vivid picture of it. Add these comparisons to your personal vocabulary list. You can use them in your writing.

Talk It Over

Speak Persuasively

When you persuade, you try to influence another person's opinions or persuade him or her to do something. In "This Farm for Sale," Melvin Spencer wanted to persuade someone to buy the farm. Work with a partner. Imagine that you are a salesperson showing the farm to a customer who has noticed the absence of a paved road, electricity, and other conveniences. Try to persuade your partner to purchase the farm. Listen closely to your partner's objections and try to think of good reasons to overcome them.

Quick Write

Write a Letter to the Editor

Besides offering news and advertisements, a newspaper is a place for people to express their ideas and opinions. Newspapers express their opinions in editorials. Readers express their opinions in letters to the editor. Imagine that you are one of the characters in "This Farm for Sale" or a reader of the newspaper mentioned in the story. Write a brief letter to the editor expressing the need for a paved road along the Tiber River.

Dear Editor:

Your newspaper has advertised the Stone's farm for sale. What a shame! The farms along our Tiber River will continue to lose value unless the town paves the old road. Horses are a thing of the past. Anyone who tries to sell a farm will discover how much we need a modern road.

Yours truly,
Concerned Neighbor

Idea Corner *Think of Topics*

Think of issues or problems that exist in your school, neighborhood, or community and about which you might like to write an editorial. You may already have some opinions that you would like to express. Write them in your journal. You might write topic ideas such as "cafeteria food" or "TV versus real life." You might design a poster or draw a cartoon that expresses your view of a problem.

PICTURES  *SEEING LIKE A WRITER*

Finding Ideas for Writing

Look at the photographs on these pages. Think about what you see. What ideas for persuasive writing do the pictures give you? Write your ideas in your journal.

1 GROUP WRITING: AN EDITORIAL

COOPERATIVE
LEARNING

Newspaper editors can write **editorials** to express opinions about important topics. The **purpose** of an editorial is to persuade an **audience** to think or act in a certain way. These points will help you write an effective editorial.

- Fact and Opinion
- Order of Reasons
- Persuasive Language

Fact and Opinion

<u>Lucia Nichols deserves to be elected to the school board.</u> First and foremost, she is experienced. Ms. Nichols developed and directed the successful after-school program. Although she has no school-age children of her own, Ms. Nichols has nevertheless served as a school volunteer for three years. Opponents to her election point to the fact that she has been a resident for only three years. However, in those three years her effect on our educational system has been clear and strong. Her interest and involvement in education make her worthy of your vote next week.

The underlined sentence expresses an opinion. An **opinion** is a statement of belief about a topic. Opinions are matters about which people are likely to disagree. You cannot prove that an opinion is true. You can, however, support an opinion with facts. **Facts** are statements that are known to be true or can be proved by study or observation.

Guided Practice: Fact and Opinion

As a class, choose one of the following topics or think of one on which you all agree. Discuss the topic and write at least one opinion about it. Then write two or three facts that support the opinion.

Example: Littering is an expensive habit.
Thousands of dollars are spent to pick up litter.
People who litter should pay the clean-up costs.

today's movies   modern music   education

Order of Reasons

When you write an editorial, state your opinion about the topic in the first sentence. In the detail sentences that follow, present the facts and reasons that support your opinion.

Look at the editorial on page 414 again. Notice the order in which the writer has arranged the supporting facts and reasons. They are arranged by **order of importance**, beginning with what the writer considered to be the most important fact.

In an editorial, organize your supporting facts in the order of their importance. First, decide which fact or reason is the most persuasive. Then decide whether to put that reason first or to save it and place it last. The editorial on page 414 might also have been organized in this way.

> Lucia Nichols deserves to be elected to the school board. Although she has no school-age children of her own, Ms. Nichols has nevertheless served as a school volunteer for three years. Opponents to her election point to the fact that she has been a resident for only three years. However, in those three years her effect on our educational system has been clear and strong. Most importantly, she is experienced. Ms. Nichols developed and directed the successful after-school enrichment program. Her interest and involvement in education make her worthy of your vote next week.

Transition Words

When you write an editorial, you can help your audience to follow your argument clearly by using transition words to present facts, to state an opinion, or to show opposition.

To Present Facts	To State an Opinion	To Show Opposition
first	I believe	on the other hand
most importantly	in my opinion	but
for example	I feel	although
in addition	I think	however

Close your editorial with a **concluding sentence** that restates your opinion and sums up your arguments. You may also use the concluding sentence to tell your readers what action you think they should take.

- What is the purpose of the concluding sentence in the editorial above?
- Do you think the concluding sentence is effective? Why or why not?

Guided Practice: Ordering Reasons

Remember the opinion that you wrote earlier in your topic sentence and the supporting arguments that you wrote in your detail sentences. As a class, discuss the supporting arguments that you based on the facts. Decide which argument is the strongest, or most likely to persuade the audience to accept your opinion. Write the facts or arguments and number them in their order of importance, with the most important argument first.

Persuasive Language

Opinions often contain judgment words that will help you recognize them. Words like *should*, *best*, *worst*, *believe*, *must*, and *probably* let you know that the writer is expressing an opinion.

When you write an editorial, use language effectively to present your arguments. Choose words that will support your opinion fairly and honestly. Read the example sentences below.

1. Having a pen pal is interesting.
2. Receiving letters from abroad helps us to understand and appreciate how other people live.

- Which sentence is more persuasive?

Remember that your purpose is to influence the opinions of your audience. Good word choice is an important skill in persuasive writing.

Putting an Editorial Together

As a class you have written an opinion for an editorial and listed facts and arguments that support the opinion. You have also arranged the supporting arguments in order of importance. Now you are ready to write your editorial.

Guided Practice: Writing an Editorial

Write a topic sentence in which you state your opinion. Then, read over the facts and arguments you have listed to make sure that they are strong enough to support your opinion. Close your editorial with an effective concluding sentence.

Share your editorial with a friend. Ask your friend if he or she thinks your editorial is persuasive.

Checklist An Editorial

When you write an editorial, one way to remember important points is to make a checklist.

Below is a sample checklist for writing an editorial. Copy it and add any other points to it that you wish to remember when you are writing an editorial. Keep the checklist in your writing folder and use it when you write.

> **CHECKLIST**
>
> - Remember purpose and audience.
> - State an opinion in the topic sentence.
> - Present strong supporting facts and reasons.
> - Use order of importance.
> - Use transition words.
> - Write a strong concluding sentence.
> - _____

2 THINKING AND WRITING: Faulty Methods of Persuasion

Consider what you have learned about persuasive writing. You know that persuasive writing attempts to convince someone to accept your opinion or take some specific action. You also know that careful organization and good choice of words are very important for success in presenting your opinion and your supporting arguments.

When you write an editorial, your arguments should also be fair and honest. Before you write, you should be able to recognize unfair or faulty methods of persuasion. Some common faulty methods of persuasion are listed below.

Slanted Facts present only one side of an issue. Strong opposing arguments are left out or hidden.

Example: This computer system will make your life a snap! It's easy to operate and fun to use.

The writer does not mention the high cost of the system or the many things that a computer will not do.

Charged Words are words that appeal to emotions. They make something sound better or worse than it really is.

Example: The candidate is known for her thrift. The candidate is known for her stinginess.

The candidate is restrained about spending. The word *thrift* makes her sound like a good candidate, while *stinginess* makes her sound like a bad choice.

Bandwagon is an attempt to persuade by arguing that "everyone else is doing it; therefore you should do it, too."

Example: Don't be the last to try *Zing!*, the fruit drink everybody's raving about.

What others are doing may not be best for you. Individuals should decide for themselves what is best.

Either-or Thinking makes you think there are only two choices, when there may be many.

Example: If you don't use *Dazzle* toothpaste, you'll develop cavities.

There may be many other ways of avoiding cavities. The argument does not present a reasonable range of options.

Thinking Like a Writer

■ Why do you think the writer of an editorial needs to recognize faulty methods of persuasion?

When you write an editorial, you should avoid faulty methods of persuasion. Remember that your purpose is to present clear facts that support your opinion. Faulty methods of persuasion are often obvious to an audience. They almost always weaken your arguments. Decide which methods of persuading others are fair and honest.

THINKING APPLICATION Faulty Methods of Persuasion

COOPERATIVE LEARNING

Each of the writers below is planning to write an editorial. Help each writer to identify the faulty method of persuasion in his or her first draft. You may wish to discuss your thinking with your classmates. In your discussions, explain how the student's editorial plan could be rewritten to avoid the faulty method of persuasion.

1. Kendra is writing an editorial in favor of weekly student-body assemblies. Which of her ideas contains a faulty method of persuasion?

   Weekly student assemblies build school pride. Without them, a sense of school spirit is impossible.

2. Daryl has written an editorial that opposes a longer school day. Which idea should he change because of a faulty method of persuasion?

   The current school day is lengthy enough. A longer day will lead to boredom and exhaustion. Only an egghead with no interests other than school would want a longer school day.

3. Sally supports a plan to teach Spanish to all students. Which idea contains a faulty method of persuasion that she should correct?

   Every other school in the district now offers Spanish. If they do it, we should do it also.

4. Alex wants to persuade his classmates that they should travel to Washington, D.C., for their end-of-year trip. Which idea contains a faulty method of persuasion?

   Going to Washington, D.C., will be wonderful! Lots of other kids have been there, so we should go too.

3 INDEPENDENT WRITING: An Editorial

Prewrite: Step 1

By now you have learned a good deal about persuasive writing. Now you are ready to choose a topic of your own for writing an editorial. Fran, a seventh-grade student, chose a topic in this way.

Choosing a Topic

First, Fran wrote a list of topics about which she had an opinion. Then, she thought about supporting arguments for each opinion. Finally, she decided on the opinion for which she had the best support.

> *sports   music*
> *broken lockers*
> *jobs – the neighborhood jobs program*

Fran decided to develop the last topic on her list. She first narrowed the topic to the summer neighborhood jobs program in town.

Fran explored her topic by making a **diagram.** Here is what her diagram looked like.

Exploring Ideas: Diagraming Strategy

jobs programs

open to seventh graders

need money   willing to work   summer camp program goes through sixth grade

for high school only

young teens too young to work   older teens need more jobs

Fran was pleased with her ideas. She decided to write an editorial on the topic for the school newspaper. Her **audience** would be the students in the school. Her **purpose** would be to persuade them to accept her opinion.

Before beginning to write, Fran imagined herself defending her opinion against someone who disagreed with it. She imagined her opponent's arguments against hers in order to see whether she had strong arguments on her side. At this point, Fran added another detail to her diagram.

jobs programs

open to seventh graders   *for high school only*

need money   *willing to work*   *summer camp program goes through sixth grade*   *young teens too young to work*   *older teens need more jobs*

already do these jobs

Thinking Like a Writer

- What did Fran add?
- Why did she add that point?
- Why did she cross out one point?

YOUR TURN

Think of a topic for an editorial. Follow these steps. Use **Pictures** or your journal to find ideas.

- Make a list of topics or issues that interest you.
- Choose the topic that concerns you most.
- Narrow your topic if it is too broad.
- Think of an opinion you hold about the topic.
- Remember your purpose and audience.

Now make a diagram to explore your topic. Write down facts and arguments that support your opinion. You may add points and remove details from your diagram at any time.

Write a First Draft: Step 2

Before she started writing her paragraph, Fran studied her diagram again and thought about the main points she wanted to make in her writing.

To help her write her first draft, Fran has made a checklist of points to remember. On her checklist she included points about purpose, audience, topic sentence, supporting facts, and concluding sentence. She used her planning checklist as she wrote her editorial.

Fran is now ready to write her first draft.

After she thought about the important parts of an editorial, Fran began to write her first draft. While writing her first draft, she did not interrupt the flow of her ideas to worry about errors. She knew she could make corrections and changes later.

Fran's First Draft

> Seventh graders should be included in the Neighborhood jobs project. The neighborhood jobs project is now being proposed by the community council. young teens are willing to work, all they need are oportunities. Seventh Graders cannot get the restaurant and department store jobs. Seventh graders are already doing the jobs the members of the community council is recommending. Without the jobs program, there will be nothing for seventh-graders to do all summer.

Planning Checklist
- Remember purpose and audience.
- State an opinion in the topic sentence.
- Include strong supporting facts and reasons.
- Use order of importance.
- Use transition words.
- Write a strong concluding sentence.

YOUR TURN

Write your first draft. As you prepare to write, ask yourself these questions.

- What is the opinion that I want to express?
- What facts and reasons will convince my audience?
- How can I best organize my reasons?
- What should I say in my concluding sentence?

TIME-OUT You might want to take some time out before you revise. That way you will be able to revise your writing with a fresh eye.

Revise: Step 3

After she finished writing her first draft, Fran read her editorial. She felt that it could be improved, so she decided to ask a classmate for comments and suggestions.

I like most of your ideas, but I didn't think your last sentence was very convincing.

Thanks, Anita. I'll have to think it over.

After she met with her friend, Fran took out her planning checklist and placed a checkmark next to the point her friend mentioned. Fran also noted another point she needed to check in her draft. Her checklist helped her remember that she needed to use order of importance and to write a strong concluding sentence for her paragraph. Fran now has a checklist to use as she revises.

Using her checklist as a guide, Fran revised her editorial. She asked herself a number of questions about her writing. Were her supporting facts strong enough? Did she use order of importance? Did any information need to be added or eliminated? She did not correct errors in spelling or punctuation. She knew she could correct her mistakes later.

Fran also thought more about the **purpose** and **audience** for her editorial. Since her purpose was to persuade, she read her editorial carefully to see if an audience of her classmates would be convinced that her opinion was reasonable.

Look at Fran's revised draft on the next page.

Fran's revisions changed her paragraph. Notice the corrections she made on her first draft.

Revising Checklist
- Remember purpose and audience.
- State an opinion in the topic sentence.
- Include strong supporting facts and reasons.
✔ Use order of importance.
- Use transition words.
✔ Write a strong concluding sentence.

Fran's Revised Draft

> Seventh graders should be included in the Neighborhood jobs project. ~~The neighborhood jobs project is~~ now being proposed by the community council. young teens are willing to work, all they need are oportunities. *Unlike older teens,* Seventh Graders cannot get the restaurant and department store jobs. Seventh graders are already doing the jobs the members of the community council is recommending. *such as baby-sitting, yard work, and helping senior citizens. The community council should consider all its young people and open the program* ~~Without the jobs program, there will be nothing for seventh graders to do all summer.~~ *to seventh graders.*

Thinking Like a Writer

- Read the last sentence. Why do you think Fran changed it?
- What information did she add? Why do you think she added this?
- What phrase did she add at the beginning of a sentence? Why do you think she added it?
- Which sentences did she combine? How does combining them improve her writing?

YOUR TURN

Read your first draft. Ask yourself these questions to see how your writing can be improved.

- How can I make the supporting facts and reasons in my editorial stronger?
- What transition words could I add in order to express my thoughts more clearly?
- How could the concluding sentence of my editorial be more effective?
- How would combining sentences with related information improve my writing?

If you wish, ask a friend to read your work and make suggestions. Then revise your editorial.

Proofread: Step 4

In revising, Fran had worked on the content and organization of her editorial. She knew, however, that her work was not complete until she proofread her paragraph. Fran made a proofreading checklist to use while she checked her work.

Fran's Proofread Draft

Seventh graders should be included in the Ɲeighbor-

hood jobs project. ~~The neighborhood jobs project is~~ now

being proposed by the community council. young teens are

willing to work; all they need are ⟨oportunities⟩ $\overset{opportunities}{}$ $\overset{=Unlike\ older\ teens,}{}$ Seventh

Ǥraders cannot get the restaurant and department store

jobs. Seventh graders are already doing the jobs the mem-

bers of the community council ~~is~~ $\overset{are}{}$ recommending. $\overset{,such\ as}{}$ ~~Without~~

~~the jobs program, there will be nothing for seventh-~~ *baby-sitting, yard work, and helping senior citizens. The community*

~~graders to do all summer.~~ *council should consider all its young people and open the program*

to seventh graders.

YOUR TURN

Proofreading Practice

Find the errors in this paragraph. Write the paragraph correctly on a separate piece of paper.

Some members of the school Comittee has recently
suggested that subjects like music, art, and drama should
be dropped from the curriculum. They recomend that the
time be spent on the basics, reading, writing, grammer,
and math. They are mistaken, music and art are basic, too.
an apreciasion of the arts are a mark of an educated
person. Also there are many carreers for which a background in the arts are necessary. finally, not all students
are good in reading and math.

Proofreading Checklist
- Did I indent each paragraph?
- Did I spell each word correctly?
- What errors in punctuation do I need to correct?
- What errors in subject-verb agreement do I need to correct?

Applying Your Proofreading Skills

Now proofread your editorial. Review your checklist as well as **The Grammar Connection** and **The Mechanics Connection** below. Use the proofreading marks to make changes.

THE GRAMMAR CONNECTION

Remember this rule about using verbs after prepositional phrases.
- Make sure that the verb in a sentence agrees with its subject and not with the object of a preposition.

The *source* of these problems **is** not known.
The *members* of the committee **work** hard.

Check your work. Does each verb agree with its subject?

THE MECHANICS CONNECTION

Remember these rules about using semicolons and colons.
- Use a **semicolon** to join parts of a compound sentence when a conjunction is not used, or when the parts are very long and subdivided by commas.

Jill will hand out the forms; Miles will collect them.
Ann, John, and Guillermo will count the votes tomorrow afternoon; and Katherine will announce the results.

- Use a **colon** to introduce a list of items that ends a sentence.

Please bring the following: tape, string, paper, and glue.

Review your writing. Have you used semicolons and colons correctly?

Publish: Step 5

To share her editorial with her classmates, Fran copied it in her best handwriting and posted it on the class bulletin board. Several of her friends discussed the editorial with her. They had not thought about the problem before and wanted to know more about Fran's opinion. Afterwards, Fran and a group of her classmates decided to present the community council with their viewpoint.

YOUR TURN

Make a final copy of your editorial in your best handwriting. If possible, use a typewriter or a computer to make your final copy. Think of ways to share your work. You might find some ideas in the **Sharing Suggestions** box below.

SHARING SUGGESTIONS

Submit your editorial to your school newspaper or magazine. If your paper has no editorial page, start an "Opinions" column.	Write your editorial as a letter to the editor of your local newspaper. Be sure to use the proper business letter form.	Read your editorial aloud to the class. Challenge your classmates to respond by telling why their opinion differs from yours.

4 SPEAKING AND LISTENING: Having a Debate

You can use what you know about persuasive writing to have a **debate**. A debate presents two sides of an issue about which people are likely to disagree.

In a debate, teams of speakers take turns speaking for or against a particular opinion, or resolution. The team speaking for the resolution is the *affirmative* side. The team speaking against the resolution is the *negative* side. In a formal debate, a judge is appointed to decide the winner of the debate. Effective debaters are those who present persuasive support for their opinions and deliver their thoughts in a clear, fair, and convincing manner.

The speakers in a debate often use note cards that they have prepared beforehand. A note card should include the main points you wish to make and important information you need to remember to support your points.

RESOLUTION: Students should not watch television during the school year.

—Students who watch less TV get better grades.

—Time spent watching television could be used for sports, hobbies, reading, and jobs.

—Watching TV takes time away from family and friends.

> **SPEAKING GUIDELINES: Debating**
>
> 1. An affirmative speaker speaks *for* the resolution, or topic.
> 2. A negative speaker speaks *against* the resolution.
> 3. A negative speaker challenges the affirmative case. An affirmative speaker challenges the negative case.
> 4. Make a note card from which to speak. List convincing arguments for your opinion.
> 5. Speak in a clear, audible voice.
> 6. Always be courteous.

- Why are notes helpful in a debate?
- Why are strong supporting facts important in a debate?

When you listen to a debate, you listen in order to decide which side has presented the more convincing argument. Strong facts and reasons to support the resolution and the speakers' ability to answer the other side's arguments can help you decide. Also listen to make sure each speaker is arguing fairly and soundly and not using faulty methods of persuasion, such as slanted facts, charged words, bandwagon, or either-or thinking.

SPEAKING APPLICATION Debating

Think of a topic that concerns you and about which you might hold a debate with a group of classmates. The topic should be one about which opinions may differ—for and against. Gather factual information to support your opinion on the topic. Make a note card and use the speaking guidelines to help you prepare. Your classmates will be using the following guidelines as they listen to the debate.

> **LISTENING GUIDELINES: Debating**
>
> 1. Listen for the opinions of each speaker.
> 2. Listen for supporting facts and arguments that are given for each opinion.
> 3. Listen for effective responses as each side answers the other's arguments.
> 4. Listen for faulty or unfair methods of persuasion.
> 5. Listen for concluding statements.

THE CURRICULUM CONNECTION

Writing About the Media

When someone mentions the *media*, what do you think of? You may think of television, which is the most popular form for delivering information to large numbers of people. Other forms you might mention are radio, newspapers, and magazines. The media are forms of communication. Each form transmits news, entertainment, and information around the world.

Many people who work in the media are journalists. They specialize in collecting news and information and reporting it to the public. Television, radio, newspapers, and magazines all use news articles and editorials that are written in some form. Besides words, photography is also important in both print and television journalism. Photojournalism is a form of news reporting that makes primary use of photographs.

ACTIVITIES

Draw a Cartoon

Creating cartoons is another way to express opinions. Such cartoons often appear on the editorial page of a newspaper. Think of an issue in your school or town about which you have an opinion. Draw a cartoon that illustrates the issue or situation. Write a caption under the cartoon. If you wish, send a copy of your cartoon to the editor of your school or town newspaper.

Be a Media Critic

Listen to two different television or radio news programs during the course of one afternoon or evening. Write a persuasive paragraph giving reasons why you think one program was better than the other. Take notes on how the two different programs cover the same news story. Did they report the same facts? If not, how were they different? Did you think that either report left out any important information? Compare the amounts of time each devotes to the story. Write your summary in a paragraph and compare your work with that of your classmates.

Respond to Literature

The following excerpt is taken from an essay called "Teenage Stereotypes" by Richard Peck. After reading the excerpt, write a response. Do you understand the author's point of view? Do you agree with his opinions?

Role Models

It has taken television an astonishingly long time to catch its first glimpse of adolescents, despite the fact that they are faithful viewers and have a large, expendable, unearned income. . . . But it is a rare teenager who sees much of himself on a television screen, and teenagers rarely look for anything else.

Television limps along in pursuit of the relevant, but the relevant issues of adults rarely compare with those of the young. Why has no one thought to ask the young themselves?

They want stories that inspire them to survive in the world as it is: in their almighty peer groups, in their middle-class standards of propriety, in their need to be accepted. They do not want the boat rocked; they want to keep from falling overboard. And so they will be drawn to situations they can rise to: success stories about young people who manage to survive in their peer groups without losing all of their individuality; stories that pit the standards of the individual against the rules of the group. There are plenty of stories that hold out a little light in the jungle of present-day youth culture, if only television can change enough to find them.

UNIT CHECKUP

LESSON 1   **Group Writing: An Editorial** (page 414)   Read the following sentences. Write whether each one is a **fact** or an **opinion**.

1. Computer education should be taught in elementary school.
2. Over half the class received a perfect score on the test.
3. Essay tests tell more about what a student has learned than multiple choice tests do.
4. The high school is the oldest school building in the city.
5. One of the most important subjects anyone can take is math.

LESSON 2   **Thinking: Faulty Methods of Persuasion** (page 418)   Read the following items. Identify the faulty method of persuasion used in each one: **slanted facts, charged words, bandwagon,** or **either-or thinking**.

1. Everybody is signing up for volunteer day. Don't be the only one in your class to miss out. Sign up now.
2. Without a pet, you will not learn the things a pet teaches: patience, responsibility, and self-discipline.
3. Taking lots of vitamins is the only way to stay healthy.
4. The candidate's ridiculous behavior and foolish comments show just how unfit for office he is.
5. The city needs a new public swimming pool because the old one contains cracks.

LESSON 3   **Writing an Editorial** (page 420)   Imagine that you are the editor of a local newspaper. You have been informed of a number of recent bicycle accidents involving injury to pedestrians in your town. Write an editorial on the subject for tomorrow's edition of the newspaper. State your opinion concerning what might be done about this problem. Include at least two reasons that support your opinion. In your editorial give reasons why you believe your solution is better than one proposed by the mayor.

LESSON 4   **Speaking and Listening: Having a Debate** (page 428)   In a paragraph summarize the guidelines for having an effective debate.

THEME PROJECT CLASS CAMPAIGN

In learning about persuasive writing and speaking, you have seen that individuals may vary in outlook. Differing outlooks create an interesting world and make the art of persuasion an important part of human interaction.

Think about the ways in which people express their outlooks: in writing, painting, sculpture, music, architecture, and politics.

Look at the picture below. This picture shows a political convention. A convention is part of a long campaign in which candidates express their opinions and outlooks in an attempt to persuade people to vote for them. Talk with your classmates about all the ways in which candidates carry their persuasive messages to voters.

With your classmates organize a campaign to elect the president of your English class. Choose one or more of the following activities, or think of an activity of your own.

- Present a speech to convince students to vote for you or the candidate of your choice.
- Make a poster urging all students to vote.
- Hold debates between the candidates.

13

Complex Sentences and Verbals

In Unit 13 you will learn about clauses, participles, gerunds, and infinitives. When you include these elements in your sentences, you can add variety to your writing.

Discuss Read the poem on the opposite page. Who is the poet remembering?

Creative Expression The unit theme is *Traditions*. Birthday celebrations often are traditional occasions. In your journal write about a traditional custom that is part of a birthday celebration in your family.

THEME: *TRADITIONS*

*Remember the smoke,
the chants, the drums,
the stick grandfather held
as he spoke in the dark
of the power of the fathers?*

—Liz Sohappy, from "Once Again"

1 SENTENCES AND CLAUSES

You know that a sentence is a group of words that expresses a complete thought. A **simple sentence** has one complete subject and one complete predicate.

> Most Americans   know about Christopher Columbus.
>
> The *Nina, Pinta,* and *Santa Maria*   were his ships.

A **compound sentence** is a sentence that contains two or more simple sentences. Each simple sentence is called an *independent clause*. An **independent clause** has a subject and a predicate and can stand alone as a complete thought.

In the compound sentences below, each independent clause is underlined.

> <u>Columbus is famous</u>, but <u>others came earlier.</u>
> <u>Vikings had visited</u>; <u>Asian people had migrated there.</u>
> <u>The Spanish were followed by the French, Dutch, and English</u>; and <u>they considered America a new world.</u>

Notice that a comma precedes the conjunction in a compound sentence. A semicolon joins the two parts if they are not joined by a conjunction. A semicolon and a conjunction join two independent clauses if a comma already appears within either part of a compound sentence.

Guided Practice

Tell whether each sentence is simple or compound.

Example: Our class studied and discussed early settlers.
          simple sentence

1. Columbus and his crew set sail from Spain on August 3, 1492.
2. A rudder broke, and they had to stop to repair it.
3. This stop at the Canary Islands was their last.
4. They had no reliable maps; the ocean was a vast unknown.
5. After two months the crew was weary and frightened.
6. Then they saw floating debris; land birds flew overhead.
7. Columbus expected to find Japan, but he was in the Bahamas.

?! THINK

- How can I decide whether a sentence is simple or compound?

REMEMBER

- A **simple sentence** has one complete subject and one complete predicate
- A **compound sentence** has two or more **independent clauses** that can stand alone as a sentence.

More Practice

A. Write each sentence. Tell if it is **simple** or **compound.** If it is compound, underline each independent clause.

Example: Columbus reached the New World.   *simple*

8. Men and women in this unknown land welcomed the sailors.
9. The natives were expert fishers, and they also swam well.
10. They swam to the ships with parrots, cloth, and other small gifts; the Spaniards gave them gifts in return.
11. Columbus communicated by means of sign language.
12. He mistook the islands for the East Indies, and so he called the people "Indians."

B. Write each sentence and identify whether it is **simple** or **compound.** If it is compound, underline the independent clauses. Add a comma or semicolon.

Example: These facts are important but many people do
not know them.   *These facts are important, but
many people do not know them.*   *compound*

13. These people were descended from the first Americans.
14. Their ancestors came from Siberia but they did not swim.
15. Thousands of years ago no water divided Asia from Alaska.
16. Vast herds moved freely and the hunters followed them.
17. Food and land were plentiful the people were mobile.
18. Under these conditions populations increased rapidly.
19. Eleven thousand years ago people had already reached the tip of South America experts have evidence of cave dwellers.
20. Evidence can consist of tools, bones, and charcoal and these are dated by special techniques.

Extra Practice, page 460

WRITING APPLICATION A Letter

Write a letter to a classmate in which you describe what you or someone you know did that was a "first." Identify your simple and compound sentences.

2 COMPLEX SENTENCES

Remember that an independent clause has a subject and a predicate and that it can stand alone as a sentence.

A **subordinate clause** also has a subject and a predicate, but it cannot stand alone as a sentence.

> **Before Columbus sailed,** Norsemen had visited North America.
>
> Lisa told me this fact **after she had read an article.**

Subordinate clauses are introduced by subordinating conjunctions.

Subordinating Conjunctions			
after	before	though	whenever
although	if	unless	where
as	since	until	whereas
because	than	when	wherever

A sentence with an independent clause and one or more subordinate clauses is called a **complex sentence.**

When a subordinate clause comes at the beginning of a sentence, use a comma after the subordinate clause. When the subordinate clause comes at the end of the sentence, you usually do not use a comma before the subordinate clause.

Guided Practice

Name the subordinate clause in each sentence.

Example: Sal knew about the Vikings before I did.
> *before I did*

1. If the Viking sagas are true, they made three landings.
2. Historians cannot be certain because there is little physical evidence.
3. Unless more sites are found, experts have only partial proof.
4. Since there is one site in Newfoundland, it is probably true.

?! THINK

- How can I tell the difference between an independent clause and a subordinate clause?

REMEMBER

- A **subordinate clause** is a group of words that has a subject and a predicate, but it cannot stand alone as a complete sentence.

- A **complex sentence** contains an independent clause and one or more subordinate clauses.

More Practice

A. Write the subordinate clause in each sentence.

Example: The Vikings arrived before Columbus did.
before Columbus did

5. Since wild grapes were growing there, the explorers named the place Vinland.
6. When they returned to Greenland, they brought vines.
7. It must have been New England if grapes were growing.
8. Wherever they were, the Norsemen found the climate mild.
9. They built shelters after they had scouted the area.
10. Whenever the weather permitted, they explored further.
11. Although their first meeting with Indians was friendly, the two groups became enemies.
12. The Indians traded furs since they were skilled trappers.

B. Write each sentence and underline the subordinate clause. Draw two lines under the subordinating conjunction.

Example: <u>Although that text is old</u>, it is excellent.

13. Although Vinland is only a legend, it is still fascinating.
14. The geographical details seem true though they are vague.
15. As it sounds like a Promised Land, it could be a myth.
16. The Viking sagas were repeated orally for two hundred years before they were written down.
17. Whenever a people tell their history, some facts are changed.
18. Although exaggeration exists, the core often can be accepted.
19. After experts have weighed the evidence, history books sometimes change.

Extra Practice, page 461

WRITING APPLICATION An Advertisement

Have you ever dreamed of a new world? Write an advertisement describing your discovery. Post your ad. Have the class identify your complex sentences.

3 ADJECTIVE CLAUSES

A subordinate clause is a sentence part that contains a subject and a predicate. Some subordinate clauses act like adjectives. An **adjective clause** modifies or describes a noun or pronoun in the independent clause.

> Native American tradition, **which centers around a love for the earth,** teaches many important lessons.

> Myths **that told about the world's origins** always taught respect for nature.

An adjective clause usually begins with a **relative pronoun,** like *who, whom, whose, which,* or *that.*

> Native Americans, **who** respect nature, seek harmony with their environment.

When an adjective clause is not essential to the meaning of a sentence, it should be set off with commas. Do not use commas to set off adjective clauses that are essential to the meaning of a sentence.

Guided Practice

Name the adjective clause in each sentence.

Example: I am reading a book that describes Indian life.
that describes Indian life

1. Groups who lived in different areas held similar views.
2. The earth, which was generous to them, deserved care and protection.
3. An idea that was honored everywhere concerned the avoidance of waste.
4. The land, which seems so vast, should not be taken for granted.
5. I admire a people whose respect for nature is so great.
6. We studied Indian agriculture, which began long ago.
7. Families who planted near their dwellings became farmers.

?! THINK

- How can I tell whether a group of words in a sentence is an adjective clause?

REMEMBER

- An **adjective clause** is a subordinate clause that modifies, or describes, a noun or pronoun in the independent clause of a complex sentence.

More Practice

A. Write the adjective clause in each sentence.

Example: The film that we saw was fine. *that we saw*

8. Others, who hunted, learned the ways of the animals.
9. The buffalo herds that roamed the plains were enormous.
10. Native American hunters, who considered themselves the buffalo's guardians, killed only what they needed.
11. The buffalo, whom the hunters cherished, grew in number.
12. The respect that Native Americans felt for nature was great.
13. Traditional crafts, which use materials from nature, are often decorated with designs from nature.

B. Write each sentence. Draw one line under each adjective clause and two lines under the word or words it modifies.

Example: Allan has a <u>sweater</u> <u>that was handmade.</u>

14. Artists whose skill produced beautiful objects were honored.
15. Pottery that is made from clay is painted.
16. Navajo blankets, which contained colorful patterns, were woven from sheep's wool.
17. Pottery and weaving, which produced items of great beauty, also produced things that were useful.
18. The hunters of the plains, whose garments were made of animal skins, often decorated their clothes.
19. Even traditional arrowheads, which were primarily useful, could be very handsome.
20. Traditional crafts that reflected nature's beauty were another form of showing reverence for the earth.

Extra Practice, Practice Plus, pages 462–463

WRITING APPLICATION An Interview

Who might be able to tell you about a craft? Interview that person and write a summary. Ask a classmate to help you to identify the adjective clauses.

4 ADVERB CLAUSES

When a subordinate clause is joined with an independent clause to form a complex sentence, the subordinate clause can act like an adverb. An **adverb clause** modifies, or describes, the verb in the independent clause.

> **Although tap dancing is a folk art,** it demands great skill. Tap dancing began **when European dance was combined with African rhythm.**

An adverb clause usually begins with a **subordinating conjunction,** such as *because, when, although,* or *if*. Like adverbs, adverb clauses tell *how, when, where, why,* or *under what conditions* the action takes place. Place a comma after a clause that comes at the beginning of a sentence.

> **When dancers have mastered this art,** they make it look easy.

Guided Practice

Name the adverb clause in each sentence.

Example: The dancers perform well when they have practiced. *when they have practiced*

1. Though tap dancing is American, its roots are in Irish step dancing.
2. If you listen carefully, you will hear distinct rhythms.
3. These rhythms can sound very complex because they are largely African.
4. Tap dancers create a form of music when they dance.
5. Because they make music, tap dancers are also musicians.
6. The rhythms are syncopated because they grew out of ragtime.

THINK

- How can I identify an adverb clause in a complex sentence?

■ An **adverb clause** modifies the verb in the independent clause of a complex sentence.

■ An adverb clause usually begins with a **subordinating conjunction,** such as *because, when, although,* or *if.*

More Practice

A. Write the adverb clause in each sentence.

Example: Tom has tap danced since he was a child.
since he was a child

7. Rhythm is syncopated when the weak beat is given a stress.

8. Although many composers wrote music in ragtime, Scott Joplin was one of the greatest.

9. Vaudeville became famous because ragtime grew popular.

10. Since there was no television, people enjoyed vaudeville.

11. As vaudeville was an important form of entertainment, it became a showcase for tap dancers.

12. Dancers liked tap because there were so many styles.

B. Write each sentence. Draw one line under the adverb clause. Then draw two lines under the verb it modifies.

Example: I <u>tightened</u> my shoe laces <u>before I performed</u>.

13. When I see an Irish jig, tap dancing comes to mind.

14. Although traditional steps were passed down, each generation added variations.

15. Tap dancing became a great art because Bill Robinson perfected it.

16. Since he made his "bones jangle," people called him "Bojangles."

17. He created a sensation when he danced on his toes.

18. Robinson had remarkable skills, though John W. Bubbles was equally talented.

19. Although tap dancing mixes European and African traditions, it is strictly American.

Extra Practice, page 464

WRITING APPLICATION An Explanatory Paragraph

Write a paragraph explaining a tradition that has come to America from another country. Identify the adverb clauses in your work.

5 PARTICIPLES AND PARTICIPIAL PHRASES

The present participle of a verb is formed by adding *ing* to the verb. The past participle is usually formed by adding *ed* to the verb. A participle can be the main verb in a verb phrase.

> The woman was **weaving.**
> The loom had been **imported.**

A participle can also function as an adjective to describe a noun or pronoun.

> The **imported** loom had foot pedals.

Sometimes other words are added to a participle to complete its meaning, forming a **participial phrase.**

> **Weaving on her loom,** the woman made fine cloth.

A participial phrase that comes at the beginning of a sentence is set off by a comma.

A participial phrase can appear before or after the word it describes. Always place the phrase as close as possible to the word it modifies, or the meaning of the sentence may become unclear.

> CORRECT: Weaving on a loom, the woman smiled at me.
> MISPLACED: The woman smiled at me, weaving on a loom.

Guided Practice

Name the participle and tell whether it is the main verb in a verb phrase or is used as an adjective.

Example: The class is studying Spanish customs.
studying   main verb

1. The living legacy of Spain is present in Puerto Rico.
2. The island was discovered by Columbus in 1493.
3. Coming from Mexico, the Spanish explored the West.
4. Spanish traditions are still passed on today.

?! THINK

- How do I decide where to place a participial phrase in a sentence?

REMEMBER

- A **participle** is a verb form that can be used as an adjective to modify nouns or pronouns.
- A **participial phrase** is a group of words that includes a participle used as an adjective and other words that complete its meaning.

More Practice

A. Write the participle in each sentence. Tell whether it is the **main verb** in a verb phrase or is used as an **adjective.**

Example: The <u>interested</u> student asked a question.   *adjective*

5. The Feast of the Three Kings is celebrated on January 6.
6. For Puerto Rican children, this is a most exciting day.
7. Guided by a star, the kings brought gifts on this day.
8. Believing children put grass and water under their beds for the king's horses.
9. Awakened in the morning, they find gifts.
10. The black king riding the white horse is a favorite.
11. He is perhaps the most giving king.
12. Statues of the kings are displayed in homes and in street processions.

B. Write each sentence and underline the participial phrase. Then draw two lines under the word the phrase modifies.

Example: The <u>girl</u> <u>speaking Spanish</u> is my friend.

13. Holy images called *santos* are part of Spanish culture.
14. Displayed in the home, they are part of family life.
15. Painted on flat surfaces, religious scenes are popular.
16. Statuettes carved in wood portray saints.
17. Hoping for help and favors, people pray to the saints.
18. The images used in festivals are larger.
19. Dressed in exotic clothing, the statuettes are unusual.
20. Defying time, traditions can last for generations.

Extra Practice, page 465

WRITING APPLICATION A Descriptive Paragraph

Is there a holiday whose traditions you particularly enjoy? What do you like about the way you celebrate this day? Write a description of these special traditions.

6 GERUNDS

Just as a participle is a verb form that can be used as an adjective, a **gerund** is a verb form used as a noun. Gerunds are formed in the same way as present participles—by adding ing to the base form of the verb. Gerunds can function as subjects or direct objects in sentences.

> SUBJECT: **Running** is an ancient sport.
> DIRECT OBJECT: Runners love **competing.**

Verb forms ending in *ing* can be used as main verbs in verb phrases, as present participles, and as gerunds. To tell how the verb form is functioning, examine the sentence. If the *ing* form describes a noun or a pronoun, it is a participle being used as an adjective. If the verb is being used as a noun, it is a gerund.

> MAIN VERB: Runners are **training** daily.
>
> PARTICIPLE USED
> AS ADJECTIVE: The **training** program is excellent.
>
> GERUND: **Training** will be difficult.

Sometimes other words are added to a gerund to complete its meaning, forming a **gerund phrase.**

> **Completing a marathon race** is a victory in itself.
> She chose **long-distance running** as her sport.

Guided Practice

Identify the underlined word as a main verb, a participle used as an adjective, or a gerund.

Example: Skiing is my favorite sport.   *gerund*

1. The Olympic Games have been growing in importance and popularity.
2. They are part of a continuing tradition of competition.
3. Participating is an honor for any athlete.
4. The ultimate triumph is winning a gold medal.

 THINK

- How can I tell if a verb form is being used as a gerund in a sentence?

REMEMBER

- A **gerund** is a verb form that ends in *ing* and is used as a noun.
- A **gerund phrase** is a group of words that includes a gerund and other words that complete its meaning.

More Practice

A. Write whether the underlined word is a **main verb,** a **participle** used as an adjective, or a **gerund.**

Example: <u>Watching</u> the Olympics is fun. *gerund*

5. The <u>dazzling</u> spectacle of the Olympics thrills many.
6. The games are <u>following</u> an ancient Greek tradition.
7. Athletes have been <u>waiting</u> for four years to compete.
8. Victory requires constant <u>practicing</u> of skills.
9. <u>Breaking</u> past records seems required of a winner.
10. Greater and greater <u>daring</u> is expected all the time.
11. <u>Aspiring</u> athletes spend time and money to prepare themselves.
12. Sometimes politics influences the <u>judging</u> of athletic performances.

B. Identify each gerund phrase and write whether it is a **subject** or **direct object.** If the sentence contains no gerund phrase, write **none.**

Example: I like participating in sports.
                participating in sports   direct object

13. Watching sports is a family activity for many.
14. The national championships are unifying events.
15. Millions of people are sharing the excitement.
16. Rooting for a team inspires strong emotions.
17. Maturity means accepting defeat gracefully.
18. Loyalty requires supporting your team.
19. Losing a championship can be bitter.
20. Everyone likes congratulating the winning team.

Extra Practice, page 466

WRITING APPLICATION Instructions

COOPERATIVE
LEARNING

Imagine that you could change the rules for playing your favorite sport or game. With a small group of classmates, write a set of instructions that explains the new rules. Identify the gerunds in your work.

7 INFINITIVES

You know that gerunds are verb forms used as nouns. An **infinitive** is another verb form that can be used as a noun. Infinitives are formed by using the word *to* with the base form of the verb.

Sometimes an infinitive is used as the subject.

> SUBJECT: **To skate** is fun.

In other sentences an infinitive may be used as the direct object of the verb.

> DIRECT OBJECT: Many people want **to learn.**

Do not confuse an infinitive with a prepositional phrase that begins with *to*. Remember that a preposition is a word that relates a noun or pronoun to another word in a sentence. A prepositional phrase begins with a preposition and ends with a noun or pronoun that is the object of the preposition.

> INFINITIVE: We plan **to practice.**
> PREPOSITIONAL PHRASE: I took my skates **to the rink.**

Sometimes other words are added to an infinitive to complete its meaning, forming an **infinitive phrase.**

> I want **to take lessons every day.**
> **To perform well** is my dream.

Guided Practice

Tell whether the underlined words are an infinitive, an infinitive phrase, or a prepositional phrase.

Example: Thelma likes <u>to watch the skaters</u>.
　　　　　　infinitive phrase

1. Many young people love <u>to move fast</u>.
2. <u>To skate</u> is one way to gain speed.
3. A faster way is <u>to ride on a skateboard</u>.
4. <u>To many youngsters</u> no sport equals skateboarding.

?! THINK

- How can I tell if a group of words is an infinitive phrase or a prepositional phrase?

REMEMBER

- An **infinitive** is formed with the word *to* and the base form of the verb.
- An **infinitive phrase** includes an infinitive and other words that complete its meaning.

More Practice

A. Write whether the underlined words are an **infinitive,** an **infinitive phrase,** or a **prepositional phrase.**

Example: I would like to try.   *infinitive*

5. To buy a skateboard was my latest project.
6. But I would have to save.
7. My father's old red scooter was given to me.
8. He also taught me how to make a soapbox scooter.
9. You attach roller skate wheels to a board.
10. To use a box as the steering post is the next step.
11. Scooters seemed to fly.
12. To young people of today, scooters seem quite old-fashioned.

B. Write and label each **infinitive phrase** or **prepositional phrase.** Then write whether the infinitive phrase is used as the **subject** or **direct object** of the sentence.

Example: To ride expertly requires much practice.   *To ride expertly,   infinitive phrase   subject*

13. You must look to California for the first skateboard.
14. One calm day a surfer wanted to do something for fun.
15. He nailed old roller skates to a water ski.
16. He rode downhill to the ocean using surfing movements.
17. The sidewalk surfer learned to skateboard the hard way.
18. To make the skateboard safe required the use of durable wheels.
19. To master the skill of skateboarding is a challenge.
20. You need to face the possibility of accidents.

Extra Practice, page 467

WRITING APPLICATION A Summary

Find out about the origins of a hobby, a sport, or a custom that interests you. Summarize the information in a brief paragraph. Then, exchange papers with a classmate and find infinitives in each other's work.

8 MECHANICS: Using Commas with Clauses

Use the following comma rules when you write sentences that contain clauses.

1. Use a comma before the conjunction *and, or,* or *but* in a compound sentence.

   Citizens can complain, or they can work for change.

2. Use commas to set off an adjective clause that gives information that is not essential to the meaning of the sentence. Do not use commas to set off an adjective clause that provides essential information.

   Immigration, which is important to any country, is the topic for my research report.
   The topic that we discussed yesterday was immigration.

3. Use a comma after an adverb clause that begins a sentence. Do not use a comma when the adverb clause comes at the end of a sentence.

   Although immigrants often had to struggle, those of the last century had hope for their children.

   It is unclear whether today's immigrants are as hopeful.

Guided Practice

Tell where a comma or commas are needed.

Example: When she visited New York Clara saw the Statue of Liberty.   *comma after York*

1. Immigrants sought freedom and they traveled far for it.
2. The Statue of Liberty which loomed on the horizon greeted immigrants.
3. Although it was only a statue the monument symbolized hope.
4. Since it was a gift from France the statue also stands for friendship.
5. The statue which impressed Clara was constructed in Paris.

?! THINK

- How do I decide whether to use commas when I write sentences with clauses?

REMEMBER

- Use a comma before the conjunction *and*, *or*, or *but* in a compound sentence.
- Use commas to set off an adjective clause that gives unessential information.
- Use a comma after an adverb clause that begins a sentence.

More Practice

A. Write each sentence, adding a comma or commas.

Example: The guide spoke French which Clara knows.
The guide spoke French, which Clara knows.

6. The sculptor always needed more money and somehow he always managed to get it.
7. Because he was encouraged the sculptor persevered.
8. Because it took so long some people ridiculed the project.
9. The size of the statue which was phenomenal amazed people.
10. At its unveiling in 1886 a million people lined the streets and all were wild with enthusiasm.

B. Write each sentence, adding commas where needed. Then write whether the sentence is **compound** or contains an **adjective clause** or **adverb clause.**

Example: Because it was a gift the statue has special meaning.   *Because it was a gift, the statue has special meaning.*   *adverb clause*

11. The French gave but Americans donated also.
12. The statue which fell into disrepair needed reconstruction.
13. Since its anniversary was in 1986 the time was right.
14. Because funds were raised repairs could begin.
15. The deadline was July 4 and the statue was repaired in time.

Extra Practice, page 468

WRITING APPLICATION A Letter

Imagine that you are an immigrant. Write a letter to a relative you left behind. Ask a classmate to check your use of commas.

9 VOCABULARY BUILDING: Suffixes

A **suffix** is a word part that is added to the end of a base word. The addition of a suffix often changes a word's meaning or part of speech.

Noun-forming Suffixes		
Suffix	**Meaning**	**Example**
an	one that is of	American
er, or	one who or that which	speak**er**, operat**or**
ian	one skilled in	beautic**ian**
ion	act, state, or result of	protect**ion**
ism	act, practice, or process of	critic**ism**
ist	one who works at, practices, or adheres to	scient**ist**
ment	act, condition, or result of	employ**ment**
ness	quality, state, or condition	sad**ness**
tion	act, state, or result of	descrip**tion**

Adjective-forming Suffixes		
Suffix	**Meaning**	**Example**
able, ible	able to, capable of being	read**able**, vis**ible**
an	of or belonging to	Shakespear**ean**
ful	full of, marked by	sorrow**ful**
ish	like, suggesting	imp**ish**
less	lacking, without	love**less**
ly	like in nature	queen**ly**
ward	moving or tending toward	east**ward**
y	showing, suggesting	dirt**y**

Guided Practice

Name the suffix in each word.

Example: government   *ment*

1. joyful   **2.** theorist   **3.** horrible   **4.** election   **5.** actor

 THINK

■ How can the addition of a suffix change a word?

REMEMBER

- A **suffix** is a word part added to the end of a base word. A suffix changes the meaning of the base word to which it is added. It also changes the part of speech of the base word.

More Practice

A. Write each word and underline the suffix. Then give the meaning of the word. Use a dictionary, if necessary.

Example: merci<u>less</u> *without mercy*

6. laborer
7. tenderness
8. lovable
9. childish
10. westward

11. brotherly
12. judgment
13. reflection
14. Mexican
15. mathematician

B. Complete each sentence. Add an appropriate suffix to the word in parentheses and use it to fill in the blank. Use a dictionary to help you.

Example: That song is _____. (joy) *joyful*

16. My aunt is a ____ of folk songs. (collect)
17. She is considered a ____ in this field. (special)
18. The discovery of a song fills her with ____. (excite)
19. Folk songs express sorrow and ____. (happy)
20. Work songs have an ____ quality. (earth)
21. The lullabies give a feeling of ____. (content)
22. Their ____ melodies soothe the spirit. (peace)
23. A folk ____ is the voice of a culture. (sing)
24. Folk music is an ____ of group life. (express)
25. Studying it is a ____ way to learn about people. (pain)
26. ____ folk songs tell a unique story. (Mexico)
27. Cultures are ____ and influence one another. (flex)
28. The music of each culture is a unique ____. (state)

Extra Practice, page 469

WRITING APPLICATION Song Lyrics

Do you think of yourself as part of a group? Do you and your family or friends share a common heritage or common interests? Write the words for a song that expresses your feelings for this group. Work with a partner to identify the suffixes you have used.

GRAMMAR
—AND
WRITING
CONNECTION

Parallel Structure

John F. Kennedy once said, "Ask not what your country can do for you but what you can do for your country." People often quote this sentiment, partly because it expresses an important idea, but also because the parallel structure of the sentence helps make the idea memorable. **Parallel structure** means that similar parts of the sentence are expressed in the same way.

Sometimes you may write a sentence that contains two or more similar items. When the items are alike in importance, they should be stated in similar ways, or in parallel structure. Parallel structure applies to nouns, verbs, adjectives, and adverbs.

> NOT PARALLEL: John F. Kennedy spoke gracefully and with wit.
>
> PARALLEL: John F. Kennedy spoke gracefully and wittily.

Working Together

COOPERATIVE
LEARNING

Rewrite each sentence to create parallel structure.

Example: The role of a historian is uncovering the truth, recording it, and to be an interpreter of its meaning. *The role of a historian is uncovering the truth, recording it, and interpreting its meaning.*

1. Archaeologists go to the sites of ancient civilizations and are investigators of their remains.
2. Historians often make use of written records, eyewitness accounts, and conduct interviews.
3. If you are interested in the past, you may want to be a historian, an anthropologist, or study archaeology.

Revising Sentences

Cecily wrote the following sentences as she gathered information for a research report. Help her to revise her sentences by using parallel structure.

4. Woodrow Wilson was a teacher, statesman, and practiced law.
5. Wilson wrote, spoke, and was a fighter for the creation of a League of Nations.
6. Wilson wisely, carefully, and with quickness altered the undergraduate program of study at Princeton University.
7. Diplomats greatly respected Wilson for high ideals and because he was honest.
8. In his first administration Wilson designed, wrote, and was a lobbyist for new laws in the banking system.
9. Wilson wrote fourteen eloquently and concise statements concerning world peace.
10. Wilson wrote about and was a speaker for the elimination of any future arms races among nations.

WRITER AT WORK

Using the theme of this unit, traditions, write an explanatory essay about the importance of the past. You may wish to choose a particular tradition and explain its origin and importance, or you may want to address the topic in a different way. When you revise your sentences, make sure you have maintained parallel structure.

UNIT CHECKUP

LESSON 1

Sentences and Clauses (page 436) Write each sentence and label it **simple** or **compound.** If it is compound, add a comma or semicolon where needed.

1. America has always been a land of people from other places.
2. The first settlers migrated from Siberia they were ancestors of the American Indians.
3. The date of the start of this migration is not known exactly but it was more than 10,000 years ago.
4. European settlement came thousands of years later.
5. Many Africans were brought here against their will.

LESSON 2

Complex Sentences (page 438) Underline the subordinate clause. Draw two lines under the subordinating conjunction.

6. America is a special place because it includes many cultures.
7. When people come to a new land, they bring their traditions.
8. They think about their roots after they feel secure.
9. Although history often tells of injustice and hardship, our past is part of our identity.
10. Until we know our roots, we know only part of ourselves.

LESSONS 3-4

Adjective and Adverb Clauses (pages 440–442) Write each sentence. Underline and label each **adjective clause** or **adverb clause.** Add commas where needed.

11. Most Jewish people who live in the United States have their roots in Eastern Europe.
12. The language that was spoken was called Yiddish.
13. Because the law demanded it, Jews lived separate from others.
14. The jobs that Jews could hold were also limited.
15. Though their lives were so restricted, the people developed a rich community and religious life.

LESSON 5

Participles (page 444) Write each participle. Then write whether it is a **main verb** or is used as an **adjective.**

16. In the Jewish religion the honored day is Saturday.
17. The Sabbath is celebrated with joy and devotion.
18. Specially prepared food is part of the tradition.
19. Candles are lighted by the woman of the house.
20. Loving children pray and sing with their elders.

LESSONS 6-7 **Gerunds and Infinitives** (pages 446–448) Identify each **gerund, gerund phrase, infinitive,** or **infinitive phrase.**

21. Tracing one's family tree can be very interesting.
22. Everyone likes discovering a famous ancestor.
23. Take the time to listen before it is too late.
24. To hear your family history firsthand is a privilege.
25. Traveling is often necessary to get missing information.
26. Do you enjoy finding out about the past?
27. To discover facts about your ancestors can be exciting.
28. To record it for future generations is important.

LESSON 8 **Mechanics: Using Commas with Clauses** (page 450) Write each sentence and add a comma or commas where needed. If the sentence needs no comma, write **correct.**

29. Many became immigrants and America welcomed them.
30. Many came to America because they faced death at home.
31. In the 1850s Ireland which is my parents' birthplace experienced hard times.
32. The immigrants were peasants and they mostly settled in American cities.
33. Churches were built and local neighborhoods grew.
34. When they could afford it many moved out of the city.

LESSON 9 **Vocabulary Building: Suffixes** (page 452) Complete each sentence. Add a suffix to the word in parentheses.

35. Many ____ came to America. (Europe)
36. An ethnic parade is a ____ of a heritage. (celebrate)
37. The ____ take pride in their unique past. (march)
38. They also point to their recent ____. (achieve)
39. They are proud to be ____ Americans. (success)
40. Flags reflect the people's ____. (patriot)
41. With great hope new citizens look ____ the future. (to)

Writing Application: Clauses and Verbals (pages 436–451) The following paragraph contains 5 errors in the use of clauses. Rewrite the paragraph correctly.

42.–46. Wherever canals link oceans ships sail quickly from sea to sea. Some ships are so large they must be pulled by a tugboat, weighing many tons. A canal, that has a lock system helps large ships sail quickly. The ship enters the channel and the canal lock behind the ship closes. Then the ship waits in the channel which fills with water.

Traveling Sentences

With a partner, list nouns having to do with transportation, for example, ships, rockets, cars, horses, submarines, and taxies. Then, list verbs describing travel, such as swim, fly, crawl, and gallop. Last, describe a travel adventure combining different modes of travel. Use as many compound sentences as possible in your adventure.

The Right Combination

The following participles have been locked up until they can be used as adjectives. That time has come! Unlock the participles by using five of them as adjectives in complete sentences.

winning	telling	screaming	forgiving
changing	giving	loving	following
relaxed	feeling	believing	swinging
learning	beginning	overturned	losing

Example: My aunt had such a *trying* day.

THE GERUND GAME

Choose a partner and take turns telling him or her about your favorite hobby—or about what you like to do best. Use gerunds whenever you can. Score a point for every gerund that is identified.

CREATIVE EXPRESSION

Blowin' in the Wind

How many roads must a man walk down
  before you call him a man?
Yes, 'n' how many seas must a white dove sail
  before she sleeps in the sand?
Yes, 'n' how many times must the cannon balls fly
  before they're forever banned?
The answer, my friend, is blowin' in the wind,
The answer is blowin' in the wind.

How many times must a man look up
  before he can see the sky?
Yes, 'n' how many ears must one man have
  before he can hear people cry?
Yes 'n' how many deaths will it take till he knows
  that too many people have died?
The answer, my friend, is blowin' in the wind,
The answer is blowin' in the wind.

How many years can a mountain exist
  before it's washed to the sea?
Yes 'n' how many times can a man turn his head
  pretending he just doesn't see?
The answer, my friend, is blowin' in the wind,
The answer is blowin' in the wind.
The answer is blowin' in the wind.

—Bob Dylan

TRY IT OUT

Song lyrics and poetry have much in common. Both often contain elements such as rhythm, rhyme, and images. Many songs also have a refrain, which is a stanza that is repeated throughout the song. Write down the lyrics of a song you like, or make up your own.

EXTRA PRACTICE

Three levels of practice

Sentences and Clauses (page 436)

LEVEL

A. Write whether each sentence is **simple** or **compound.**

1. Baseball has been a national pastime for more than one hundred years; the first game was in June 1846.
2. It was played in Hoboken, New Jersey, but that game looked quite different from today's game.
3. For example, pitchers had to throw underhand, and it took nine balls to get a base on balls.
4. The New York Nine and the New York Knickerbockers were the opposing teams.
5. That day the New York Nine won by a score of 23 to 1.
6. The history of baseball had begun; America had found its favorite sport.

LEVEL

B. Write whether each sentence is **simple** or **compound.** If it is compound, underline the independent clauses.

7. The basic idea of baseball was borrowed from cricket.
8. The rules were developed by Alexander Cartwright, but Abner Doubleday is often given the credit.
9. Cartwright was a surveyor and an amateur athlete.
10. The first professional team was the Cincinnati Red Stockings; they did not lose a game in their first year.
11. The National League was formed in 1876, and the same league continues today.
12. By 1900 baseball was played more or less like today's game.

LEVEL

C. Write each sentence and label it as a **simple** or **compound sentence.** If it is compound, underline the independent clauses and add a comma or semicolon where needed.

13. In the 1870s batters could request a high or low pitch.
14. The rules were changed and pitchers started trying new throws.
15. In the 1880s gloves were not used thin strips of leather were placed over the palm.
16. Later gloves were worn but they were smaller than today's.
17. Only two or three baseballs would be used in one game.
18. Pitches may still be high or low but we also have knuckle-balls, sliders, and fastballs.

EXTRA PRACTICE

Three levels of practice

Complex Sentences (page 438)

LEVEL

A. Write whether each sentence is **simple** or **complex.**

1. Baseball has become an American tradition because it has been loved by so many for so long.
2. The arrival of spring is eagerly awaited.
3. If you are a fan, you are following games in March.
4. The past is as important as the present in baseball.
5. As every player matures, he is compared with the greats.

LEVEL

B. Write each sentence. Underline the subordinate clause and draw two lines under the subordinating conjunction.

6. Unless a player breaks an earlier record, he cannot join the circle of all-time heroes.
7. Although today's athletes are generally faster and stronger, no one has forgotten Babe Ruth or Ty Cobb.
8. These and other names are constantly heard whenever fans talk about baseball.
9. Their reputations live on as their feats are retold to new fans.
10. When Hank Aaron broke Ruth's home run record, it had taken him four thousand more times at bat.
11. Today the game of baseball has its heroes, though the heroes of the past seem like giants.

LEVEL

C. Write each sentence and underline the subordinate clause. Then draw two lines under the subordinating conjunction, and add a comma where needed.

12. Baseball is still popular although it has much competition from other professional sports.
13. If you find it too slow you may prefer basketball.
14. When you want a contact sport football offers more.
15. The strategic aspect of football is obvious whereas baseball strategy is more subtle.
16. Since they have different seasons you can avoid the choice between baseball and football.
17. Baseball is a natural sport for summer since the heavy shoulder pads are not needed.

EXTRA PRACTICE

Three levels of practice

Adjective Clauses (page 440)

LEVEL
A. Write the adjective clause in each sentence.

1. Columbus, who was seeking India, found America.
2. Haiti, which he thought was India, was one of his first stops.
3. All of the islands that he explored are now called the West Indies.
4. The Native Americans, whose homeland he entered, have often been called Indians.
5. Columbus found a people who had discovered the continent long before.
6. The people who lived on this continent were called Arawaks.

LEVEL
B. Write each sentence. Draw one line under the adjective clause and two lines under the relative pronoun.

7. Europeans desired India's riches, which included gold.
8. The idea that Columbus discovered America is true in one way.
9. The people of Europe, who thought the world was flat, knew nothing about America.
10. Columbus, whom the King and Queen of Spain supported, discovered a land completely new to them.
11. For Europeans these islands, which clearly had nothing to do with India, were a new world.

LEVEL
C. Write each sentence. Draw one line under the adjective clause and two lines under the noun it modifies. Add commas where they are needed.

12. Leif Eriksson who sailed from Greenland also discovered America.
13. The Vikings whose ship landed in Newfoundland discovered America only for themselves.
14. The voyage that reached America took place hundreds of years before Columbus's birth.
15. This fact which many people do not know was a significant event in history.
16. The honor for discovering America which everyone awards to Columbus really belongs to Native Americans.

PRACTICE + PLUS

Three levels of additional practice for a difficult skill

Adjective Clauses (page 440)

LEVEL

A. Write the adjective clause in each sentence.

1. The snow that fell last night has melted.
2. I saw a weather map that showed a snowstorm in the west.
3. The storm, which moved slowly, was the worst of the year.
4. The first snowflakes, which melt quickly, are falling now.
5. Dad is getting out the sled that Mom gave us last year.
6. Many children play in the snow, which delights everyone.
7. Alice and Ted made a snowman whose nose was a carrot.
8. Its scarf was donated by their father, who later caught a cold.

LEVEL

B. Write each sentence. Draw one line under the adjective clause and two lines under the relative pronoun.

9. Many people listen to the weather forecast, which can help them in many ways.
10. Greek thinkers wrote essays that told about the weather.
11. Weather stations, which were first built in the nineteenth century, gave valuable information to scientists.
12. Today's weather forecasters, who have satellite maps, can make accurate predictions.
13. The cold front that is approaching our area will lower the temperature.
14. Light rain, which will begin this afternoon, will end tonight.

LEVEL

C. Write each sentence. Draw one line under the adjective clause and two lines under the noun it modifies. Add commas where they are needed.

15. People who now ride bicycles use them for pleasure or sport.
16. Bicycle races which are very popular today began in the last century.
17. There are many people whose main interest is bicycling.
18. Some amateurs who practice a great deal become experts.
19. Many messenger services that depend on speed use cyclists.
20. Many people who live in large cities commute by bicycle to their homes.

EXTRA PRACTICE

Three levels of practice

Adverb Clauses (page 442)

LEVEL

A. Write the adverb clause in each sentence.

1. Gina learned about Phaethon while she was studying myths.
2. Although it is old, Phaethon's story has meaning today.
3. His friends made fun of him because Phaethon claimed the Sun as his father.
4. "If what you say is true, prove it."
5. His friends would believe him if he asked the Sun for proof.
6. After he had told them of his plan, Phaethon traveled eastward toward the Palace of the Sun.

LEVEL

B. Write each sentence. Draw one line under the adverb clause and two lines under the subordinating conjunction.

7. What happened after Phaethon started his journey?
8. Phaethon knew the way because every morning the Sun rode from the Palace in a blazing chariot.
9. Although the path was steep, Phaethon climbed to the Palace.
10. When the Sun welcomed him, Phaethon boldly asked for visible proof of his birthright.
11. "Because you are my child, I will grant you any wish."
12. "If you are really my father, lend me your blazing chariot."

LEVEL

C. Write each sentence. Draw one line under the adverb clause and two lines under the verb it modifies. Add commas where they are needed.

13. Although he had sworn to keep his promise the Sun argued strongly against Phaethon's request.
14. When Phaethon would not relent the Sun gave him lessons on handling the fiery horses.
15. After the boy took the reins the horses leapt wildly.
16. The Sun foresaw only disaster when the blazing chariot shattered stars and scorched the earth.
17. When the Sun cast a thunderbolt Phaethon fell from the sky.
18. The story ends after Phaethon falls.
19. If you wish to read this myth ask Gina.
20. She will lend you the book when she is finished with it.

EXTRA PRACTICE

Three levels of practice

Participles and Participial Phrases (page 444)

LEVEL
A. Write whether the underlined participle is the **main verb** in a verb phrase or is used as an **adjective.**

1. The <u>farming</u> Indians of Puerto Rico lived simply.
2. They made their homes with palm boards and <u>tied</u> cane.
3. The round roof was <u>covered</u> with palm fronds.
4. The *hamaca* was a bed <u>suspended</u> from the beams of the roof.
5. These hammocks were <u>created</u> from thread or plant fibers.
6. The farmers also made small stools, <u>called</u> *dujos*.
7. The <u>crafted</u> stools were sturdy.
8. Have you ever <u>constructed</u> anything?

LEVEL
B. Write each sentence. Then underline the participle and write whether it is the **main verb** in a verb phrase or is used as an **adjective.**

9. The *dujos* of the chiefs were decorated with designs.
10. The carved designs were often in the form of animals.
11. For cooking purposes the Indians made clay pots.
12. They had used the clay from around the villages.
13. First, the soft clay was shaped into pots or bowls.
14. Then, covering the vessels with branches, they baked them.
15. The potters had learned their craft well.
16. These pleasing objects were also useful.

LEVEL
C. Write each sentence and underline the participial phrase. Then draw two lines under the word the phrase modifies. Add commas where needed.

17. Decorating their vessels the Tainos created beautiful objects.
18. Using plants such as the achiote they made paints.
19. Drawn on the soft clay colorful designs were added.
20. Made of clay little heads were attached to the soft pots.
21. They used the *higuera*, a kind of gourd growing on trees.
22. They carried food in baskets woven from vines.
23. Using natural materials these Indians made practical tools.
24. These objects created for work also pleased the eye.
25. Researching Indian crafts I found many fascinating facts.

EXTRA PRACTICE

Three levels of practice

Gerunds (page 446)

LEVEL

A. Write whether the underlined word is a **main verb,** a **participle** used as an adjective, or a **gerund.**

1. My class is <u>making</u> a study of the history of rock music.
2. <u>Admiring</u> fans are no longer limited to teenagers.
3. Rock finally is <u>getting</u> the serious study it deserves.
4. The <u>beginning</u> goes all the way back to the 1950s.
5. <u>Tracing</u> the musical roots of rock takes us back even further.
6. Our research requires <u>listening</u> to old records.
7. <u>Researching</u> this topic is enjoyable.
8. It is an <u>entertaining</u> project.

LEVEL

B. Write each sentence. Then underline the gerund or gerund phrase in each.

9. Reading is the other way we are getting information.
10. Searching for old records is like a treasure hunt.
11. The old recordings are often frustrating to find.
12. The ongoing search often demands much patient waiting.
13. Finding a rare song or singer is a lasting triumph.
14. Success means hearing the connecting links between the old and the new.
15. Listening carefully to old records can reveal new insights.
16. I have always enjoyed discovering rare records.

LEVEL

C. Identify each gerund phrase and write whether it is used as the **subject** or the **direct object** of the sentence. If the sentence contains no gerund, write **none.**

17. Singing the blues expresses the pain of life.
18. Adding gospel rhythms to blues created a new musical style.
19. Coming out of the black experience in America, rhythm and blues is the foundation of rock music.
20. Musical sensitivity requires appreciating many styles.
21. We all like following the latest developments in rock.
22. This evolving music had been embraced around the world.
23. Do you enjoy studying the history of music?
24. Becoming a music historian is a goal of mine.
25. Each musical style is interesting and unique.

EXTRA PRACTICE

Three levels of practice

Infinitives (page 448)

LEVEL
A. Write whether the underlined words are an **infinitive,** an **infinitive phrase,** or a **prepositional phrase.**

1. To do research is sometimes hard work.
2. To my class this research project was easy.
3. We each wanted to choose the right topic.
4. The subject of rock music was interesting to everyone.
5. Listening to rock music did not seem like research.
6. To work was a pleasure in this case.
7. The last step was to write the paper itself.
8. To share one's work is rewarding.

LEVEL
B. Write each sentence and underline any infinitive phrase. If the sentence contains no infinitive phrase, write **none.**

9. Writing has always been a challenge to me.
10. I have always wanted to express my thoughts in words.
11. To write well is an art.
12. To my great surprise I enjoyed writing this paper.
13. Now I must continue to build on this experience.
14. I have started to keep a daily journal.
15. A journal can be a source of inspiration to a writer.
16. To put thoughts into words can be very difficult.

LEVEL
C. Write and label each **infinitive phrase** or **prepositional phrase** beginning with *to.* Then write whether each infinitive phrase is used as a **subject** or **direct object.**

17. For inspiration musicians listen to the work of others.
18. Writers like to read the work of other writers.
19. To imitate others is a way of learning the basics.
20. Later, a creative person will begin to develop a personal style.
21. To reach other people is the purpose of most art.
22. Both books and music have communicated to millions.
23. I am beginning my writing by adding words to my favorite music.
24. To compose lyrics is fun.
25. Let's add more lyrics to this song.

EXTRA PRACTICE

Three levels of practice

Mechanics: Using Commas with Clauses (page 450)

LEVEL

A. Add a comma or commas where they are needed.

1. Because all cultures enjoy music folk music is universal.
2. Although the sounds differ widely the emotions expressed are quite similar.
3. Folk songs which have a down-to-earth quality come out of everyday experience.
4. Folk dances often reenact daily activities or they dramatize ancient stories or myths.
5. When people dance traditional dances they are learning about their past.

LEVEL

B. Write each sentence and add a comma or commas if they are needed. If no commas are needed, write **correct.**

6. Perhaps the early Africans in America held fast to their music because they were forced to live in exile.
7. Since music was a link with home they kept it alive.
8. Music can offer comfort in sorrow and it can be an expression of joy in happy times.
9. African musical influence which is found in almost every form of popular American music is widespread.
10. We learned about these elements in our music class.

LEVEL

C. Write each sentence and add a comma or commas where they are needed. Then write whether you added a comma or commas to punctuate a **compound sentence,** an **adjective clause,** or an **adverb clause.**

11. Mardi Gras which is celebrated in New Orleans also has African roots.
12. Whereas people complain about the commercialization of Mardi Gras very few want to end it.
13. Since it occurs on the last day before Lent Mardi Gras is a Christian festival.
14. Traditions like Mardi Gras change over time but the essence often remains alive for centuries.
15. Mardi Gras which is related to the carnival festivals in Brazil and in the Caribbean is a folk tradition.

EXTRA PRACTICE

Three levels of practice

Vocabulary Building: Suffixes (page 452)

LEVEL

A. Write each word. Then underline the suffix in each.

1. Texan
2. cheerless
3. filthy
4. employable
5. skyward

6. trainer
7. tension
8. Catholicism
9. operation
10. resentment

LEVEL

B. Write each word in the first column and underline the suffix in each. Then match it with the correct meaning of the suffix.

11. director
12. pitiable
13. woeful
14. keenness
15. tactless
16. biologist
17. organization
18. landward
19. saucy
20. paganism

a. practice of
b. one who works at
c. one who
d. capable of being
e. quality or state
f. lacking, without
g. showing, suggesting
h. marked by
i. moving toward
j. act or result of

LEVEL

C. Complete each sentence. Add a suffix to the word in parentheses to fill the blank. If necessary, use a dictionary to help you.

21. Only a ____ person would dislike holidays. (joy)
22. What could be more ____ than a party! (enjoy)
23. ____ agree on the benefits of recreation. (therapy)
24. Tired ____ need relief from their daily labors. (work)
25. The ____ calendar provides many opportunities for celebration. (America)
26. One of the most ____ is Thanksgiving. (cheer)
27. On that day we are ____ for our blessings. (thank)
28. Certainly the most ____ is the Fourth of July. (noise)
29. Halloween pranks have an ____ quality. (imp)
30. The most ____ days are the family holidays. (memory)

MAINTENANCE

UNIT 1: SENTENCES

Complete Subjects and Complete Predicates, Simple Subjects and Simple Predicates (pages 4, 6) Write each sentence. Underline the complete subject once and the complete predicate twice. Circle the simple subject and the simple predicate. If the complete subject is understood, write (*You*).

1. A pizza chef in a white uniform makes a dough.
2. He tosses the dough in the air.
3. Does this showy act stretch the dough?
4. Here is some kneaded dough for you.
5. Show me some more tricks with dough.

Correcting Fragments and Run-on Sentences (page 12) Write each group of words, identifying and correcting the sentence fragments and run-on sentences. Write **correct** next to any word group that is a sentence.

6. The lives of many wild animals are endangered, these animals may become extinct.
7. Many new animal parks in remote areas.
8. Land for the animals is becoming scarce.
9. Offer sanctuary from hunters and poachers.
10. Worldwide efforts are being made, people hope to save the animals.

UNIT 3: NOUNS

Possessive Nouns (page 72) Write each word. After each one write its possessive form.

11. juries
12. chiefs
13. heroes
14. Hartz
15. prince
16. thief
17. women
18. mouse
19. classes

UNIT 5: VERBS

Action Verbs (page 136) Write each sentence. Draw a line under each action verb. Then, write whether the verb expresses a **physical** or a **mental** action.

20. Elmer views the night sky through his telescope.
21. The rings of Saturn shine brightly.
22. Elmer wonders about Saturn's satellites.
23. The young astronomer turns his telescope excitedly toward Jupiter.
24. He thinks about a future trip to the planet.

Verbs with Direct Objects, Linking Verbs (pages 138, 142)   Write each sentence. Draw one line under each verb and identify each direct object, predicate noun, or predicate adjective. Label each verb as **transitive, intransitive** or **linking.**

25. Dora puts a worm on her fishing line.
26. The small schools of speedy fish are silvery in the clear water.
27. All of a sudden Dora's line pulls with the weight of a large fish.
28. Dora anxiously releases the line a bit.
29. After a while Dora is the proud owner of a beautiful catch.

Verbs with Indirect Objects (page 140)   Write each sentence. Then, underline each action verb and identify each **direct object** and **indirect object.**

30. The farmer sold his neighbor some oats.
31. The neighbor loaned the farmer a tractor with many wonderful features.
32. The farmer's wife bought her husband some new farm implements.
33. He handed her their paid-up mortgage.
34. Both the farmer and his wife gave their friends a mortgage-burning party.

Present, Past, and Future Tenses; Verb Phrases; Perfect Tenses (pages 144, 146, 150)   Write each sentence. Underline the verb or main verb once and the helping verb (if any) twice.

35. Postage rates are rising again this year.
36. Rates have steadily climbed over the years.
37. Next year I will send fewer letters and cards to my friends and family.
38. My mailing list had become much too large.
39. I regret the loss of some of my correspondents.

Irregular Verbs I, Irregular Verbs II (pages 152, 154) Write each sentence, using the correct form of the verb shown in parentheses. Then, write whether the verb is in the **past** or **past participle** form.

40. The surfer has (swim) far out from the shore.
41. The waves had (grow) quite high.
42. The surfer (spring) onto his surfboard.
43. He (hold) on fast as he skipped over the waves.
44. He has (ride) safely to shore.

Subject-Verb Agreement (page 156)   Rewrite the sentences so that all verbs agree with their subjects.

45. Square dancers listens to the words of the caller.

46. Have the band found a good fiddler yet?
47. At the back of the room is some good dancers.
48. There is some well-trained musicians in the band.
49. The main thing to learn in square dancing are the steps.

Using Commas to Separate Parts of a Sentence (page 158)   Rewrite each sentence by adding a comma or commas where needed.

50. Have you tried any of the exotic fruits and vegetables now on sale Cassie?
51. Yes jicamas are tasteless but crunchy.
52. I like sugar-snap peas pearl onions and spaghetti squash though.
53. Paul don't you think kiwi fruit is overrated?
54. No but I'd like to know what tamarillos pipinios and kiwanos taste like!

UNIT 7: PRONOUNS

Using Pronouns Correctly (page 220)   Write each sentence, choosing the correct pronoun or pronouns in parentheses.

55. Carl, Ella, and (me, I) will start a stamp club.
56. (He, Him) and Mary Lou just bought new albums.
57. Carol told (Ella and I) (Ella and me) about her first-day cover collection.

58. It was (him, he) who gave Ella some colorful commemorative stamps.
59. (He and I) (Him and I) have examples of the entire Great Americans series.

Possessive Pronouns (page 222)   Write each sentence, replacing each underlined possessive noun with the correct possessive pronoun.

60. Tina's Monopoly game is set up for play.
61. Now it is Scott's turn to play.
62. That hotel on Atlantic Avenue is Mabel's.
63. A doorbell ring interrupts the players' fun.
64. Scott and Mabel's brother has brought a really delightful surprise.

UNIT 9: ADJECTIVES AND ADVERBS

Adjectives, Articles and Proper Adjectives (pages 290, 292)   Write each sentence. Draw one line under each descriptive adjective and two lines under each proper adjective. Label each article.

65. Dave brought a large, slender Afghan hound to the pet show.
66. Mona's pet was a friendly gray Siamese cat with dark paws.
67. Clara carefully brushed the smooth, silky coat of a Boston terrier.

68. The rough wiry coat of an Irish wolfhound also needed attention.

69. Did the black Persian lamb really win a blue ribbon?

Comparative and Superlative Adjectives I, Comparative and Superlative Adjectives II

(pages 294, 296)   Write each sentence. Fill in each blank with the correct comparative form of the adjective.

70. Lake Superior is the ____ of the five Great Lakes.   (long)

71. Lake Titicaca in South America is located at a ____ elevation than any other lake in the world.   (high)

72. Lake Baikal in Asia is the world's ____ lake.   (deep)

73. The Caspian Sea is four and one-half times ____ than Lake Superior.   (large)

74. The Finger Lakes of New York are some of the ____ lakes anywhere.   (beautiful)

Adverbs

(page 300)   Write each sentence. Draw one line under each adverb and two lines under the word it modifies. Write whether the word is a **verb, adjective,** or another **adverb.**

75. Julia Morgan's California architecture delights visitors often.

76. She designed San Simeon, the extremely ornate mansion of William Randolph Hearst.

77. Her skills developed rather remarkably.

78. She clambered deftly over scaffolding to direct the workers.

79. Nearly eight hundred buildings from 1900 to the late 1950s were designed by Julia Morgan.

Comparative and Superlative Adverbs

(page 302)   Write each sentence. Fill the blank with the correct form of the adverb in parentheses.

80. Eve solves crossword puzzles ____ than Al.   (quickly)

81. She grabs the morning paper ____ than anyone else in the entire family.   (soon)

82. She concentrates ____ of anyone in the family.   (intensely)

83. Today Al got the paper ____ than Eve.   (early)

84. He solved the puzzle ____ than he ever has before.   (well)

Avoiding Double Negatives

(page 304)   Rewrite each sentence, correcting the double negative.

85. The candidates for student government hadn't never looked so good before.

86. No one at the rally had never heard them speak before.

87. The first candidate didn't make no campaign promises to the citizens.

88. There wasn't no speech as exciting as the one the second candidate gave.
89. Hardly no one at the rally will fail to vote when election day arrives.

Using Adjectives and Adverbs

(page 306)   Write each sentence. Choose the correct modifier to complete each sentence.

90. The clowns perform (real, really) funny antics.
91. They chug (excited, excitedly) around the ring in an undersized locomotive.
92. They sweep the floor (bad, badly) with toothbrushes and odd-looking brooms.
93. The lion tamer moves a (tremendous, tremendously) barrier into their path.
94. The ringmaster asks for a (good, well) round of applause.

Using Commas with Dates, Addresses, and Names (page 308)   Write the following sentences, adding commas wherever needed.

95. This Abigail Adams letter came into the museum on June 28 1988.
96. It was donated by Peter MacGregor D.D.S.
97. Dr. MacGregor has been collecting historical autographs since April 1969.
98. The museum is located at 135 Adams Street Quincy Massachusetts.

99. A letter was signed "A friend of the Adams National Historic Site Peter MacGregor D.D.S."

Synonyms and Antonyms

(page 310)   Write whether each pair of words are **synonyms** or **antonyms**.

100. extreme, moderate
101. novel, uncommon
102. bleak, bare
103. renew, exhaust
104. cease, commence
105. zealous, enthusiastic
106. thoughtful, heedless
107. narrate, recount
108. lazy, brisk
109. gruff, polite

UNIT 11: PREPOSITIONS, CONJUNCTIONS, AND INTERJECTIONS

Prepositions and Prepositional Phrases (page 364) Write each prepositional phrase. Then, draw one line under the preposition and two lines under its object.

110. Eddy must get his project to the fair.
111. He constructed a large diagram of a black hole.
112. Will it go through the door?
113. He has studied black holes for several years.
114. The diagrams in his exhibit are well drawn.

Using Pronouns in Prepositional Phrases (page 366)
Write each sentence, replacing each incorrect pronoun with a correct one. Underline the prepositional phrase in which the pronoun appears.

115. Edna showed the mirage to me and him.

116. She often explains the wonders of nature to ourselves.

117. A person like I appreciated Edna's explanations.

118. Edna asked me to walk farther into the desert with he and she.

119. She began a discussion of mirages between they and I.

Using Verbs after Prepositional Phrases (page 370)
Write the sentences, choosing the form of the verb that will correctly complete the sentence.

120. The most successful of the many utopian communities of the nineteenth century (was, were) the Amana group.

121. A visit to the Iowa villages (provide, provides) an interesting vacation.

122. Members of the Amana Society still (run, runs) the seven villages of the community.

123. One of the museums (contain, contains) original kitchen tools and appliances, doesn't it?

124. Nowadays members of the Society (own, owns) shares in the community.

Conjunctions (page 372)
Write and label the coordinating and correlative conjunctions.

125. Both Joanna and Link read books in their spare time.

126. Joanna reads about spies or detectives.

127. Link not only reads books but also acts in plays.

128. Joanna has acted in plays, but her music lessons now interfere.

129. Neither Joanna nor Link has time for watching very much television.

Making Verbs Agree with Compound Subjects (page 374) Write each sentence, choosing the correct form of the verb in parentheses. Underline each conjunction used.

130. Neither Mr. Barnes nor his employees (want, wants) another sale soon.

131. Both the geraniums and the African violets (was, were) sold out early.

132. Some begonias or a jade plant (was, were) the only choice left.

133. Pedestrians and merchants still (talk, talks) about the crowds at the sale.

134. Either more plants or a better plan (is, are) needed for the next sale, if we are to make a profit.

Prefixes (page 380)   Write each word and underline its prefix. Then write the meaning of the word and the meaning of its prefix. Use a dictionary if you need help.

135. irregular
136. forefather
137. preschool
138. mislead
139. decode
140. reorder
141. indirect
142. impartial
143. illegible
144. bilingual
145. nonessential
146. interchange
147. subtitle
148. postelection
149. dishonor

UNIT 13: COMPLEX SENTENCES AND VERBALS

Sentence and Clauses, Complex Sentences (pages 436, 438)   Write each sentence. Underline each independent clause once and each subordinate clause twice. Then write whether the sentence is **compound** or **complex.**

150. The word *laser* is an acronym; it stands for "Light Amplification by the Stimulated Emission of Radiation."
151. Unfortunately, early lasers had few applications because they were too hot.

152. In contemporary times cooler lasers are used because they cause fewer problems.
153. Laser beams shine in movie special effects, laser light shows, and supermarket price scanners; but their most important consumer use is in communications.
154. When laser beams are combined with fiber optics, they can carry over 10,000 telephone calls at once.

Adjective Clauses, Adverb Clauses (pages 440, 442) Write each sentence. Then underline and label the **adverb clause** or the **adjective clause** in the sentence.

155. The eccentric who became the "firebrand of the Revolution" was Sam Adams.
156. Although he failed at many jobs, Sam Adams found his true life's work in the field of politics.
157. He wrote hundreds of circulars, newspaper articles, and letters, which he signed with various names.
158. His one-man propaganda factory stated many arguments that later became doctrines of the Revolution.
159. Since he worked mostly behind the scenes, many people don't know of his leading role in the Boston Tea Party.

Participles and Participial Phrases (page 444)   Write each sentence. Draw one line under each participle, and write whether it is used as part of a verb or as an adjective in the sentence.

160. As long ago as the sixteenth century, Filipino hunters were trapping animals with the use of yo-yos.
161. The Tagalog people used the yo-yos as incapacitating weapons.
162. In the 1920s an American named Duncan saw the Filipino weapons.
163. Scaling down the size of the weapon, he changed the yo-yo into a toy.
164. As a toy the yo-yo has retained the original Tagalog word as its name.

Using Commas with Clauses (page 450)   Write each sentence, adding a comma where needed. If the sentence needs no commas, write **correct.**

165. Since pterodactyls are extinct a California company made a replica of one for a movie.

166. The replica which was guided by a tiny computer actually flew.
167. It flapped its wings in actual flight after a towline took it aloft.
168. Machinery simulated muscles and a motor made them work.
169. When the pterodactyl had completed its movie role it was given to the Smithsonian Institution in Washington, D.C.

Suffixes (page 452)   Write each sentence. Complete each one by using the word in parentheses with its correct suffix, from the list below, to fill the blank.

able   ful   ian   ish   ism   ly

170. ___ is a frequent theme in literature. (Hero)
171. In fantasies a ___ may be a character. (magic)
172. The villain is often ___. (fiend)
173. Fantasy, villains, and adventure make a ___ tale. (live)
174. A ___ writer weaves these elements into an ___ story. (skill) (enjoy)

UNIT

14

Writing Research Reports

Read the quotation and look at the picture on the opposite page. Talk about different sources you can use to learn more about a subject of interest.

When you write a research report, you will want to share with your audience important information you have gathered on a topic.

Focus A research report is an explanation of a topic based upon information compiled from different sources.

What would be a good topic for a research report? On the following pages you will find an article about a fascinating topic. You will see some pictures, too. You can use them to find ideas for writing.

*With many hours of interviewing and many more hours
of poring over books, I've learned how to learn what
I need to know in order to write a book.*

—Carolyn Meyer

AWARD
WINNING
SELECTION

Have you ever been on a treasure hunt? What was it like?
Why do you think people enjoy treasure hunts?

For Alberto Ruz Lhuillier, the ultimate treasure hunt was an
archaeological dig—one with the possibility of real treasure at
the end. By interpreting the clues he found, Ruz was able to
discover the secrets of an ancient Mayan pyramid that had
puzzled others for more than a century.

As you read the selection, look for the ways in which the
authors have explained Ruz's discovery and its importance.

The Secrets
of a
TOMB

Carolyn Meyer and Charles Gallenkamp

Alberto Ruz Lhuillier stared at the flagstone floor of the Temple of Inscriptions, high atop a terraced pyramid at the ancient city of Palenque. There was something peculiar about it. Near the center of the room lay an unusually large stone with circular holes drilled around its edges, all filled with plugs to conceal them. No one had been able to figure out what they were for—and the site had been studied intensively since Stephens and Catherwood had stopped there more than a century before. But Ruz, an archaeologist from the Center for Maya Studies in Mexico, noticed something other explorers had missed: the walls of the temple seemed to continue on below the floor, as though another room lay beneath it. On a hunch, Ruz decided to raise the stone.[1]

As workmen struggled to lift the heavy slab, Ruz could make out the outlines of a narrow opening completely filled with large stones and clay. There was nothing to do but haul out this debris. After a few days of digging, a series of stone steps began to appear, an interior staircase leading down into the pyramid. Ruz resolved to follow the stairway to its end, even though he knew it would involve an enormous amount of labor.

For two and a half months Ruz and his men struggled against heat, humidity, and choking dust while they hauled up the heavy rocks with ropes and pulleys. It took them four such stretches—a total of ten months—to clear the staircase. By the end of the first season, in the summer of 1949, only twenty-three steps had been uncovered. At the end of the third season they had dug out sixty-six steps and were down about seventy-three feet beneath the temple floor, near ground level. They still had no idea where the stairway was leading and no clues to its original function. No inscriptions were visible on the walls, no sculpture had been found. But at the bottom of the stairs they did find a box of offerings—pottery dishes, jade beads, jade earplugs, and a beautiful tear-shaped pearl. They knew they were getting close.

During the summer of 1952 the diggers encountered a wall. "The wall turned out to be more than twelve feet thick," Ruz wrote, "breaking through it took a full week of the hardest labor of the entire expedition. The mortar held so firmly that the stones often broke before they separated, and the wet lime

1. The writers use the 5 W's and H to introduce their subject: who, what, when, where, why, and how.

burned and cracked the women's hands. Finally we got through and came upon a rude masonry box or chest.''

Inside the box were six human skeletons, at least one of them female. "Unquestionably this was a human sacrifice," Ruz wrote, "young persons whose spirits were forever to guard and attend him for whom all this entire massive pyramid had been made—and whom we now soon hoped to find.''

Excitement mounted. Next they discovered a low triangular doorway sealed by an enormous stone, and they managed to loosen it enough for Ruz to squeeze behind it and into a vaulted room. He knew instantly that his four seasons of exhausting labor had been rewarded.

"Out of the dim shadows emerged a vision from a fairytale, a fantastic, ethereal sight from another world. . . . Across the walls marched stucco figures in low relief. Then my eyes sought the floor. This was almost entirely filled with a great carved stone slab, in perfect condition. . . . Ours were the first eyes that had gazed on it in more than a thousand years!''

The chamber was about twenty-nine feet long by thirteen feet wide, the steeply vaulted ceiling twenty-three feet high. Human figures modeled in stucco relief, probably representing the gods of the underworld, paraded around the walls. A colossal monument filled up most of the room: a beautifully carved stone slab resting on another immense stone which in turn was supported by six huge chiseled blocks.

Ruz believed that he had found a ceremonial burial place, but he would have to wait to find out. It was mid-July; the rains had come, and funds for that phase of the exploration were gone. Ruz had to leave Palenque and his exciting project until November.

When he returned, Ruz had a narrow hole drilled into the base stone, and when the bit reached a hollow space he poked a wire through the opening. The particles of red paint that stuck to the wire told him this was not an altar but an incredible coffin. But to prove this he would have to lift the sculptured stone slab, weighing about five tons and a masterpiece of Maya art. Ruz spent two days getting ready. Hardwood logs cut in the forest were brought to the pyramid and lowered by cables through the interior staircase. Then jacks were placed under the corners of the slab, reinforced by the logs.[2]

2. The writers organize facts in chronological order.

"On November 27, at dusk, after a twelve hour working day, the soul-shaking manoeuvre took place." Inch by inch they raised the slab. Ruz saw that a cavity had been carved in the huge base stone, and the cavity was sealed with another polished stone, also fitted with plugs. When the slab had been lifted up about fifteen inches, Ruz could stand the suspense no longer. He squeezed under it, removed the plugs from the inner cover, and peered in.

Green jade ornaments, red-painted teeth and bones, the fragments of a mask—Ruz gazed at the remains of the man for whom all of this had been created. A treasure of jade ornaments had been placed on the dead man at the time of his burial— headdress, earplugs, bead collar, breastplate, rings on every finger, bracelets, and sandal beads. A single jade bead had been placed in his mouth to make sure that the spirit of this king or high priest could buy food in the afterlife.

The body had been wrapped in a cotton shroud painted red and sprinkled with powdered cinnabar, a red mineral. A magnificent mask made of jade mosaic with shell and obsidian inlays for the eyes had been fitted over the face of the corpse. The mask is so lifelike that it was probably an actual portrait made while the noble was still alive.

For years before the dignitary died, the whole community had helped to prepare the tomb. After his death the body was carried down the stairway to the crypt, probably accompanied by a procession of priests in elaborate ceremonial dress, and laid in the stone coffin, the inside of which had been painted red, the color of death. Then they closed the coffin and moved the massive carved slab into place. Jewels were placed on the slab and some clay containers with food and drink were left behind, along with two beautiful heads modeled in stucco. The crypt was sealed by sliding the stone block into position in the narrow entrance. Then the six young people were killed— maybe sons and daughters of important nobles—to accompany and serve the dead man in the next world. Through a stone duct that Ruz found, which ran along the wall of the stairway all the way to the floor of the temple, the priests could communicate with the spirit of the dead man below.

Ruz's discovery yielded an enormous amount of information about this civilization. The complicated structure of the temple proves the skill of Maya architects. The carved slab over the stone coffin and the two stucco heads place Maya sculptors among the world's finest. The magnificent jade ornaments demonstrate their talent as craftsmen.[3]

Palenque, perhaps the most beautiful of Maya ruins, represents the peak of Maya achievement during the Classic period. It also shows the huge amount of effort that could be summoned from engineers, artists, stonemasons, and laborers, and the lengths to which the Maya people would go to honor a priest-king.

3. The writers present specific reasons explaining the importance of the discovery.

Thinking Like a Reader
1. Why was Alberto Ruz Lhuillier's discovery of the Mayan tomb so important?
2. Have you ever discovered something that was important or valuable to you? What was it?

Write your responses in your journal.

Thinking Like a Writer
3. How does the way the authors present their information help to hold the reader's interest?
4. In what order are the details presented?
5. Which details do you think are most important? Why?
6. If you were writing about an important discovery about the past, how would you gather information?

Write your responses in your journal.

LITERATURE

Brainstorm *Vocabulary*

In "Secrets of a Tomb," the authors use terms such as "vaulted ceiling," "stucco relief," "sculptured," and "chiseled," to describe the tomb. These words are part of the special vocabulary of art and architecture. Think of a topic about which you would like to do research and write a report. It might be an event in history, a place, an object, or a living thing. In your journal, write any special words and phrases that you associate with your topic. You can use your personal vocabulary list when you write about your topic.

Talk It Over
Explain a Process

When you explain a process, you tell how to do or make something. In "Secrets of a Tomb," the authors tell how Alberto Ruz uncovered the tomb. Think of something you have done or something you know how to do. Work in a group to explain the process. Be sure to include all the important steps or details and to keep them in the right order.

If you wish, use the following list of topics to help you get ideas.

> woodworking
> training pets
> making bread
> using a calculator

Quick Write
Write a Definition

When you explain something that is unfamiliar to your audience, you often have to include a definition. Write a definition of something unusual that is known to you. In your definition, tell what kind of thing you are writing about. Then, tell what it looks like and what it does. End with interesting information about your topic. For example, imagine that you were writing a definition of *obsidian*.

Obsidian is glass that is naturally formed when a volcano erupts and great heat melts certain minerals. It is usually black or brownish and very shiny. Obsidian can be carved like stone and is used to make art objects such as figurines.

Idea Corner
Think of Research Topics

Make a list of topics about which you would like to write a research report. Think of topics that interest you most or which arouse your curiosity. Write them in your journal. You might write general topics, like "American history" or specific ideas, like "the Boston Tea Party." You might wish to discuss possible topics with a classmate.

PICTURES SEEING LIKE A WRITER

Finding Ideas for Writing

Look at the pictures. Think about what you see. What ideas for a research report do the pictures give you? Write your ideas in your journal.

Storyteller, Ivory Coast, Africa

Pre-Columbian earrings from Peru

1 GROUP WRITING: A RESEARCH REPORT

COOPERATIVE
LEARNING

You know that a research report is a report based on outside sources of information. Its **purpose** is to inform an **audience** of interested readers about a topic. What are the steps you take to write an effective research report?

- Finding Information and Note Taking
- Making an Outline
- Writing Paragraphs from an Outline

Finding Information and Note Taking

When you do research, you look in encyclopedias, magazines, books, and other resources for information on the topic you have chosen. The sources you use in preparing your report must be listed in a **bibliography**, which appears at the end of the report. For each source, you make a bibliography card, which is a 3 1/2 x 5 inch note card with information about the book, magazine, or other source. Look at the following examples of bibliography cards.

author	Secrist, Elizabeth Hough	
title	"Arbor Day"	
	World Book Encyclopedia Vol. 19	encyclopedia
date	1984 edition	

author	Ickis, Marguerite	
title	The Book of Holidays and Festivals Around the World	book
location	New York, Dodd, Mead	publisher
date	1970	

author	Winkleman, P. H.
title	"New York's Arbor Day Centennial"
	The Conservationist magazine
	Vol. 42, pages 44-49 volume and page
date	March/April 1988

Keep a record of the information you find by summarizing it in your own words on a note card.

Read the following paragraph from an article about Arbor Day. Then read the note card below.

On the first Arbor Day in Nebraska, April 10, 1872, thousands of people turned out to plant trees. There was a festival atmosphere as holes were dug and rows of small trees went up along streets, in yards, and at the edges of farmland. Later, officials calculated that over one million trees had been planted to help save Nebraska's soil.

title	"Arbor Days of Old"
author	Janis Zbrezney
subject	first Arbor Day
summary	estimated one million trees planted "to help save Nebraska's soil."
page	p. 45

On each note card, identify the source from which you took information and write a heading that gives the subject of the notes. Be sure to include the page number as well.

The summary on the note card gives you a general idea of what the source says. Notice that on the card above the student put quotation marks around words taken directly from the source.

Guided Practice: Finding Information and Taking Notes

As a class, choose a topic from the list, or think of one on which you all agree. Then, individually, find one source for your topic and make a bibliography card and a note card using that source. Compare your cards with those of your classmates.

folk songs	Veterans' Day	Halloween
soccer	the rodeo	Native American crafts

Making an Outline

Once you have gathered information on note cards, arrange the cards in categories according to the types of details recorded on the cards. You can also see which details do not fit any category. You may either discard those cards or decide to gather additional related information.

Review your cards to see what information they contain, and think about what you want to say about your topic. Write a statement that summarizes all the main points your report will make.

In a **topic outline** you organize information logically into main topics and subtopics. Look at this example.

Arbor Day

I. What it is
   A. Day set aside for planting trees
   B. Observed at different times in different states
      1. Observed in March in California
      2. Observed in April or May in the North

II. History of Arbor Day
   A. Sterling Morton in Nebraska
      1. Concerned about dry soil
      2. Knew trees would protect soil
      3. Persuaded state to set aside a special day for planting trees
   B. Idea picked up by other states

III. Importance of Arbor Day
   A. Beautifies landscape
   B. Conservation

In an outline, place roman numerals before main topics. Place capital letters before subtopics. Your outline must always have at least two main topics and two subtopics. That is, if you have a I, you must have a II; if you have an A, you must have a B. The first word of each entry begins with a capital letter.

Guided Practice: Making an Outline

Recall the subject for which you have gathered information and made note cards. Organize your cards into categories. Then use your note cards to write a topic outline for your research report. Be sure that your outline has three topics and at least two subtopics for each topic.

Writing Paragraphs from an Outline

Your outline is a guide from which to write your report. Each paragraph of the report corresponds to a main topic in your outline. The main topics in the outline become topic sentences for your paragraphs. The subtopics become supporting sentences.

Begin the first paragraph of your report with a topic sentence that introduces your first main idea. Then write the supporting details for that topic sentence.

Your report should have at least three paragraphs. In the first paragraph include an introduction that tells readers what the report is about. The last paragraph will state your conclusion. The middle of the report will contain the facts and information you have learned from your research.

Look at this example of a three-paragraph report.

Arbor Day

Arbor Day is an important holiday for people today and in the future. Arbor Day is a day set aside for planting trees. In some states it is a state holiday, and in others it is proclaimed each year by the governor. Different states celebrate at different times, according to the best time for tree-planting. In the South and Hawaii, it may be held any time from December to March. In the North, it is usually held in April or May. California celebrates Arbor Day on March 7, the birthday of the naturalist, Luther Burbank.

Arbor Day was begun in Nebraska by Sterling Morton, a newspaper publisher. He was concerned that the soil in his state was drying up and blowing away. He knew that trees would help to hold the soil and keep it moist. He persuaded the state to set aside a day for planting trees. One million trees were planted on the first Arbor Day, April 10, 1872. Soon other states picked up the idea and began to hold Arbor Days of their own.

Arbor Day celebrations add trees that beautify the landscape for the future. The holiday also helps to make people aware of the importance of conserving the trees and woodlands we have to keep the earth healthy. It is truly a festival for the future.

At the end of your report, on a separate sheet of paper, list your bibliography—the sources you used in preparing the report. Organize your list alphabetically by the authors' last names.

Bibliography

Hall-Quest, Alfred Lawrence, "Holidays and Holy Days," Colliers Encyclopedia, Vol. 12, 1987 ed.

Ickis, Marguerite, The Book of Holidays and Festivals the World Over, New York, Dodd, Mead, and Company, 1970, pp. 86–87

Putting a Research Report Together

With your classmates you have gathered information and arranged your note cards for a research report. You have also developed a topic outline to organize your information.

Guided Practice: Writing a Research Report

Use your outline to write a three-paragraph research report. For your first paragraph, write roman numeral I of your outline as a topic sentence. Write detail sentences for the subtopics. Then begin your next paragraph. Use details from the notes you have gathered. Remember to include a bibliography at the end of your report. Use the sample bibliography on the opposite page to organize your information.

Share your report with a friend. Ask your friend if he or she learned anything new about the subject from reading your report.

Checklist A Research Report

When you write a research report, you will want to keep in mind some important points.

One way to remember the important elements of a research report is to make a checklist. The checklist will remind you of the things you need to do to write an effective research report, including making an outline and writing a conclusion.

Look at this checklist. Make a copy of the checklist and add other points you wish to remember. Keep a copy of it in your writing folder. You can use it when you write your own research report.

CHECKLIST

- ✔ Remember purpose and audience.
- ✔ Find information and take notes.
- ✔ Organize note cards into groups.
- ✔ Make an outline.
- ✔ Write paragraphs from the outline.
- ✔ Include a good introduction and conclusion.
- ✔ _____

2 THINKING AND WRITING: Cause and Effect

Think over what you have learned about research reports. You know that the purpose of a report is to explain and inform—to help your readers answer such questions as *How?* or *Why?* about a subject.

A writer can help readers understand a subject by identifying causes and effects. A **cause** is the reason why something happened. An **effect** is what happened as a result of the cause. Read the list below. What causes and effects can you add?

Cause	Effect
drought	crop failure
tooth care	decay prevention
immigration	increased population
medical research	vaccine

Now look at this page from a writer's journal. The writer has jotted down her thoughts about a possible research report topic that interests her.

Native American cliff dwellings
　　built like apartments in cave walls
Why in this place?
　　natural protection from weather, enemies
Eventually abandoned-- reason unknown
　　perhaps lack of water, the people left
Importance of water
　　drinking, raising crops, livestock

The writer plans to write a paragraph about cliff dwellings of early Native Americans. She wants to present possible reasons, or causes, for the dwellings to have been abandoned. Her notes list several causes and effects.

Thinking Like a Writer

■ What effects does the writer mention? Which causes do you think help to explain these effects?

The writer's explanation will be clearest if she chooses strong, logical causes to explain the effects. One item she lists—that the people left—is not a cause, because it does not tell *why* they left. Lack of water might be a cause, since without water for themselves, their livestock, and their crops, the people would have to go elsewhere.

When you write a research report, you will have to identify causes and effects, too. You will have to find the reasons why things happened and use them in your writing.

 THINKING APPLICATION Understanding Cause and Effect

Each of the writers mentioned below is writing a research report and has written notes on his or her topic. Help each writer to decide which notes to use in explaining causes and effects related to his or her topic.

1. Hector is reporting on the blizzard of 1888. He wants to show causes and effects connected with the storm. Which items should he choose?

   The storm began on March 12 and lasted three days.
   The storm was not forecast; so people were unprepared.
   People were blown off their feet by the strong winds.
   Train stations were open; so people stayed in them.

2. Rachel is writing about the hazards of ocean dumping. She believes that plastic causes special problems. Which effects can she use to support her claim?

   Dolphins become entangled in plastic nets and drown.
   People are careless with plastic goods.
   Birds and animals may eat plastic and die.
   There are more plastic containers than ever before.

3. Dawn feels that showing causes and effects will strengthen her report on the art of quilting. Which items showing causes and effects should she choose?

   Quilts are warm because their layers trap warmth.
   Most pioneer women made quilts for their homes.
   Made from scraps, quilts were economical.
   Quilting bees had both social and practical goals.

3 INDEPENDENT WRITING: A Research Report

Prewrite: Step 1

You have learned the important elements in writing a research report. In this lesson, you will choose a topic of your own and write a research report. Daryl, a student your age, chose his topic in this way.

Choosing a Topic

First, Daryl wrote a list of subjects that interest him. Next, he thought of questions about each subject that might be answered by research. He knew his purpose would be to inform. Below is a list of topics that he brainstormed in his writing journal.

> *Labor Day*
> *Thanksgiving*
> *jazz*
> *sports — just the Olympic Games*
> *weather forecasting*

Daryl liked the fourth topic on his list best, but felt that it was too broad. He narrowed his topic to the Olympic Games. Since his gym teacher had mentioned the Olympic Games in a class recently, he decided that the members of his gym class might make a good audience. Then he read an encyclopedia article about the Olympic Games to get an overview of his topic. He decided that he should narrow his topic still further. Notice below how he narrowed his subject down to a specific topic.

Sports	GENERAL
The Olympic Games	LESS GENERAL
The Ancient Olympic Games	SPECIFIC

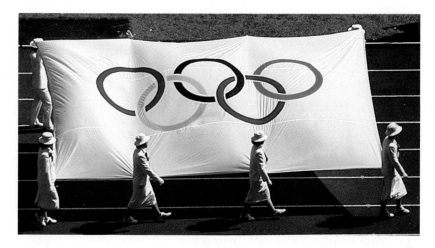

Daryl realized that he would need at least three sources to write his research report. He used the library card catalog to find books on his topic. He also used the *Readers' Guide to Periodical Literature* to help him find magazine articles in which to look for information.

Exploring Ideas: Note Taking and Outlining

To help him keep track of his sources, Daryl made a bibliography card for each book, magazine article, or encyclopedia article he read. These cards became his working bibliography. When his report is finished, Daryl will select the cards for the sources he actually used, arrange them in alphabetical order, and list them at the end of his report as a final bibliography. Look at this bibliography card that Daryl made for his report.

Author	Glubok, Shirley and Alfred Tamarin	
Title	Olympic Games in Ancient Greece	
Location	New York, Harper and Row	Publisher
Date	1976	

Keeping track of his sources now will save Daryl a trip back to the library to locate the information later.

Next, Daryl located his sources and read them for information. As he read, he took notes summarizing the information he found. He recorded the information on note cards like the one on the next page.

Olympic Games in Ancient Greece

Glubok, Shirley and Alfred Tamarin

Contests

The <u>pentathlon</u> included discus throw, long jump,
javelin throw, a foot race, and wrestling (all in
Olympics today).

When he had collected a number of note cards, Daryl read
through them and grouped them according to subject. He
discarded cards that did not fit into any group. He then used
the cards to make a topic outline.

I. History and purpose of the games
    A. First recorded in 776 B.C. but much older
    B. Held in Olympia—a sacred place
    C. Displayed Greek ideals of courage, sportsmanship

II. The games themselves
    A. Contests for skills needed in war
    B. Chariot racing, running, throwing, wrestling
    C. To the honor of Zeus, Greek king of the gods

III. The modern games
    A. Revived in 1896
    B. Modeled after ancient games

Before beginning to write, Daryl imagined that he was a representative of the Olympic committee explaining the Olympic Games to a group of students. This helped him think of the kinds of questions his report should answer. At this point, he made some changes in part of his outline.

I. History and purpose of the games
   A. First recorded in 776 B.C. but much older
   B. Held in Olympia—a sacred place
   C. Displayed Greek ideals of courage, sportsmanship

II. The games themselves
   A. Contests for skills needed in war
   B. Chariot racing, running, throwing, wrestling
      No women allowed
   C. ~~To the honor of Zeus, Greek king of the gods~~

III. The modern games
   A. Revived in 1896
   B. Modeled after ancient games
   C. *To encourage sportsmanship, promote world peace*

Thinking Like a Writer
- What did Daryl add?
- What did he take out?
- Why do you think he made these changes?

YOUR TURN

Think of a topic on which you would like to write a research report. Follow these steps. Use **Pictures** or your journal to help you think of ideas.

JOURNAL

- Make a list of topics.
- Choose the one you like best.
- Narrow your topic if it is too broad.
- Think of questions you would like to answer about it.
- Think about your purpose and audience.

Make an outline. Remember, you can add to or take away from your outline at any time.

Write a First Draft: Step 2

Daryl knows what a research report should include. To help him remember, he has made a checklist. On his checklist Daryl included reminders to organize his notes, make an outline, and write an effective introduction and conclusion for his research report. Look at Daryl's planning checklist. Daryl is now ready to write his first draft.

After he reviewed the important elements to include in his research report, Daryl began to write his first draft. As Daryl was writing his first draft, he concentrated on getting his ideas on paper. He did not worry about errors, because he knew he could go back and correct them later.

Part of Daryl's First Draft

> The modern Olympic Games have much in common with the ancient games held in Greece, arousing enthusiasm around the world. The Olympic Games were first recorded in 776 B.C. They had probaly begun long before that. They were held in olympia. Representatives of states, that were at war, could come there to arrange a Truce. During the games the truce was declared so that everyone could play. The games displayed all the things the Greeks honored.

Planning Checklist
- Remember purpose and audience.
- Find information and take notes.
- Organize note cards into groups.
- Make an outline.
- Write paragraphs from the outline.
- Include a good introduction and conclusion.

YOUR TURN

Write the first draft of your research report. As you prepare to write, ask yourself these questions.

- What does my audience need to know?
- What is the main idea I want to state?
- How can I best use my outline to write the paragraphs of my report?
- What facts and details will explain my main point?
- What important ideas should I state in my introduction and conclusion?

TIME-OUT You might want to take some time out before you revise. That way you will be able to revise your writing with a fresh eye.

Revise: Step 3

After Daryl finished writing his first draft, he read it over. He noticed that there were several changes and corrections he needed to make. Then, he shared his draft with a classmate and asked for some suggestions for improvement. In their conference, Daryl's friend pointed out that some parts of the report would benefit from additional facts to clarify the ideas discussed.

Daryl then looked back at his planning checklist. He noticed that he had forgotten one point. The conclusion he had written in his first draft needed to be stronger. He checked it off so that he would remember this point when he revised.

Using his checklist as a guide, Daryl revised his report. He asked himself several questions to help him improve his research report. Did he write paragraphs that covered the topics on his outline? Were his introduction and conclusion strong? Did any information need to be added or eliminated? He did not correct errors such as those in spelling or punctuation. He would fix those mistakes later.

Daryl also thought more about the **purpose** and **audience** for his research report. He reminded himself that his primary purpose was to write a clear and informative explanation of his topic for his classmates.

Look at some of Daryl's revisions on the next page.

Revising Checklist
- Remember purpose and audience.
- Find information and take notes.
- Organize the note cards into groups.
- Make an outline.
- Write paragraphs from the outline.
- ✔ Include a good introduction and conclusion.

The revisions Daryl made changed his report. Here is part of his revised draft.

Part of Daryl's Revised Draft

The modern Olympic Games have much in common with

the ancient games held in Greece, arousing enthusiasm

around the world. The Olympic Games were first recorded

in 776 B.C.ₐ*,but* They had probaly begun long before that. They

were held in olympiaₐ *,a sacred place to the Greeks.* Representatives of states, that were

at war, could come there to arrange a Truce. During the

games the truce was declared so that ~~everyone~~ *competing athletes* could play.

The games displayed all the ~~things~~ *ideals* the Greeks honored.ₐ*,such*

as courage, physical strength, beauty, and good sportsmanship.

Thinking Like a Writer

WISE
WORD
CHOICE

- Which details about the Olympic Games did Daryl add? How do they improve the report?
- Which words did he change? How does changing them improve his writing?
- What sentences did he combine? How does combining them improve his writing?

YOUR TURN

Read your first draft. Ask yourself these questions about the important parts of a research report.

- How can I make my topic sentences clearer? Do they state my main points?
- How can I organize my information more logically? Have I used my outline effectively?
- How can my introduction and conclusion be stronger?
- How can combining sentences that have related information improve my writing?

If you wish, ask a friend to read your work and make suggestions. Then revise your research report.

Proofread: Step 4

Daryl was pleased with the changes in content and sentence structure that he made in his revision, but he knew that his report was not complete until he proofread it thoroughly. He made a proofreading checklist to use while he proofread.

Part of Daryl's Proofread Draft

The modern Olympic Games have much in common with the ancient games held in Greece, arousing enthusiasm around the world. The Olympic Games were first recorded in 776 B.C. They had probably begun long before that. They were held in olympia, a sacred place to the Greeks. Representatives of states that were at war could come there to arrange a truce. During the games the truce was declared so that competing athletes could play. The games displayed all the ideals the Greeks honored, such as courage, physical strength, beauty, and good sportsmanship.

YOUR TURN

Proofreading Practice

Below is a paragraph that you can use to practice your proofreading skills. Find the errors. Write the paragraph correctly on a separate piece of paper.

Carrying many famous people the *Titanic* set out from Southhampton england. She was the largest ship in the world and people thought her the most seccure. Four days out from port, she struck an Iceberg. the ship quickly began to fill with water, ripped open by collision. People raced for Lifeboats but to few boats had been provieded. The great ship sank in just three hours.

Proofreading Checklist
- Did I indent each paragraph?
- Did I spell all words correctly?
- What punctuation errors do I need to correct?
- What capitalization errors do I need to correct?
- What errors in the placement of phrases do I need to correct?

Applying Your Proofreading Skills

Now proofread your research report. Review your checklist as well as **The Grammar Connection** and **The Mechanics Connection** below. Use the proofreading marks to make changes.

THE GRAMMAR CONNECTION

Remember this rule about placing participial phrases correctly.

■ Place a participial phrase as close as possible to the noun or pronoun it describes.

MISPLACED:	The snow closed the road, drifting to eight feet.
CORRECT:	**Drifting to eight feet,** the snow closed the road.
CORRECT:	The snow, **drifting to eight feet**, closed the road.
MISPLACED:	A large German shepherd chased the squirrel, barking loudly.
CORRECT:	**Barking loudly,** a large German shepherd chased the squirrel.
CORRECT:	A large German shepherd, **barking loudly,** chased the squirrel.

Review your writing. Have you placed participial phrases correctly?

THE MECHANICS CONNECTION

Remember these rules about using commas in sentences with clauses.

■ Use a comma before the conjunction *and*, *or*, or *but* in a compound sentence.
  The years passed, and the city prospered.
  The city grew, but taxes were high.

■ Use commas to set off an adjective clause that gives information that is not essential to the meaning of the sentence.
  My research topic, which I selected last night, focuses on prehistoric art.

■ Use a comma after an adverb clause or a participial phrase that begins a sentence.
  After the war ended, the country began to rebuild.
  Finding no game, the hunters returned to camp.

Check your writing. Have you used commas correctly in sentences with clauses?

Proofreading Marks

Indent ¶
Add ∧
Add a comma ∧
Add quotation marks ˅ ˅
Add a period ⊙
Take out ⅁
Capitalize ≡
Lower-case letter /
Reverse the order ∩

Publish: Step 5

Daryl had decided to share his report with the members of his gym class. He copied it neatly in his best handwriting and posted it on the bulletin board near the locker room. Several of his classmates asked him questions about the ancient Olympic Games. He found that his research had enabled him to answer most of their questions. He decided to do more research to answer the remaining questions.

YOUR TURN

Make a final copy of your report. Use your best handwriting, or use a typewriter or computer. Think of a way to share your report. You might find some ideas in the **Sharing Suggestions** box below.

SHARING SUGGESTIONS

Form a small group with other classmates and read your reports aloud. Challenge each other by asking questions about each topic.	Make an illustrated booklet of your report and present it to interested people who live in a nursing home.	With other classmates, collect your reports into an encyclopedia of information. Arrange the reports alphabetically by subject, and create an index.

WRITING PROCESS

4 SPEAKING AND LISTENING: Giving an Effective Oral Report

Writing a research report involves a number of steps, including locating sources, taking notes, and organizing those notes into an outline. You can use the same skills to gather information and prepare for an oral report.

Begin by choosing and narrowing a topic. Then identify sources and gather information. Group your information into topics, and discard any notes that do not fit into the groupings. When you have organized your information, you will be ready to plan the report itself.

When you give an oral report, you speak from note cards or from an outline. The cards or outline will help to remind you of what you want to say. Look at this note card.

ORAL REPORT ON JAZZ--THE AMERICAN ART FORM

I. Only art form to originate in America
    A.   West African rhythms--also gospel songs and spirituals, work songs, popular music of the 1800s
    B.   Mostly not written down--improvised. Musicians can play any notes as long as they don't clash. Langston Hughes, black writer, said "jazz began with people playing for fun."

Notice that the points of the report are listed in outline form, but that some specific details are included as well. They will allow the speaker to make particular points or to give quotations exactly.

When you give an oral report, keep the following guidelines in mind. They will help you prepare and deliver your report.

SPEAKING GUIDELINES: Giving an Oral Report

1. Keep your **purpose** in mind when you plan. Consider questions that your **audience** might ask.
2. Prepare note cards from which to speak. Include the main points of your report and any important details.
3. Practice with a friend or with a tape recorder.
4. Follow your outline or notes. Begin each part of your report with a clear topic sentence.
5. Look at your listeners frequently. Speak to them directly. Avoid reading your report word for word.
6. Speak clearly and distinctly. Vary the speed, volume, and tone of your voice. Use gestures where appropriate.

- Why is it important to begin each part of the report with a clear topic sentence?
- How does quoting sources make a report stronger?

SPEAKING APPLICATION An Oral Report

Prepare an oral report. You may speak on any subject of interest to you. Gather information by reading about your subject and taking notes. Organize your notes and prepare an outline or note cards from which to speak. Use the speaking guidelines to help you prepare. Your classmates will be using the following guidelines as they listen to your report.

LISTENING GUIDELINES: Listening to a Report

1. Listen for the speaker's main idea.
2. Listen for the details that provide information about the topic and that support the main idea.
3. Listen for points about which you would like to know more. Ask the speaker questions to find out more information.

THE CURRICULUM CONNECTION

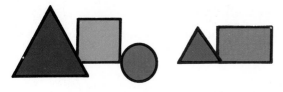

Writing About Mathematics

When you think about mathematics, you probably think first of the problems you see in your math book. The world of mathematics, however, extends to almost every facet of daily life. Mathematicians see principles of mathematics in art, science, geography, music, and sports, among other things. How often do you use math in your everyday life?

You recognize math in such activities as purchasing items or measuring a piece of wood. But you are also using mathematics when you decide what the chances are that you will have a quiz in history today. A mathematician would call it the law of probability. People who write about computer programs, business and finance, and games are often writing about mathematics. Clear, direct writing about mathematics helps readers form an accurate understanding of many aspects of the world in which we live.

ACTIVITIES

Visualize a How-to Project
Think of an object that you would like to make. It might be a birdhouse or a garment, for example. Draw a diagram of the object. Label your diagram with measurements and list the materials you will use along with their amounts. Then, write a brief explanation of how you would make the item. Share your project with an interested friend.

Explain Uses of Mathematics
Imagine a hardware or grocery store. How many things in it would require you to use your mathematics skills? To begin, make a list of items and the skills they would require. Then use these as examples in a paragraph on mathematics in daily life. Remember to begin with a topic sentence. Post your paragraph on the bulletin board.

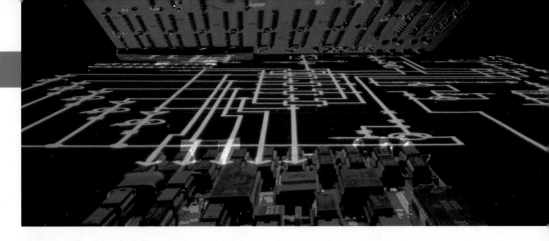

Respond to Literature

Write a response to the ideas in the selection below. Your response might be a story, an essay, or a research report.

Computers and You

A computer consists essentially of five functional elements—input, arithmetic, control, storage (or "memory"), and output. Through the input element it receives information (generally in numerical form) and adds, subtracts, multiplies, divides, rearranges, sorts, files, and extracts that information as instructed.

These capabilities are not startling by themselves. The speeds at which they are performed are, however. It would take one man a lifetime to do the calculating our fastest computers can do in three minutes.

Computers are not only much faster than man, but have better memories, are more accurate and more reliable.

In their exhaustive study of the year 2000, Herman Kahn and Anthony J. Wiener state: "Individual computers . . . will become essential equipment for home, school, business, and profession, and the ability to use a computer skillfully and flexibly may become more widespread than the ability to play bridge or drive a car (and presumably much easier)."

The computer is not, however, the machine to end all machines. Contrary to the image it inevitably projects, it is not perfect. As writer William Gilman has pointed out, it can't be programmed for judgment or courage; it is blind to emotion.

But such defects are desirable in that they remind us that the computer is only a tool of man (Superslave?), not a potential master, or even an equal.

UNIT CHECKUP

LESSON 1
Group Writing: A Research Report (page 488)   Read the following paragraph from a book entitled *Eskimo Folk Art* by Matilda Zim. Then prepare a note card for the paragraph. Be sure to include all the necessary information.

> Eskimo carvers produce some of the most beautiful stone and ivory carvings of any folk artists. Traditionally, carvings have been made of the animals of the Arctic hunted by the Eskimo: seals, walruses, bears, sea birds, wolves, and whales. Today, human figures engaged in kayaking or hunting may be found among the sculptures as well.

LESSON 2   **Thinking: Cause and Effect** (page 494)   Imagine that you are writing a science report on the causes and effects of the common cold. Which of the following items show cause and effect? Identify each cause and each effect.

1. Many work and school days are lost due to colds.
2. A cold is the result of an attack by a virus.
3. Colds may occur in either summer or winter.
4. The symptoms of a cold are due to the body's defenses against the virus.
5. Wet feet and drafts are harmless without the virus.
6. Some people only rarely develop colds.

LESSON 3   **Writing a Research Report** (page 496)   Imagine that you are a researcher who will write a report on computers. Narrow your topic. Then identify sources and gather information for a three-paragraph report. Organize your notes into an outline. Be sure to include an effective introduction and conclusion in your research report. Also include a bibliography at the end of your report. Remember to revise and proofread your report carefully. Then think of a way to share your research report with the audience you have chosen.

LESSON 4   **Speaking and Listening: Giving an Effective Oral Report** (page 506)   In a paragraph, summarize the steps for presenting an oral report effectively.

THEME PROJECT

CRAFTS

Think about the many kinds of traditions with which you are familiar. There are national traditions, local traditions, and family traditions. Ethnic foods and costumes are traditions. So are folklore and legends.

Look at the picture below. This picture shows a craftsperson at work. Talk with your classmates about different kinds of traditional crafts that you have seen or tried. How are they practiced? How did they begin?

Think of a traditional craft that interests you. It might be a useful craft such as weaving or basket making or a decorative craft like carving or paper folding. Then do one of the following as a group, class, or individual project.

- Interview a person who works at the craft or who sells craft items.
- Create a poem or picture based on the craft.
- Give an oral presentation about the craft.
- Organize a display of pictures or actual objects representing the craft.

Writer's Reference

CONTENTS

Language Study Handbook   513

Thesaurus for Writing   527

Letter Models   545

Spelling Strategies   547

Overview of the Writing Process   551

Writer's Resources
Study Strategies   552
Using the Parts of a Textbook   556
Using a Dictionary   557
Using the Library   560
Using Reference Works   562
Skimming and Scanning   564
Note Taking   566
Outlining   568
Atlases and Almanacs   570

Sentence Structure: Diagraming Guide   574

Glossary   583

LANGUAGE STUDY

H A N D B O O K

GRAMMAR

Sentences

A **sentence** is a group of words that expresses a complete thought.

There are four sentence types.
A **declarative** sentence makes a statement.

> This is an interesting book. (ends with a period)

An **interrogative** sentence asks a question.

> Who wrote the book? (ends with a question mark)

An **imperative** sentence gives a command or makes a request. (ends with a period)

> Look at that car.

An **exclamatory** sentence expresses strong feeling. (ends with an exclamation mark)

> I just won one million dollars!

The **complete subject** of a sentence includes all the words that tell what or whom the sentence is about.

> *The cold, dreary rain* fell for hours.

The **complete predicate** of a sentence includes all the words that tell what the subject does or is.

> The heavy clouds *slowly thickened across the sky.*

A **compound subject** is two or more simple subjects with the same predicate.

> *Lions and tigers* are both cats.

A **compound predicate** is two or more simple predicates with the same subject.

> Tigers *sleep, hunt, and prowl.*

A **run-on sentence** joins together two or more sentences that should be written separately.

> I had just sat down when the phone rang and I got up to answer it and I fell over the dog and it started to bark and then the phone stopped ringing.

Divide a run-on sentence into several sentences. The sentences may be simple, compound, or complex.

> I had just sat down when the phone rang. I got up to answer it. I fell over the dog, and it started to bark. Then the phone stopped ringing.

A **sentence fragment** is a group of words that is only part of a sentence. It does not have both a subject and a predicate, and it does not express a complete thought.

> The ways of the world. (fragment: no predicate)
> Cannot always be understood. (fragment: no subject)

Add a subject or a predicate to complete a fragment.

> The ways of the world cannot always be understood.

A **compound sentence** contains two or more simple sentences joined by *and*, *but*, or *or*.

> We collected money, *but* others collected clothing.

An **independent clause** has one complete subject and one complete predicate. It expresses a complete thought, and it can stand alone as a sentence.

> We packed boxes.

A **subordinate clause** is a group of words that has a subject and a predicate, but it cannot stand alone as a complete sentence.

> While others counted supplies.

A **complex sentence** contains an independent clause and one or more subordinate clauses.

> We packed boxes while others counted supplies.

An **adjective clause** is a subordinate clause used as an adjective to modify a noun or pronoun in an independent clause.

> I like movies *that tell about space travel.*

An **adverb clause** is a subordinate clause used as an adverb to modify the verb in an independent clause.

> I see science fiction movies *whenever I can.*

Nouns

A **noun** is a word that names a person, place, thing, or idea.

officer   classroom   bell   freedom

A **concrete noun** names something that you can see or touch.

book   skin   hall   feather

An **abstract noun** names something that you cannot see or touch, such as emotions or ideas.

joy   peace   honesty   anger

A **proper noun** names a specific person, place, or thing.

Pocahontas   Utah   Washington Monument

A **collective noun** names a group of people or things.

committee   family   club   collection

A **compound noun** is formed from two or more words that work together as a single noun.

dining room   Abraham Lincoln   son-in-law

A **plural noun** is a noun that names more than one person, place, thing, or idea.

officers   classrooms   bells   freedoms

An **appositive** is a word or group of words that follows and identifies a noun.

George Washington, *our first President,* was a Virginian.

Verbs

An **action verb** is a word that expresses action.

run   play   shout   sleep

A **linking verb** is a verb that links the subject of a sentence to a noun or an adjective in the predicate.

Lewis and Clark *were* brave explorers.

A **direct object** is a noun or pronoun that receives the action of a verb. A verb that takes a direct object is a **transitive verb**.

John Paul Jones fought several *battles.*

An **indirect object** is a noun or pronoun that answers the question *to whom? for whom? to what?* or *for what?* after an action verb.

I gave *Mother* the vase of flowers.

The time expressed by a verb is called its **tense**. The three simple tenses are **past** (the action has already happened), **present** (the action is happening now), and **future** (the action will happen in the future).

> We *watched* the football game.   (past)
> We *watch* the football game.   (present)
> We *will watch* the football game.   (future)

A **verb phrase** consists of a main verb and all of its helping verbs.

> I *would choose* a darker red.

The **progressive** form of a verb expresses action that is or was continuing for some time.

> I *am singing.*   (present progressive)
> I *was singing.*   (past progressive)

The **present perfect** tense of a verb expresses action that happened at an indefinite time in the past.

> I *have eaten.*   (present perfect)
> Before I left, I *had eaten.*   (past perfect)
> By noon, I *will have eaten.*   (future perfect)

Most verbs add **d** or **ed** to form the past tense. (wait—*waited*; close—*closed*) An **irregular verb** does not use this pattern. You must memorize the irregular verb forms. Here are some examples of irregular verbs.

Present	Past	Past with Helping Verb
be	was	been
begin	began	begun
blow	blew	blown
come	came	come
drive	drove	driven
go	went	gone
hide	hid	hidden
set	set	set
take	took	taken

Pronouns

A **pronoun** takes the place of one or more nouns and the words that go with the nouns.

> The black dog barked. *It* barked.

An **antecedent** is a word or group of words to which a pronoun refers.

> *Betsy Ross* picked up a needle, and then *she* smiled.

A **subject pronoun** is a pronoun that is used as the subject of a sentence.

> I, you, he, she, it, we, they

An **object pronoun** is a pronoun that is used as the object of a verb or as the object of a preposition.

> me, you, him, her, it, us, them

A **possessive pronoun** shows who or what owns something.

> my, your, his, her, its, our, their

An **indefinite pronoun** is a pronoun that does not refer to a particular person, place, or thing.

> all, any, anyone, each, every, everybody, few, nobody

A **reflexive pronoun** points the action of the verb back to the subject. Reflexive pronouns end in *self* or *selves*.

> He gave the speech *himself*.

An **interrogative pronoun** is a pronoun used to form questions.

> *Who* is that?   *Whom* did you ask?

A **demonstrative pronoun** is a pronoun that points out specific persons, places, things, or ideas and stands alone in a sentence.

> this   that   these   those

Adjectives

An **adjective** is a word that describes a noun or pronoun.

> *important* papers   *frequent* travelers

The words *a*, *an*, and *the* are special adjectives called **articles**. *A* and *an* are **indefinite articles** because they do not refer to a particular noun or pronoun. *The* is called a **definite article** because it identifies a specific person, place, thing, or idea.

A **proper adjective** is formed from a proper noun and begins with a capital letter.

> *Spanish* lace   *Chinese* alphabet

A **comparative adjective** compares two nouns. To form a comparative adjective, add *er* or use the word *more*.

> the *smaller* model   the *more intelligent* dog

A **superlative adjective** compares more than two nouns. To form a superlative adjective, add *est* or use the word *most*.

> the *largest* barn   the *most beautiful* garden

A **demonstrative adjective** points out something and describes nouns by answering the question *which one?* or *which ones?*

> *this* car   *that* coat   *these* gloves   *those* shoes

Adverbs

An **adverb** is a word that modifies a verb, an adjective, or another adverb.

> The cat climbed *carefully*.
> The tree was *very* tall.
> The children watched *really quietly*.

An **intensifier** is an adverb that emphasizes or intensifies an adjective or adverb.

> That is an *extremely* old statue.
> Examine it *very* carefully.

A **comparative adverb** compares two actions. Comparative adverbs are usually formed with the word *more*.

> swam *more beautifully*

A **superlative adverb** compares more than two actions. Superlative adverbs are usually formed with the word *most*.

> worked *most carefully*

Prepositions

A **preposition** is a word that relates a noun or pronoun to another word in a sentence.

> I walked *to* the store.

A **prepositional phrase** is a group of words that begins with a preposition and ends with a noun or pronoun.

> I walked *to the store*.

The noun or pronoun that completes a prepositional phrase is called the **object of the preposition**.

> I walked to the *store*.

If a prepositional phrase tells *how*, *where*, or *when*, it is an **adverb phrase**.

> He played *near the lake*.

If a prepositional phrase tells *how many* or *which one*, it is an **adjective phrase**.

> I watched the dog *in the corner*.

Conjunctions

A **conjunction** is a word that joins words or groups of words. A **coordinating conjunction** is a single word that joins words, groups of words, or sentences.

> Dave *and* Linda need a book of facts *or* a new encyclopedia.
> Dave is finished, *but* Linda hasn't begun.

Correlative conjunctions are pairs of words used to join words or groups of words.

> *both* black *and* white   *neither* blue *nor* yellow

Interjections

An **interjection** is a word or group of words that expresses strong feeling.

> Wow!   Gee!   Oops!   Oh, no!

Verbals

A **participle** is a verb form used as an adjective.

> The *finished* house was ready for occupancy.
> The *traveling* salesperson rang our doorbell.

A **participial phrase** is a group of words that includes a participle and other words that complete its meaning.

> *Using a rusted fork*, the prisoner dug a tunnel.

A **gerund** is a verb form that ends in *ing* and is used as a noun.

> *Swimming* is fine exercise.

A **gerund phrase** is a group of words that includes a gerund and other words that complete its meaning.

> *Choosing the proper sport* is a serious decision.

An **infinitive** is formed with the word *to* and the base form of a verb. An infinitive is often used as a noun in a sentence.

> *To practice* is the secret of success.

An **infinitive phrase** is a group of words that includes an infinitive and other words that complete its meaning.

> Success means *to do your best consistently*.

MECHANICS

Punctuation

Periods

Use a period to show the end of an abbreviation.

Ms.   Sr.   Rev.   Ave.

Use a period after initials.

C.S. Lewis   T.S. Eliot

Colons

Use a colon after the greeting in a business letter.

Dear Sir or Madam:

Commas

Use commas before the conjunction in a compound sentence.

I wanted to stay, but I knew I had to go.

Use commas between names of cities and states.

Springfield, Illinois   Midland, Texas   Salem, Oregon

Use a comma to separate the day and year in a date.

January 1, 1863   July 20, 1969

Use commas to separate words in a series.

Oahu, Maui, and Lanai are some of the Hawaiian Islands.

Use commas after the greeting and closing in a letter.

Dear Lao,   Sincerely,

Use commas after introductory words or phrases.

No, this is not the way out of the tunnel.
As a matter of fact, we are going the wrong way.

Use commas to set off words in direct address and appositives.

You, Luisa, will make the final decision.
Luisa, the class president, agreed with me.

Apostrophes

Use apostrophes (') in contractions to show where letters are missing.

shouldn't   o'clock   isn't

Use apostrophes with nouns to show possession. Add **'s** to singular nouns or plural nouns that do not end in **s**.

Hobson's choice   children's hour
Bess's eyeglasses   Leon Jones's sisters

Add **'** to plural nouns ending in **s**.

bees' knees   whales' tails
the Joneses' new house

Semicolons

Use a semicolon (;) to connect two simple sentences in a compound sentence when a conjunction is not used.

The earth turns; slowly, night becomes day.

Dashes

Use a dash to show that a thought was unfinished or interrupted. If the sentence continues, use a second dash to mark the end of an interruption.

The astronaut spoke about the need for training in simulators because—but you know the rest.

Hyphens

Use a hyphen to show the division of a word at the end of a line. Always divide the word between syllables.

Astronauts operate spacecraft and conduct engineering and medical experiments in space.

Use a hyphen in compound numbers from twenty-one through ninety-nine.

seventy-six trombones   twenty-three flights

Titles

Underline the titles of full-length books. Put quotation marks around the titles of movies, short stories, poems, and plays.

A Wrinkle in Time
"Beauty and the Beast"

Capitalize the first word and all important words in the titles of books, plays, short stories, poems, movies, and television shows.

Little Women
"Star Wars"

Writing Quotations

Capitalize the first word of a quotation.

> We asked, "**W**ill there be enough for everyone?"

Do *not* capitalize the first letter of the explanatory words unless they are the first words of a sentence.

> "**W**ill there be enough for everyone?" **w**e asked.

Do *not* capitalize the second part of an interrupted quotation unless it begins a new sentence.

> "**W**ill there," we asked, "**b**e enough for everyone?"

Use a comma to separate a quotation from the explanatory words at the beginning of a sentence.

> King said, "I have a dream."

Use a comma instead of a period at the end of a statement or command in a quotation at the beginning of a sentence.

> "I have a dream," said King.

Punctuate quoted questions or exclamations in the usual way. The end punctuation goes *before* the second quotation mark unless the punctuation mark is part of the entire sentence and not part of the quotation. The first explanatory word is not capitalized.

> "We won the game!" the students cheered.
> Did Ms. Osmond say, "Jumbo jets entered airline service in 1970"?

Abbreviations

Abbreviations are shortened forms of words. An abbreviation ends with a period.

> *Prof.* Amanda Mercado   Edward S. Lunes, *Jr.*

There are many common abbreviations used in addresses.

> St. (street)   Blvd. (boulevard)   Ave. (avenue)

You will often see these abbreviations in company names.

> Co. (company)   Inc. (incorporated)

Some abbreviations use all capital letters.

> P.M.   B.C.   M.D.

Some abbreviations do not use a period at the end.

> NATO   AFL-CIO   OAS   USMC

Postal Abbreviations

Use the United States Postal Service abbreviations for state names. Notice that each abbreviation consists of *two* capital letters. No period follows these abbreviations.

AL (Alabama)	LA (Louisiana)	OH (Ohio)
AK (Alaska)	ME (Maine)	OK (Oklahoma)
AZ (Arizona)	MD (Maryland)	OR (Oregon)
AR (Arkansas)	MA (Massachusetts)	PA (Pennsylvania)
CA (California)	MI (Michigan)	RI (Rhode Island)
CO (Colorado)	MN (Minnesota)	SC (South Carolina)
CT (Connecticut)	MS (Mississippi)	SD (South Dakota)
DE (Delaware)	MO (Missouri)	TN (Tennessee)
FL (Florida)	MT (Montana)	TX (Texas)
GA (Georgia)	NE (Nebraska)	UT (Utah)
HI (Hawaii)	NV (Nevada)	VT (Vermont)
ID (Idaho)	NH (New Hampshire)	VA (Virginia)
IL (Illinois)	NJ (New Jersey)	WA (Washington)
IN (Indiana)	NM (New Mexico)	WV (West Virginia)
IA (Iowa)	NY (New York)	WI (Wisconsin)
KS (Kansas)	NC (North Carolina)	WY (Wyoming)
KY (Kentucky)	ND (North Dakota)	

Capitalization

Capitalize the names and initials of specific persons, places, or things.

> John **F.** Kennedy   Baton **R**ouge   Uncle **H**enry

Capitalize titles of respect or their abbreviations when they are part of a specific name.

> **G**eneral Moses   **D**r. Elizabeth Blackwell

Always capitalize the first-person pronoun *I*.

Capitalize words that show family relationships only when they are used as substitutes for a person's name.

> I asked **M**other for permission to see the movie.
> (*but:* My **m**other had already seen the movie herself.)

Capitalize the names of religious books.

> The **B**ible is divided into many books.

Capitalize the days of the week and the months of the year.

> Tuesday   Thursday   March   November

Capitalize names of holidays and religious days.

Valentine's **Day**   Labor **Day**   Yom **Kippur**

Capitalize names of cities, states, countries, and other specific geographic locations.

Miami   **Kentucky**   **Egypt**   **Pike's Peak**

Capitalize titles of specific clubs and organizations.

Corps of Engineers   **New York Philharmonic Orchestra**

Capitalize the names of political and ethnic groups.

Democrats   **Republicans**   **Sioux**   **Hispanics**

Capitalize proper adjectives.

Peruvian   **Australian**   **Californian**   **Japanese**

Capitalize all words in the greeting of a letter.

Dear Reader,

Capitalize only the first word in a letter's closing.

Very truly yours,

Capitalize the names of important historical eras, events, and documents.

Renaissance   **Declaration of Independence**
Great Depression

Capitalize names of languages.

English   **Swahili**

USAGE

Verbs

Subjects and verbs must agree in **number.** If a subject is singular, the verb must be singular as well. If a subject is plural, the verb must be plural as well.

> The busy *student works* hard.(singular subject and verb)
> The busy *students work* hard. (plural subject and verb)

If a compound subject is connected by *and,* use a plural verb. If a compound subject is connected by *or,* use the verb that agrees with the second part of the subject.

> North *and* South Dakota *were* admitted together. (plural)
> North Dakota *or* South Dakota *is* the 39th state. (singular)

The subject and verb must agree even when the subject appears after the verb.

> Where in the world *are* Alex and Jonny?

Sometimes a phrase comes between the subject and the verb.

> The *cat* with the white paws *hisses* at the children.

Pronouns

When a pronoun is in a compound subject, use a subject pronoun.

> The dog and *he* went for a walk.

When a pronoun is in a compound object, use an object pronoun.

> Give the charts to Sally and *him.*
> I saw Mark and *her* at the show.

Use *I* or *me* last when it appears in a compound subject or compound object.

> Al and *I* swim.   Tell Joe and *me.*

Pronoun Antecedents

Be sure pronoun antecedents are clear. Some sentences have to be reworded so that the antecedent is clear.

> Steve had questions about his homework, so he asked Mark for help. (clear)
> Steve asked Mark questions about his homework. (unclear)

Adjectives

Do not use *more* or *most* with adjectives that already show comparison.

China is *larger* than India.   (correct)
China is *more larger* than India.   (incorrect)

Some adjectives are **irregular**. That is, they do not form their comparison forms in the usual way.

Adjective	Compares Two Nouns	Compares More Than Two Nouns
good	better	best
bad	worse	worst
much	more	most
little	less	least

To make an adjective into an adverb, add **ly** to the end of many adjectives.

honest—*honestly*   careful—*carefully*

Adverbs

Negatives (*never, none, not, nothing, can't, don't*) are words that mean *no*. Use only one negative in a sentence. A **double negative** is the incorrect use of two negatives in a sentence.

I was doing *nothing*.   (correct: single negative)
I was *not* doing *nothing*.   (incorrect: double negative)

Good-Well, Bad-Badly

Good and *bad* are adjectives. They tell about nouns.

He was a *good* student.   They made a *bad* mistake.

Well and *badly* are adverbs. They describe verbs.

The play began *well*.   It was written *badly*.

Use *well* when talking about health.

I am not feeling *well* today.

Misplaced Modifiers

Place phrases as close as possible to the words they modify. Otherwise, the sentence may be confusing.

On her way to play, Mary saw the old woman. (clear)
Mary saw the old woman *on her way to play*. (misplaced)

THESAURUS FOR WRITING

What Is a Thesaurus?

A thesaurus is a reference book that can be very useful in your writing. It provides synonyms for many common words. **Synonyms** are words that mean almost the same thing.

The thesaurus can help you choose more interesting words and more exact words to use in your writing. For example, you may write this sentence: The land was dry from the long drought. *Dry* is not a very interesting word; nor is it very exact. If you look up the word *dry* in the thesaurus, you will find these words: *arid, desiccated, parched, sere.* Each of these words means "dry," but each one suggests a certain kind of dryness.

Using the Thesaurus

The words in a thesaurus are listed in alphabetical order. If the word is listed in the thesaurus, you will find an entry. For example, if you looked up *neat,* you would find this entry.

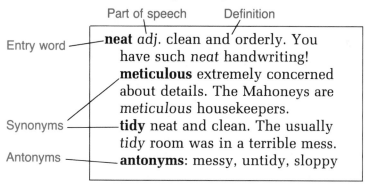

The word *neat* is called an entry word. The information that follows is called the entry. The entry for *neat* gives the part of speech, a definition of the word, and an example sentence. Below that are synonyms. Each synonym is defined, especially in how it differs from *neat,* and is used in an example sentence.

Cross-References

In some cases you will find cross-references. For example, if you look up the word *allow,* you will find this cross-reference: "See *let.*" This means that you should look up the word *let;* the word *allow* will be listed under *let.*

A

agree *v.* to say "yes"; to have the same opinion; to be in harmony. You *agreed* to baby-sit on Friday.
assent to express acceptance (of an idea, proposal, etc.). Dad quickly *assented* to Brian's plan.
concur to have the same opinion. I *concur* with your views.
consent to give permission or approval. Did your parents *consent* to your being on the team?

allow *See* let.

angry *adj.* feeling or showing anger. The *angry* cat hissed at us.
choleric easily irritated or angered. Jack's *choleric* nature makes him hard to get along with.
enraged filled with rage; angry beyond control. *Enraged* by their teasing, the bull chased the boys.
furious extremely angry. Dina was *furious* to find her tools broken.
incensed filled with anger. Herb was *incensed* by the misleading report.
resentful feeling bitter or indignant. The man's co-workers were *resentful* of his promotion.
Other synonyms: outraged, irate, infuriated, irascible, cross, irritated, displeased

answer *v.* to give a spoken or written response. No one *answered* when I knocked on the door.
reply to say in response. What should I *reply* if she asks me?

respond to give an answer. Did you *respond* to the invitation?
retort to reply, usually sharply, to criticism or a remark. Gerry quickly *retorted* to Howard's insult.
antonyms: ask, inquire

ask *v.* to put a question to. *Ask* that woman what time it is.
inquire to seek information by asking questions. A man called to *inquire* about buying our old car.
query to seek a formal answer to a question. The reporter *queried* the scientists about their work.
question to try to get information (from someone). Mr. Drew *questioned* the kids about their plans for the evening.
antonyms: *See* answer.

awful *adj.* causing fear, dread, or awe. Look at this *awful* spider.
dreadful causing great fear. Entire villages were wiped out by the *dreadful* disease.
frightful causing fright. The bear let out a *frightful* growl.
horrible arousing feelings of horror. Kay couldn't forget the movie's *horrible* ending.
terrible causing terror or awe. The king was in a *terrible* rage.
Other synonyms: dire, shocking, ominous, horrifying, ghastly

B

beautiful *adj.* full of beauty; having qualities that are pleasing. This book contains *beautiful* illustrations.

attractive appealing or pleasing, but not in an exceptional way. Pam has an *attractive* haircut.

gorgeous extremely beautiful or richly colored. The flower-covered hillside was a *gorgeous* sight.

lovely beautiful in a comforting way. Nate has a *lovely* smile.

pretty pleasing or attractive, often said of something small or dainty. What a *pretty* necklace!

antonyms: ugly, unattractive
Other synonyms: stunning, striking, appealing, handsome

big *adj.* of great size. We picked a *big* bunch of daisies.

enormous much greater than the usual size. The waiter brought me an *enormous* dish of spaghetti.

gigantic like a giant in size. Dinosaurs were *gigantic* animals.

huge extremely big. A *huge* wave nearly capsized the boat.

large of great size; big. That coat is too *large* for you.

antonyms: See little.
Other synonyms: monstrous, massive, titanic

brave *adj.* willing to face danger; without fear. The *brave* rescuers made their way toward the wreck.

bold showing courage; fearless. Challenging the country's dictator was a *bold* move.

courageous having courage. One *courageous* boy rescued the group.

daring willing to take risks. Are you *daring* enough to jump off the high diving board?

antonyms: afraid, fearful
Other synonyms: intrepid, fearless, dauntless

break *v.* to come apart; to separate into pieces. Who *broke* the clock?

crack to break without fully separating. Tim *cracked* a plate while he was doing the dishes.

fracture to break or split a bone. She *fractured* her wrist when she fell.

shatter to break suddenly into many pieces. The bottles *shattered* as we tossed them into the bin.

Other synonyms: split, splinter, smash, burst

bright *adj.* filled with light; shining. I saw a *bright* spotlight.

brilliant shining or sparkling with light. The case was filled with *brilliant* jewels.

glistening shining with reflected light. By moonlight, we paddled across the *glistening* lake.

luminous giving off light. All that remained of the fire was a few *luminous* coals.

shiny shining; bright. The child was delighted by the *shiny* penny.

antonyms: dark, dull

C

cheap *adj.* low in price; inferior in quality or value. Where can we get a *cheap* meal?

cut-rate sold or selling at a reduced or cheap price. Green's is a *cut-rate* department store.

economical operating cheaply; inexpensive. Our new car is very *economical* to run.

gaudy tastelessly bright or ornate. Lou hated the *gaudy* orange sweater he received.
inexpensive low in price. They want to buy an *inexpensive* camera.
antonym: expensive

clean *adj.* without dirt or stain. "Put on a *clean* shirt," said Mom.
immaculate perfectly clean. The kitchen was *immaculate*.
pure free from contamination. The hiker drank the *pure* spring water.
spic-and-span fresh, neat, and clean. The apartment was *spic-and-span* when we arrived.
spotless extremely clean. Vera's new sneakers were *spotless*.
antonyms: dirty, filthy, messy

cold *adj.* having a low temperature; lacking warmth or heat. Milk tastes better when it's *cold*.
chilly uncomfortably cool. The wind made James feel *chilly*.
frigid extremely cold. Few people live in the *frigid* Arctic region.
icy very cold. I rubbed her *icy* hands to warm them.
antonyms: See hot.
Other synonyms: frosty, nippy, raw, bitter, wintry

collect *v.* to gather or bring (things) together. *Collect* your dirty clothes so I can wash them.
assemble to gather or bring together, especially people. We *assembled* at the wedding.

compile to collect and put together (information), as in a list or report. The teacher will *compile* a summer reading list.
gather to bring together in one place or group. The girl *gathered* flowers to decorate the table.

cook *v.* to prepare food for eating, using heat. Pat *cooked* an egg.
bake to cook in an oven. Mrs. Kaye likes to *bake* her own bread.
broil to cook by exposing to a flame or other source of intense heat. Let's *broil* some steaks.
fry to cook in a pan over direct heat, using hot oil or fat. Jack plans to *fry* the fish he caught.
roast to cook with very little moisture, in an oven or over an open fire. The campers put ears of corn in the campfire to *roast*.
Other synonyms: sauté, boil

crazy *adj.* not having a sound or normal mind. You'd have to be *crazy* to go out in such a storm.
insane mentally ill. *Insane* people can often be cured.
mad out of one's mind. Harold was almost *mad* with jealousy.
Other synonyms: deranged, lunatic, berserk

cry *v.* to shed tears. The big kids teased Nan to make her *cry*.
bawl to cry loudly. The child *bawled* when his parents left.
sob to cry with short gasps. Ted *sobbed* as he told about the fire.
weep to show grief, joy, or other strong emotions by crying. We *wept* at the news of Fred's recovery.

whimper to cry with weak, broken sounds. The sick baby just lay in the crib and *whimpered*.
whine to make a high-pitched, mournful cry of pain or distress. The stray dog *whined* with hunger.
antonyms: See laugh.

D

do *v.* to carry out. Please *do* your homework before you go out.
achieve to bring about an intended result. The athlete will try to *achieve* a new record.
contrive to bring about, especially with difficulty. How did they *contrive* their escape?
execute to complete, often when told to do so; to put into effect. Mr. Brooks *executed* his instructions.
perform to carry out to completion. A priest *performed* the wedding ceremony.

dry *adj.* not wet; free of moisture. You can put the *dry* dishes away.
arid dry as a result of having little rainfall. One *arid* region has not had rain for five years!
desiccated completely dried up. I found a *desiccated* old apple on the window sill.
parched dried out by heat. Her skin was *parched* from the sun.
sere withered; dry. The crops in the field were brown and *sere*.
antonyms: See wet.

E

easy *adj.* requiring little mental or physical effort; not difficult. Sweeping is an *easy* chore.

effortless seeming to require little effort. Everyone admired the skater's *effortless* moves.
facile not hard to do or achieve; done easily and quickly. A *facile* solution may not be the best one.
simple not complicated. Do you have any *simple* recipes?
antonyms: difficult, hard

F

far *adj.* a long way off; not near. Is it *far* from here to your house?
distant extremely far. We heard the whistle of a *distant* train.
remote far away, in an out-of-the-way place. The monks lived in a *remote* monastery.
antonyms: near, close

fast *adj.* moving or done with speed. Most of the kids prefer *fast* dances.
quick done in a very short time. Dad took a *quick* look at his mail.
rapid with great speed, often in a continuing way. The reporter made some *rapid* notes on his pad.
speedy characterized by rapid motion. The winner of the race was a *speedy* little sailboat.
swift moving with great speed, often said of animals or people. Cheetahs are *swift* runners.
antonym: slow

funny *adj.* causing laughter. Cartoons are meant to be *funny*.
amusing causing smiles of enjoyment or laughter. Cathy wrote an *amusing* story about her dog.

comical causing laughter through actions. It was *comical* to watch Uncle Henry dance.

hilarious very funny; usually noisy. The pictures from Meg's surprise party were *hilarious.*

humorous funny in a mild or regular way. Ernie did not find Will's joke *humorous* at all.

G

get *v.* to go for and return with. Please *get* some milk at the store.

acquire to come into possession of through effort. Over the years, he *acquired* great wealth.

earn to gain through effort. Did you *earn* much in your summer job?

obtain to get as one's own, often with some difficulty. Tickets must be *obtained* ahead of time.

procure to get hold of through effort. The sailor *procured* some rope from another boat.

give *v.* to turn over possession or control of; to make a present of. Brent forgot to *give* me my book.

confer to give as an honor. The President will *confer* a medal on the soldier.

contribute to give or supply in common with others. Each family will *contribute* to the bake sale.

grant to give in response to a request. The teacher *granted* the class more time to prepare their reports.

present to give in a formal way, usually something of value. Mr. Gray will *present* the diplomas.
antonyms: See take.

good *adj.* above average in quality; not bad. She writes *good* poems.

excellent extremely good. Pat is an *excellent* cook.

fair somewhat good; slightly better than average. The movie was *fair*, but I wouldn't see it again.

fine of high quality; very good. The table was set with *fine* china.

antonyms: bad, poor
See also great.

great *adj.* of unusual quality or ability. Most people agree that Lincoln was a *great* president.

remarkable having unusual qualities. Mr. Liang reread Lyle's *remarkable* essay.

superb of greater quality than most. Let's eat at that *superb* restaurant on Green Street.

wonderful very good; excellent. You should see the Drama Club's *wonderful* new play.
See also good.

H

happy *adj.* having, showing, or bringing pleasure. Ann is *happy* to be going to camp.

gay full of joy and fun. The *gay* music made Rena feel like dancing.

glad feeling or expressing joy or pleasure. Brian was *glad* to see Nick.

joyful very happy; filled with joy. Ana called to share her *joyful* news.

merry happy and cheerful. Cal's *merry* laughter made us laugh, too.

pleased satisfied or content. Kim was *pleased* with her report card.

antonyms: *See* sad.

Other synonyms: delighted, contented, ecstatic, elated, jubilant, overjoyed

hard *adj.* not easy to do or deal with. The jar was *hard* to open.

difficult hard to do; requiring effort. Len's sore throat made talking *difficult*.

tough difficult to do, often in a physical sense. It was *tough* to fit everything in one box.

antonym: easy

help *v.* to provide with support; be of service to. Marie *helped* her brother climb over the fence.

aid to give help to (someone in trouble). The lifeguard *aided* me when I got a cramp.

assist to help, often in a cooperative way. The clerk can *assist* you in picking out a gift.

remedy to cause to heal or improve. What can we do to *remedy* this bad situation?

succor to give help, assistance, or relief to. The woman did what she could to *succor* the refugees.

high *adj.* located or extending a great distance above the ground. Their apartment has *high* ceilings.

elevated raised; high. The train runs on *elevated* tracks.

lofty very high; of grand or inspiring height. The hawk soared at a *lofty* height.

tall having a height greater than average, but with a relatively narrow width. Our town has very few *tall* buildings.

towering of great or imposing height. The little girl looked up at her *towering* father.

antonyms: low, short

hot *adj.* having a high temperature; having much heat. Watch out for the *hot* coals.

fiery as hot as fire; burning. The sick child's skin was *fiery*.

scalding hot enough to burn, often said of liquids. The hot water in the shower is *scalding*.

scorching intensely hot, enough to cause burning or drying. The air near the fire was *scorching*.

tepid slightly warm; lukewarm. A baby's bath water should be *tepid*.

torrid extremely hot, often said of weather. Parts of Kenya are quite *torrid*.

antonyms: *See* cold.

Other synonyms: blistering, blazing, sweltering

hurt *v.* to cause pain or damage. It *hurt* when Jeffy pulled my hair.

bruise to cause a bruise on the surface of; to injure or hurt slightly. The false rumors *bruised* the senator's reputation.

damage to injure or harm in a way that causes loss. An unexpected frost *damaged* the tomato plants.

harm to do damage to. The hen thought we would *harm* her.

injure to cause physical damage. Gladys *injured* her knee playing basketball.

I

important *adj.* having special value, meaning, authority, or influence. The President will make an *important* speech on Tuesday.
consequential important, usually because of an actual or expected outcome. His book contains a number of *consequential* new ideas.
noteworthy worthy of special notice or attention. Several *noteworthy* remarks were made during the debate.
prominent well-known or important. Margot's father is a *prominent* lawyer.
significant having special meaning or importance that may not be immediately apparent. The fossil was a *significant* find.
antonyms: insignificant, unimportant, trivial
Other synonyms: momentous, crucial, critical

information *n.* knowledge or facts. Where can I find *information* about the 1849 gold rush?
data information from which conclusions can be drawn; facts and figures. The scientist is collecting *data* about rainfall.
facts information known to be true or real. Just give me the *facts*, not your opinions.
statistics numerical data. The *statistics* show an increase in population.

interesting *adj.* arousing or holding interest or attention. We saw an *interesting* exhibit.
captivating capturing and holding the attention of by beauty or excellence. The singer gave a *captivating* performance.
fascinating causing and holding interest through a special quality or charm. India is a *fascinating* country.
inspiring having a rousing effect; arousing interest. The band played some *inspiring* music.
antonyms: dull, boring
Other synonyms: engrossing, gripping, absorbing, thought-provoking

L

large *See* big.

laugh *v.* to make the sounds and facial movements that show amusement. That comedian loved to make people *laugh*.
chortle to chuckle gleefully. "You'll never guess the surprise!" *chortled* Marisa.
chuckle to laugh softly, especially to oneself. Howie *chuckled* each time he remembered Paul's joke.
giggle to laugh in a silly, high-pitched, or nervous way. The girl *giggled* whenever Pete spoke to her.
guffaw to laugh loudly. Someone in the audience *guffawed*.
snicker to laugh slyly, in a disrespectful way. Cleo *snickered* when her brother got in trouble.
antonyms: *See* cry.
Other synonyms: titter, crow, cackle, whoop

let *v.* to give permission to. Please *let* me go with you.
allow to grant permission to or for, usually in relation to rules. Will the school *allow* us to have a dance in the gym?
concede to grant or yield; to give in. The candidate *conceded* the election to his opponent.
permit to allow (a person) to do something. Ms. Rufus will not *permit* anyone to leave early.
antonyms: deny, refuse, forbid

like *v.* to take pleasure in (something); to feel affection for (someone). I don't *like* eggs.
admire to have affection and respect for (someone). Katie *admires* her older sister.
enjoy to take pleasure in (something). After dinner, they both *enjoy* a good game of chess.
love to like (something) a lot; to feel great affection for (someone). Lee *loves* to cook.
antonyms: dislike, hate
Other synonyms: relish, savor, cherish, appreciate, approve

little *adj.* small in size; not big. We found some *little* lavender flowers.
small not large. He has very *small* feet for such a big man.
tiny extremely small. The plant's stem was covered with *tiny* hairs.
wee very small. Can you believe that big dog was once a *wee* puppy?
antonyms: See big.
Other synonyms: puny, minute, minuscule

look *v.* to see with one's eyes. Tommy *looked* out the window.
glance to look quickly. The woman *glanced* up when we came in.
peer to look closely. Tina *peered* out through a crack in the door.
regard to look at attentively. The students *regarded* the chalkboard during the lesson.
stare to look at for a long time with eyes wide open. Mike *stared* at me as though I were crazy.
Other synonyms: behold, perceive, discern, inspect, scan
See *also* see.

loud *adj.* having a strong sound. The lion let out a *loud* roar.
deafening loud enough to make one deaf. His radio was so loud that the sound was *deafening*.
noisy full of sounds, often unpleasant. The gym is very *noisy* during basketball games.
raucous loud and rowdy. A *raucous* crowd gathered in the street.
vociferous characterized by a loud outcry. *Vociferous* boos followed the referee's call.
antonyms: See quiet.

M
mad See angry; *see* crazy.

many *adj.* consisting of a large number. Will there be *many* people at the party?
myriad of indefinitely large number; countless. They have had *myriad* arguments on this subject.

numerous a great many. *Numerous* people have asked for this book.

plenty (of) enough, or more than enough, suggesting a large number. Take *plenty* of change for the bus.

several more than a few but less than many. He bought *several* pens.

antonym: few

mean *adj.* lacking in kindness or understanding. That *mean* man scowled at the children.

cruel willing to cause pain or suffering to others. Pam says it is *cruel* to put animals in cages.

malicious desiring to cause pain, injury, or misfortune to another. Some *malicious* person slashed the tires on our bikes.

nasty resulting from hate. Who would start such a *nasty* rumor?

selfish concerned only about oneself. The *selfish* boy kept all the cookies for himself.

spiteful filled with ill feelings toward others. Allen's *spiteful* words hurt Judy's feelings.

antonyms: See nice.

N

neat *adj.* clean and orderly. You have such *neat* handwriting.

meticulous extremely concerned about details. The Mahoneys are *meticulous* housekeepers.

tidy neat and clean, often said of a place. The usually *tidy* room was in a terrible mess.

well-groomed carefully dressed and groomed. Mother insists that we leave for school *well-groomed*.

antonyms: messy, untidy, sloppy

new *adj.* having just come into being, use, or possession. We got a *new* bird feeder today.

fresh new or seeming new and unaffected by time or use. This looks like a *fresh* coat of paint.

innovative newly introduced or changed. Mr. Hutchins liked the architect's *innovative* plans.

modern having to do with the present time; up-to-date. The museum's *modern* art collection is in the west wing.

novel new and unusual. This catalog offers *novel* gifts for the person who has everything.

recent referring to a time just before the present. Did you read the *recent* article on tornadoes?

antonym: old

nice *adj.* agreeable or pleasing. We live on a very *nice* street.

agreeable to one's liking; pleasant. They spent an *agreeable* afternoon in the park.

gentle mild and kindly in manner. Be *gentle* when you hold the puppy.

kind/kindly gentle and friendly; good-hearted. People like Ann because she is *kind* to everyone.

pleasant agreeable; giving pleasure to. I hope you had a *pleasant* visit.

sweet having or marked by agreeable or pleasing qualities. He was *sweet* to send flowers.

antonyms: See mean.

O

often *adv.* many times; again and again. He *often* walks to work.
frequently happening again and again. She was *frequently* ill.
regularly happening at fixed times. Have you ever exercised *regularly*?
repeatedly over and over again. That pesky salesman has called us *repeatedly*.
antonyms: seldom, rarely

old *adj.* having lived or existed for a long time. These *old* toys belonged to my grandfather.
aged having grown old. Mr. Fox's *aged* aunt lives upstairs.
ancient of great age; very old; of times long past. The expedition found an *ancient* city.
hoary white or gray with age; very old. Grandpa's long white beard makes him look *hoary*.
antonym: young
Other synonyms: archaic, elder, venerable, senior, antique

P

particular *adj.* separate or distinct from any other; of or for a single definite person, group, or thing. Do you have a *particular* color in mind?
certain definite but not named; agreed upon or determined. She can't eat *certain* foods.
specific distinctly or explicitly named. The recipe calls for a *specific* kind of cheese.

plain *adj.* not distinguished from others in any way. Karen thought her face was too *plain*.
common average or standard; not distinguished. Sparrows are *common* birds.
homely of a familiar or everyday nature. Lisa's *homely* ways made her guests feel at ease.
ordinary average. Willie's "monster" was really just an *ordinary* frog.
antonym: special; *see also* unusual.

possible *adj.* capable of existing, happening, being done, or being proven true. It's *possible* that Uncle Ray will visit this week.
imaginable capable of being imagined. She has given every *imaginable* excuse for being late.
plausible apparently true or acceptable; likely. Mr. Maxwell offered a *plausible* explanation for what we had seen.
potential capable of being or becoming; possible but not actual. She gave us a list of *potential* volunteers.
antonym: impossible

proud *adj.* having a sense of one's own worth, usually in a positive way. Winning the spelling bee made Rem Thuc *proud*.
conceited having too high an opinion of oneself, in a negative way. Marcy's *conceited* attitude annoyed her friends.
haughty having or showing much pride in oneself. Since he won the election, Ned has become *haughty*.
immodest boastful; taking too much praise or credit. Juan's *immodest* claim that the plan was his idea is just not true.

vain overly concerned with or proud of oneself. The *vain* woman admired herself in the mirror.
antonym: humble

Q

quiet *adj.* with little or no noise. It is *quiet* in the library.
calm free of excitement or strong feeling; quiet. It is important to remain *calm* during an emergency.
peaceful calm; undisturbed. Jana looks *peaceful* when she's asleep.
serene not disturbed or troubled. Mrs. Hobbs remained *serene* in spite of the uproar around her.
silent completely quiet; without noise. The phone rang three times and then was *silent*.
still without sound; silent. Late at night, the street was *still*.
tranquil of a calm or peaceful nature. Henry is a *tranquil* person who is not easily angered.
antonyms: loud, noisy

R

ready *adj.* fit for use or action. "Dinner's *ready*!" called Mom.
alert watchful and ready. Stay *alert* and you might see a heron.
handy nearby; ready for use. The writer kept a notebook *handy*.
prepared ready or fit for a particular purpose. They are *prepared* for any emergency.
set ready or prepared to do something. We were all *set* to leave when the phone rang.

really *adv.* in fact. You aren't *really* going to go, are you?
actually in fact; really. That "log" was *actually* an alligator.
indeed really; truly. Deena was *indeed* born in an elevator.
truly in fact; really. She *truly* wants to be your friend.

rich *adj.* having great wealth. His oil wells made him a *rich* man.
affluent wealthy; prosperous. She comes from an *affluent* family.
opulent showing wealth or affluence. The ballroom was filled with people in *opulent* dress.
wealthy having many material goods or riches. Being *wealthy*, they can afford servants.
antonym: poor

right *adj.* free from error; true. Am I *right* that the party is at four o'clock?
accurate without errors or mistakes. The newspaper gave an *accurate* account of the local incident.
correct agreeing with fact or truth. Check the dictionary for the *correct* spelling of the word.
exact very accurate; completely correct. It is important that the measurements be *exact*.
precise strictly accurate; clearly defined. The map he drew for us was not very *precise*.
antonyms: wrong, mistaken
Other synonyms: just, fit, fitting, appropriate, apt

rude *adj.* not polite; ill-mannered. It's *rude* to interrupt.
discourteous without good

manners. A *discourteous* guest is one who is always late.

impolite not showing good manners. It was *impolite* of her to keep whispering.

insolent offensively rude or arrogant. Being *insolent* to her parents got Nola into trouble.

uncouth lacking social polish or culture. The man's *uncouth* remarks embarrassed his companion.

antonyms: polite, courteous

run *v.* to go quickly on foot. If we *run*, we can still make it on time.

dash to go very fast; to run with sudden speed. Pete *dashed* around the house, trying to get ready.

race to run very fast; to run in competition with. The brothers always *race* each other to school.

scurry to move hurriedly. A mouse *scurried* across the kitchen floor.

sprint to run at top speed for a short distance. Larry *sprinted* to catch up with his friends.

Other synonyms: bolt, lope, trot, gallop, scamper, streak, scuttle

S

sad *adj.* feeling or showing unhappiness or sorrow. Cora was *sad* about losing her ring.

depressed feeling low. After being sick for so long, the patient began to feel *depressed*.

downcast low in spirits. Mike was quite *downcast*.

miserable extremely unhappy. The boys' teasing made Ana *miserable*.

wretched very unhappy; deeply distressed. Lyle was *wretched* the whole time he was away from home.

antonyms: See happy.

same *adj.* being just like something else in kind, quantity, or degree. Ashur and Dan are the *same* age.

alike similar, showing a resemblance. His sisters look *alike*.

equal the same in size, amount, quality, or value. Make sure all the ropes are *equal* in length.

equivalent equal in value, effect, or meaning. A meter is *equivalent* to 39.37 inches.

identical the same in every detail. The woman knitted *identical* sweaters for each of her children.

antonym: different

say *v.* to make known or express in words. What did you *say*?

declare to make known publicly or formally. The company *declared* itself bankrupt.

pronounce to say formally or officially that something is so. Jan and Renee *pronounced* it a great success.

speak to express an idea, fact, or feeling. If you are interested in going, *speak* to Ms. Halsted.

state to express or explain fully in words. Ima *stated* her reasons for refusing to obey.

talk to express ideas or information by means of speech; to speak. Jia called just to *talk*. See *also* tell.

Other synonyms: proclaim, exclaim

scared *adj.* afraid; alarmed. The child cried because he was *scared*.
afraid feeling fear, often in a continuing way or for a long time. Are you *afraid* of bees?
fearful filled with fear. "Who's there?" said a *fearful* voice.
frightened scared suddenly, or for a short time. We found the *frightened* dog under the bed.
terrified extremely scared; filled with terror. For some reason, she is *terrified* of ants.
Other synonyms: petrified, aghast, awestruck

see *v.* to receive information, impressions, etc., through use of the eyes. Did you *see* any bears?
observe to notice. They *observed* a new bird at the feeder.
perceive to become aware of through sight or other senses. He *perceived* that something was moving.
view to see or look at, usually for some purpose. The class will *view* the fossil exhibit at the museum.
See also look.

shy *adj.* uncomfortable in the presence of others. Paul is *shy* around people he does not know.
bashful easily embarrassed; very shy. The *bashful* girl was afraid to ask the librarian for help.
demure quiet and modest, often in an artificial way. Lila wore a *demure* blue dress to church.
reticent restrained or reserved, especially in speech. The actor is *reticent* about discussing his personal life.
retiring avoiding society or publicity. He is a *retiring* person who prefers his own company.
timid showing a lack of courage; easily frightened. The *timid* girl jumped when Mr. More spoke to her.
antonym: bold

sick *adj.* having poor health. She got *sick* from eating too much.
ailing in poor health, especially over a period of time. The *ailing* child stayed indoors all month.
ill not healthy; sick. He had to miss the party because he was *ill*.
infirm physically weak, especially from old age. Gram may be *infirm*, but her mind is sharp.
nauseated feeling sick to one's stomach. I felt *nauseated* the whole time I was sailing.
unwell not feeling well. Nadine was *unwell* and had to leave early.
antonyms: well, healthy

small See little.

smart *adj.* intelligent; bright; having learned a lot. Pigs are *smart* animals.
clever mentally sharp; quick-witted. You have to be *clever* to figure out these puzzles.

intelligent able to learn, understand, and reason. Some dogs seem almost as *intelligent* as humans.

shrewd clever or sharp in practical matters. Buying property was a *shrewd* decision.

sly clever about tricky or secret matters. You will have to be very *sly* to keep Jeb's party a secret.

wise able to know or judge what is right, good, or true, often describing a person with good sense rather than one who knows many facts. Hattie seems very *wise* for someone her age.

antonym: stupid

smile *v.* to have, show, or give a smile, in a happy or friendly way. Fred *smiled* when he saw Elsie.

beam to smile joyfully. The newlyweds *beamed* at each other.

grin to smile broadly, with great happiness or amusement. The good news made Larry *grin*.

simper to smile in a silly or artificial way. Van did not like the way Patti *simpered* at him.

smirk to smile in a silly or self-satisfied way. Ray's little sister *smirked* as he got scolded.

antonyms: frown, scowl

strange *adj.* differing from the usual or the ordinary. Anteaters are *strange* animals.

bizarre strikingly out of the ordinary; startlingly odd. People stared at Glen's *bizarre* haircut.

odd not ordinary. That's a very *odd* kite up there, isn't it?

peculiar strange or odd, but in an interesting or curious way. Many of their relatives are *peculiar*.

weird strange or odd, in a frightening or mysterious way. We saw some *weird* lights out in the field. See *also* unusual.

strong *adj.* having great strength or physical power. We need someone *strong* to help us move the piano.

brawny strong and muscular. The lifeguard was tall and *brawny*.

muscular having well-developed muscles; strong. Her arms grew *muscular* from lifting heavy boxes.

powerful having great strength, influence, or authority. *Powerful* legs make the frog a good jumper.

stalwart morally or physically strong. Mrs. Jay remained *stalwart* all through her husband's illness.

antonym: weak

Other synonyms: hardy, vigorous, mighty, potent, irresistible

sure *adj.* firmly believing in something. He was *sure* he had heard someone calling his name.

certain free from doubt; very sure. Karen was *certain* she had returned Lenore's sweater.

confident firmly trusting; sure of oneself or of another. I am *confident* you will do a good job.

definite positive or certain, often in a factual way. When can you give them a *definite* answer?
antonyms: doubtful, unsure

surprised *adj.* feeling sudden wonder. Leroy sounded *surprised* that I had called.
amazed overwhelmed with wonder or surprise. Luis was *amazed* at how fast Bert could run.
astonished greatly surprised; shocked. We were *astonished* to run into our neighbors in Quebec.
astounded greatly surprised; stunned. I am *astounded* that you have never heard of Tom Sawyer.
awestruck filled with awe or wonder. They stood in *awestruck* silence on the edge of the canyon.

T

take *v.* to get into one's hands or possession; to obtain. Did you *take* my boots by mistake?
grab to take roughly or rudely. The man *grabbed* his hat and left.
seize to take suddenly and by force. Gwen *seized* the matches out of her baby sister's hand.
snatch to take suddenly and quickly, often in secret. He *snatched* the money and ran off.
antonyms: See give.

talk See say.

tell *v.* to put or express in written or spoken words. Did you *tell* them about the window yet?

announce to state or make known publicly. The senator will *announce* his candidacy tomorrow.
narrate to tell about events, especially a story. The lecturer *narrated* the town's history.
recount to tell in detail; to narrate. Gramps loved to *recount* the adventures of his youth.
relate to tell or report events or details. The newspaper *related* the details of the accident.
See also say.

thin *adj.* not fat. The sick child was *thin* and pale.
lean with little or no fat, but often strong. Swimming has made Jan very *lean*.
skinny very thin, in a way that suggests poor health. Ryan is so *skinny* that his socks fall down.
slim thin, in a good or healthy way. That outfit makes you look *slim*.
antonyms: fat, plump, chubby

think *v.* to occupy one's thoughts (with). It is hard to *think* in such a noisy place.
contemplate to give long and close attention to. John lay in bed and *contemplated* the pattern on the ceiling.
meditate to think seriously and carefully. Tanya *meditated* about her plans for the future.
muse to think in an idle or unconcerned manner. Mrs. Adams sat on the porch and *mused*.
ponder to consider or think over carefully. I may come up with a solution if I *ponder* for a while.

U

unusual *adj.* not usual, common, or ordinary. He wore an *unusual* ring.

exceptional much above average in quality or ability. The restaurant serves *exceptional* seafood.

extraordinary very unusual; beyond the ordinary. That is an *extraordinary* cactus.

rare seldom happening, seen, or found. It is *rare* for an owl to hunt during the day.

uncommon rare or unusual. Coral snakes are *uncommon* around here.

unique having no equal or match; one of a kind. Each of the carver's works is *unique*. See also strange.

antonyms: usual, common; *see also* plain.

Other synonyms: abnormal, queer, singular, irregular

upset *adj.* feeling uneasy; distressed. Bill was *upset* because Lily ignored him.

anxious uneasy or fearful of what may happen. Jim was *anxious* to do well in his new job.

concerned troubled or worried. Her partner was *concerned* when Louise did not show up for work.

disturbed in an unsettled state of mind. Gloria was *disturbed* by what she heard.

nervous emotionally tense or restless; apprehensive or fearful. Are you *nervous* about tomorrow's performance?

worried uneasy or troubled about something. We were *worried* about Lad until he finally came home.

antonym: calm

Other synonyms: agitated, distraught

V

very *adv.* to a great extent. It is *very* muggy today.

considerably to a large or important degree. Your house is *considerably* bigger than ours.

extremely greatly or intensely. His note made me *extremely* angry.

somewhat a little, to some extent. Josh felt *somewhat* confused about the assignment.

W

walk *v.* to move or travel on foot. The girls *walk* home together.

march to walk with regular steps. The Boy Scouts always *march* in the Memorial Day parade.

stride to walk with long steps, usually with a purpose. They watched Guy *stride* up the walk.

stroll to walk in a relaxed or leisurely manner. We *strolled* through town that afternoon.

strut to walk in a vain or very proud way. To see him *strut*, you would think he owned the world.

want *v.* to have a desire or wish for. Do you *want* something to eat?

crave to want badly, often in an uncontrollable way. The hot sun made the hiker *crave* water.

desire to have a strong wish for. All he *desired* was a chance to prove himself.

wish to have a longing or strong need for. Lorraine *wished* she had her own room.

yearn to feel a strong and deep desire. The homesick camper *yearned* to see his family.

wet *adj.* covered or soaked with water or other liquid. You'd better take off those *wet* socks.

damp slightly wet. The air in the basement is *damp*.

moist slightly wet; damp. Her hair was *moist* from the steam.

soggy damp and heavy. We hung the *soggy* towels on the clothesline.

sopping extremely wet; dripping. "Stay outside in those *sopping* bathing suits!" said Dad.

antonyms: See dry.

Other synonyms: drenched, dank

whole *adj.* made up of the entire amount, quantity, or number. She broke the *whole* dozen eggs.

complete having all its parts. Do you have a *complete* set of chessmen?

entire whole; having all its parts. They talked throughout the *entire* movie.

total whole, full, or entire, often referring to numbers. The *total* number of voters was 5,890.

Y

yell *v.* to call or cry out loudly. "Hey, Ramon!" *yelled* Jesse.

bellow to cry out in a loud, deep voice. The man *bellowed* in anger.

holler to yell, especially in a rough-sounding way. The boys started to *holler* at each other.

scream to cry out in a loud, shrill, piercing way. We heard Nina *scream* and ran to help her.

shout to cry out loudly. The coach *shouted* to the players.

LETTER MODELS

A Friendly Letter

We communicate with people in many ways. Often we speak with others in person. Sometimes we talk to individuals by telephone.

Letters are sometimes the best way to communicate with friends. Writing allows you time to say exactly what you mean. Also, a letter can be read over to keep thoughts fresh. Letters written to friends and family are called friendly letters. You use **informal,** or everyday, language in friendly letters.

Read the friendly letter below. Notice how it is organized in five main parts. Thank-you letters and letters of invitation follow the same form.

Heading	414 E. Roy Street Seattle, Washington 98102 February 12, 19—
Greeting	Dear Robin,
Body	We are working on a new project at our school. Some students cannot afford school supplies. Since a good education is everyone's right, we started a "Bill of Rights" program. Those students who can afford it donate a "bill" to help less fortunate students. So far we have collected $103.00. We have bought new notebooks and gym shoes for twelve students. This program has made us feel very good. Please let me hear from you. How did you do at orchestra tryouts? When are you coming to visit?
Closing	Your friend,
Signature	Lee

A Business Letter

Sometimes you want to obtain information, make a complaint, or place an order. You might perform these tasks by phone. However, it is usually better to write a business letter. First, your letter is a written record of your business. Also, a letter gives you time to express yourself clearly and politely.

The style of a business letter is a little different from the style of a friendly letter. A business letter is briefer, and the language is more **formal.** The letter should include all of the necessary information.

Read the following business letter.

Heading	15 Maple Drive Pine Bluff, Arkansas 60211 November 4, 19—
Inside Address	Adopt-a-Child Plan P.O. Box 23 Chicago, Illinois 60645
Greeting	Dear Adopt-a-Child Plan:
Body	Our class learned about your organization in social studies. We would like to "adopt" a child in South America. Our teacher, Ms. Harriet Warren, is in charge. A committee of seventh graders will give money, write letters, and send holiday presents. Could you please send us more information about your organization? We look forward to hearing about our new "family member." Thank you.
Closing	Yours truly,
Signature	*Jerome Cohen* Jerome Cohen

SPELLING STRATEGIES

In your writing, it is very important to spell every word correctly. Otherwise, the meaning of what you write may not be clear to your reader. Follow these steps to help improve your spelling.

1. Learn some basic spelling rules.
2. Learn to spell some commonly misspelled words.
3. Learn to spell words by syllables.
4. Check your work carefully when you have finished writing.
5. Whenever you have a question about how a word should be spelled, use a dictionary to check the spelling.

Spelling Rules

Here are rules to help you spell certain kinds of words correctly.

Words with *ie* and *ei*

Spell the word with *ie* when the sound is $\bar{e}$, except after *c*.

Examples: relief, believe, shield, deceit, perceive, ceiling

Spell the word with *ei* when the sound is not $\bar{e}$, especially if the sound is $\bar{a}$.

Examples: neigh, weight, eighty, sleigh

Exceptions: either, seize, weird, friend

Words with *cede*, *ceed*, and *sede*

There are three words in English that end with *ceed* (*proceed*, *succeed*, and *exceed*). There is only one word that ends with *sede* (*supersede*). All other words with a similar-sounding ending are spelled *cede*.

Examples: precede, concede, secede, recede

Making Nouns Plural

Sometimes when you make a noun plural, the spelling of the word changes. Here are some rules to help you spell these words.

Adding *s* and *es*

In most cases, *s* can be added to a noun without changing the spelling.

Example: trick + s = tricks

If the word ends in *ch*, *s*, *sh*, *x*, or *z*, add *es*.

Examples: wrench/wrenches, suffix/suffixes

Changing _f_ to _v_	For most words ending in _f_ or _fe_, change the _f_ to _v_ when you add _s_ or _es_.
	Examples: sheaf/sheaves, scarf/scarves, self/selves

There are some exceptions to this rule.

> **Exceptions:** roof/roofs, chief/chiefs

Words ending in _o_	For most words that end in _o_ following a vowel, add _s_ to form the plural: studio + s = studios, cameo + s = cameos. For most words that end in _o_ following a consonant, add _es_: potato + es = potatoes, echo + es = echoes.
	For words from the Italian language that refer to music, add _s_: pianos, solos.
Irregular nouns	Some words become plural in irregular ways.
	Examples: ox/oxen, child/children, mouse/mice, tooth/teeth, goose/geese
	Some words stay the same when singular or plural, as in: fish, sheep, deer, series.
Compound nouns	To form the plural of a compound noun written as one word, add _s_ or _es_: leftovers, spoonfuls, stopwatches. If the compound is made up of a noun and modifiers, usually joined by hyphens, make the noun plural: editors-in-chief, presidents-elect, attorneys-general. The plural forms of some compound nouns are irregular: ten-year-olds, drive-ins, lean-tos.
Foreign words	For some words taken from foreign languages, the plural in English is the same as the plural in the original language.
	Examples: datum/data, alumnus/alumni, alumna/alumnae, crisis/crises, criterion/criteria
	For other foreign words, the plural form from either the foreign language or English would be correct: index/indexes or indices, chateau/chateaus or chateaux.

Numbers, letters, signs, and words

To form the plural of a number, letter, sign, or word considered as a word, add an apostrophe and *s*.

Examples: 7's, two x's, several #'s, too many *dear's*

Adding Endings

With many kinds of words, if you add an ending such as *es*, *ed*, *ing*, *er*, or *est*, the spelling of the word may change.

Changing *y* to *i*

If the word ends in a consonant and *y*, change the *y* to *i* before any ending that does not begin with *i*.

Examples: tally + es = tallies
hurry + ed = hurried
skinny + est = skinniest

However, for most words that end in a vowel and *y*, keep the *y* when adding an ending.

Examples: overjoy + ed = overjoyed
delay + ing = delaying

Doubling the final consonant

In most cases, if a one-syllable word ends in one vowel and one consonant, double the consonant when adding an ending that begins with a vowel.

Examples: skip + ed = skipped
grim + er = grimmer
chop + ing = chopping
thin + est = thinnest

For most two-syllable words ending in one vowel and one consonant, double the consonant only if the accent is on the second syllable.

Examples: prefer + ed = preferred
compel + ing = compelling

Silent *e*

If the word ends in a silent *e*, drop the *e* when adding an ending that begins with a vowel.

Examples: sure + er = surer
strive + ing = striving
lame + est = lamest
graze + ed = grazed

Adding Prefixes and Suffixes

When a prefix is added to a word, the spelling of the word stays the same: bi + weekly = biweekly, sub + marine = submarine, fore + warn = forewarn.

When a suffix is added to a word, the spelling of the word may change. If the word ends in a silent e, drop the e when adding a suffix that begins with a vowel, as in: reptile + ian = reptilian, future + ist = futurist.

However, for most words ending in silent e, keep the e when adding a suffix that begins with a consonant.

> **Examples:** shame + less = shameless
> side + ward = sideward
> prince + ly = princely

> **Exceptions:** true + ly = truly, judge + ment = judgment

When adding the suffix *ness* or *ly*, the spelling of the word usually does not change, as in: ripe + ness = ripeness, cruel + ly = cruelly. However, if the word ends in y and has more than one syllable, change the y to i.

> **Examples:** gloomy + ness = gloominess
> sneaky + ly = sneakily

Words Often Confused

There are many pairs of words that sound alike, or similar, but are spelled differently and have different meanings. Knowing what these words mean will help you choose—and spell—the correct word when you use it in your writing. Here are some examples. If you do not know what these words mean, look them up in the dictionary.

affect/effect	complement/compliment	council/counsel
accept/except	stationary/stationery	weather/whether
capital/capitol	principal/principle	

OVERVIEW OF THE WRITING PROCESS

In this book you have learned that writing is a process. When you write, you follow certain steps. Sometimes you move back and forth between steps, but basically you proceed from the beginning to the end of the process.

Prewrite

- Decide on a purpose and audience for your writing.
- Choose a topic that would be suitable for your purpose and audience.
- Explore ideas about your topic. You could brainstorm, make a cluster, or make a list.
- Narrow your topic if it is too broad to cover adequately.

Write a First Draft

- Use your prewriting ideas to write your draft.
- Do not worry too much about making errors. Your goal is to get your ideas on paper.

Revise

- Read your draft. Share it with someone else to get a response.
- Ask yourself these questions about your draft.
  What else will my audience want to know? What details can I add?
  How can I make my purpose clearer?
  How can I make my writing easier to understand?
  How can I improve the organization of my writing?

Proofread

- Read your revised draft.
- Ask yourself these questions about your revised draft.
  Have I followed correct paragraph form?
  Have I used complete sentences?
  Have I used capitalization and punctuation correctly?
  Have I spelled all words correctly?

Publish

- Make a clean copy of your revised and proofread draft.
- Share your writing with the audience you selected.

WRITER'S RESOURCES

STUDY STRATEGIES

Whenever you study, you should plan your time carefully. Keep a list of assignments. Decide how much time to spend on each task. Find a quiet, comfortable place to work. Make sure you have study materials handy—paper, pens and pencils, and reference works such as dictionaries. Keep your work area clean and neat.

The SQ3R Method

There are many different ways to study. One method is called "SQ3R." The name stands for the five steps you should follow.

1. **Survey**. Survey or scan the whole chapter or article you are going to read to get a general idea of what it covers.
2. **Question**. Prepare questions to help you understand the work. Use the title and any important headings to make up questions.
3. **Read**. Read the chapter or article. Look for answers to the questions you made up, and look for important points in what you read.
4. **Record**. Write down the answers to the questions and the important points.
5. **Review**. Look back over the article and the notes you have written.

The PROTO Method

The SQ3R Method is most useful for reading a chapter or an article. The PROTO Method can be used in studying all kinds of material. The PROTO Method includes five steps: Preview, Read, Organize, Take Notes, and Overview.

1. **Preview**. First, preview the material to identify the general idea. Look at the title of the selection. Look at the major headings.
2. **Read**. Second, read the material. Look at the headings again before you read each part. Identify the most important points in each section. If you don't understand part of what you read, look for clues in the headings and read the material again.

3. **Organize**. After you have read the material once, figure out how the important points should be organized. Information may be organized by sequential order, classification, cause-effect, or comparison-contrast.
4. **Take Notes**. Use the method of organization when taking notes. Write down the important points in what you have read. You may want to write down each major idea or title, and then write notes under each idea. Or you may want to use an outline, a time line, or a flow chart.
5. **Overview**. Finally, read through your notes and the list of important ideas again to form an overview or summary of what you have read.

The PROTO Method can help you to study just about any kind of material.

Here are some additional skills that will help you use the PROTO Method.

Special Study Tips

Following Directions
For many assignments, your teacher will give you directions before you begin. Sometimes the directions will be spoken, sometimes written. Pay close attention to the directions.
1. Identify the steps you should follow.
2. Ask questions about any steps you are not sure you understand.
3. Collect the materials you will need for the assignment.
4. Follow the directions step by step.

Setting a Purpose
Before you begin studying, identify the purpose of your work. Your goal might be to identify the causes of an event, to find examples to support a theory, or to contrast two events or documents. Use the directions to help you identify the purpose of your study. Then stick to the purpose as you work.

Outlining
One way to organize your work and take notes about the material is to use an outline. An outline helps you decide what is most important and helps you put each important note in the right place. You can organize an outline by sequential order, classification, cause-effect, or comparison-contrast.

Mapping

Mapping is similar to outlining, but it uses a diagram or picture to organize ideas. You may choose to outline the information in an article by using a map, a time line (listing things in the order in which they happened), a diagram (a picture of how all the parts work together), a flow chart (a diagram showing how each event leads to the next one), or a cluster (key words and phrases organized on the page).

Using Graphic Aids

Many selections include graphic aids such as maps, charts, tables, graphs, and diagrams. In many cases, the graphic aid provides a summary of important points in the selection. Look at the graphic aid carefully to figure out what it means, how the information relates to the selection, and why it is important. Read keys and labels carefully.

Memorizing

When you study something, you will want to remember it. Here are a number of methods to help you memorize important information.

1. **Speak and write**. First, say it aloud. Then write it down. Hearing and seeing what you want to remember will help you to memorize it.

2. **Classify ideas.** Think of a way to classify the information you want to remember. For example, you might list important events in chronological order. You might list important facts in alphabetical order, or in groups related to categories such as "Causes" and "Effects" or "Comparisons" and "Contrasts."

3. **Invent memory joggers**. A "memory jogger" might be a word or a funny sentence that helps you to remember things. For example, in chemistry there are six important inert gases: Helium, Neon, Argon, Krypton, Xenon, and Radon. You can remember them by making up a name, such as "HaNA KiXeR," or a silly sentence: "Have Now Acquired King's Xylophone Recordings." The first letter in each word of the sentence is the first letter in the name of each gas.

4. **Repeat** things as many times as you can. Repeating information often will help you to remember it.

Taking Tests

Taking tests is an important part of your schoolwork. You can use many of the study skills you have learned to make test taking easier.

1. **Preview the test**. Look through the test quickly to see what it covers and how long it is.

2. **Plan your time**. Your teacher will tell you how much time you have to finish the test. Decide how much time to spend on each part of the test. Some parts may take longer than others. Reading stories, for example, will usually take longer than answering vocabulary questions. Keep track of the time as you work.

3. **Follow directions**. Listen to any directions your teacher gives you. Then read the test directions carefully before you begin the test. As you work through the test, read any directions you see at the beginning of each new section.

4. **Read questions carefully**. Read each test question carefully. Figure out exactly what the question means. Use key words to figure out what kind of answer is required. (Key words might include "why," "when," "who," "because," "after," and "what.") Then decide on your answer.

5. **Complete easy questions first**. Work through the test and finish every question for which you know the answer. Leave the difficult questions for last. Then go back and work on each difficult question.

6. **Mark your answers carefully**. If you are taking a multiple-choice test, fill in only one bubble for each question and fill it in completely. If you are writing your answers, write each one clearly and neatly so that the teacher can read it.

7. **Check your work**. When you have answered all the questions, use the time you have left to go back and check your work. Make sure that you have answered each question.

USING THE PARTS OF A TEXTBOOK

1. To get a general idea of what the book covers and how it is organized, examine the **table of contents** near the front. The table of contents lists the book's units or chapters and the pages on which they begin; it will also list any special sections found at the back of the book.

2. As you read a textbook chapter or unit, pay careful attention to any **opening or closing features** that identify or summarize key points. Textbook chapters often begin with objectives that tell you what you are about to learn; they often end with a list or paragraph that sums up the main points.

3. Pay careful attention to **highlighted features** within the chapter or unit. Textbooks often highlight key terms, definitions, and other important information by using headings and sub-headings, bold (dark) or italic (slanted) print.

4. Make use of **handbooks, glossaries,** or any other **special features** at the back of the textbook. A **glossary** is an alphabetical list of words and their meanings; a **handbook** lists important facts or rules.

5. To find specific information in a textbook, consult its **index** at the back. The index is an alphabetical list of all the topics discussed in the book, along with their page numbers.

Practice   Answer the following questions about *this* textbook.

1. What area of English is covered in all the even-numbered units?
2. What topic is covered in Unit 4? What more specific topic is covered in Lesson 2 of Unit 4?
3. On what page does Unit 7 begin?
4. What special section appears near the end of every unit? What special sections are included in the back of the book?
5. On what page will you find a story by Jesse Stuart?

 WRITING APPLICATION An Explanation

Examine another of your school textbooks, and in a few sentences explain how its body is organized. Also list any special features found at the start or end of the book's chapters or units, and list any special sections found at the back of the book.

USING A DICTIONARY

A **dictionary** is a book containing an alphabetical list of words and their definitions. Each word listed is called an **entry word**; **guide words** at the top of each page show the first and last entry on the page. **Homographs**—words with the same spellings but very different meanings and origins—are listed as separate entry words, each followed by a small raised number called a super-script. The following sample dictionary entries appeared on a page with the guide words *mole/mushroom. Mush*[1] *and mush*[2] are homographs.

---

mole·hill (mōl′hil′) *n.* a small mound or ridge of earth formed by a mole burrowing underground. **—to make a mountain out of a molehill.** to give too much importance to something unimportant.
mol·lie (mol′ē) *also,* **mol·ly.** *n. pl.,* **mol·lies.** any of a group of tropical fish that bear their young alive. [Named for François N. *Mollien*, 1758–1850, French statesman.]
mol·lusk (mol′əsk) *also,* **mol·lusc.** *n.* any of a large group of animals without backbones, including clams, oysters, and snails. [Latin *molluscus* soft.]
mol·to (mōl′tō) *adv. Music.* much; very. [Italian *molto.*]
mo·men·tum (mō men′təm) *n. pl.,* **mo·men·ta** or **mo·men·tums.** 1. *Physics.* the property of a moving body, measured by multiplying its mass by its velocity. 2. the force or speed resulting from motion; impetus: *The rock gained momentum as it rolled down the hill.*
mush[1] (mush) *n.* 1. a thick porridge made by boiling corn meal. 2. any soft, thick mass. 3. *Informal.* anything overly sentimental or romantic. [Probably a form of *mash.*] **—mush′y,** *adj.*
mush[2] (mush) *interj.* go or go faster (said to a team of dogs pulling a sled). **—***v.i.* to travel by dog sled. [Possibly from French *marche* go.]**—mush′er,** *n.*

---

at; āpe; fär; câre; end; mē; it; īce; pîerce; hot; ōld; sông, fôrk; oil; out; up; ūse; rüle; pull; tûrn; chin; sing; shop; thin; this; hw in white; zh in treasure. The symbol ə stands for the unstressed vowel sound heard in **a**bout, tak**e**n, penc**i**l, lem**o**n, and circ**u**s.

Dictionary entries provide the following information.

1. The entry word is broken into **syllables**. Divisions are made with dots, dashes, or spaces; in the sample entries, dots are used. The syllable divisions show where to divide a word if you need to break it at the end of a line.

2. The entry word also shows the correct **spelling**. If a word has more than one correct spelling—such as *mollie,* which is also spelled *molly*—the most common spelling is given first. Plural, past tense, and past participle forms are shown if they need clarification. For example, the entry for *momentum* clarifies its two plurals.

3. The **pronunciation** appears right after the entry word, usually in parentheses. Accents (′) show which syllables to stress; other symbols are part of the phonetic alphabet and are explained in the dictionary's **pronunciation key**. A short form of the key generally appears on each right-hand page; in the sample, it is boxed.

4. Abbreviations tell you the word's **part of speech**. For example, *mush¹* is a noun; *mush²* can be either an interjection or an intransitive verb (*v.i.*). All abbreviations used in a dictionary are explained in a **key to abbreviations** at the front or back of the book.

   adj. adjective   *prep.* preposition   *v.* verb
   adv. adverb   *pron.* pronoun

5. The word's **definition** appears after its part of speech; if it has more than one definition as a particular part of speech, each definition is numbered. Definitions are sometimes clarified with *examples,* phrases or sentences that show the meaning in context. Such an example is provided for definition 2 of *momentum.*

6. **Usage labels** indicate definitions with limited or special usage. For instance, definition 1 of *momentum* is a technical definition used in *physics*; definition 3 of *mush¹* is used only in *informal* English.

7. Dictionaries often include an entry word's **etymology,** or history, in brackets or parentheses near the beginning or end of the entry. In the sample entries, etymologies appear in brackets near the ends of entries.

8. Dictionaries also may show **additional forms** of the entry word, such as the noun form *musher* at the end of the entry for *mush².* They also list and define **idioms** in which the entry word appears. An idiom is an expression in which words are used in a sense different from their usual meaning. The entry for *molehill* includes the idiom *to make a mountain out of a molehill.*

Practice

A. Use the sample entries and pronunciation key to answer these questions.

1. How many syllables does *molehill* have?
2. What is the less common spelling of *mollusk*?
3. What is the plural of *molly*?
4. Does *molto's* first syllable rhyme with *doll* or *dole*?
5. In pronouncing *momentum*, which syllable is stressed?
6. As what part of speech is *molto* used?
7. In what field is *molto* used?
8. Which sentence uses *momentum* correctly?
   a. *Winning the primary gave her campaign momentum.*
   b. *Losing the primary gave her campaign momentum.*
   c. *Voting took only a momentum.*
9. From what language does *mollusk* come?
10. What is the adjective form of *mush*¹?

B. Use the sample dictionary entries below to answer these questions.

11. What does the word *caterwaul* mean?
12. What part of speech is the word *caterer*?
13. How many syllables are in the word *caterpillar*?
14. What does a *caterer* do?
15. What is the noun form of the word *caterwaul*?
16. What is the etymology of the word *caterpillar*?
17. Which of the three entry words does not begin with a syllable pronounced like the word *cat*?

ca•ter•er (kā′ tər ər) *n.* a person who caters, especially one who provides food and other services, as for a party. **cat•er•pil•lar** (kat′ ər pil′ ər) *n.* a larva, especially of a butterfly	or moth, that resembles a furry worm. [Old French *catepelose* literally, hairy cat.] **cat•er•waul** (kat′ ər wôl′) *v.i.* to howl or screech like a cat. *–n.* such a howl or screech.

WRITING APPLICATION A Dictionary Entry

Using the style of the sample entries, create a dictionary entry for an imaginary word. Show the word's syllables, pronunciation, and part(s) of speech as well as one or more definitions. Also include other dictionary features, such as an alternative spelling, a usage label, or a made-up etymology.

USING THE LIBRARY

The library is a storehouse of information of many kinds. To help you locate library books, every book is catalogued. A library's catalog may consist of index cards filed in drawers or of computer printouts on microfilm or in booklets. While catalog systems vary, every system provides similar information. Nonfiction books are listed by author, title, and subject; fiction books, by author and title. Listings are alphabetical, with authors alphabetized by last name and titles by their first word, excluding *A*, *An*, and *The*. The library's three-way catalog system enables you to find a book when you know only its author or only its title, or to find nonfiction books on a particular subject when you do not know their authors or titles. Below are three sample catalog listings for the same nonfiction book.

Most libraries use the Dewey decimal system or the Library of Congress system to catalog books. In both systems, nonfiction books are assigned **call numbers** based on their subjects. (The

Author Card

call
number

796.357	Angell, Roger.
A	Late Innings: A Baseball Companion.
	New York: Simon & Schuster, c. 1982.
	448p.: illus.

Title Card

Late Innings: A Baseball Companion.

796.357	Angell, Roger.
A	Late Innings: A Baseball Companion.
	New York: Simon & Schuster, c. 1982.
	448p.: illus.

Subject Card

```
                    BASEBALL

796.357    Angell, Roger.
A              Late Innings: A Baseball Companion.
           New York: Simon & Schuster, c. 1982.
           448p.: illus.
```

call number for the book in the sample listings is from the Dewey decimal system.) Since nonfiction books are arranged by call numbers on library shelves, you can locate a nonfiction book once you have obtained its call number from one of its catalog listings. To locate the book in the sample listings, you would go to the 700s section of the library shelves and then follow the numerical sequence of call numbers on the spines of books until you reached 796.357A.

Most libraries shelve reference books in a special section; their call numbers are usually preceded by *Ref* or *R*. Fiction books are not assigned call numbers but instead are kept in a special section arranged alphabetically by authors' last names.

Practice

A. Answer these questions about finding library books.

1. In which catalog listing (author, title, or subject) and under what letter would you look to find names and call numbers of books by Edith Hamilton?

2. In which catalog listing (author, title, or subject) and under what letter would you look to find the author and call number of the book *The Greeks*?

3. In which catalog listing (author, title, or subject) and under what letter would you look to find names and call numbers of books about the city of Athens?

4. When you look up a nonfiction book in the library catalog, what single item of information must you obtain in order to locate the book on the library shelves?

5. Under what letter would *Oliver Twist* by Charles Dickens be alphabetized in the fiction section?

6. How many catalog listings would Harper Lee's novel *To Kill a Mockingbird* have?

B. Use this catalog listing to answer questions 7-15.

	Hop, Skim, and Fly: An Insect Book.
595.7	Hutchins, Ross Elliot.
H	Hop, Skim, and Fly: An Insect Book.
	New York: Magazine Press, c. 1970.
	64p.: illus.

---

7. Is this an author, title, or subject listing?

8. Who wrote this book?

9. What is the book's title?

10. How long is the book?

11. In what year was the book published?

12. Who published the book?

13. In what city was the book published?

Using Reference Works

Nonfiction books are a good source of specific information for your research. For more general information, you can consult an encyclopedia in the library's reference section. An **encyclopedia** is a multivolume reference work with articles arranged alphabetically by subject. To learn which articles cover your research topic, look up the topic in the encyclopedia's index.

Books are not the only research sources available at libraries. Most libraries have other print materials—like magazines and newspapers—as well as nonprint materials like records and videocassettes. Magazines and newspapers, which are called **periodicals** because they are published at regular periods, can be a useful source of up-to-date information. Libraries usually keep recent issues of periodicals in a special reading area.

To learn which periodical contains an article on a particular topic, you have to consult one of the library's **periodical indexes.** The most widely used periodical index is the *Readers' Guide to Periodical Literature,* which lists magazine articles alphabetically by subject (and sometimes by author). Each issue of the *Readers' Guide* lists articles published in a specified time period. To find information on recent articles, consult a recent issue.

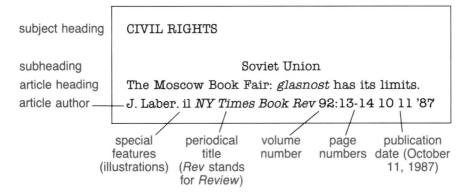

subject heading	CIVIL RIGHTS
subheading	Soviet Union
article heading	The Moscow Book Fair: *glasnost* has its limits.
article author	J. Laber. il *NY Times Book Rev* 92:13-14 10 11 '87

special features (illustrations)   periodical title (*Rev* stands for *Review*)   volume number   page numbers   publication date (October 11, 1987)

Practice

Use this *Readers' Guide* entry to answer the questions.

SPRINGFIELD, MASSACHUSETTS
Galleries and museums
Binding Ties. K. Simmons. il *Horizon* 30:43 N '87

14. What is the subject heading for this entry?
15. Under what subheading does the entry appear?
16. In what magazine does the article appear?
17. What is the volume number of the magazine?
18. What is the date of publication?
19. On what page or pages does the article appear?
20. What is the article's title?
21. Who wrote the article?
22. What special feature does the article contain?

WRITING APPLICATION A List

Choose a research topic. Then use the library catalog, *Readers' Guide*, and reference section to prepare a list of four nonfiction books, two magazine articles, and one encyclopedia article that could help you research the topic. For each book, list the title, author, publisher and city, copyright date, and call number. For each magazine article, list the article's title and author; the name, volume number, and date of the magazine; and the page or pages on which the article appears. For the encyclopedia article, list the article's title and the name and copyright date of the encyclopedia.

SKIMMING AND SCANNING

Skimming and scanning can help you make effective use of your study time. **Skimming** is the process of looking quickly at written material to get a general idea of its content. For instance, you might skim a book's table of contents to get a general idea of what the book is about and how it is arranged; or you might skim a chapter in a nonfiction book to see if it covers information that could be useful to your research.

Scanning is the process of reading quickly to find a specific piece of information. For instance, if you wanted to learn the pages on which transitive verbs are discussed in this book, you would scan the book's index. If you then wanted to find the definition of the term *transitive verb,* you would scan the pages that discuss transitive verbs until you came to the definition.

Practice

A. Skim the table of contents below. Then cover it with a slip of paper and answer the questions below it.

Contents

Part A. The Beginnings of Science Fiction

Chapter 1. Science Fiction Before 1800 5
Chapter 2. Mary Shelley's *Frankenstein* and Other
           Romantic Age Science Fiction   27
Chapter 3. True Science Fiction: Verne and Wells 59

Part B. The Golden Age

Chapter 4. Science-Fiction Magazines 79
Chapter 5. Utopian and Dystopian Novels 111

Part C. Postwar Science Fiction

Chapter 6. Asimov, Bradbury, and Other Masters 126
Chapter 7. Recent Trends in Sci-Fi Literature 181

Bibliography of Science-Fiction Literature 213
Index 221

---

1. What general subject is the book about?
2. Into how many parts is the body of the book divided?
3. In addition to the index, what special section appears at the back of the book?

4. If you were researching Ray Bradbury's science-fiction novels, would this book probably be useful? If you were researching Isaac Asimov's nonfiction writing, would the book probably be useful?

5. Which one of these research topics does the book cover?
   (a) science-fiction films
   (b) science fiction before *Frankenstein*
   (c) the Golden Age of ancient Greek civilization

B. Scan the index below to answer the questions that follow.

Adventure (magazine), 81–2	LeGuin, Ursula, 184–5
Amazing Stories (magazine), 81	monsters in science fiction, 23–6,
Asimov, Isaac, 126–32	84
Bradbury, Ray, 126, 133–45	Orwell, George, 120, 122
Clarke, Arthur C., 146–7	Pohl, Frederick, 88
dystopian novels, 120–8	Shelley, Mary, 23–6
Fantasy and Science Fiction	space travel
(magazine), 84–5	in early science fiction, 63,
Frankenstein—see Shelley	84–5
Hawthorne, Nathaniel, 27	since 1969, 188–9
Heinlein, Robert, 179	utopian novels, 111–20
Herbert, Frank, 148–50	Verne, Jules, 50–9, 78
Huxley, Aldous, 124	Wells, H.G., 50, 59–78

6. On what pages of the book would you look to find a definition of the term *dystopian novel*?

7. On what pages is *Frankenstein* discussed?

8. Where would you look to find information on how space travel is depicted in recent science fiction?

9. How many magazine titles does the index list?

10. Does the book have information on Steven Spielberg?

WRITING APPLICATION Questions

Select a short section in one of your school textbooks. Write five questions about its general content—questions that could be answered by skimming the section. Then write five questions about specific information in the section—questions that could be answered by scanning the section. Exchange textbooks and questions with a classmate, and answer his or her questions by skimming and then scanning the section your classmate chose.

NOTE TAKING

Whether you are listening in class or reading your textbooks, taking notes will help you learn the information. Writing something down helps you to remember it, and your notes will be helpful when you study for tests. In addition, when you do research, you will need to take notes from library books and other sources.

Follow these guidelines for successful note taking.

Guidelines for Note Taking

1. Label your notes. For class notes, write the date and the class or subject; you should also organize your notebook into sections by subject. For notes from your textbooks, write the chapter and page numbers in addition to the subject. For library books, write the title, author, editor (if any), publisher, city of publication, publication date, and page numbers.

2. Paraphrase and summarize your notes. Paraphrasing means rewriting ideas in your own words, a process that will help you to learn and remember the information. **Summarizing** means writing only the main ideas and important details, a process that saves time and helps you to focus on the information you most need to know. In class you cannot possibly write down everything your teacher says; however, by summarizing the information, you can still take effective notes.

3. Use key terms. Be sure to include in your notes key terms, definitions, and other important information that your teacher or textbook highlights. Teachers usually highlight important information by speaking more slowly or by writing it on the chalkboard. Textbooks usually highlight important information by using headings and subheadings; bold (dark), italic (slanted), or colored print; special boxes; or illustrations such as tables and maps. They may also include special sections that summarize or list the important information in a chapter or unit.

4. Use words and phrases. Save time by taking notes in words and phrases instead of full sentences. You can also use abbreviations, but be sure you will understand them later.

5. Organize your notes. Group related ideas together, and list specific details under the main points that they support or illustrate.

Practice

Take notes on the textbook passage below.

Ancient Mesopotamia

Mesopotamia is often called "the cradle of civilization," for in this ancient region were born many of the customs and achievements that we associate with civilized life. Mesopotamia was located between the Tigris and Euphrates rivers in what today is the mideastern nation of Iraq; in fact, the name *Mesopotamia* means "land between the rivers." From about 3500 B.C. the southeastern part of Mesopotamia was dominated by a people called the Sumerians, and the region they inhabited was known as Sumer.

In this hot, dry region, rivers were a source of life, for their flood waters were needed to help farm crops grow. To build devices to control these flood waters, Sumerian farmers began to band together. The almost constant warfare in the area also spurred them to join forces and build protective walls to keep out invaders. As Sumerian farmers joined together in small, walled communities, the world's first cities were born. The largest of the Sumerian cities was Ur, on the banks of the Euphrates River.

The Sumerians were also the first known people to devise a writing system to record their stories. Their written language employed wedge-shaped marks now called **cuneiform** (from the Latin for "wedge"). Using a sharp instrument called a *stylus*, specially trained writers, or *scribes*, carved cuneiform onto clay tablets that were then hardened by baking. Because the area is so dry, many of these tablets have been preserved over the centuries and are studied today to teach us more about Sumerian civilization.

—*World History*, Chapter 2, p. 41

WRITING APPLICATION A Report

Choose another ancient civilization—for example, the ancient Egyptians or the Aztecs—and research its achievements in science, art, religion, writing, or another area. Take notes from the library books you used. Then prepare and deliver an oral report on the information, and have your classmates take notes.

OUTLINING

Creating an **outline** is one of the clearest ways to list information about a subject. The special visual pattern of an outline immediately shows which items of information are most important and how all the items are related to one another. A **formal outline** uses a standard pattern of indentation, numbers, and letters. Main topics are listed with Roman numerals (I, II, and so on). Subtopics supporting the main topics are indented and listed with capital letters. Details supporting the subtopics are indented further and listed with Arabic numbers (1, 2, and so on). Details that support those details are indented even further and are listed with small letters. Study the following example of a formal outline that a writer prepared before writing a research report about the works of Isaac Asimov.

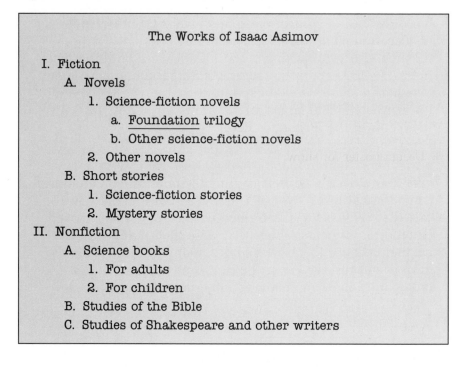

The Works of Isaac Asimov

I. Fiction
   A. Novels
      1. Science-fiction novels
         a. <u>Foundation</u> trilogy
         b. Other science-fiction novels
      2. Other novels
   B. Short stories
      1. Science-fiction stories
      2. Mystery stories
II. Nonfiction
   A. Science books
      1. For adults
      2. For children
   B. Studies of the Bible
   C. Studies of Shakespeare and other writers

As you can see, the title of the outline is centered at the top. The first word of each listing begins with a capital letter, and the Roman-numeral listings align on the periods after the numerals. A formal outline must also have at least two items at each level of information—for instance, you cannot have a I without a II, or an A without a B.

When you prepare an outline for your teacher or someone else to read, you should usually use formal outline style. On the other hand, there are times when you will find it helpful to prepare an outline for your own use only. For example, you can use an outline to organize your class notes or the notes you take from textbooks or library sources. You can also use an outline to organize your thoughts before answering an essay question or writing a composition or research report. In such cases, since no one will see the outline but you, you need not follow every rule of formal outline style. Nevertheless, you should still use some sort of number-and-letter system to show how the information is related.

Practice

A. Rewrite this outline in correct outline form for a two-paragraph composition on the topic, planning a talent show. Use Roman numerals I and II and capital letters A, B, and C.

1. Place ads in store windows.
2. Arrange the program.
3. Advertise the show.
4. Sign up talent.
5. Organize order of acts.
6. Print copies of sign.
7. Audition each performer.
8. Design poster for show.

B. Rearrange the items below into a formal outline with the title School Studies. If you are not sure where to place some of the items, look them up in a dictionary.

Geology	Biology	Physics
Grammar	History	English
Chemistry	American History	Geometry
Arithmetic	World History	Science
Mathematics	Literature	Writing
Ancient History	Medieval History	Modern History
Social Studies	Algebra	Geography

 WRITING APPLICATION An Outline

Write a formal outline on the subject you researched for the **Writing Application** activity on page 567 or on another subject you recently studied.

ATLASES AND ALMANACS

Atlases and almanacs are both useful reference books. An **atlas** is a book of **maps**, drawings that show an area of the earth's surface. A map helps you to picture an area and understand the locations of its features. Maps may also appear in newspapers, magazines, textbooks, encyclopedias, and other books.

Some maps give a general picture of an area; others focus on specific features. For instance, a **topographical map** focuses on physical surface features such as mountains; a **street map** shows the streets of a town or a city; and a **weather map** shows temperatures, high and low fronts, and other information about an area's weather. A map's title usually clarifies the information shown. The map below is a general map of Japan.

Most maps include a **key** or **legend** that explains the colors and symbols they use. In some atlases, a general key appears in the front of the book. Maps also include a **north indicator** or a **direction indicator** that clarifies directions on the map. Once you know north, you know that east is to the right of north, west is to the left, and south is directly opposite.

Most maps are drawn *to scale*; that is, the real distances of the area they show are scaled down proportionately. Maps usually include the scale that was used; on the map of Japan, a **scale of miles.** It shows that 200 miles equals about ⅞-inch on the map. If you mark off the scale's 200-mile point on the edge of a paper and then put the edge between Nagasaki and Hiroshima, you will find that the actual distance between the cities is about 200 miles.

Practice   Use the map of Japan to answer these questions.

1. What is the capital of Japan?
2. What ocean lies to the south and east of Japan?
3. What is the largest Japanese island?
4. On which Japanese island is Nagasaki located?
5. What body of water separates Japan from North Korea?
6. Which city is farther west, Kyoto or Osaka?
7. What mountain is southwest of Tokyo?
8. At their closest points, is the distance between Japan and South Korea (a) under 100 miles, (b) about 350 miles, or (c) over 500?
9. About how far is Hiroshima from Kyoto?
10. Which statement is not true? (a) Except for its coastal areas, Japan is mostly plains. (b) Japan is an island. (c) Japan's closest neighbor is South Korea.

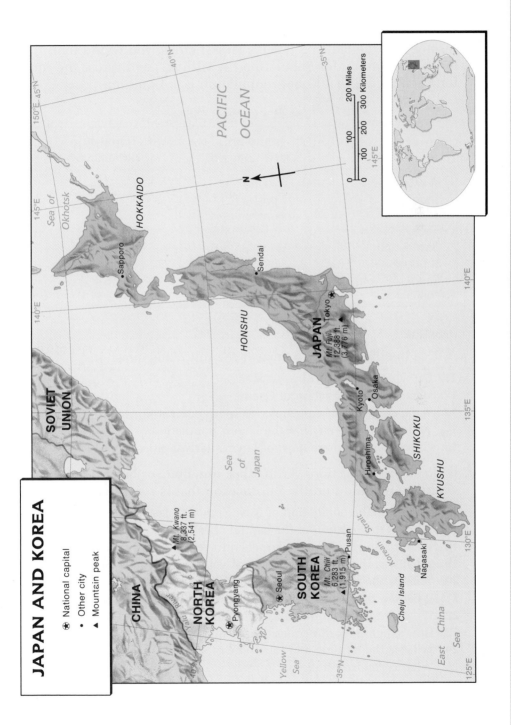

JAPAN AND KOREA

⊛ National capital
• Other city
▲ Mountain peak

SOVIET
UNION

CHINA

NORTH
KOREA
⊛ Pyongyang

SOUTH
KOREA
⊛ Seoul

Pusan

Mt. Kwano
8,337 ft.
(2,541 m)

Mt. Chiri
6,283 ft.
(1,915 m)

Yalu River

Yellow
Sea

Cheju Island

Korean Strait

Nagasaki

KYUSHU

East
China
Sea

Sea
of
Japan

Hiroshima

SHIKOKU

Kyoto
Osaka

JAPAN

Mt. Fuji
12,388 ft.
(3,776 m)

Tokyo ⊛

HONSHU

Sendai

HOKKAIDO

Sapporo

Sea of
Okhotsk

PACIFIC
OCEAN

N

100 Miles
0
100   200

0   100   200   300 Kilometers

200 Miles

125°E
130°E
135°E
140°E
145°E
150°E
145°E
140°E

35°N
40°N
35°N
45°N
40°N

An **almanac** is an annually published book of facts. Much of its information appears in **tables**, lists that give information in vertical columns and horizontal rows. To find specific information on a table, you read down a column and across a row. For instance, in the table on Japan's largest cities, you would look down the column for Population (in Millions) and across the row for Kobe to find that Kobe's population is 1.4 million.

Japan's Largest Cities

	Island on Which Located	Population (in Millions)
Kitakyushu	Kyushu	1.0
Kobe	Honshu	1.4
Kyoto	Honshu	1.4
Nagoya	Honshu	2.1
Osaka	Honshu	2.6
Sapporo	Hokkaido	1.5
Tokyo	Honshu	8.4
Yokohama	Honshu	2.9

Practice

A. Use the table above to answer the following questions.

11. On what island is Tokyo located?
12. What is the population of Osaka?
13. Which city has more people, Sapporo or Kyoto?
14. Which Japanese city has the largest population?
15. On which island are most of Japan's largest cities?

B. Read each question. Write **atlas, almanac,** or **both** to tell where you would find the information that is requested.

16. What was the population of New York City last year?
17. What is the location of the capital of India?
18. What route should one take when traveling from Paris to Zurich?
19. What was the average rainfall last year in the United States?
20. What is the largest body of water in Africa?
21. What are the names of the senators from Texas and California?
22. What country won the most gold medals in the last Olympics?
23. How much milk did Americans drink last year?
24. What is the latitude and longitude of Greenwich, England?
25. What is the largest city in Europe?

Almanacs may also contain **graphs** to present information. A **circle graph** shows the parts of a whole. For instance, in the circle graph of the Japanese labor force, the whole circle is divided into parts that show the fraction or percentage of the Japanese labor force working in various labeled fields. Because a bit less than one fourth, or 25 percent, of the circle is labeled *trade*, you know that a bit less than one fourth, or 25 percent, of the Japanese labor force works in trade.

The Japanese Labor Force

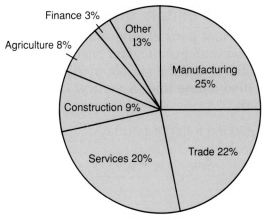

Practice

Use the circle graph to answer the following questions.

26. Is the percentage of the Japanese labor force working in services (a) less than 10 percent, (b) about 20 percent, or (c) about 50 percent?

27. What fraction of the Japanese labor force works in manufacturing?

28. Do more Japanese work in construction or in trade?

29. Do more Japanese work in finance or in agriculture?

30. In which area are the most Japanese employed?

 WRITING APPLICATION A Table

Draw a map of an imaginary country with mountains, bodies of water, and other features. Use a scale in which one inch equals 50 miles, and include the scale on your map. Also include a north indicator and a key that explains the symbols and colors you use. After you have finished, create a table and a circle graph that both present imaginary facts about the places shown on the map.

SENTENCE STRUCTURE:
Diagraming Guide

A **sentence diagram** uses lines to show the relationship of the words in the sentence. In these lessons, you will begin by diagraming the most important words in the sentence. As you continue through the section, you will learn how to diagram every word in a sentence.

Simple Subjects and Simple Predicates (pp. 6-7)

The two most important parts of any sentence are the subject and the predicate. The sentence diagram begins with these two parts. The simple subject and the simple predicate are written on a horizontal line called a **base line.** A vertical line separates the subject from the verb.

The class is making a list of holidays.

class	is making

The subject of an imperative sentence is understood to be *you*. This is because the word *you* does not appear in the sentence. See how the subject of an imperative sentence is diagramed.

Suggest some holidays for the list.

(you)	Suggest

Practice   Diagram the simple subject and simple predicate.

1. Several students suggested Independence Day.
2. Thanksgiving appears on the list.
3. A clever girl suggested Arbor Day.
4. Halloween was named by several students.
5. The teacher was writing each holiday on the chalkboard.

Compound Subjects and Compound Predicates (pp. 8-9)

A compound subject or compound predicate has more than one part. Each part is written on a separate horizontal line. The conjunction (usually *or*, *and*, or *but*) is written on a dotted line that connects the two parts.

Mom, Dad, and I discussed and planned our vacation.

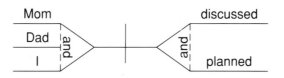

Practice Diagram the simple or compound subject and the simple or compound predicate in each sentence.

1. Mom and I collected and studied maps.
2. Dad bought and read travel books.
3. My parents and I chose a train trip.
4. Suitcases and bags were gathered and packed.
5. Our neighbors and friends waved and cheered.

Predicate Nouns and Pronouns (pp. 142-143)

Predicate nouns are written on the base line. A slanted line separates the verb from the predicate noun. The slanted line shows that the subject and the predicate noun name the same thing. Remember a pronoun can take the place of a noun; so there are predicate pronouns as well as predicate nouns.

The poodle is a very popular dog.

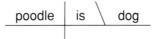

Their biggest fan is she.

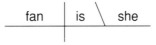

Practice Diagram the subjects, verbs, and predicate nouns or pronouns in each sentence.

1. Spaniels and shepherds are also popular breeds.
2. Many young people are very happy owners.
3. Interested owners are they.
4. My favorite dog is the collie.
5. Dobermans are now favorites.

Predicate Adjectives (pp. 142-143)

A predicate adjective is diagramed in the same way as a predicate noun. It is written on the base line, and a slanting line separates the verb from the predicate adjective. The slanting line means the predicate adjective modifies the subject.

Soccer is very popular.

The game is fast, fun, and exciting.

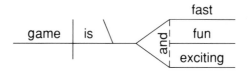

Practice   Diagram the subjects, verbs, and predicate adjectives in these sentences.

1. Most players appear eager.
2. My sister and I are confident.
3. Many teams have become successful lately.
4. The equipment is common, lightweight, and inexpensive.
5. Fans and players seem excited.

Direct Objects (pp. 138-139)

A direct object is written on the base line after the verb. A vertical line separates the verb from the direct object. This line does not go below the base line.

My sister built a bicycle.

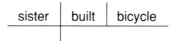

A sentence can also have a compound direct object.

She also made a radio, a telephone, and a telegraph.

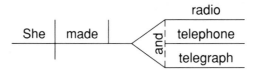

Practice Diagram the subjects, verbs, and direct objects in each sentence.

1. The radio had a loud signal.
2. The telephone and telegraph won several prizes or awards.
3. My mother and father give her encouragement.
4. Mother praises her work.
5. My sister shows her prizes and awards.

Indirect Objects (pp. 140-141)

In a diagram, an indirect object is written on a horizontal line under the base line. A slanting line connects the indirect object to the verb.

Mother made us a picnic.

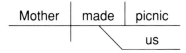

Practice Diagram the subjects, verbs, direct objects, and indirect objects in each sentence.

1. Mrs. Hunan offered me an orange slice.
2. I handed my sister the plates and cups.
3. Mom and Dad gave everyone a napkin.
4. Mom told the guests the recipes and ingredients.
5. Dad brought me a special dessert.

Adjectives (pp. 292-299)

An adjective is written on a slanting line below the word it modifies. Adjectives in a series are joined by a dotted line. The word *and* or *or* is written on the dotted line. Remember that the articles *a*, *an*, and *the* are special adjectives. Diagram articles as you would other adjectives.

The funny play had tall, short, and medium actors.

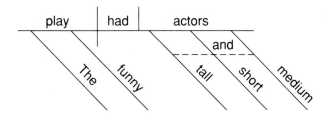

Practice Diagram every word in these sentences.

1. The different heights seemed strange and funny.
2. A tall, clumsy actor wore a green, red, and blue bow tie.
3. Some enthusiastic actors danced a fast and intricate polka.
4. A short boy and a tall girl sang a silly, old French song.
5. Happy, weary, and proud actors took many deep bows.

Adverbs (pp. 300-303)

If an adverb modifies a verb, write it on a slanting line below the verb. If the adverb modifies an adjective or another adverb, write it on a line parallel to the word it modifies. A line connects the adverb to the adjective or adverb it modifies.

The quite simple party happened easily and very nicely.

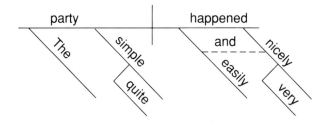

Practice Diagram every word in these sentences.

1. A very tasty soup was served early.
2. Rather hungry guests waited quite eagerly.
3. The hostess spoke simply, quietly, and very warmly.
4. Many happy songs were sung loudly and often.
5. A very funny poem was repeated often.

Prepositional Phrases (pp. 364-371)

To diagram a prepositional phrase, write the preposition on a slanted line below the word the phrase modifies. Write the object of the preposition on a line parallel to the base line.

The house on the corner was painted by a crew with a truck.

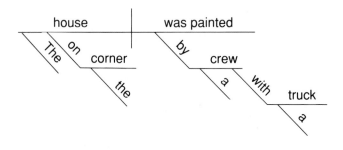

Practice Diagram every word in these sentences.

1. The girl with the red cap painted under the porch.
2. The owner selected paints of many colors.
3. The crew from town worked in the heat of the day.
4. The boy beside the well in the garden seems ill.
5. His idea of work includes a nap in the shade after lunch.

Appositives (pp. 76-77)

An appositive is diagramed in parentheses after the noun or pronoun it identifies. Modifiers are written in the usual way.

The Appalachians, an old mountain range, are famous.

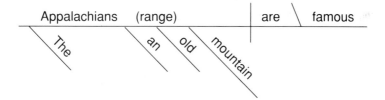

Practice Diagram every word in these sentences.

1. The Rockies, a Western range, are much younger.
2. Pike's Peak, a famous mountain, rises in the Rockies.
3. It was discovered by Zebulon Pike, an early explorer.
4. Mount St. Helen's, an active volcano, is now famous.
5. Many mountains are in Colorado, the Centennial State.

Participles and Participial Phrases (pp. 444-445)

A participial phrase is diagramed like a prepositional phrase. The participle is written on a slanting line connected to a horizontal line. If the participle has an object, write it on the horizontal line.

Singing a song, the campers awaited the expected guest.

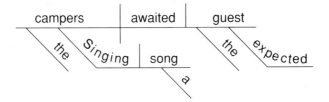

Practice Diagram every word in these sentences.

1. Awaiting him patiently, they ate a hastily cooked meal.
2. Demanding a story, they stamped their feet in the dust.
3. Their leader, from his seat, told the demanded story.
4. Fighting shivers, they listened with growing interest.
5. The delayed guest arrived, making apologies to everyone.

Gerunds and Gerund Phrases (pp. 446-447)

Gerunds and gerund phrases are written on a special line called a **standard**. This standard is placed where it belongs in the diagram; for example, where the subject or direct object is placed. The gerund is written in a curve on the standard.

Swimming requires practicing constantly.

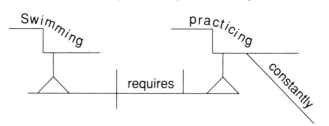

Practice Diagram every word in these sentences.

1. Swimming on a team means improving skills.
2. Diving can be a challenge.
3. Having a handy pool is certainly a big help.
4. The members of a team practice kicking properly.

Infinitives and Infinitive Phrases (pp. 448-449)

An infinitive is placed on a standard when it is the subject, direct object, or predicate noun. If the infinitive is a modifier, diagram it as you would a prepositional phrase.

To become the best means to work constantly.

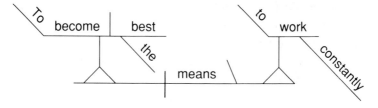

Practice Diagram every word in these sentences.

1. The goal of every person should be to do well.
2. We want to succeed.
3. To do your best is admirable.
4. Many choose to try and dare to try again.
5. To live successfully seems a reasonable dream.

Compound Sentences (pp. 10-11)

Each clause of a compound sentence is diagramed as if it were a separate sentence. The conjunction is written on a line between the two clauses. A dotted line connects the conjunction to the verb in each clause.

> A boy in my class learns quickly, but his mother helps him.

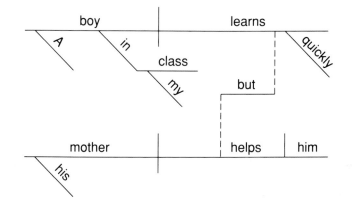

Practice Diagram every word in these sentences.

1. I study daily, but it is hard work.
2. I take notes, or my dad asks me questions.
3. The system works, and my grades prove it.
4. Studying is important, and I take it seriously.
5. Tests and quizzes prove my system, and I use it often in my room at home.

Adverb Clauses (pp. 442-443)

Diagram an adverb clause as a separate sentence. Place it below the independent clause of the sentence. The subordinating conjunction is written on a dotted line connecting the verbs in the clauses. Look at the example on the next page.

When we move, I will attend a new school.

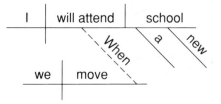

Practice Diagram every word in these sentences.

1. If we move now, I will go to Mariner Junior High.
2. It will be Baxter School unless we move soon.
3. After we arrive, I will find the school office.
4. They will have my records before I make the appointment.
5. Until I am a student, I must have a pass for classes.

Adjective Clauses (pp. 440-441)

An adjective clause is written like the independent clause. It is placed below the independent clause. A dotted line connects the relative pronoun to the word that the clause modifies. Diagram the relative pronoun according to its function in the sentence. See how the adjective clause is diagramed in this sentence.

The teacher who is my favorite gives me special assignments.

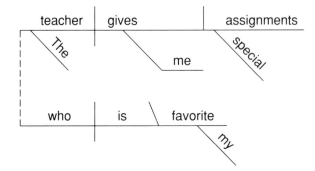

Practice Diagram every word in these sentences.

1. I write reports that require research in the library.
2. The last report, which has been graded, took two weeks.
3. The library where I study is on a busy street in our town.
4. The building, which is rather new, is low and handsome.
5. The library replaces an older building that closed in the fall.

G L O S S A R Y

OF WRITING, GRAMMAR, AND LITERARY TERMS

WRITING TERMS

audience the reader or readers for whom a composition is written

bibliography a list of books, articles, and other sources used in writing a research paper

brainstorm to list any thoughts—words, phrases, questions—that come to mind about a writing topic

chronological order the arrangement of events in the order in which they happen in time

first draft the first version of a composition, in which the writer gets his or her basic ideas down on paper

overall impression the general idea or feeling expressed in a description

personal narrative a piece of writing in which the writer tells about something that has happened in his or her life

prewriting the stage in the writing process in which the writer chooses a topic, explores ideas, gathers information, and organizes his or her material before writing a first draft

prewriting strategies particular ways of gathering, exploring, planning, and organizing ideas before writing the first draft of a composition

- **charting** a way to gather ideas under different headings—especially useful in comparing and contrasting

	Similarities	Differences
Type:	both hair seals, not fur seals	
Habitat:	both Antarctic	elephant seal —also Arctic
Appearance:		crabeater seal—most beautiful seal, gray-white pelt, soft brown eyes, whiskers, my favorite
		elephant seal —most terrifying seal, largest seal, 6,000 pounds
Behavior:		crabeater seal—graceful, playful
		elephant seal —clumsy, inflates nose, howls

- **clustering** a way to explore ideas by gathering details related to the writing topic

motor off · hour trip · boat · Cape Cod · quiet · whale watching · huge · noisy little kids · 2 whales · came close

- **diagraming** a way of exploring ideas by showing visually how details relate to a writing topic

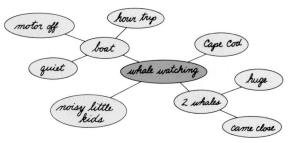

jobs programs

open to seventh graders

for high school only

need money · willing to work · summer camp program goes through sixth grade · young teens too young to work · older teens need more jobs

- **outline**   a way to organize topic-related ideas in the order in which they will be discussed—especially useful in drafting a research report

> The Works of Isaac Asimov
>
> I. Fiction
>   A. Novels
>   1. Science-fiction novels
>   a. Foundation trilogy
>   b. Other science-fiction novels
>   2. Other novels
>   B. Short stories
>   1. Science-fiction stories
>   2. Mystery stories
> II. Nonfiction
>   A. Science books
>   1. For adults
>   2. For children
>   B. Studies of the Bible
>   C. Studies of Shakespeare and other writers

- **story chart**   a way to gather ideas and details under headings important for story writing

Who are the main characters? What are they like?	Brother and younger sister—sister likes to act bratty sometimes, but they really care about each other.
What is the setting?	Summer cabin in the woods. House where they live—ordinary house.
What is the central problem in the plot?	Brother and sister alone in house. Power goes off. It's dark and scary. Brother sees something moving. What is it?

- **time line**   a way to arrange events in time order

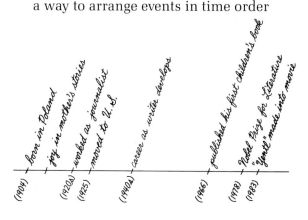

proofread	to correct errors in punctuation, capitalization, spelling, and grammar in a writing draft
publish	to share a composition with an audience
purpose	the writer's reason for writing a composition—for example, to explain, to entertain, or to persuade
revise	to improve the first draft of a composition by adding or taking out information, rearranging sentences, or changing word choice according to one's purpose and audience
supporting details	facts, examples, or sensory details that give more information about the main idea of a paragraph
topic sentence	sentence that states the main idea of a paragraph
transition words	words or phrases that link sentences in a paragraph, such as *finally* and *in the meantime*
writing conference	a meeting in which a writer discusses his or her writing with the purpose of improving it
writing process	the steps for writing a composition, including prewriting, writing a first draft, revising, proofreading, and publishing

GRAMMAR TERMS

action verb	a word that expresses action Ducks *swim* across the pond.
adjective	a word that describes a noun or a pronoun Hasn't it been a *cool* summer?
adverb	a word that modifies a verb, an adjective, or another adverb Walk *quickly* to the police station.

antecedent a word or group of words to which a pronoun refers
Holly sings, but she doesn't perform often.

appositive a word or group of words that follows and identifies a noun
Vanessa, *my cousin*, is quite artistic.

article the special adjective *a, an,* or *the*
The noises in this room are *a* nuisance.

common noun a noun that names any person, place, thing, or idea
I ate a delicious *apple*.

complete predicate all the words that tell what the subject of a sentence does or is
This movie *appeals to both children and adults*.

complete subject all the words that tell whom or what a sentence is about
The last house on the block is for sale.

complex sentence a sentence that contains an independent clause and one or more subordinate clauses
They play soccer *when the weather permits*.

compound sentence a sentence that contains two or more sentences joined by a comma and the word *and, or,* or *but*
The flag is torn, *but* John will repair it.

conjunction a word that joins other words or groups of words in a sentence
Manuel *or* Donna will help you.

direct object a word that receives the action of a verb
The mayor gave a *speech*.

gerund a verb form that ends in *ing* and is used as a noun
Swimming is my favorite sport.

indefinite pronoun a pronoun that does not refer to a particular person, place, or thing
Everyone listened carefully.

independent clause a group of words that contains one complete subject and one complete predicate, and that can stand alone as a sentence
The streets in this neighborhood need stoplights, and *many residents have complained.*

indirect object	a noun or pronoun that answers the question *to whom? for whom? to what?* or *for what?* after an action verb We gave *Justine* a locket.
infinitive	the base form of a verb preceded by the word *to* Have you ever tried *to draw*?
interjection	a word or group of words that expresses strong feeling *Hey!* Watch out for that falling branch!
intransitive verb	a verb that does not take a direct object The horse *jumped* gracefully.
irregular verb	a verb that does not form the past tense by adding *d* or *ed.* The chorus *sang* numbers from Gilbert and Sullivan.
linking verb	a word that connects the subject of a sentence to a noun or an adjective in the predicate That chair *is* a priceless antique.
noun	a word that names a person, place, thing, or idea Describe the *story* for me.
object of a preposition	the noun or pronoun that follows the preposition in a prepositional phrase The students gathered in the *auditorium.*
object pronoun	a pronoun that is used as the object of an action verb or as the object of a preposition The last scene in the movie scared *them.*
participle	a verb form used as an adjective *Swaying* trees glittered in the sunlight.
participial phrase	a group of words that includes a participle and other words that complete its meaning, all acting together as an adjective *Swaying in the breeze,* the trees glittered.
possessive noun	a noun that shows ownership The *dog's* fur was white with tan patches.
possessive pronoun	a pronoun that shows who or what owns something Did you find *your* hat?

preposition	a word that relates a noun or pronoun to another word in a sentence *The guests sat by the window.*
prepositional phrase	a group of words that begins with a preposition and ends with a noun or pronoun *The raft floated across the river.*
pronoun	a word that takes the place of one or more nouns and the words that go with the nouns *The actors were nervous, but they performed well.*
proper adjective	an adjective formed from a proper noun *German cars are growing more expensive.*
proper noun	a noun that names a particular person, place, thing, or idea *Hector is from Brazil.*
run-on sentence	two or more sentences that have been joined together incorrectly *The Alps are the highest mountains in Europe they are a skier's paradise.*
sentence	a group of words that expresses a complete thought *The underground city fascinated the explorers.*
sentence fragment	a group of words that does not express a complete thought *A tall woman with red curly hair and blue eyes.*
simple predicate	the main word or words in the complete predicate of a sentence *Tom showed four of his paintings in the art show.*
simple subject	the main word or words in the complete subject of a sentence *A child in a straw hat stood outside the store.*
subject pronoun	a pronoun that is used as the subject of a sentence *She knows all about redwood trees.*
subordinate clause	a group of words that has a subject and a predicate but cannot stand alone as a complete sentence *They discussed the issue while they waited.*
transitive verb	a verb that takes a direct object *Two men planted young trees along the fence.*

LITERARY TERMS

alliteration   the repetition of the same first letter or initial sound in a series of words—for example, "Four fellows fled the fire."

conflict   the central problem in the plot of a story

dialogue   the conversations in a story or a play

haiku   a poem that has three lines and usually seventeen syllables, and that frequently describes something in nature

idiom   an expression whose meaning is different from the individual words composing it—for example, "She had her head in the clouds."

metaphor   a figure of speech in which a comparison is made without using the word *like* or *as*—for example, "The pond was a mirror."

meter   the systematic pattern of beats in a poem

mood   the particular feeling suggested by a description

onomatopoeia   the use of a word that imitates the natural sound of the thing described—for example, "The bee *buzzed*."

personification   a description in which human qualities are given to something that is not human—for example, "The bright sky smiled down on the travelers."

plot   the sequence of events in a story

point of view   the position from which a story is told

resolution   in a story, the working out of the problem presented in the plot

setting   the time and place in which a story occurs

simile   a figure of speech in which a comparison is made using the word *like* or *as*—for example, "The rabbit's ear felt as soft as silk."

INDEX

A

a, an, the, 292-293
Abbreviations
  of titles, capitalizing, 80-81
  using, 232-233
Abstract nouns, 68-69
Action verbs, 136-137
Active voice, 162-163
Addresses
  capitalizing, 80-81
  using commas with, 308-309
Adjective clauses, 440-441
  commas setting off, 450-451
Adjective-forming suffixes,
  452-453
Adjective phrases, 368-369
Adjectives, 290-329
  adverbs confused with,
    306-307
  comparative forms of, 294-297
  demonstrative, 230-231,
    298-299, 300-301
  participles used as, 446-447
  predicate, 142-143, 290-291
  prepositional phrases as,
    368-369
  proper, 292-293
  superlative forms of, 294-297
  using, 306-307
Adverb clauses, 442-443
  commas setting off, 450-451
Adverb phrases, 368-369
Adverbs, 300-329
  adjectives confused with,
    306-307
  comparative forms of, 302-303
  irregular comparisons with,
    302
  kinds of, 300-301
  prepositional phrases as, 368-
    369
  superlative forms of, 302-303
  using, 306-307

Agreement, subject-verb. See
  Subject-verb agreement
Almanacs and atlases, 570-573
and, or, or *but,* 8-9, 10-11
Anecdotes, telling, 60-61
Antecedents, 218-219
  pronouns and, 218-219
Antonyms and synonyms, 310-311
Apostrophes
  in contractions, 78-79
  in possessive nouns, 72-73, 78-79
  using, 222-223
Appositives, 76-77
Articles, 292-293
  definite, 292-293
  indefinite, 292-293
Atlases and almanacs, 570-573
Audience, 46, 55, 114, 123, 194,
    203, 268, 277, 342, 351, 414,
    423, 488, 501
Authors
  on bibliography cards, 488-489
  in book reports, 130-131

B

bad and *badly,* 306-307
bad, worse, worst, 294-295
badly, worse, worst, 302-303
Bandwagon method, 418
Base words, 380-381
be, **forms of,** 152-153
because, 442-443
Beginning sentences, 46-49
Beginnings of short stories, 114
better, best, good, 294-295
better, best, well, 302-303
Bibliography, 488
Bibliography cards, 488-489
Biographical sketches, 268-287
  elements of, 268-271
  writing, 274-281
Blends, 82-83
blow, **forms of,** 154-155

Body
   of biographical sketch, 269
   of book report, 130-131
Book reports, 130-131
Books, using parts of, 556
Borrowed words, 82-83
both . . . and, 372-373
break, **forms of,** 154-155
bring, **forms of,** 152-153
burst, **forms of,** 154-155
Business letter
   colons after salutations of,
      378-379
   commas after closings of,
      308-309
but, or, **or** *and,* 8-9, 10-11
buy, **forms of,** 152-153

C

Capital letters
   abbreviations beginning with,
      232-233
   proper adjectives beginning
      with, 292-293
   proper nouns beginning with,
      80-81
   sentences beginning with, 2-3
   subtopics in outlines
      beginning with, 491
Catalogs, 210
catch, **forms of,** 152-153
Cause and effect, 494-495
Characters in short stories,
   115-116
Charged words, 418
Checklist
   biographical sketches, 271
   descriptions, 345
   editorials, 417
   explanations, 197
   personal narratives, 49
   research reports, 493
   short stories, 117
choose, **forms of,** 154-155
Chronological order, 47-48
   arranging events in, 269, 272

Cities, capitalizing names of,
   80-81
Class discussions, 128-129
Classifying, 346-347
Clauses
   adjective. See Adjective clauses
   adverb. See Adverb clauses
   commas with, 450-451
   independent, 436-437
   sentences and, 436-437
   subordinate, 438-439
Clipped words, 82-83
Collective nouns, 74-75
Colons
   introducing lists of items,
      378-379
   in time of day, 378-379
   using, 378-379
Combining Sentences
   with adjective clauses, 236-237
   with adjectives, 382-383
   with adverb clauses, 18-19
   with appositives, 84-85
   into compound sentences, 10-11
   with participles, 312-313
   with prepositional phrases,
      382-383
Commas
   after adverb clauses at
      beginnings of sentences,
      442-443
   with appositives, 76-77
   with clauses, 450-451
   in compound sentences, 10, 14-15
   before coordinating
      conjunctions, 372-373
   with dates, addresses, and
      names, 310-311
   with direct address, 158-159
   with direct quotations, 126-127
   afer interjections, 376-377
   with interrupting phrases,
      158-159
   after introductory words,
      158-159
   in letter parts, 310
   preceding conjunctions in

compound sentences,
436-437
in a series, 158-159
setting off participial phrases,
444-445
after subordinate clauses,
438-439
Common nouns, 68-69
Comparative forms
of adjectives, 294-297
of adverbs, 302-303
Comparatives, double, 296-297
Comparing and contrasting,
198-199
Complete predicates, 4-5, 436-437
Complete subjects, 4-5, 436-437
Complex sentences, 438-443
Composition. *See* Writing
Compound nouns, 74-75, 82-83
Compound objects, 220-221,
366-367
of prepositions, 372
Compound predicates, 8-9, 372
Compound sentences, 10-11,
372-373, 436-437
Compound subjects, 8-9,
220-221, 372
making verbs agree with,
374-375
Computers, 509
Concluding sentences, 196, 416
Conclusions
of biographical sketches, 270
of book reports, 130-131
of short stories, 114-115
Concrete nouns, 68-69
Conjunctions, 372-373
coordinating, 8-9, 10-11,
372-373, 378-379
correlative, 372-373
subordinating, 438-439, 442-443
Connotations of words, 160-161
Context, words in, 16-17
**Continents, capitalizing names
of,** 80-81
Contractions, 230-231
forming, 78-79

in negatives, 304-305
Contrasting and comparing,
198-199
Conversation, 116
Coordinating conjunctions, 8-9
10-11, 372-373, 378-379
Correlative conjunctions, 372-373
Countries
capitalizing names of, 80-81
commas with names of, 308
Curriculum Connection
writing about art, 358-359
writing about health, 284-285
writing about literature, 130-131
writing about mathematics,
508-509
writing about media, 430-431
writing about science, 210-211
writing about social studies,
62-63

D

Dashes, 521
Dates, using commas with,
308-309
Days
capitalizing names of, 80-81
periods in abbreviations of,
232-233
times of. *See* Times of day
Debates, having, 428-429
Declarative sentences, 2-3
Definite articles, 292-293
Degrees
abbreviated, commas with, 309
capitalizing, 80-81
Demonstrative adjectives, 298-299
Demonstrative pronouns, 230-231
Denotations of words, 160-161
Descriptions, 342-361
elements of, 342-345
oral, 356-357
writing, 348-355
Details
listening for, 356-357
ordering, 47-49, 344

sensory, 343-347
supporting, 46-49, 195-196
Diagraming sentences, 574-582
Dialogue in short stories, 116
Dictionaries, 16
meanings in, 558
parts of entries, 557-558
using, 557-559
Differences, 198-199
Direct address, nouns of, 158-159
Direct objects, 138-139
gerunds as, 446-447
infinitives as, 448-449
verbs with, 138-139
Discussions, class, 128-129
do, **forms of,** 152-153
Double comparatives, 296-297
Double negatives, avoiding,
304-305
draw, **forms of,** 154-155
drink, **forms of,** 152-153
drive, **forms of,** 154-155

E

eat, **forms of,** 154-155
Editorials, 414-433
elements of, 414-417
writing, 420-427
Effects and causes, 494-495
either . . . or, 372-373
Either-or thinking, 418
Endings. See Conclusions
English language. *See* Language
Enrichment, 22-23, 88-89,
166-167, 240-241, 316-317,
386-387, 458-459
er
for adjective comparison,
294-297
for adverb comparison, 302-303
est
for adjective comparison,
294-297
for adverb comparison, 302-303
Events, historical, capitalizing
names of, 80-81

Exclamation marks
ending sentences, 2-3, 14-15
after interjections, 376-377
Exclamatory sentences, 2-3,
376-377
Explanations, 194-213
Explanatory paragraphs, 194-197
Explanatory sentences, 2-3
Exploring story ideas, 120-121
Extra Practice, 24-33, 90-99,
168-181, 242-252, 318-329,
388-397, 460-469

F

Facts
opinions and, 414
slanted, 418
far, farther, further, 302-303
Faulty methods of persuasion,
418-419
feel, **forms of,** 152-153
First-person point of view,
118-119
fly, **forms of,** 154-155
Formal discussions, 128-129
Formal language, 546
Fragments, sentence, 12-13
freeze, **forms of,** 154-155
Friendly letters
commas after closings of, 308
commas after salutations of, 308
further, farther, 302-303
Future perfect tenses of verbs,
150-151
Future tenses of verbs, 144-145

G

Gender, 218-219
General terms, 50-51
Geographical features,
capitalizing names of, 80-81
Gerund phrases, 446-447
Gerunds, 446-447
give, **forms of,** 154-155
go, **forms of,** 154-155

good and *well,* 294-295, 306-307
Group discussions, 128-129
grow, forms of, 154-155

H

have, forms of, 152-153
Helping verbs, 144, 146-147
here, adding, 298
hold, forms of, 152-153
Holidays, capitalizing names of, 80-81
Homophones and homographs, 234-235
Hours, colons in writing, 378-379
How-to projects, 508
Hyphens, 521

I

Ideas, story, exploring, 120-121
Idioms, 22
if, 442-443
Images, 344, 459
Imperative sentences, 2-3, 4-5
Impression, overall, 342
Indefinite articles, 292-293
Indefinite pronouns, 224-225
  subject-verb agreement with, 226-227
Independent clauses, 436-437
Independent Writing
  biographical sketches, 274-281
  descriptions, 348-358
  editorials, 420-427
  explanations, 200-207
  personal narratives, 52-59
  research reports, 496-505
  short stories, 120-127
Indirect objects, 140-141
  verbs with, 140-141
Infinitives, 448-449
  prepositional phrases and, 448-449
Informal language, 545
Information, finding, 488-490
Initials, capitalizing, 80-81

Institutions, capitalizing names of, 80-81
Instructions, giving, 202-209
Intensifiers, 518
Intensive pronouns, 228-229
Interjections, 376-377
  commas after, 376-377
  common, 376-377
  exclamation marks after, 376-377
Interrogative pronouns, 230-231
Interrogative sentences, 2-3, 4-5
Interviews, conducting, 282-283
Intransitive verbs, 138-139
Introductions to book reports, 130-131
Introductory paragrphs, 268
Inventions, 210
Irregular adverb comparisons, 302
Irregular verbs, 152-155

J

Journals, 42, 43, 44, 53, 110, 111, 112, 121, 190, 191, 192, 201, 264, 265, 266, 275, 338, 339, 340, 349, 410, 411, 412, 421, 484, 485, 486, 499
just as . . . so, 372-373

K

know, forms of, 154-155

L

Language
  how it changes, 82-83
  persuasive, 416
Languages, capitalizing names of, 80-81
Language Study Handbook, 513-526
least, less, little, 296-297, 302-303
leave, forms of, 152-153
lend, forms of, 152-153
Letter models, 545-546

Letters
    business. *See* Business letters
    friendly. *See* Friendly letters
    using commas in, 308-309
Libraries, using, 560-563
Linking verbs, 142-143, 220
Listening
    conducting interviews, 282-283
    for details, 356-357
    giving instructions, 208-209
    having class discussions, 128-129
    having debates, 428-429
    oral reports, 506-507
    telling anecdotes, 60-63
Lists of items, colons
    introducing, 378-379
Literature
    "Charles" (Shirley Jackson), 104-110
    "Homesick" (Jean Fritz), 36-42
    The Incredible Journey (Sheila
      Burnford), 332-338
    "The Marriage of Sea and
      Space" (Margaret Poynter
      and Donald Collins), 184-190
    "The Secrets of a Tomb"
      (Carolyn Meyer and Charles
      Gellenkamp), 480-484
    The Story of Stevie Wonder
      (James Haskins), 258-264
    "This Farm for Sale" (Jesse
      Stuart), 400-410
little, less, least, 302-303
***look,* forms of,** 144-145, 148-149

M

Main idea, 47, 50, 61, 194, 202, 507
Main verbs, 146-147, 444-445
Maintenance, 100-101, 253-255,
    470-477
***make,* forms of,** 152-153
many, much, more, most, 294-297
Mechanics
    capitalizing proper nouns, 80-81
    forming possessive nouns and
      contractions, 78-79
    punctuating sentences, 14-15

    using abbreviations, 232-233
    using commas to separate parts
      of sentences, 158-159
    using commas with clauses,
      450-451
    using commas with dates,
      addresses, and names,
      308-309
    using semicolons and colons,
      378-379
***me* in compound objects,** 366-367
Metaphors, 344
Months
    capitalizing names of, 80-81,
      232-233
    commas with, 308
    periods in abbreviations of,
      232-233
**Monuments, capitalizing names
    of,** 80-81
Mood, 116
more* and *most, 294-297
    for adverb comparison, 302-303
much, more, most, 294-295

N

Names, 68-69
    using commas with, 308-309
Narratives, personal. *See*
    Personal narratives
Narrowing topics, 195
**Nationalities, capitalizing names
    of,** 80-81
Negatives, avoiding double,
    304-305
Negative side in debates, 428
neither . . . nor, 372-373
not only . . . but also, 372-373
Note cards in debates, 428
Note taking, 488-490, 566-567
***not,* used in negatives,** 306-307
Noun-forming suffixes, 452-453
Nouns, 68-69
    abstract, 68-69
    collective, 74-75
    common, 68-69

compound, 74-75, 82-83
concrete, 68-69
of direct address, 158-159
kinds of, 68-69
plural, 70-71
possessive. *See* Possessive
    nouns
predicate, 142-143
proper. *See* Proper nouns
singular, 70-71
Number, in pronouns, 218-219

O

Object pronouns, 216-217,
    366-367
Objects
compound. *See* Compound
    objects
direct. *See* Direct objects
indirect. *See* Indirect objects
Opinions and facts, 414
Oral descriptions, 356-357
Oral reports, 506-507
or, and, or *but,* 8-9, 10-11
Order
See Chronological order
of reasons, 415
Ordering details, 47-49, 344
**Organizations, capitalizing
    names of,** 80-81, 232-233
Outlines
making, 490-491
topic, 490-491
writing paragraphs from,
    491-492
Outlining, 568-569
Overall impression, 342

P

Paragraphs
explanatory, 194-197
introductory, 268
writing, from outlines, 491-492
Parallel structure, 454, 455
Participial phrases, 444-445

Participles
participial phrases and,
    444-445
used as adjectives, 446-447
Parts of speech. *See* Adjectives;
    Adverbs; Conjunctions;
    Interjections; Nouns;
    Prepositions; Pronouns;
    Verbs
Passive voice, 162-163
Past participle
of irregular verbs, 152-155
of regular verbs, 146-147,
    444-445
Past perfect tenses of verbs,
    150-151
Past progressive forms of verbs,
    148-149
Past tense
of irregular verbs, 152-155
of regular verbs, 144-147
People, capitalizing names of,
    80-81
Perfect tenses of verbs, 150-151
Periods
ending abbreviations with,
    232-233
ending sentences with, 2-3,
    14-15
in outlines, 490, 499, 568
Personal narratives, 46-65
understanding elements of,
    46-49
writing, 52-59
Personal pronouns, 216-217
Persuasion, faulty methods of,
    418-419
Persuasive language, 416
Phrases
adjective, 368-369
adverb, 368-369
gerund, 446-447
participial, participles and,
    444-445
prepositional. *See*
    Prepositional phrases
verb, 146-147

Pictures, 44-45, 112-113, 192-193, 266-267, 340-341, 412-413, 486-487

Plots, 114-115

Plural indefinite pronouns, 224-227

Plural nouns, 70-71

Plural pronouns, 216-217

Poetry

"All Day I Hear" (James Joyce), 213

"Drawing by Ronnie C., Grade One" (Ruth Lechlitner), 359

Haiku, 387

"Stopping by Woods on a Snowy Evening" (Robert Frost), 167

"Who Am I?" (Felice Holman), 89

Point of view, understanding, 118-119

Possessive nouns, 72-73, 222-223

forming, 78-79

Possessive pronouns, 222-223

Practice Plus, 30-31, 96-97, 179, 245, 327, 392, 463

Precision in writing, 310-311

Predicate adjectives, 142-143, 290-291

Predicate nouns, 142-143

Predicates

complete, 4-5, 436-437

compound, 8-9, 372-373

simple, 6-7

Prefixes, 380-381

Prepositional phrases, 364-365

as adjectives and adverbs, 368-369

infinitives and, 448-449

prepositions and, 364-365

pronouns in, 366-367

verbs after, 370-371

Prepositions, 364-371

compound objects of, 372

object of, 364-365

prepositional phrases and, 364-365

Present participles, 146-147, 444-445

Present perfect tenses of verbs, 150-151

Present progressive forms of verbs, 148-149

Present tense of verbs, 144-147

Prewriting, 52-53, 120-121, 200-201, 274-275, 348-349, 420-421, 496-499

Principal parts of verbs, 146-147

Progressive forms of verbs, 148-149

Pronouns, 216-252

antecedents and, 218-219

demonstrative, 230-231, 298-299

indefinite. See Indefinite pronouns

intensive, 228-229

interrogative, 230-231

object, 216-217, 366-367

personal, 216-217

plural, 216-217

possessive, 222-223

in prepositional phrases, 366-367

reflexive, 228-229, 366-367

relative, 440-441

singular, 216-217

subject, 216-217

using correctly, 220-221

Proofreading, 57-58, 125-126, 205-206, 279-280, 353-354, 425-426, 503-504

Proofreading marks, 206

Proper adjectives, 292-293

Proper nouns, 68-69

capitalizing, 80-81

Publishing, 59, 127, 207, 281, 355, 427, 505

Punctuating sentences, 14-15

Punctuation marks, 2-3; *see also* Apostrophes; Colons; Commas; Exclamation marks; Quotation marks; Semicolons

Q

qt., 232

Question marks, ending
  sentences with, 2-3, 14-15
Quotation marks, 126
  with titles of works, 521
  around words taken directly
    from sources, 489

R

*Readers' Guide to Periodical
  Literature,* 497
real and *really,* 306-307
Reasons, order of, 415
Reference works, using, 562-563
Reflexive pronouns, 228-229,
  366-367
Regular verbs, *152; see also* Verbs
Relative pronouns, 440-441
Reports
  book, 130-131
  oral, 506-507
  research. *See* Research reports
Research reports, 488-511
  elements of, 488-493
  writing, 496-505
Resolution, in debates, 428
Responding to Literature, 43,
  111, 191, 265, 339, 411, 485
Revising, 55-56, 123-124,
  203-204, 277-278, 351-352,
  423-424, 501-502
Rhyme, 167
Rhythm, 167
ride, forms of, 154-155
Roman numerals before main
  topics in outlines, 491
run, forms of, 152-153
Run-on sentences, 12-13

S

Salutations
  of business letters, colons after,
    378-379
  of friendly letters, commas after,
    308-309
say, forms of, 152-153

see, forms of, 154-155
Semicolons
  in compound sentences, 10,
    14-15
  joining parts of compound
    sentences, 436-437
  using, 378-379
Sensory details, 343-347
Sentence fragments, 12-13
Sentences, 2-33
  beginning, 46-49
  clauses and, 436-437
  complex, 438-443
  compound, 10-11, 372-373,
    436-437
  concluding, 196, 416
  declarative, 2-3
  diagraming, 574-582
  exclamatory, 2-3, 376-377
  explanatory, 2-3
  imperative, 2-3, 4
  interrogative, 2-3, 4
  kinds of, 2-3
  punctuating, 14-15
  reviewing structure of, 574-582
  run-on, 12-13
  simple, 10-11, 436-437
  topic, 47, 194-195
  using commas to separate parts
    of, 158-159
Sequence, understanding, 272-273
set, forms of, 154-155
Settings of short stories, 114-116
shall or *will,* 144-145
Sharing. *See* Publishing
Short stories, 114-133
  elements of, 114-117
  putting together, 116
  writing, 120-127
Similarities, 198-199
Similes, 344
Simple predicates, 6-7
Simple sentences, 10-11, 436-437
Simple subjects, 6-7
sing, forms of, 152-153
Singular indefinite pronouns,
  224-227

Singular nouns, 70-71
Singular pronouns, 216-217
sit, forms of, 152-153
Sketches, biographical. *See* Biographical sketches
Skimming and scanning, 564-565
Slanted facts, 418
Sources, quotation marks around words taken directly from, 489
speak, forms of, 154-155
Speaking
    conducting interviews, 282-283
    giving instructions, 208-209
    having class discussions, 128-129
    having debates, 428-429
    listening for details, 356-357
    oral reports, 506-507
    peer revision, 55, 123, 203, 277, 351, 423, 499
    telling anecdotes, 60-61
Specific terms, 50-51
Spelling Strategies, 547-550
spring, forms of, 152-153
States
    abbreviations for, 232-233
    capitalizing names of, 80-81
    commas with names of, 308
Stories, short. *See* Short stories
Story ideas, exploring, 120-121
Streets
    capitalizing names of, 80-81
    periods in abbreviations of, 232-233
Structure, parallel, 454-455
Study skills
    atlases and almanacs, 570-573
    note taking, 566-567
    outlining, 568-569
    skimming and scanning, 564-565
    study strategies, 552-554
    using dictionaries, 557-559
    using libraries, 560-563
Study Strategies, 552-554
    taking tests, 555
    using parts of textbooks, 556
Subject pronouns, 216-217

Subjects
    agreement with verbs. *See* Subject-verb agreement
    complete, 4-5, 436-437
    compound. See Compound subjects
    gerunds as, 446-447
    infinitives as, 448-449
    simple, 6-7
    verb agreement with. *See* Subject-verb agreement
Subject-verb agreement, 156-157
    with collective nouns, 74-75
    with compound subjects, 374-375
    with indefinite pronouns, 226-227
    after prepositional phrases, 370-371
Subordinate clauses, 438-439
Subordinating conjunctions, 438-439, 442-443
Suffixes, 452-453
    adjective-forming, 452-453
    noun-forming, 452-453
Summarizing, 566
Superlative forms
    of adjectives, 294-297
    of adverbs, 302-303
Supporting details, 46-49, 195-196
swim, forms of, 152-153
swing, forms of, 152-153
Synonyms and antonyms, 310-311

T

take, forms of, 154-155
talk, forms of, 146-147
teach, foms of, 152-153
tear, forms of, 154-155
Telling anecdotes, 60-61
Tenses of verbs. see verbs
Test taking, 555
Textbooks, using parts of, 556
that, 440-441

Theme Project, 65, 133, 213, 287, 361, 433, 511

there, **adding,** 298

Thesaurus for Writing, 527-544

think, **forms of,** 152-153

Thinking, either-or, 418

Thinking Skills
    cause and effect, 494-495
    classifying, 346-347
    comparing and contrasting, 198-199
    distinguishing between general and specific, 50-51
    faulty methods of persuasion, 418-419
    understanding point of view, 118-119
    understanding sequence, 272-273

Third-person limited point of view, 118-119

this, that, these, those, 230, 298-299

throw, **forms of,** 154-155

Time lines, 274-275

Time order. See Chronological order

Times of day
    capital letters and periods in writing, 232-233
    colons in writing, 378-379

Titles
    abbreviated, commas with, 308
    on bibliography cards, 488-489
    of book reports, 130-131
    capitalizing, 80-81
    of people, using commas with, 308-309
    periods with, 232-233

to, **beginning infinitives with,** 448-449

Topic outlines, 490-491

Topics
    choosing, 52, 120, 200, 274, 348, 420, 496
    main topics in outlines, 490-491
    narrowing, 195

Topic sentences, 47, 194-195

Transition words, 47, 196, 269, 415

Transitive verbs, 138-139

U

Underlining titles of books, 521

Unit Checkups, 20-21, 64, 86-87, 132, 164-165, 212, 238-239, 286, 314-315, 360, 384-385, 432, 456-457, 510

Units of measure, 232-233

V

Verbals, 444-449; *see also* Gerunds; Infinitives; Participles

Verb phrases, 146-147

Verbs, 136-181
    action, 136-137
    agreement with subjects. See Subject-verb agreement
    consistency in tense, 206
    with direct objects, 138-139
    future perfect tenses of, 150-151
    future tenses of, 144-145
    helping, 144-147
    with indirect objects, 140-141
    intransitive, 138-139
    irregular, 152-155
    linking, 142-143, 220
    main, 146-147, 444-445
    past participles of, 146-147, 444-445
    past perfect tenses of, 150-151
    past progressive forms of, 148-149
    past tenses of, 144-147
    perfect tenses of, 150-151
    after prepositional phrases, 370-371
    present participles of, 146-147, 444-445
    present perfect tenses of, 150-151
    present progressive forms of, 148-149

present tenses of, 144-147
principal parts of, 146-147
progressive forms of, 148-149
regular, 152
subject agreement with. *See*
Subject-verb agreement
transitive, 138-139
Verb-subject agreement. *See*
Subject-verb agreement
View, point of, understanding,
118-119
Vocabulary
context clues, 16-17
homophones and homographs,
234-235
how language changes, 82-83
prefixes, 380-381
suffixes, 452-453
synonyms and antonyms,
310-311
word choice, 160-161

W

wear, **forms of,** 154-155
well **and** *good,* 294-295, 306-307
well, better, best, 302-303
when, 442-443
whether . . . or, 372-373
which, 440-441
who, whom, 230, 440-441
whose, who's, 230
will **or** *shall,* 144-145
Words
base, 380-381
blends, 82-83
borrowed, 82-83
charged, 418
choice of, 160-161
clipped, 82-83
connotations of, 160-161

in context, 16-17
denotations of, 160-161
general, 50-51, 68-69
quotation marks around words
taken directly from sources,
489
specific, 50-51, 68-69
transition, 47, 196, 269, 415
Words in context, 16-17
worse, worst, bad, 294-295
worse, worst, badly, 302-303
write, **forms of,** 154-155
Writer's Reference, 512-582
Writing, 54, 122, 202, 276, 350,
422, 500
Independent. *See* Independent
Writing
Thesaurus for, 527-544
Writing, forms of
biographical sketches, 268-271
descriptions, 342-345
editorials, 414-417
explanatory paragraphs, 194-
197
personal narratives, 46-49
research reports, 488-493
short stories, 114-117
Writing Process. *See* Prewriting;
Writing; Revising;
Proofreading; Publishing
Writing Process Overview, 551

Y

Years, commas before and after,
308-309
You **as understood subject,** 4-5

Z

Zip codes, commas and, 308

Excerpt from "The Highwayman" by Alfred Noyes is reprinted by permission of Hugh Noyes for Alfred Noyes Literary Estate.

Excerpt from "Long Trip" from *Selected Poems of Langston Hughes*. Copyright 1926 by Alfred A. Knopf, Inc. and renewed 1954 by Langston Hughes. Reprinted by permission of the publisher.

Brief quotation from "Peter Pan, the Pilgrims, a Pirate and a Cat" by Jean Fritz in *Once Upon a Time*. Copyright © 1986 by G. P. Putnam's Sons. Reprinted by permission.

"Stopping by Woods on a Snowy Evening" is from *The Poetry of Robert Frost*, edited by Edward Connery Lathem. Copyright 1923 by Holt, Rinehart and Winston, Inc. and renewed 1951 by Robert Frost. Reprinted by permission of Henry Holt and Company, Inc. Reprinted also by permission of Jonathan Cape Ltd.

Brief quotation by M. B. Goffstein from *Once Upon a Time*. copyright © 1986 by G. P. Putnam's Sons. Reprinted by permission.

Haiku by Shiki is from *Cricket Songs*, Japanese haiku translated by Harry Behn. Copyright © 1964 by Harry Behn. All rights reserved. Reprinted by permission of Marian Reiner.

Anonymous haiku and other haiku by Shiki excerpted from *An Introduction to Haiku*, edited by Harold G. Henderson. Copyright © 1958 by Harold G. Henderson. Reprinted by permission of Doubleday, a division of Bantam, Doubleday, Dell Publishing Group, Inc.

Excerpt about Margaret Mead from *Dreams into Deeds: Nine Women Who Dared* by Linda Peavy & Ursula Smith. Copyright © 1985 by Linda Peavy and Ursula Smith. Reprinted by permission of Charles Scribner's Sons, an imprint of Macmillan Publishing Company.

James Haskins quotation is from *Something About the Author Autobiography Series*: Volume 4. Edited by Adele Sarkissian. Copyright © 1987 by Gale Research Company. Reprinted by permission of the publisher.

Excerpt from and full poem "Vern" in *Bronzeville Boys and Girls* by Gwendolyn Brooks. Copyright © 1956 by Gwendolyn Brooks Blakely, renewed 1984 by Gwendolyn Brooks Blakely. Reprinted by permission of Harper & Row, Publishers, Inc.

Brief quotation from *A Gift from the Sea* by Anne Morrow Lindbergh. Copyright © 1955, 1975 by Anne Morrow Lindbergh. All rights reserved. Reprinted by permission of Pantheon Books, a division of Random House, Inc.

"Gold Medalist" from *The Break Dance Kids* by Lillian Morrison. Copyright © 1985 by Lillian Morrison. Reprinted by permission of Lothrop, Lee & Shepard Books (A Division of William Morrow and Company, Inc.).

"A Computer Will Not Take Your Place" by John L. Chapman is excerpted from the article of that name which appeared in *West* magazine, June 30, 1968. Extensive research failed to locate the copyright holder of this work.

ILLUSTRATION CREDITS: Dan Bridy, 184–191; Jack Brusca, 22–23, 88, 166, 240–241, 316–317, 386, 458; Eva Vagreti-Cockrille, 65, 133, 213, 287, 332–339, 346, 361, 400–411, 433, 511; Fernando, 36–43; Ketti Kupper, 104–111; Ondre Pettingill, 258–265; Jan Pyk, 44, 62, 112, 130, 192, 210, 266, 284, 340, 358, 412, 430, 486, 508

PHOTO CREDITS: ART RESOURCE: Scala, 76; Joseph Martin, 217. BETTMANN ARCHIVE: 219, 223, 236. BLACK STAR: Fred Ward, 454. LEE BOLTIN: 483, 487BL. BRUCE COLMAN: James Carmichael, 78: Phil Degginger, 383R; Nicholas deVore, 63; Jessica Ehlers, 68; Kenneth W. Fink, 459; M.L. Fogden, 295; David Madison, 131; Chris Newbert, 163R; Frank Oberle, 83; David Overcash, 167; Norman Owen Tomalin, 7, 455R. THE COUSTEAU SOCIETY: 162. CULVER PICTURES: 85R, 195, 451. DUOMO: Paul J. Sutton, 497. FOCUS ON SPORTS: 267TR, 301, 447. GAMMA-LIAISON: J. Rubin, 267B. GLOBE PHOTOS: 112. HISTORICAL PICTURE SERVICE: 85L. MICHAEL HOLFORD: 480, 484–485 (border). THE IMAGE BANK: Morton Beebe, 113R; Nancy Brown, 113TL; Don Carroll, 211; David Hamilton, 8; Walter Iooss, 193T; Robert Kristofik, 267TL; Michael Melford, 491; Peter Miller, 115; Co Rentmeester, 369; Barrie Rokeach, 412TL; Sobel/Klonsky, 441; Alex Stewart, 331; Frank Whitney, 1. THE IMAGE WORKS: Bob Daemmrich, 73, 486; David Hall, 147; Joe Soha, 45BR. KEN KARP: 49, 55, 59, 60, 66, 67, 117, 123, 126, 127, 128, 197, 203, 206, 207, 214, 268, 271, 277, 280, 281, 288, 345, 351, 354, 355, 359, 381, 417, 423, 426, 427, 428, 431, 501, 505, 506. LEO DE WYS: Casimir, 307; Fridmar Damm, 19L; Henry Kaiser, 341T; Jean-Paul Nacivet, 357; Steve Vidler, 192L; Rocky Weldon, 134. DAVID MADISON: 215, 256, 266, 312, 313L, 313R, 498. MAGNUM PHOTOS: Cornell Capa, 237R; Raymond Depardon, 133. JOE MCNALLY: 103, 511. METROPOLITAN MUSEUM OF ART: The Cloisters Collection, Munsey Fund, 1932, detail, The Nine Heroes Tapestries, 84. MKD PRODUCTIONS: 257. OUTLINE: Jack Mitchell, 442. PETER ARNOLD: Martha Cooper, 45BL; Harry Haralambou, 387; Jeff Rotman, 163L, 193B; Bruce Silverstein, 81; Clyde Smith, 330; G. Ziesler, 299. PHOTOGRAPHERS ASPEN: Nicholas deVore, 213; David Hiser, 455L. PHOTO RESEARCHERS: Linda Bartlett, 304; Ron Church, 192R; Paul Crum, 340B; John Dommers, 412B; Richard Elis, 143, 150; R.D. Estes, 229; Rapho/Rick Golt, 235; Soames Summer-